The Life and Times of Godwine, Earl of Wessex

Hubert John Grills

Published 2009 by

Anglo-Saxon Books
www.asbooks.co.uk

25 Brocks Road
EcoTech Business Park
Swaffham, Norfolk PE37 7XG

PL

© Hubert J Grills

All rights reserved. No part of this publication may be reproduced or transmitted in any form or by any means, electronic or mechanical including photo-copying, recording, or any information storage or retrieval system, without prior permission in writing from the publisher, except for the quotation of brief passages in connection with a review written for inclusion in a magazine or newspaper.

This book may not be lent, resold, hired out or otherwise disposed of by way of trade in any form of binding or cover other than that in which it is published, without the prior consent of the publisher.

ISBN 978 1 898281528

To my grandchildren
Richard, Amy and Ben

Contents

Contents 4

Acknowledgements 7

Foreword 8

A Note On Sources 10

Glossary 10

Introduction 11

1. Godwine's Background 14
    Godwine's Ancestry 15
    Æthelgifu 18
    Wulfnoth Cild 20
    Danes and Danegeld 23
    Intrigues at Court 24
    Seizing of the English Fleet 26
    The Man Named 'Ælfmær' 28

2. Godwine's Early Years 31
    Family, Birth and Early Life 31
    Swein and Cnut 33
    Death of Æthelstan and Rise of Edmund 36
    Godwine and King Edmund 37
    Godwine's Holdings in Kent 40

3. Godwine's Rise To Power 45
    Cnut's Reign and Godwine's Favour 45
    Godwine and Gytha 49
    Cnut's Brothers-in-Law 51
        Eilifr 51
        Ulfr 55
    Gytha and her Father 58
    Styrbjörn 59

4. Earl Godwine in the Reign Of King Cnut 63
    Godwine's Marriage and Elevation 64
    Cnut and Rome 68
    Norway Divided 71
    Leofric 73

- Archbishop Æthelnoth 79
- Lyfing 80
- Normandy 80
- Cnut's Death 83
- English Earldoms 84
  - East Anglia 84
  - Northumbria 84
  - Mercia 85

5. Godwine, Loyalty and the Royal Succession 88
   - Cnut's successors 88
   - Æthelred's sons 97
   - Abingdon attitudes 103
   - Scots and Welsh 104
   - Harold Harefoot's death 106

6. Earl Godwine the Scapegoat 109
   - Harthacnut in England 111
   - Earl Siward 119
   - Encomium Emmae Reginae 123
   - Osgod and Tovi 124
   - Harthacnut the King 126

7. The Premier Earl 128
   - Godwine's Offspring 128
   - Edward the King 136

8. The Gathering Shadows 147
   - Earl Swegn 148
   - Robert Champart, Edward's favourite 161

9. Exile of the Godwinesons 171
   - Eustace's mission 171
   - Ireland 183
   - Godwine in exile 185

10. Godwine's Homecoming 191
    - Godwine's Planned Return 191
    - Godwine in London 195
    - Godwine's Restoration 197
    - Godwine's Death and Legacy 200
    - Godwine's Line 208
    - England after Harold 217

Appendix 1	220
The Lands of Godwine & Gytha	220
Appendix 2	231
Sources for the Life of Godwine	231
The Anglo-Saxon Chronicle (ASC)	231
Manuscript 'C'	231
Manuscript 'D'	231
Manuscript 'E'	232
Manuscript 'F'	232
Anglo-Norman Sources	233
John of Worcester	233
William of Malmesbury	233
Henry of Huntingdon	234
Encomium Emmae Reginae	234
Vita Ædwardi Regis	234
Scandinavian	235
Knytlingasaga	235
Gesta Danorum	235
Heimskringla	236
Abbreviations & Citations	237
Bibliography	239
Primary Sources	239
Secondary Sources	243
Articles	246
Index	249

Acknowledgements

In the process of writing this life of Godwine I have become increasingly aware of how great is the debt owed to the generations of scholars who have studied different aspects of the period and made such enormous strides in our knowledge of Anglo-Saxon history.

It is with great pleasure that I acknowledge my gratitude for the advice and encouragement received from Professor Frank Barlow; to Professor Richard Perkins and Eric Christiansen for their help on many Scandinavian questions; to Professor Simon Keynes and Dr David Roffe; to Dennis Corner who furnished me with maps and information about Porlock, and to Alison Swan replying for the church wardens of Southover, Lewes, East Sussex in connection with the tablet in memory of Magnus. I am also indebted to the 'Office de Tourisme, Canton De La Chaise Dieu' for the courteous reply received. In addition, my thanks are due to the Exeter Reference Library and to the staff of Tavistock Library for their consideration and kindness in obtaining for me a great many books over a long period.

I owe a very special debt to Dr Ann Williams whose encouragement and assistance has enabled me to avoid many errors and has greatly enriched my understanding of Anglo-Saxon history. Any inaccuracy which does occur, and any suggestions I have advanced, are my own responsibility entirely.

I am also pleased to acknowledge my considerable debt to Stephen Pollington for revising some of the text, compiling the index, and re-organising the text for publication.

I gratefully acknowledge the help received from my daughter, Tamzin, and son-in-law, Antony, with their help in the word processing of my manuscript. Also I would like to express my gratitude to Alison and Cyril who encouraged me with advice and interest. I appreciate my family's tolerance and forbearance during the time devoted to research and writing this book.

H.J. Grills

Foreword

By Stephen Pollington

The subject of this book, Earl Godwine, was one of the most important and influential figures in 11th century history. The story of his life is scattered in many source documents, both contemporary and later, in which fact is mingled with legend and polemic. In this important work, H.J. Grills has taken the opportunity to review all the available sources –Anglo-Saxon, Scandinavian and Norman – and to subject them to a new analysis based on more than a century of published scholarship. Grills' familiarity with the texts - and with the inherent bias in each of them – allows him to bring a fresh approach to the study of a mediaeval lifestory.

Godwine was an independent-minded, dominant and courageous man who came to hold a great deal of power – both political and military – in England in the 11th century. Mediaeval kings relied on men of Godwine's kind for support and for execution of their policies; it was a confident king who could afford to ignore the interests and wishes of such powerful magnates. When the interests of the king and his leading men coincided, the country could enjoy an effective administration; when these interests conflicted, ruinous and unnecessary strife resulted and it was by no means certain that the authority of the king would prevail over that of his followers. Godwine was perhaps fortunate in that both the kings whom he served were to some extent outsiders – Cnut was a Dane trying to pass himself off as an Anglo-Saxon king, while Edward was an Anglo-Saxon trying to pass himself of as a Norman king. Godwine clearly enjoyed considerable support among the English and Anglo-Danish thanes and landowners; it was this which made him such a dangerous enemy as well as a valuable ally.

The times of Godwine and his famous sons were an important crossroads in European history, with many significant political and religious developments shaping the course which Christendom would take for several centuries. It would be too large a claim to suggest that Earl Godwine was in any way directly responsible for subsequent events – the Norman problem, the Norwegian problem, the papal interventions and religious appointments – but it is interesting to speculate that if his relations with King Edward had been more cordial, or simply more stable, then England might not have been sucked into the orbit of competing continental and Scandinavian polities and many English lives would not have been squandered in the fruitless quest for power.

Godwine was appointed to the dignity of 'Earl of Wessex' in 1023. Wessex – *West Seaxe*, formerly the kingdom of the West Saxons – was an important powerbase for the later Anglo-Saxon rulers, whose lineage was drawn from the West Saxon kings from the time of Alfred the Great and his father Æþelwulf. Godwine had come by this title upon marrying Gytha (*Gyþa*), the sister of King Cnut. The young Cnut had fought a bitter and lengthy campaign against the West Saxon prince Edmund, known as Ironside; they were both rivals for the throne, Edmund through his paternal ancestry and Cnut through his father, Swein Forkbeard (*Sven Tviskeggi*), having seized control of England in 1014 at the culmination of a long and ruinous campaign against King Ethelred (*Æþelræd*). While Cnut and Edmund had both won significant victories, none of them had been in any way decisive, and so, in 1016, an uneasy truce was arranged whereby Edmund would retain the West Saxon lands in the south and Cnut would take the former Danelaw territories to the north and east. Edmund died shortly after the peace treaty was concluded, and it seem highly probable that both the marriage to Gytha and the elevation to the rank of earl were sweeteners aimed at keeping the leader of the West Saxon contingent content. Godwine had fought bravely and with determination for Edmund and the Wessex cause during the turbulent years of campaigning, and Cnut doubtless recognised in the English leader a person who could be either a bitter foe or a valuable ally. Godwine allegedly took control of the English forces in Cnut's later Scandinavian campaigns.

The earl's relations with Edward the Confessor were strained: Edward was evidently suspicious of his over-mighty subject, and the king allowed himself to be swayed by his Norman appointees who had their own agenda – in which Godwine and his family figured only as victims.

The title of 'Earl of Wessex' was not continued in the post-Norman invasion peerage. After Godwine's death in 1053, his son Harold (later King Harold the Second) was appointed the second earl. When Harold was killed at the battle of Hastings, the title lapsed and the lands of Wessex were divided and apportioned amongst the followers of Duke William. However, on the 19th of June 1999 Queen Elizabeth II conferred on her youngest son, H.R.H Prince Edward, the title of Earl of Wessex on the occasion of his marriage to Sophie Rhys-Jones.

In the history of England there have only been three Earls of Wessex – Godwine, Harold and, now, Prince Edward. This book concentrates on the first Earl – Godwine: his life, his character and loyalties.

A Note On Sources

The sources available for the study of Godwine – and his political and social context – are too numerous to list in full in so small a book as this. My own primary source is 'Old English History for Children', by E. A. Freeman which I read as a boy and which piqued my interest in things Anglo-Saxon. The book having captured my imagination, as the years passed I read every publication and article that could be obtained, passing from the Anglo-Saxon to the Norman authorities such as the writings of J. H. Round, David Douglas, R.H. C. Davis and R. Allen Brown. The result of my long hours of research and consideration is this book.

I need hardly say that to attempt to write a biography of someone who lived over a thousand years ago presents difficulties that would not be encountered when dealing with a more modern celebrity. The first step is to track down the primary sources for the period, and then to evaluate their reliability. First and foremost for any work of political history in the first millennium AD is the *Anglo-Saxon Chronicle*. The different versions ('recensions') of the chronicle which affect the eleventh century are known as Manuscripts 'C', 'D', 'E' and 'F'. Details of these documents are given in Appendix 2.

Glossary

Ætheling	Æþeling, nobleman, prince of the royal blood
Æthelred	Ethelred
A.S.C.	*Anglo-Saxon Chronicle*
Bernicia	Old Anglo-Saxon kingdom based on Bamburgh, roughly equivalent to Northumberland
Deira	Old Anglo-Saxon kingdom based on York, roughly equivalent to Yorkshire
fyrd	Regional military force
Mercia	Old Anglo-Saxon kingdom based on Tamworth, roughly equivalent to the Midlands
T.R.E.	"in the time of King Edward"
Þorkel Hávi	Thorkel the Tall

Introduction

King Edgar and his Successors

The reign of King Edgar was looked back on by English writers of the 11th century as the Golden Age, but almost immediately portents of impending evil were seen in the autumn sky. A comet appeared, foretelling famine and discord: hostility arose regarding the nomination of Edgar's successor. The king had left two sons, Edward and Æthelred, by different spouses. Edward's mother was Æthelflaed[1], Æthelred's was Ælfthryth. Æthelflaed had never been crowned as queen, Ælfthryth had. Edward was probably thirteen years of age at the time, Æthelred only seven. Edward's cause was championed by Æthelwine the ealdorman of East Anglia. Æthelred's supporters included Ælfhere, ealdorman of Mercia, himself a scion of the royal house of Wessex. The enmity which had existed between the two men intensified and civil war was only narrowly averted.[2] Edward was crowned during the same year; within nineteen months he was murdered.

The portents of approaching calamity were more than justified. Æthelred was crowned at Kingston 'with great rejoicing', but rejoicing soon gave way to fear and confusion: within months the Vikings struck in a new campaign of mayhem and turmoil aimed at destabilising the English crown, winning plunder and silver, and enriching the leaders of the Danish host. English resistance was occasionally determined and courageous, but most often fragmented, poorly organised, badly led and ineffectual. When Ealdorman Byrhtnoth fell at Maldon in 991, the death of so great a warrior sent a dire warning to the English nobility: resistance would carry a heavy cost. Eventually, the English leaders decided to buy off the invaders with payment of the Danegeld. It must have been about the time when Godwine was born that the nature of the raiding changed. Ólafr Trygvason of Norway and King Swein of Denmark arrived at the walls of London with a considerable fleet. Suffering repulse, 'they travelled from there and wrought the greatest harm which any raiding army could ever do, burning and raiding and slaughter of men, both along the sea coast in Essex and in the land of Kent and in Sussex and in Hampshire.'[3]

---

[1] A. Williams, 'Dark Age Britain' p. 22.
[2] A. Williams, 'Princeps Merciorum Gentis; the family career and connections of Æthelhere of Mercia,' pp..160-170.
[3] A.S.C 'E' AD 994. Quoted from 'AS Chronicles', M. Swanton p.129.

As a boy, Godwine grew up in surroundings permeated with violence and uncertainty. Perhaps his career and influence did help to give his country a degree of stability and continuity during several years of the eleventh century. Arguably Earl Godwine attained a greater degree of power than any other English statesman. In spite of, or perhaps because of this, there are few distinguished politicians whose characters are more difficult to assess. It is baffling to try to reconcile the actions of the man who obtained the dissolution of Berkeley nunnery or the possession of Bosham by trickery and fraud[4] with the 'father' of the English nation as portrayed in the *Vita Ædwardi Regis*.[5] His involvement in the murder of the Ætheling Alfred has remained a stain on his character to this day, yet this seems oddly at variance with the returning exile for whom the men of the south-east were prepared to live and die.[6] What follows is an attempt to evaluate the motives and aims of the man who, more than any other, inspired the hatred of so many and yet was able to inspire such loyalty in the hearts of the populace in his own heartland.

---

[4] 'De Nugis Curialum'; Berkeley pp.416-419: Bosham pp.418-421 Dist v c 3.
[5] 'Vita' pp. 8-47.
[6] A.S.C 'C', 'D' s.a 1052; 'Vita' pp.40-41.

The English Royal Genealogy

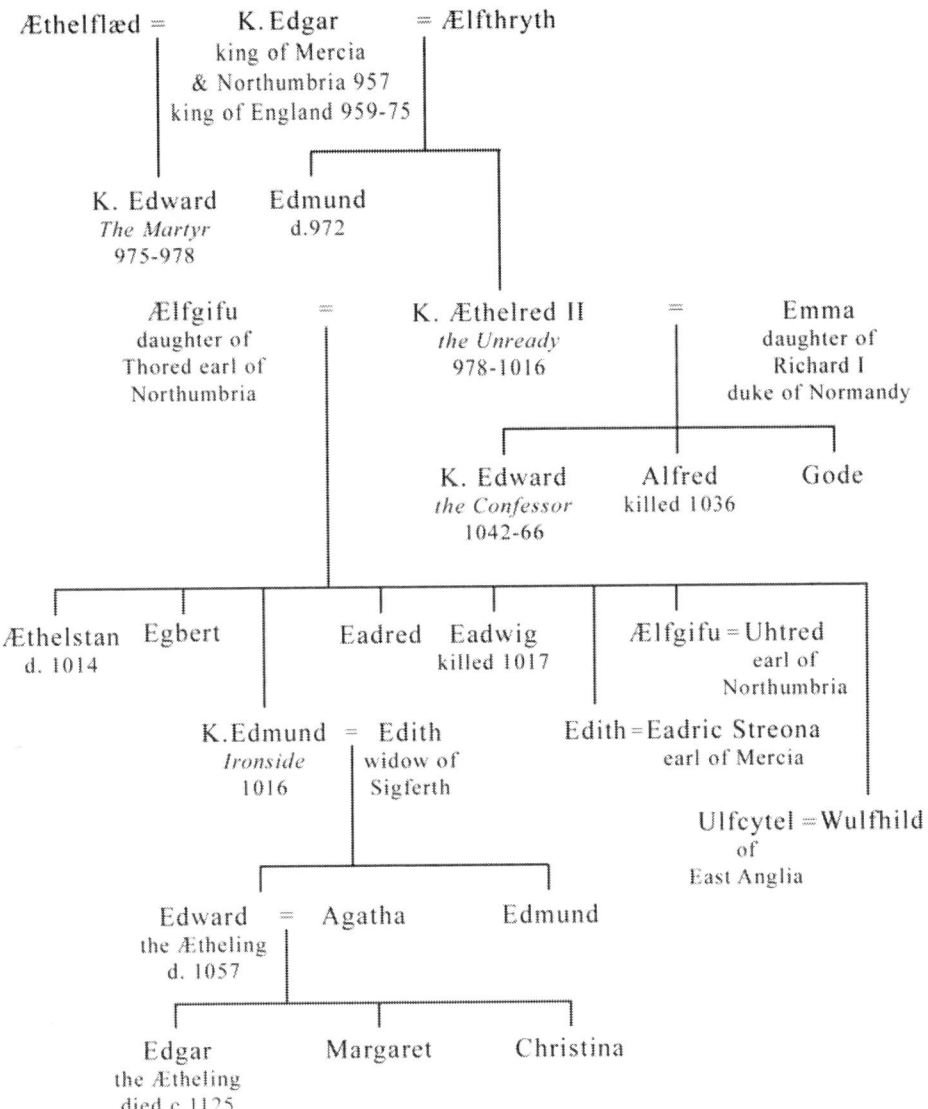

1. Godwine's Background

We may begin the tale of Godwine by looking into the family background of the earl, whose rise to political dominance was so remarkable due to the family's apparent lack of eminence previously. The charismatic magnate Godwine appears to come from nowhere, and this fact allowed – indeed, encouraged - later embellishment of his origins.

Many of the Anglo-Norman and Norman chroniclers gave Godwine a far from favourable character. To Henry of Huntingdon he was a 'consummate traitor';[1] to William of Jumièges, 'another Judas Iscariot';[2] Eadmer, the Canterbury monk, called him 'a bitter enemy of the Church of Canterbury' and wrote that 'he died an evil death';[3] to Walter Map, a Welsh Canon of Hereford, Godwine was 'ignoble, grasping and unprincipled';[4] and Roger of Wendover has King Edward call him 'a dog and a traitor; unworthy of Christian burial'.[5] Even the author of the *Vita Haroldi* writes that his hero's father, Godwine, and other members of his family 'had been heavily branded with the mark of treason and other crimes' and speaks of his 'incredible cunning and audacity'[6]. It must be remembered in this respect that some of the chronicle writers were anxious to ingratiate themselves with their wealthy Norman patrons for obvious reasons; others, from the storehouse of their own lively imaginations were loath to spoil a good story for want of a little embellishment.

Stories were told to show Godwine's humble background; theories were advanced to claim his descent from the kings of Wessex and genealogies produced to link the Earl to the Mercian Eadric Streona of great ill-repute. The stories will be shown to have no substance; the theories can be discredited and the genealogy is incorrect.

Putting aside these improbable claims for the time we are left with two solid facts: an entry in the *Anglo-Saxon Chronicle* and the will of King Æthelred II's eldest son. A starting point is the name of Godwine's father. On this there seems to be mutual agreement that he was called Wulfnoth. The *Chronicle* entry records under the year 1009 'Wulfnoth, the South Saxon, father of Earl Godwine,' and a nobleman of Sussex in another version. The term 'nobleman' or *cild* implies that he was a wealthy landowner with military obligations. Part of his duties required the guardianship of the Sussex coastline. The words of the

---

[1] 'Historia Anglorum' sa 1042 Bk6 p.201.
[2] W. J. G. N. D. ch vi pp.121-122; William of Poitiers speaks of Godwine's 'nefarious guile and wicked treachery' and goes on to say, 'whose name even after death is infamous and hateful', ch3 pp.4-5 and ch3 pp.2-5 PART ONE.
[3] 'Historia Novorum' pp.6-7.
[4] 'De Nugis Curialum' Dist v ch3 pp.416-417.
[5] 'Flowers of History' p.312 s.a 1054.
[6] 'Vita Haroldi' pp.14-15, 113, 114.

will of Æthelstan shows that Wulfstan's sympathies lay with the sons of King Æthelred by his earlier marriage who were in danger of being marginalised in favour of Edward, the child of Emma, the king's second wife. This will become more apparent as the story of deceit and court intrigue unfolds.

Among some later scribes there was a desire to portray the earl as having originated from the humblest beginnings. During the twelfth and thirteenth centuries this formed the basis of some romantic accounts of his rise to fame. Walter Map tells the story of King Æthelred II losing his way while hunting in mid-winter and seeking shelter in the cottage of a lowly herdsman. The son, not recognising their visitor, fed and tended to his horse, and generally made the king welcome. Æthelred was so impressed that he adopted Godwine and eventually appointed him earl of Gloucester.[7]

A later and more likely version of the story appeared in the *Knytlinga Saga*, attributed to Ólafr Thordarson, an Icelandic poet of the mid-thirteenth century. Jarl Úlfr, escaping from the battlefield of Sherston, was befriended by the youngster, Godwine, and taken to his father's house. Wulfnoth, a prosperous yeoman farmer, entertained the Danish leader. After guiding him back safely to the Danish fleet, Godwine was rewarded by Úlfr's friendship and his sister's hand in marriage. As a result of the jarl's patronage, King Cnut granted him an earldom.[8] In 1854, E.A. Freeman admitted that, with certain modifications, he was inclined to accept the story as a probable explanation of Godwine's rise to fame. (This was before weighing the implications of the will of the Ætheling Æthelstan and the supporting evidence of the Domesday Survey.)[9]

Further reference to the lowly status of Godwine's family background is given in the *Liber de Hyda*, a short fragment which dealt with the years from 1055 to 1121. Ralph the Black, writing during the reign of Henry II, alludes to 'Godwine's lowly family'. To the stories of Walter Map and the *Knytlinga Saga* may be added a line from the *Roman de Rou* of Robert Wace which was written in the mid-twelfth century[10], and the complete absence in the *Vita Ædwardi Regis* of any mention of Godwine's ancestry.

Godwine's Ancestry

The first attempt to trace the earl's antecedents was made by John of Worcester under the year 1007. He records of Eadric Streona, the newly created ealdorman of Mercia: 'His brothers were Brihtric, Ælfric, Goda, Æthelwine, Æthelweard and Æthelmaer, father of Wulfnoth, father of Godwine, ealdorman of the West Saxons.'[11]

---

[7] 'De Nugis Curialum' Dist v ch3 pp.412-415.
[8] 'Kyntlinga Saga' ch11 pp.32-34.
[9] F. N. C. i Appendix Note ZZ pp.704-705.
[10] 'Roman de Rou' line 9809.
[11] J. W. vol ii pp.460-461.

As Freeman pointed out, if this were correct it would mean that King Edward married his brother-in-law's great granddaughter:[12]

It must be admitted that King Edward's half sister, Eadgyth, may have been twelve or fifteen years older than Edward, and Godwine's daughter could plausibly have been fifteen years younger than her husband. Even so, this still leaves a gap of two generations, an interval of at least forty or possibly even fifty years. The linking of Godwine and Eadric Streona in John of Worcester's genealogy gives an implied association of the evil reputation of the latter - his greed, treachery and cunning - with an attempt to blacken the character of the former. In addition to the pedigree being chronologically impossible, if correct, this would have meant that in AD 1009 Brihtric would have been engineering the ruin of his own nephew.

Although there are flaws in the family tree quoted by John of Worcester, three people provided a link which gives the clues necessary to clarify the result. They are king Æthelred II, Eadric Streona and Earl Godwine. The trees quoted may have caused John of Worcester to provide the faulty family tree that appeared in his chronicles.

In each case, the family tree quoted is adapted for a special purpose and not to supersede the more comprehensive ones. For example, the English Royal Family is not a substitute for the family tree here, which is only concerned with the link which caused John of Worcester's error in connecting Earl Godwine's family tree Eadric Streona's. The same applies to the family tree of Godwine. All of these will be given their appropriate page reference later.

In 1913, an attempt was made by Alfred Anscombe to trace the family descent of Earl Godwine in a paper read to the Royal Historical Association on January 16th of that year.[13] Using the will of King Æthelred's eldest son. Æthelstan, he identified Ælfmaer with Ealdorman Æthelmaer, the son of Æthelweard the Chronicler. The wording of the will reads: 'And I grant to Ælfmaer the estate at Hamelandene which he had before; and I beseech my father, for God Almighty's sake and for mine, that he will permit this grant which I have made to him. And I grant to Godwine Wulfnoth's son the estate at Cumtune which his father possessed.'[14] Anscombe noted that these three names occurred in close proximity, also that Æthelmaer was in disgrace with the king on account of his having led the western thegns to submit to King Swein of Denmark two years before. This would explain the earnest entreaty to have the bequest ratified, and imply that Wulfnoth was either disgraced or dead when the will was drafted.

The combination of this evidence was sufficient to give some credence to his theory. In addition to this Æthelmaer's father had stated in his chronicle: 'I am

---

[12] F. N. C. i Appendix Note ZZ pp.701-705; W. G. Searle, 'A. S. Bishops, Kings and Nobles' No 50 pp.358-359.
[13] Transactions of the Royal Historical Association 3rd series, volume vii pp.129-150.
[14] D. Whitelock, 'Wills' XX pp.56-63.

descended from King Æthelred', and later, writing of the sons of King Æthelwulf: 'The fourth was Æthelred, who succeeded to the kingdom after Æthelbyrht, and who was my great, great grandfather.'[15] Anscombe concluded from this that Æthelhelm, King Æthelred's eldest son, was Æthelweard's great grandfather,[16] but was unable to account for the two intervening generations.

This lack was supplied forty four years later by Lundie W. Barlow of Boston, Massachusetts in an article which appeared in the *New England Historical and Genealogical Register* entitled *The Antecedents of Earl Godwine 0f Wessex*..[17] With the charters S 367 and S 1484 as evidence, he concluded that the Ealdorman Æthelfrith who had the title deeds of land at Risborough, Buckinghamshire renewed was the grandfather of Ælfgifu who made a bequest of land at Risborough to the Old Minster, Winchester in her will. Ælfgifu was Æthelweard the Chronicler's sister and also the divorced wife of King Eadwig. Godwine's forefathers were given as King Æthelred I, Æthelhelm, Æthelfrith, his son Eadric, Æthelweard, Æthelmaer, Wulfnoth and Godwine. More recent scholarship has questioned some of Lundie Barlow's findings. It is doubtful that King Æthelred's son, Æthelhelm, was the ealdorman of Wiltshire - which both Anscombe and Lundie Barlow seem to accept.[18] In King Alfred's charter to 'Æthelhelm comes' he is not spoken of as 'kinsman'[19], nor is there any evidence in either chronicle or charter that he ever married or had children.[20]

Ælhelfrith's relationship to King Æthelred is not mentioned either in any known source. Moreover, the link between Ælfgifu and Æthelfrith is doubtful. The latter's thirty hide estate at Risborough has been identified as Monks Risborough, whilst the neighbouring Princes Risborough would almost certainly be the residence of Ælfgifu with her royal connections. In 1086, it was a royal estate and Monks Risborough a manor of the archbishop.[21] In fact there is no real evidence for any relationship between Æthelhelm and Æthelfrith or his family.

There is no doubt that the relationship between Æthelweard and his son Æthelmaer is correct. This is shown by their shared cultural and religious interests; their patronage of Ælfric the Homilist; and the fact that when Æthelmaer founded

---

[15] 'Chronicle of Æthelweard' pp.2 and 39.
[16] 'King Alfred's Will', F. Harmer, S. E. H. D. pp.91-103, S 1507.
[17] Volume LXI 1957 pp.30-38.
[18] S. Keynes and M. Lapidge, 'Alfred' p.321 n66; B. Yorke, 'Æthelwold' p.70 and n46, although P. Stafford accepts that he was, 'Unification' p.41 and 'Queens, Concubines and Dowagers', pp.43-44.
[19] S 348.
[20] A. Williams in a private correspondence.
[21] M. Gelling, 'Early Charters of the Thames Valley'; Monk's Risborough No 147, Note 148 p.74 and App179; Princes Risborough No 152 p.75. For the further history of Monk's Risborough No 154 p.76, N157 p.77, No 158 p.78; F. G. Pearson, 'Some Additional Notes on the name of Risborough' in 'Records of Buckinghamshire' XIII.

the abbey of Cerne in Dorset, he gave estates to endow it which had been left to him by his father.[22]

The family of Æthelweard is endorsed by the will of Ælfgifu. In it she bequeaths the estates of Mongewell and Berkhamstead to 'Ælfweard and Æthelweard and Ælfwaru in common for their lifetime' and in the next sentence refers to Ælfwaru as 'my sister'.[23] Their mother was Æthelgifu. This is confirmed in a charter concerning an exchange of land arranged between Bishop Brihthelm of Wells and Abbot Æthelwold of Abingdon, with King Eadwig's sanction. This was witnessed by Ælfgifu, the king's wife, Æthelgifu, the king's wife's mother, the bishops of Winchester, Ramsbury and Worcester, Ealdorman Byrhtnoth (the hero of Maldon), Ælfheah and his brother Eadric, the king's kinsmen.[24] Æthelgifu was still alive when Ælfgifu's will was drawn up possibly as late as 975. In it her daughter appeals to Bishop Æthelwold to act as 'an advocate on my behalf and that of my mother'.[25]

It is at this point that the problems arise. There is no evidence to prove the identity of Æthelgifu's husband. Using the doubtful devolution of Risborough from Ealdorman Æthelfrith and his wife Æthelgyth to Ælfgifu, Lundie W. Barlow came to the conclusion that it would have been Eadric, the youngest of Æthelfrith's sons. Dr Cyril Hart, on the other hand, suggests that Ælfstan, the eldest, was probably her spouse.[26]

However, assuming that Ælfgifu was approximately the same age as King Eadwig (who was fifteen in 955) this poses some problems. The charter witness lists indicate that Ælfstan died in 934; Eadric lived until 949. Of the two other sons of Æthelfrith, Æthelwold seems to have been a bachelor and left no children while the offspring of Æthelstan 'Half-King' are all well documented.[27] There is, in fact, no real reason to believe that either Æthelfrith or either of his sons was related to the West Saxon royal house. The only source to suggest it is the flagrantly untrustworthy biography, the *Vita Oswaldi* by Byrhtferth of Ramsey.[28]

Æthelgifu

It would seem that the only thing that can be stated with any degree of reliability is that the royal connection between Æthelweard the Chronicler and King Æthelred[4] was through Æthelgifu, and that she was the granddaughter of one of his children.

A charter of the king's dated 868 was witnessed by Queen Wulfthryth and by Oswald who is styled *filius regis* 'the son of the king'. Whether the latter was their

---

[22] S 1217.
[23] D. Whitelock, 'Wills' No viii pp.20-23, 118-121; S1484; C. Hart, 'The Danelaw', ch14 pp.455-465.
[24] A. J. Robertson, 'Charters' No XXXI, pp.58-57 and p.315.
[25] D. Whitelock, 'Wills' No viii pp.20-23, 118-21, S1484.
[26] 'The Danelaw' p.571; 'Athelstan Half-King' p.117.
[27] 'The Danelaw' pp.572-574.
[28] I am indebted to Dr Ann Williams for this reference.

son or nephew, he must have died at an early age. He last attested a charter c. 875 and was already dead when King Alfred's will was drafted.[29] The only other recorded children of Æthelred were Æthelhelm and Æthelwold. The descent which Æthelweard claimed in his *Chronicle* must either have been through one of them, or through an unrecorded daughter.

Having assumed, through lack of any evidence, that neither Æthelfrith nor either of his sons was descended from King Æthelred it follows that the descent must have been through Æthelgifu. This does not necessarily disprove the theory that Godwine was of royal lineage. As long as the relationship through Æthelweard could be maintained it would still be viable. Unfortunately, the key to this is the establishment of the identity of Ealdorman Æthelmaer with the Ælfmaer of the Ætheling Aethelstan's will. This cannot be substantiated.

The confusion of the prefix Æthel- with Ælf-maer did not occur until after the Norman Conquest.[30] It is true that Bishop Æthelmaer of Elmham, Stigand's brother does appear as Ælfmaer, but this is in the Domesday Survey of 1086. Another example occurs in the name of Æthelwine. In the contemporary Abingdon recension of the *Chronicle* the name is given in its original form; in the late eleventh or early twelfth century annal written at Worcester it is given as Ælfwine. Æthelstan's will is contemporary and exists in two early eleventh century manuscripts. This demonstrates that confusion between the two names could not have existed at that time. Nor is this the only reason that the pedigree seems unlikely to be correct. From Æthelred to Æthelmaer there is an almost unbroken line of names with the element Æthel- which then alters to Wulf- and Godwine.[31] The author of the *Vita*, speaking of Godwine says, 'among the new nobles of the conquered kingdom attached to the King's side was that Godwine, whom we have just mentioned'.[32]

Of course it can be argued that times change and the preference for names alters; also, that the term 'new noble' merely meant that Godwine was a comparative stranger to Cnut and his Danish appointed earls. The absence of any direct reference to his ancestry in the *Vita* could be explained by Eadgyth's disapproval of her father's Scandinavian associations or perhaps because of her grandfather Wulfnoth's disgrace in 1009.

One argument in favour of some relationship of Wulfnoth with the royal family is their preference to promote their own closeknit kin to positions as ealdormen, discthegns and high positions in the church. Thus Ælfhere was nominated as the ealdorman of Mercia in 956, his brother Ælfheah as *discthegn* and then as ealdorman of Hampshire. Bryhthelm who is called 'kinsman' by the kings Eadwig and Edgar was appointed to the bishopric of Selsey and then to Winchester. Æthelweard was assigned to the ealdormanry of the Western Shires and Æthelmaer his son succeeded him. Ælfheah had two sons. One of them, Godwine, became the

---

[29] D. Sturdy, 'Alfred' pp.117; 136.
[30] Dr A. Williams in a private correspondence.
[31] F. Barlow, 'The Godwins' pp.18, 19.
[32] 'Vita' pp.8, 9.

ealdorman of Lindsey. There was a close relationship between the families of Ælfheah and Æthelweard: in the former's will he left land in Buckinghamshire to his 'kinsman' Æthelweard and in Wiltshire for Ælfweard, probably Æthelweard's brother. In the Eynsham charter Godwine son of Ælfheah exchanged some land with Æthelmaer son of Æthelweard where the same relationship is mentioned.[33] The brothers Ælfgar and Byrhtferth signed high on the witness lists and in one charter were both styled as 'consul'. Ælfgar held the office of *discthegn* in King Edgar's court and after his death the office passed to his brother.[34] Similarly Edward the Confessor promoted his relatives Odda and Ralph to earldoms in 1047 and 1051.[35] This only proves that high offices could be held by the king's own kin, but does nothing to establish Wulfnoth's status or nobility. The *Chronicle* calls him 'Wulfnofh *cild* the South Saxon.' The Latin annal, in the bilingual Canterbury version, composed towards the end of the eleventh century states 'The father of Earl Godwine, the Nobleman, Wulfnoth.'[36] John of Worcester speaks of 'Wulfnoth, the ealdorman of the South Saxons'.[37] William of Jumièges writing in 1070 or soon after says that Godwine was of noble parentage'.[38]

Wulfnoth Cild

To summarise, there is general agreement that Godwine's father was called Wulfnoth whatever his status or provenance. In Norse tradition he was called *Úfnaðr*. He is mentioned in *Fagrskinna*[39], in Snorri's *Ólafr's Saga Helga*[40] and in his *Saga of Haraldr Harðraða Sigurðson*[41], in the *Knytlinga Saga*[42] and in the *Flateyjarbok*.[43]

---

[33] Ælfheah 'Royal Kinsman' in S 564, 585 and 586; Ælfhere S 555; Byrhthelm S 615, 683; Ælfgifu, S 737, 738. For Godwine of Lindsey and Æthelmaer see A. Williams, 'Ælfhere' p.171, 172 note 141 and S911; for Byrhthelm see B. Yorke, 'Æthelwold' p.75 n91; for kinship between the families of Ælfheah and Æthelweard see D. Whitelock, 'Wills' IX pp.22-5 and S1485 and B. Yorke, 'Æthelwold' pp.77 notes 104-107 for Ælfhere A. Williams 'Ælfhere' p.145 n4.

[34] A.S.C 'A' s.a 962.

[35] For Odda's relationship to King Edward see A. Williams, 'Odda of Deerhurst' particularly p.3, 16, 17.

[36] A.S.C 'C', 'D', 'E', 'F'; 'Wulfnoth Cild', 'C' omits calling him 'a South Saxon'.

[37] J. W. ii pp.460-461.

[38] G. N. D. vol ii pp.108; 109 6(9); W. P. pp.20-21 writes of 'hostages of noble birth, a son and grandson of Earl Godwine'.

[39] Fagrskinna ch 58 p.218 'Haraldr, son of Goini Ulfnaoarson and of Gyoa, dóttur þorgils sprakaleggr' trans A Finlay.

[40] 'Olafs Saga' ch CLXII p.312.

[41] 'Saga of Harald the Stern' ch LXXV p.219.

[42] 'Knytlinga Saga' ch11 p.33.

[43] Flateyjarbok ch215 p.387. 'Systir Úlfs jarl var Gyoa, er átti Guoini Úlfnaosson'.

Table 1. Sequence of Events 991 to 1014

AD 991	Olafr Tryggvason invades England; Byrhtnoth defeated and slain at Maldon.
AD 993	Probable date of Godwine's birth.[44]
AD 994	Olafr and Swein of Denmark attack London. First payment of Danegeld. Olafr and Swein return to their native countries.
AD 995	Ólafr crowned king of Norway.
AD 995-6	Swein succeeds his father in Denmark.
AD 997	Eadric Streona witnesses his first charter.[45]
AD 1000	Death of Ólafr at the battle of Svold.
AD 1002	Marriage of King Æthelred and Emma of Normandy. Pallig and his wife Gunnhildr supposedly murdered in St Brice's Day massacre.
AD 1003-4	Possible birth of Edward the Confessor.
AD 1004	Swein raiding in England.
AD 1005	Famine in England. Swein and the Danes return to Denmark. Ealdorman Æthelmaer and Ordulf retire from public life.
AD 1006	Wulfnoth disgraced; Ælfhelm murdered, his sons blinded. The Danes return. Death of King Æthelred's son Ecgberht.
AD 1007	Eadric created ealdorman of Mercia; Northumbria united under Uhtred of Bamburgh.
AD 1008	Building of the fleet.
AD 1009	Brihtric accuses Wulfnoth of treachery. Death of King Æthelred's son Edgar.
AD 1012-3	Death of King Æthelred's son Eadred
AD 1014	Death of King Æthelred's son Æthelstan.

---

[44] F. Barlow, 'The Godwins' p.20.
[45] 'Atlas' Table LXIII 2 of 9 S 890.

In all the versions of the *Chronicle* Wulfnoth is styled '*cild*'. This poses the question of what the term implies of office or position. Benjamin Thorpe considered it to be almost equivalent to an *Ætheling*.[46] To Anscombe it referred to the youngest son who, as such, inherited by law certain lands.[47] It has also been suggested that the term may have been used to differentiate between men of the same name,[48] or perhaps to signify some position preparatory to that of *discthegn* or ealdorman. Professor Swanton regards it as indicative of high rank and points out that it was used of Edgar Ætheling.[49] In the *Chronicles*, charters and the *Domesday* Survey there are many men who were classified as 'cild'. Some of these are recorded as being extensive landowners. Amongst them was Ælfric who became the ealdorman or Mercia in 983, Æthelnoth and Brihtsige of Kent, Wulfmaer and Eadric of the Western Shires, Wulfsi of Nottinghamshire, Turkil of Harringworth, Godwine Tokisson of Northamptonshire and Lincolnshire, Leofwine of Bacton owner of estates in Suffolk and Essex, Eadric 'the Wild' of Herefordshire and Shropshire and Wulfnoth of Kent. Uhtred was a member of the royal household of King Eadred; Ulf and Edward were both king's thegns; Edgar, grandson of King Edmund Ironside was of royal blood; Turkil of 'Harringworth' may have been the son of Thorkell Hávi by Eadgyth and thus King Æthelred's grandson[50]; Eadric 'the Wild' too had a more distant link with Eadgyth and her father, and Dodda may have been a kinsman of Earl Odda[51] and thus of King Edward. There is too little evidence available about the remainder to draw any conclusions. Ælfmaer is known to us only in a charter of the late tenth century[52]; Ælfsige from two Kentish Charters[53]; Ælfweard of Buckinghamshire, Wulfric of Northamptonshire and Suffolk and another Ælfsige are little more than names.[54] The most common denominator amongst most of them would seem to be the extent of their landed possessions or wealth. According to the *Domesday* record Æthelnoth cild and 'those like him' were expected to supply the king with a bodyguard for six days each year, it was also obligatory to attend the shire court in their area.[55] This would seem to imply an office of some kind with military obligations. From this we would expect the Wulfnoth who was Godwine's father would have been a considerable landowner in his native Sussex. This is confirmed by the extent of Godwine's eventual holdings in the shire together with those of

---

[46] Quoted from F. Barlow, 'The Godwins' ch1 p.25 note 7.
[47] 'The Pedigree of Earl Godwine' pp.133-134.
[48] Lundie Barlow, 'The Antecedents of Earl Godwine' p.37 Notes and References Note 2.
[49] A. S. Chronicles p.138 note 7; A.S.C 'E' s.a 1009, 1067.
[50] 'The Danelaw' pp. 636-642 particularly p.636-640 and n42 on p.636; for Leofwine of Bacton see A. Williams, 'Land and Power' p.179 and 'A West Country Magnate' p.47.
[51] F. N. C. i Note MM p.649.
[52] A. J. Robertson, 'Charters' No LXXI pp.144-5 and p.389.
[53] ibid No LXXVII pp.150-151 and LXXV pp.148-149; S 1461 and 1220.
[54] 'The Danelaw' p.227 for Ælfsige.
[55] A. Williams, 'Lost Worlds' p.73.

his family.[56] His military obligations would almost certainly have been connected with his naval expertise, as indicated in 1009.

The annal for the year 1009 in the *Chronicle* records that Brihtric, the brother of Eadric Streona, accused Wulfnoth to the king of treachery, and that the latter enticed away twenty ships and fled.[57] To understand the enormity of the disaster this created, it is necessary to go back to the England of the early 990s. Up to that time, the country had been suffering attacks from Viking armies on a recurrent but relatively small scale for many years. Because of the mobility afforded by their warships, the raiding hosts were able to penetrate the country at will, plunder to their hearts' content and return to their vessels laden with booty.

Danes and Danegeld

The situation changed in 991. Ólafr Tryggvason, fresh from marauding adventures in the Baltic, arrived in England with a fleet of ninety three ships. He landed at Folkestone; pillaging and ravaging as they went, his host eventually reached Maldon in Essex where they were confronted by the elderly Byrhtnoth and the eastern troops. After an heroic defence, the ealdorman was slain and his army defeated. The enemy which the men of Essex faced that day was a large invading force and the loss sustained was a grievous setback.

Three years later Ólafr attacked London. This time he was accompanied by Swein Forkbeard, the son of Haraldr Gormson the King of Denmark. The doughty citizens drove them off and the Viking army were forced to vent their lust for destruction in Kent, Sussex and Hampshire. It was at this point that the king and his councillors decided on the advisability of offering the first payment of the Danegeld and the promise of provisions and safe harbourage at Southampton for the winter. Ólafr accepted, agreed to be baptized, and with his share of the geld returned to claim the throne of Norway. He received a hero's welcome; old grievances were forgotten, and Ólafr was proclaimed king in Trondheim. Meanwhile, Swein sailed west, harrying along the coast of Wales and then back to wrest the crown of Denmark from his ageing father who was forced to seek refuge in Wendland where he died of his wounds. With both Ólafr and Swein occupied in their native countries, a Danish army was raiding in Wessex with hardly any opposition from 997 onwards. The *Chronicle* graphically records the suffering and hardship endured and the utter futility of the resistance given.[58]

In the year AD1000 a wounded Ólafr Tryggvason leapt from the gunwale of his ship, the 'Long Serpent' and plunged to his death in the Oresund. His kingdom of Norway was partitioned amongst the confederacy that had defeated him. This not only enhanced King Swein's power in Scandinavia, it also gave his ambitions in England free rein.

---

[56] A. Williams, 'Lands and Power' pp.176-177.
[57] A.S.C 'E' s.a 1009; 'F' s.a 1009.
[58] A.S.C 'E' s.a 997, 998, 999,1001; A.S.C 'A's.a 1001.

On November 13 1002 King Æthelred gave the order 'for all the Danes who were among the English race to be killed, because it was made known to the king that they wanted to ensnare his life'.[59] It has been plausibly suggested that this may have been connected with the treachery of Pallig the previous year who, in spite of the estates and gifts which Æthelred had given him, had defected to the Danes when they had attacked Devon.[60] How widespread the extent of the massacre was is doubtful. Later tradition asserted that amongst those murdered was Pallig, his wife and child. His wife, the story claims, was Swein's own sister, and in revenge he returned. The only determined opposition he encountered was from Ulfkell Snilling, a leading East Anglian magnate who, although he lost the battle, won the grudging admiration of his opponents. The following year the country experienced a famine so severe, 'that no one ever remembered so grim before', so bad that Swein and his Danes retired to their native land.

Intrigues at Court

This was not the only calamity that beset England in the year 1005; both Æthelmaer and Ordwulf retired from public life. Both had been the king's most trusted advisors and had with three exceptions headed the witness lists since 994.[61] Æthelmaer may have entered the monastery he had established at Eynsham and Ordwulf his monastic foundation in Tavistock. Both these men were related to the king, Æthelmaer by descent, Ordwulf as King Æthelred's brother-in-law. They and their fathers had long records of loyal service and the subsequent turmoil is symptomatic of the political atmosphere of tension and suspicion that existed in the royal circles. This was just the tip of the iceberg that was to become apparent in the following months.

The first casualty was Wulfgeat, whom the king 'had loved almost more that all others.'[62] His possessions and status were taken from him because of 'unjust judgements and arrogant deeds'. Wulfgeat had witnessed charters from 986 until his disgrace. He must have been a regular attendant at court and, from 995,[63] usually signed in third or fourth position after Æthelmaer and Ordulf, and witnessed almost every charter.[64] His wife seems to have been implicated in his crimes.[65]

There may have been some justification for the fall of Wulfgeat but what followed seems to defy any logical explanation. In 994 Sigeric, the Archbishop of Canterbury, confirmed a grant by Wulfrun to the minster of St Mary in Wolverhampton which she had founded. The grant records that Wulfrun had a

---

[59] A.S.C 'E' s.a 1002; A.S.C 'F'1003.
[60] A. Williams et al, 'Dark Age Britain' p.201.
[61] S. Keynes, 'Atlas', Table LXIII 2 of 9; S 877, 883 and 893.
[62] J. W. pp.456, 457 s.a 1006.
[63] S 884; 'Atlas', Table LXIII 2 of 9; witnessed first in 988, S 870.
[64] S. Keynes, 'Atlas', Table LXIII 2 of 9
[65] A. J. Robertson, 'Charters' No LXIII pp.130.-131 and 376; A.S.C 'E' s.a 1006; J. W. pp.456-457; S 918, 934.

daughter called Ælfthryth and a kinsman named Wulfgeat, whose crimes needed reparation.[66] Wulfrun was the mother of Wulfric Spot whose vast estates were spread over ten shires. Her daughter Ælfthryth was probably the great grandmother of the earls Eadwin and Morcar and of Ealdgyth who was successively the wife of King Gruffydd of Wales and King Harold Godwineson. Wulfrun was also the mother of Ealdorman Ælfhelm and the grandmother of Wulfheah and Ufegeat. It is not surprising therefore that, in the witness lists from 985 until 1002 when Wulfric attested for the last time, the names of Wulfgeat, Wulfric and Wulfheah are invariably found together. After Wulfric's death in 1002 the same proximity applied to Wulfgeat and Wulfheah until the fateful year of 1005.[67]

An even more sinister occurrence was to follow. On the pretext of friendship, Eadric arranged a feast and invited Ælfhelm to join him. During the visit the Northumbrian ealdorman was enticed to participate in a hunt, during which he was ambushed and murdered. The king himself was involved in the blinding of Ælfhelm's sons, Wulfheah and Ufegeat, shortly afterwards when they were at his royal residence at Cookham.[68] There is no evidence of any trial or charge being brought forward against Ælfhelm or his sons. Ufegeat witnessed no extant charter. He received a bequest in his uncle Wulfric's will of an estate at 'Northtune', 'in the hope that he may be a better friend and supporter of the monastery'.[69] Ælfhelm had been the ealdorman of Deiran Northumbria for thirteen years, and there seems to have been no motive for his murder or of the blinding of his sons. He came from a wealthy and respected Mercian family and the three incidents, Wulfgeat's disgrace, Ælfhelm's murder and the blinding of his sons, all with the king's full approval smacks of court politics of the most sinister kind. It could be said that, in the interests of co-ordinating defence, Ælfhelm was eliminated so that Northumbria could again be united under Uhtred of the ancient house of Bamburgh. King Æthelred may also have revived the ealdordom of all Mercia the following year for the same reason. The position had remained vacant after Ælfric was banished in 985. The murderer of Ælfhelm was rewarded with the appointment.

A hint of things to come appears in the last charter in which both Wulfgeat and Wulfheah witnessed. The two were separated; Wulfheah was pushed down to fourth place with Eadric Streona in second, Wulfgeat in third, and Æthelric, Eadric's father in fifth.[70] This makes it difficult to escape the conclusion that Eadric and his family were ingratiating themselves with the king for the advancement of their interests, and were prepared to mete out violence to anyone who stood in their path.[71]

---

[66] P. Sawyer, 'Charters of Burton Abbey' pp. XL-XLIII for Ælfthryth; p.XL and pp.32-33 for Wulfgeat.
[67] S. Keynes, 'Atlas', Table LXIII 2 of 9 and 3 of 9.
[68] J. W. pp.458-459.
[69] P. Sawyer, 'Charters of Burton Abbey' pp. xxii, xxvi and xlii.
[70] S 912, 'Atlas', Table LXIII 3 of 9.
[71] S. Keynes, 'Diplomas' pp.210-215.

Of those who incurred the king's displeasure or felt no longer able to work with him can be listed Æthelmaer, Ordwulf, Ælfhelm and his sons, Wulfnoth, Ælfmaer, Sigeferth, Morcar and Leofwine. It is no coincidence that the last five names appear in the will of the Ætheling Æthelstan together with his brothers Edmund and Eadwig. In that document there is no bequest for his two young step-brothers. This leads to the conclusion that a party was forming in opposition to the king's avowed intention of making Emma's son his heir. In this the king had found willing allies in the family of Eadric Streona.

Seizing of the English Fleet

With a fresh air of determination, in the year 1008, Æthelred ordered a fleet of warships to be built. Plans were set afoot which stated that each area of 310 hides was to provide one warship and every 8 hides to supply the necessary armour for a member of the crew.[72] Sussex consisted of 3375 hides.[73] If the estates that were exempt from paying geld were not answerable, Sussex would only have been responsible for providing ten vessels. It may be that the figure of 310 hides which is mentioned in all versions of the *Chronicle* and John of Worcester [with the exception of 'D'] is a hypothetical one. It seems possible that one person in a given area was made accountable for the construction or requisitioning of the required quota. It is obvious, therefore, that some of the fleet which elected to follow Wulfnoth into exile were either his own personal contribution or were sympathisers from among the men of Kent and Hampshire. All over England the shipyards reverberated to the sounds of hammering, sawing and planing of timber, while the forests were filled with the noise of the felling of trees and the plodding of horses and oxen as they dragged heavy logs to their destination.

By the following year through sheer hard work and enthusiasm a fleet, according to the records, larger than any that had been assembled before,[74] was moored at Sandwich in readiness to repel a 'foreign' invader. It was natural to place the command under men with naval experience, men such as Wulfnoth who, as thegn in Sussex, would have had ample experience of the sea and its treacherous moods.

Overall command was apparently in the hands of Brihtric who, John of Worcester tells us, was tainted with all the evil traits of his brother.[75] Brihtric accused Wulfnoth of treachery towards the king. John says that the accusation was unjust.[76]

It is impossible to discover the reasons advanced for this incrimination. The most likely cause was probably that Wulfnoth's sympathies were with the Æthelings, Æthelstan and Edmund, whom Æthelred was prepared to pass over in favour of the son of his second marriage. The author of the *Vita Ædwardi Regis* gives some

---

[72] A.S.C C-F; J. W. pp.460-461.
[73] Phillimore D. B. Sussex, Notes.
[74] A.S.C 'C'-'F' sa 1009; J. W. s.a 1008 pp.460-461.
[75] J. W. pp.460-461.
[76] ibid.

credence to his intention: he writes 'When the royal wife of old King Æthelred was pregnant in her womb, all the men of the country took an oath that if a man-child should come forth as the fruit of her labour, they should await in him their lord and king who would rule over the whole race of the English'.[77] It seems that history was repeating itself fifteen years later: before the lady was prepared to become the bride of Cnut she refused, unless 'he would affirm to her by oath, that he would never set up the son of any wife other than herself to rule after him.'[78]

Before his marriage to Emma, Æthelred had been married to Ælfgifu, the daughter of Thored the ealdorman of Deiran Northumbria. She was the mother of his six sons and three daughters. The eldest son would have been sixteen or seventeen when his father married again. Æthelstan's grandfather Thored fell from favour in 992 after the failure of an expedition of which he was one of its leaders.[79] It is feasible that, when Æthelred sought to marry Emma, her brother Duke Richard II of Normandy would have demanded that a son born to her would take precedence as heir to the throne over a son of the previous marriage. Æthelred was no longer young, he had fathered many sons and his country was threatened continuously by Viking raids. Emma, although young, was very much alive to her own interests and her Norman relatives needed to see some advantages in the match to the future of Normandy.

It is not surprising therefore that Æthelstan should seek support from the established nobility. Certainly from the year 1014 when Edward was sent as 'his father's representative' to meet the Witan to arrange his return, if not before, Æthelstan was aware that his own position was being undermined. Probably he had already started to count his friends and make alliances.

It was in this context that Ælfhelm and his family may have fallen foul of the king.[80] The same could well have applied to Wulfnoth; sympathy and support for Æthelstan and his brother Edmund could well have been the reason for Brihtric's allegation. The South Saxon thegn was not going to wait to be murdered in ambush like Ælfhelm, or to have his sight destroyed like Wulfheah and Ufegeat. He took flight, to avoid being taken prisoner, and with him the crews of twenty warships who preferred exile with Wulfnoth than to stay to serve under Brihtric's command: the latter was quick to seize the opportunity to enhance his own prestige with the king. He set out with eighty ships of the fleet in order to capture Wulfnoth 'dead or alive'.[81] In pursuit of his quarry his flotilla was caught in a heavy storm which, with superior seamanship, Wulfnoth was able to avoid. Brihtric's vessels were buffeted by heavy seas, dashed to pieces and tossed up on the shore. Turning on his pursuers Wulfnoth set fire to what was left of the battered hulks.

---

[77] 'Vita' pp.12-13.
[78] E. E. R. 16, p.33.
[79] A. S. Chronicles 'E' s.a 992 and notes 16 and 17. M. Swanton.
[80] N. Higham, 'Death of A.S England' pp.46-47.
[81] A.S.C s.a 1009 'C' – 'F'; J. W. s.a 1008 pp.462-463.

Brihtric may have perished in the storm; if he escaped it is likely that he returned to Sandwich in disgrace. His name ceases to appear on the witness lists after that year. According to a late tradition one of Eadric's brothers was murdered in Kent. Eadric expected the king to see that justice was done, but Æthelred took the view that it was nothing more than he deserved.[82] It is possible that this brother may have been Brihtric who must have provoked the fury of many who had a great deal of sympathy for Wulfnoth. His actions had been the cause of the ruin of all the hard work and hopes of the previous year 'and thus lightly let the whole nation's labour waste' and 'then it was as if everything was in confusion, and the king took himself home - and the ealdorman and the chief councillors - and thus lightly abandoned the ships'.

After some raiding along the coast to obtain provisions, nothing more is heard of Wulfnoth. It seems that he was dead when the Ætheling Æthelstan made his will in 1014. There seems a plausible reason to believe that he found a refuge in Flanders with Count Baldwin IV which could have been the origin of Godwine's later friendship with Baldwin V.[83]

Wulfnoth's attendance at court must have been rare. He witnessed only four charters; the first was in 986 when he signed in the twentieth position;[84] in 995 he attested a grant of land in Kent to the bishopric of Rochester where his name appeared in tenth place;[85] three years later he was at court to witness Æthelred's permission to convert the community of Sherborne to the Benedictine rule and to confirm grants of land in Dorset and Devon to the abbey.[86] On this occasion he was in seventh place. Last, he was in attendance to testify the confirmation of Æthelmear's foundation charter of Eynsham. He witnessed on that occurrence eighteenth amongst forty seven, following Æthelweard, Æthelwine and Brihtric who were presumably Eadric Streona's brothers.[87] This was in the fateful year of 1005 when already tension was mounting to boiling point.

The Man Named 'Ælfmær'

The Ælfmær mentioned in Æthelstan's will in close proximity to Wulfnoth and Godwine could well have been another supporter of the Ætheling and his brother Edmund. He must have done something to have caused King Æthelred's deep displeasure, to induce the king's eldest son to write 'and I beseech my father, for God Almighty's sake and for mine, that he will permit this grant which I have made him', in connection with a bequest of 'the estate at Hamlandene'.[88]

---

[82] Sir Henry Wharton, 'Anglia Sacra' II p.132 1691; A. Williams et al, 'Dark Age Britain' p.65.
[83] 'Vita' pp.36-37, 38-39.
[84] 'Atlas; Table LXIII 7 of 9; S 862.
[85] ibid 8 of 9; S 885.
[86] ibid; S 895.
[87] ibid; 9 of 9; S 911.
[88] 'The Will of the Ætheling Æthelstan', D. Whitelock 'Wills', No XX pp.57-63 and pp.167-74.

Ælfmær was still alive when the will was drawn up in 1014. He is probably the same Ælfmaer who witnessed charters in 981, 997, twice in 1004, 1005, 1012, 1014 and possibly 1018.[89]

There is one tenuous link which could provide a connection between Godwine and the West Saxon royal family. In his will, King Alfred bequeathed 'to Ælhelm, my brother's son, the residence at Aldingbourne, Compton, Crondall, Beeding, Beddingham, Barnham, Thunderfield and Eashing'.[90] Aldingbourne, Beeding, Buddington and Barnham have been identified as estates in Sussex[91], Thunderfield and Eashing in Surrey and Crondall in Hampshire. Compton could refer to one of the Comptons in Surrey, Somerset or Hampshire, but it seems likely that, as it is included in the text of the will between four other Sussex properties [the exception being Crondall] that one of the Sussex Comptons is meant.[92] In Totnore Hundred in East Sussex King Harold was later in possession of 4 hides from King Edward, which indicates that at some stage it had been absorbed into the royal demesne.[93] The other Compton, in Westbourne Hundred, was a 10 hide estate which Esbearn held from Earl Godwine[94] This was almost certainly the Compton that Wulfnoth had possessed in 1009, but was it the Compton which King Alfred bequeathed to Æthelhelm on his death in 899, one hundred and ten years earlier? If Compton had been passed down to Wulfnoth's forebears through five generations it is just possible that Lundie W. Barlow's suggestion that it may have been through his parents that the family were descended from King Æthelred could have some value.[95]

---

[89] S 890, Table LXIII 2 of 9; S 906, 907, 911, 916, 915, 918 and 933; Table LXIII 3 of 9, S 890 and perhaps S 953 Table LXIV 1 of 3.
[90] F. Harmer, S. E. H. D. No 11 pp.15-19; 91-103.
[91] ibid p.97 N 128.
[92] Keynes and Lapidge, 'Alfred' p.321 note 68, also p.322 notes 69, 70, 74.
[93] Phillimore, D. B. Sussex 10-23.
[94] ibid, D. B. Sussex 11-36.
[95] 'Antecedents of Earl Godwine' p.37 note 27.

Pedigree of Godwine

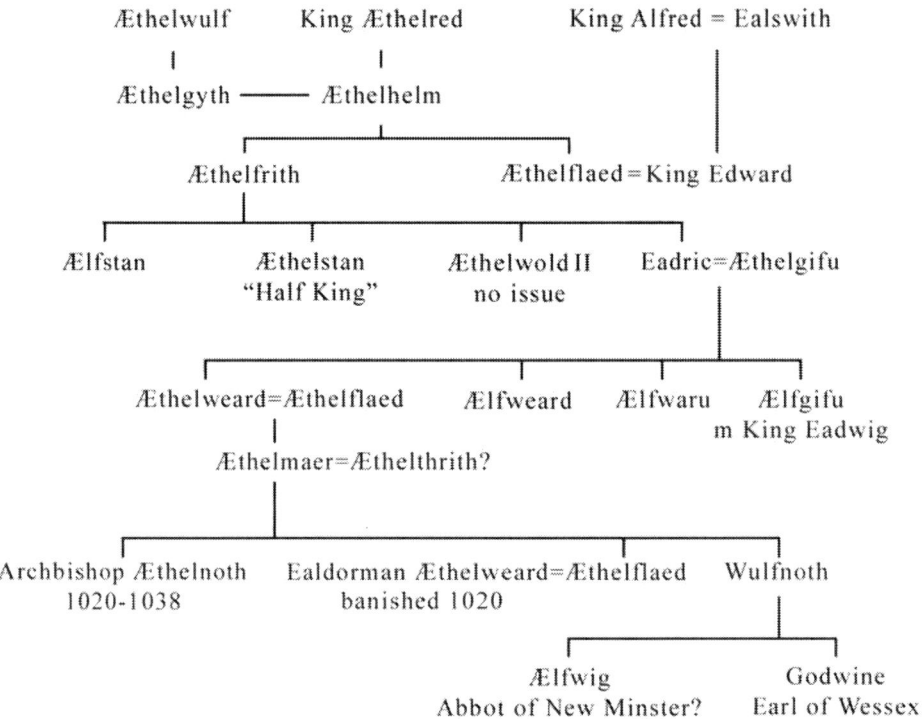

A. Anscombe *The Pedigree of Earl Godwin*,
Trans. R.Hist.Soc., 3rd ser., vii (1913) 129-50

Lundie W. Barlow, *The Antecedents of Earl Godwin of Wessex*,
New England Historical and Genealogical Registere, lxi (1957) 30-38

(See Chapter I for criticism of this simplified genealogy)

2. Godwine's Early Years

Any account of Godwine's early life is sure to contain a certain amount of speculation. The name *Godwine* 'friend of God' or 'good friend' was quite popular in the early eleventh century, particularly in south-east England. Two facts emerge which seem indisputable, however: first, that his father was Wulfnoth, a thegn of at least local importance; and second, that his birthplace was in Sussex.

Family, Birth and Early Life

Godwine was probably born in the early 990s and most likely in 992 or 993.[1] This would mean that in 1009, when his father was exiled, he would have been around eighteen years of age, old enough to rebuild the family fortunes. At the time when the Ætheling Æthelstan's will was drawn up, Godwine's services were of use to the young prince, and in 1018 he was of an age (about twenty seven) for King Cnut to advance him to the position of earl. He cannot have been born much earlier than 992/3, since it is improbable that he would still have been campaigning in 1052 if he was then much over the age of sixty. However, there are examples of vigorous older men from this time: Ealdorman Byrhtnoth, who fell at Maldon, was also over sixty years old at the time of his death in 991.

Godwine's father, Wulfnoth, is not well documented although Wulfnoth was not a very common name. Apart from the signatures to Æthelred's charters, which were probably those of Godwine's father, there was only one Wulfnoth witnessing in the reign of Cnut[2] and perhaps only one in the reign of Edward the Confessor.[3] However, this hypothesis rests on the evidence that Halton (held by Toki and Æthelflaed, inhereited from Wulfnoth) was held some thirty odd years later by Leofwine, Godwine's son, which seems altogether too flimsy in view of the way grants were made from the royal demesne to newly appointed earls.

Nothing is known of the name or identity of Godwine's mother. It is a possibility that, since he called his youngest son Wulfnoth after his own father, he may have named his youngest daughter Ælfgifu after his mother[4]. If it is correct that he did have a brother Ælfwig and perhaps a nephew Ælfric[5] then the first element *ælf-* of these names could provide some corroboration for this suggestion.

---

[1] F. Barlow, 'The Godwins' p.20.
[2] 'Atlas', Table LXX 2 of 2; S 961 AD 1024, S 979 AD 1027X 1032, S 969 AD 1033, S 975 AD 1035 and S 993 AD 1042
[3] 'Atlas' No LXXV 2 of 2, S 999 AD 1043, S 1005 Ad 1044; S 1004 AD 1044; S 1027 AD 1059.
[4] Phillimore DB 4-21.
[5] 'Vita' pp.30-31.

A late tradition gives Godwine a brother named Ælfwig. It is accepted that a man of this name was the abbot of New Minster, Winchester, appointed in 1063 and killed at the battle of Hastings together with other members of his community. According to the manuscript *Destructio Monasterri de Hydâ* this Ælfwig was an uncle of King Harold, which supports his position as Godwine's brother[6] It seems unlikely, though not impossible, that a brother of Godwine's should not have held a more prominent position in the church. Ælfwig, if the tradition is reliable, may have been a good deal younger than his more famous brother if he was still of an age to be on the battlefield in 1066 (by which time Godwine would have been seventy four years old if he had survived). There was also another relation, perhaps a nephew or cousin, called Ælric or Ælfric, a monk of Christ Church, whom the community wanted to nominate as Archbishop of Canterbury on the death of Eadsige in 1050.[7]

Lundie W. Barlow credited Godwine with a possible sister, named Æthelflaed (*Æþelflæd*). This theory is based on the authority of an agreement made between Archbishop Æthelnoth and the thegn, Toki, in connection with an estate at Halton in Buckinghamshire[8]. His wife, Æthelflaed, had died and Toki informed the primate that her father, Wulfnoth, had bequeathed the estate to Christ Church on their death and requested that he might be allowed to continue to live there until his own death.[9] At a later date, when Eadsige had succeeded Æthelnoth as archbishop, Toki sent messengers renewing his appeal.[10]

During Godwine's childhood he would have experienced the Viking raids in his native Sussex. He was little more than an infant in 994 when Ólafr and Swein, frustrated by their failure to take London, landed with their army in Kent and then spread into Sussex and Hampshire, slaughtering men, burning homesteads and according to the *Chronicle*, wreaking indescribable harm.[11] In 998 the raiding host came again. After plundering in Devonshire and Cornwall, their fleet had harboured in the Isle of Wight the previous year, and they "ate out of Hampshire and Sussex".[12] The shire was again attacked in 1009. Wulfnoth had been exiled by that time, and the fleet so enthusiastically mustered disbanded when Thorkel the Tall (*Þorkell inn Hávi*) and his horde landed at Sandwich, shortly to be joined by reinforcements from all over Scandinavia under the leadership of Hemmingr and Eilifr, the man who, years later, was to become the young Godwine's brother-in-law.[13]

---

[6] F. N. C. ii Note G.G. pp.644-645; D. Knowles, C. N. L. Brooke, London V.C.M, 'The Heads of Religious Houses, England and Wales 940-1216' p.81.
[7] 'Vita' pp.30-31.
[8] A. J. Robertson, 'Charters' No LXXX pp.154-155.
[9] ibid pp.402-403.
[10] ibid No XC pp.174-175.
[11] A.S.C 'E' s.a 994.
[12] A.S.C 'E' s.a 998.
[13] J.W. pp.462-463.

This would have been about the time when Godwine commended himself to the patronage of the Ætheling Æthelstan. The undertaking constituted a ceremony of homage which bound him to loyalty to the prince in return for his patronage and influence.[14] Wulfnoth's later supposed treachery stemmed from his sympathy and support for this son of Æthelred by his first marriage, against the king's plan to make the young Edward (the Confessor) his heir.

The suggestion has been advanced that Wulfnoth and his fleet may have joined forces with Thorkell in 1009, which could provide the explanation for Godwine's rise in status in Cnut's service.[15] The *Chronicle* does say that Wulfnoth "raided everywhere along the south coast, and wrought every kind of harm", and John of Worcester adds that he "made frequent raids along the coast"[16]. It had long been the custom for exiles to obtain provisions by raiding the coastal towns. As for Wulfnoth's joining Thorkell, the suggestion does nothing to explain why his son, Godwine, should have found favour with Æthelstan whose ambition was to succeed his father on the English throne.

At some point previously, the family of Godwine had formed a long lasting friendship with the counts of Flanders, Baldwin IV and his son Baldwin V. This relationship lasted for all the earl's lifetime, and Flanders provided a haven of safety for the family on several occasions, even united by the ties of marriage. The author of the *Vita* speaks of "their old alliance",[17] that could well have had its origin when Wulfnoth found sanctuary at the Flemish court.

Swein and Cnut

Just over a year before Æthelstan's death, the Danish King Swein Forkbeard had established his headquarters at Gainsborough. The regional powers of Northumbria, Lindsey, the Five Boroughs and East Anglia immediately submitted to him in 1014. South of the Watling Street, both Oxford and Winchester surrendered and, driving westward to Bath, Swein received the submission of Mercia and of the thegns of Wessex. Finally when London itself capitulated, Æthelred and the royal family took refuge in Normandy. A month after Æthelred's virtual abdication, Swein died. Æthelred was asked to return, and he sent his son Edward as his envoy and representative to the English Council with promises that his father would be "a gracious lord to his subjects and improve each of the things which they all hated."[18] How well these promises were kept, the future would show.

---

[14] F. Stenton, 'A.S.E.' pp.490-491; F. Barlow, 'The Godwins' p.20; I. Walker, 'Harold' p.5.
[15] E. John in 'The Anglo-Saxons' ed J. Campbell ch8 col 2 p.209.
[16] A.S.C 'E' s.a 1009; J.W. pp.460-461.
[17] 'Vita' pp.36-37; 82-83.
[18] A.S.C s.a 1014; J. W. 478-479.

By the year 1014, Godwine had proved himself sufficiently to figure prominently in Æthelstan's will. This document is invaluable for providing an insight into the members of the nobility whom the Ætheling counted as his friends and supporters. Æthelstan obviously had the wholehearted backing of his brother Edmund, and of the foremost thegns of the Danelaw, Sigeferth and his brother, Thurbrand, leader of the Anglo-Danes of York, Ulfkell of East Anglia and, most probably, Leofwine the ealdormen of the Hwicce. Included amongst these prominent magnates were Godwine of Wessex and Ælfmaer of Hampshire. The will also reveals the rift which had developed between the surviving sons of Æthelred's first marriage and their father, over his intention of gaining closer links with Normandy, perhaps extending to military aid. The established nobility was largely opposed to this policy.

Ælfgifu, the mother of Æthelstan, was, as the daughter of Ealdorman Thored, one of their own class. Ælfthryth, King Edgar's second wife, had brought Æthelstan up.[19] Ordwulf, Ælfthryth's brother, probably knew the young prince well on this account and no doubt he saw in the young man the makings of another warrior king such as the country needed. Because of his loyalty to Æthelstan, Ordwulf had relinquished his office in 1005 in protest at the king's pro-Norman policies and the new associates he was promoting.

Bishop Ælfsige had been appointed to Winchester on the death of Æthelwold II in 1012. He witnessed charters from the following year and continued in office until his death in 1032.[20] Brihtmaer must have become abbot about the same time, for his name appeared on charters from 1012 until 1016.[21]

It is noteworthy that the lay magnates mentioned above include noblemen from all areas of the country. Earls Sigeferth and Morcar may well have been related to the Ætheling through his mother: Sigeferth was certainly related by marriage to the family of the murdered Ealdorman Ælfhelm of Northumbria. Ulfkell's loyalty to the sons of Ælfgifu could well have been the reason for his not receiving the title or status of ealdorman, even although he had all the responsibilities of such a post. It could also explain why Leofwine was relegated to a subordinate position as the thegn Eadric Streona in 1007, in spite of his holding the office of ealdorman of the Hwicce for the previous eleven years.

---

[19] 'Ætheling Æthelstan's Will', D. Whitelock, No XX pp.56-63; 'and for the soul of Ælfthryth my grandmother who brought me up…' pp.62-63.
[20] A.S.C 'E' s.a 1032; Atlas Table LXVI.
[21] 'Atlas', Table LXI 4 of 4.

The Family of Sigeferth and Morcar
After P. Sawyer, The Charters of Burton Abbey

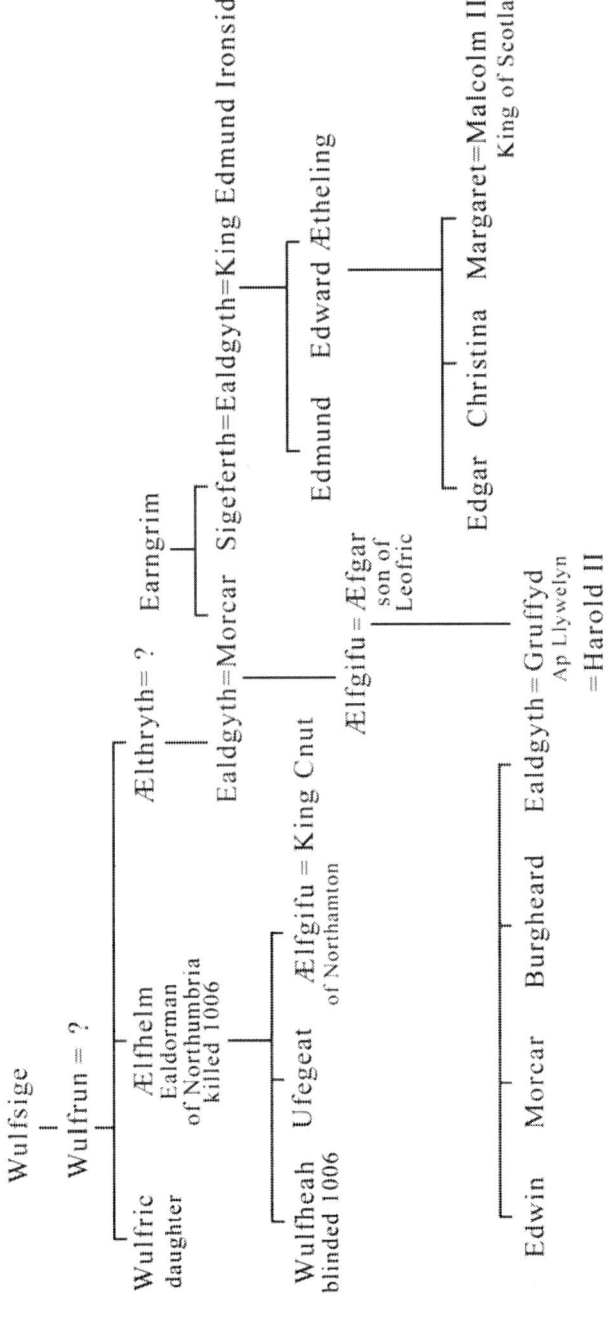

Thurbrand's reasons for supporting Æthelstan were a little different. Æthelred had appointed Uhtred in succession to Ælfhelm as the ealdorman of southern Northumbria, in addition to the northern province which he had governed for the previous eleven years. The king also gave Uhtred his daughter in marriage. Uhtred's loyalty was to his father-in-law. Unlike Eadric Streona, Uhtred was probably not involved in the hostilities centred on the succession; at his court in Bamburgh, he was too far removed to have strong feelings either way. The tract *De Obsessione Dunelmi* quotes him as saying, "As long as King Æthelred lives, I shall serve him faithfully. He is my lord and also my father-in-law, by whose gift I have sufficient honour and riches. I will never betray him."[22] There can be little doubt that, as one of the most distinguished Anglo-Danish noblemen of York, Thurbrand deeply resented Uhtred and seized the opportunity to ally himself with the Ætheling in opposition to the king.[23]

As noted above, Godwine was a common name in the early 11th century and it is therefore difficult to state with any certainty that Godwine son of Wulfnoth witnessed any charters during Æthelred's reign. It is, however, quite possible that, as an associate of the Æthelings, some of the signatures to charters may have been his.

Death of Æthelstan and Rise of Edmund

Dr Keynes has convincingly shown that Æthelstan's death occurred on 25 June 1014.[24] The young Ætheling lay ill, perhaps either from wounds or from the malady responsible for the premature deaths of many of Æthelred's children by his first wife. He realised that the end was near and sent Ælfgar, the son of Æffa, to his father entreating him permission to grant the estates and possession he had acquired as he wished. On Friday, after the feast of midsummer (24th June) Æthelstan received the king's reply confirming the request. His brother, Edmund, was with the dying prince, as was Bishop Ælfsige to minister to his spiritual needs and to perform the last rites. There also was Abbot Brihtmaer who was probably responsible for preparing a draft of the prince's will, and Ælfmaer, the prince's discthegn. To these nobles fell the duty of acting as witnesses to the will. Edmund and Bishop Ælfsige acted as his executors, with the task of seeing that his last wishes were carried out.[25] Æthelstan died the following day and was buried, as he had wished, in the church of Christ and St Peter in Winchester. Æthelstan always headed the list of Æthelings in the charter attestations and he was accorded the singular honour of being interred in the hallowed precincts normally reserved for those who had worn the crown. Surely this signifies the dept of sympathy that existed for him in the country, a commiseration that it was impossible for the aging king to ignore. Perhaps, at the last, King Æthelred himself had some misgivings of remorse and guilt.

---

[22] Quoted from 'The Early Charters of Northern England and the North Midlands' ch IX pp.143-150.
[23] A. Williams, 'Dark Age Britain' pp.227; W. E. Kapelle; N.C. of the North' pp.17-20.
[24] S. Keynes, 'Diplomas of Æthelred' p.267.
[25] D. Whitelock, 'Wills' No XX pp.56-63; 167-74.

After his brother's death, Edmund became the rallying focus for the noblemen estranged by the increasing influence of Eadric Streona and the king's own lack of purpose and initiative. The years when Eadric was the premier ealdorman were characterized by a complete lack of effective leadership, which degenerated into an absence of any national concerted effort against the Danish enemy.

In spite of Æthelred's assurance of good government when he returned from Normandy, assassinations and treachery were still a feature of the king's government. At an assembly held in Oxford early in 1015 Sigeferth and Morcar were, according to the *Chronicle* and John of Worcester, lured by Eadric into his chamber and there murdered[26]. That this treacherous deed was done with the king's full knowledge and approval is demonstrated by his seizure of their property, commanding that Sigeferth's widow be confined to the nunnery at Malmesbury. Edmund ignored his father's orders, rescued and married her, and then rode north to the Five Boroughs where he received the inhabitant's allegiance.

While Æthelred lay seriously ill at Cosham, on his royal estate in Hampshire, a concerted attempt was made to gather a national army. Edmund and Eadric both gathered forces, but distrust and doubt resulted to another fiasco. Edmund's fears were justified: Eadric's next move was to desert the king and, prevailing on forty ships crews to join him, the Mercian leader went over to Cnut, the son of Swein. The next we hear is that together Cnut and Eadric were devastating Warwickshire, which lay in Eadric's own ealdordom. The Mercian ealdorman was faced with a dilemma: he had plenty to fear from Edmund, since his hostile attitude to the elder Æthelings and the murder of Sigeferth and Morcar were not likely to be forgotten. On the other hand, Cnut's wife, Ælfgifu, could have felt nothing but hatred for the man who was responsible for the murder of her father, and Cnut was counting on the goodwill of his wife's kindred. It must have been a blow to Edmund when Thurbrand switched his support and those of the Anglo-Danes of York to join Cnut. Uhtred of Nortumbria had joined forces with Edmund and it was perhaps natural that his arch enemy defected to Cnut.

Godwine and King Edmund

While the old king still lived, the troops were loath to fight unless the king was with them.[27] However, neurotic fears and failing health prevented this and Æthelred died on 23rd April 1016. Edmund was immediately elected King by the chief councillors of London. For the next six months, Edmund fought courageously against his Danish rival. Of the supporters who had gathered around Æthelstan, both Sigeferth and Morcar were dead; changing alliances in the north had resulted in the loss of Thurbrand's influence and Leofwine's support was presumably passive.[28] Ulfkell would have been in the vanguard of the army of

---

[26] A.S.C 'E' s.a 1015; J.W. pp.478-481.
[27] A.S.C 'D' 'E' s.a 1016; J.W. pp.482-483.
[28] For Leofwine see A. Williams, 'Cockles Amongst the Wheat' pp.7-8; S. Keynes, 'Cnut's Earls' pp.74-75; C. Hart, 'Early Charters of Northern England', pp.344-345.

Edmund, and there are good grounds for thinking that Godwine, then in his early twenties, was also with Edmund.

According to the *Vita* Godwine earned a reputation as a warrior. In 1052, when in exile in Flanders preparing to attempt a return by force if necessary, he remembered "his old valour and the many achievements of his youth."[29] Henry of Huntingdon preserves the tale that three years after Edmund's death, Godwine was leading the English contingent in Cnut's war against the Slavic Wends with considerable success[30]. (William of Malmesbury transferred Godwine's display of military leadership to a later date.)[31] The skill displayed by Godwine on the shores of the Baltic could well have been gained fighting in the army of King Edmund.

Five times Edmund met his adversary in battle. At Penselwood in Dorset he was victorious; they were opposed in late June at Sherston (either Gloucestershire or Wiltshire) where the result was inconclusive. The battles at London and Brentford were again victories for the English king. Pursuing the Danish army he overtook them at Ashingdon in Essex, joined by the forces of Eadric Streona. The annalists of the *Chronicle* expresses amazement that Edmund should have accepted his assistance, or been misguided enough to trust him.[32] Eadric must have had a great deal of personal charisma or persuasiveness to gain the king's confidence after his record of deceit and treachery.

The two armies confronted each other on the hill called "Ashtree Hill"[33] and, in the thick of the battle, Eadric led away his contingent of men of Shropshire and Hereford in flight "as he had so often done before, and thus betrayed his royal lord and the whole nation"[34]. Among the slain that day was the redoubtable Ulfkell[35].

Richard Fletcher[36] suggests that Eadric's reputation for treachery is due to the monk of Abingdon who was responsible for the entries in the "C" version of the *Chronicle* and he notes that these annals were composed after Eadric's execution in 1017, perhaps in the year 1023, with the implication that the character of Eadric was impugned with the benefit of hindsight. This is of course correct, but the evil reputation given to him is also consistent with the account of the Worcester monk, Hemming, with that of John of Worcester, and with the almost contemporary *Encomium Emmae Reginae.*[37] Few of Eadric's peers could have anything but

---

[29] 'Vita' pp.40-41; Could some credence be given to Walter Map when he writes, 'Gathering a large and strong force of soldiers he [Godwine] summoned Edmund, the son of Æthelred, and they met Cnut who was hurrying to oppose them at Deerhurst in the Vale of Gloucester, on the Severn?' Dist V ch4 pp.422-5.
[30] 'Historia Anglorum', Bk VI p.197.
[31] G.R. Bk 2, ch 181 pp.322-325.
[32] A.S.C 'D', 'E', 'F' s.a 1016.
[33] E.E.R. Bk ch 7-8 pp.24-25.
[34] A.S.C 'D', 'E' p.152, A.S.C p.153.
[35] For Ulfketel/Ulfkell see FNCi Note MM p.639-640; A. Campbell, 'E.E.R' pp.70-71,77.
[36] 'Who's Who in Roman and Saxon England', p.198.
[37] Hemingi Charularium pp.280-281; Hemming was the first to use the byname 'Streona'; E.E.R Bk II ch9 pp.24-27

distrust and contempt for him, especially Godwine whose father's humiliation had been engineered by his brother Brihtric or by the wives of both Edmund and Cnut.

It may have been at Ashingdon that Edmund sustained the wound which eventually resulted in his death, but not before he and Cnut had met on an island in the river Severn and agreed to a peace treaty which divided the country between them. Apparently Eadric was foremost amongst the councillors who advised this compromise,[38] knowing full well that his only hope of survival lay in playing Edmund and Cnut off against each other. For a few months his fears were allayed when Cnut renewed his appointment as the Earl of Mercia, a course which he found expedient until such time as he was sufficiently established to dispense with Eadric's support. In the meantime Cnut introduced Hrani, one of his Danish followers, as earl of a West Mercian earldom based on Herefordshire to keep a check on Eadric.[39]

Cnut, who had succeeded to all England on Edmund's death, had taken notice of two English nobles who had steadfastly proved themselves reliable and loyal in their support of Edmund. His reason for promoting Godwine and retaining Leofwine is summed up in the words of the anonymous author of the *Encomium Emmae Reginae:* "It was accordingly the case that he [Cnut] loved those whom he had heard to have fought previously for Edmund faithfully and without deceit, and that he so hated those whom he knew to have been deceitful and to have hesitated between the two sides with fraudulent tergiversation, that on a certain day he ordered the execution of Eadric..."[40]

To sum up, from the evidence of Æthelstan's will it may be assumed that Godwine was a supporter, perhaps even a friend of Æthelstan and Edmund and that Cnut was sufficiently impressed with him to appoint him to an earldom at the first opportunity. The territory of his first earldom is open to some doubt, but there are reasons to think it may have been Kent (see below). However, charter evidence exists to show that from 1019 the shire was under the jurisdiction of *'Sired dux'* and continued so until 1023.[41] A more probable alternative is that he succeeded Ælfric, who was killed at the battle of Ashingdon in 1016. Ælfric's earldom included Hampshire, Wiltshire and quite possibly Sussex. From 999 he usually witnessed first among the ealdormen until he was gradually replaced by Eadric Streona. In spite of the character of cowardice given him in the *Chronicles* Ælfric had died fighting bravely.[42]

---

[38] A.S.C 'D', 'E', 'F' s.a 1016; J.W pp.492-493.
[39] A. Williams, 'Cockles Amongst the Wheat' for Cnut's Mercian appointments: S. Keynes, 'Cnut's Earls' pp.60-61 for Hrani.
[40] E.E.R ch15 pp.30-31.
[41] S 1389; Robertson 'Charters' No LXXXIX pp.174-5. 'I, Æthelnoth, Archbishop of Canterbury have bought the estate at Godmersham from Earl Sired for 72 marks of pure silver...' Æthelnoth gave Godmersham to Canterbury in 1023 and Sired witnessed as Earl S 960 in AD 1023.
[42] A.S.C 'D', 'E', 'F' s.a 1016; JW pp.490-491.

Godwine's Holdings in Kent

There are two charters which some authorities claim might throw some light on Godwine's early life. Both are published in Miss A.J. Robertson's *Anglo-Saxon Charters*. The first concerns a grant of swine pasture in Kent to Leofwine the Red at Sarrenden; at his death, Leofwine records the wish that the pasture should pass to whoever was the owner of the land at Boughton, one Godwine. The document was witnessed by Archbishop Lyfing, Abbot Ælfmaer and the communities of Christ Church and St Augustine's, Sired, Ælfsige cild and Æthelric. If this does apply to Godwine, Wulfnoth's son, it must have been drawn up prior to 1018 when he became an earl. As he did hold both Boughton Alaph and Boughton Malherbe "it is possible that this is correct".[43]

The great difficulty in accepting this proposal is the other charter, known as the *Kentish Marriage Agreement*,[44] which a certain Godwine made with Brihtric at Kingston in order to persuade the latter's daughter to accept him as her suitor. To achieve this, he gave her a pound's weight in gold, an estate at 'Street' and one hundred and fifty acres of land at Burmarsh, as well as thirty oxen, twenty cows, ten horses and ten slaves. The agreement was made with the approval of King Cnut and Archbishop Lyfing. This wording either excludes the Godwine we are discussing, or dates the document to before 1018 when he became an earl. The witness lists of both charters are substantially the same, but in the second the presence of the king and archbishop and the size of the bride's dowry all serve to indicate that the bridegroom and the bride's parents were people of considerable wealth and importance. It is interesting to note in this context King Cnut's charter to Christ Church, Canterbury, which granted the revenues of the port of Sandwich " for the support of the monks".[45] Amongst the witnesses were Earl Godwine, Brihtric, Sired, Godwine and Eadmaer. The latter all sign as 'minister' (i.e. thanes) and all of them are mentioned in the *Kentish Marriage Agreement*. The charter prompted Mr C.T. Chevalier in the *Introduction* to *The Norman Conquest; Its Setting and Impact* to suggest that "it seems possible that this Godwine was the Earl, although the name was common." He further speculates that Godwine's family had settled in the Folkestone area of Kent, and that the marriage settlement between Godwine and Byrhtric/Brihtric's daughter may have implied a reconciliation, brought about by King Cnut, between the son of Wulfnoth and the Brihtric who had been responsible for Wulfnoth's disgrace in 1009. As Chevalier pointed out, if this Godwine was the future earl then the bride from Brihtling near Battle in Sussex, who was brought to live with her husband in the Folkestone area presumably soon died childless.

---

[43] A.J. Robertson 'Charters' No LXXV pp.148-9; and p.394 for Miss Robertson's comments; DB Kent Phillimore, Boughton Alulph 10-2 Boughton Malherbe 5-79.
[44] Robertson, 'A.S Charters' No LXXVII pp.150-151, 397-399.
[45] ibid No LXXXII pp.158-161 and pp.406-411.

The fact that the name Godwine was a common one is amply borne out; in the Agreement under discussion there are five Godwines mentioned. Also, it is most unlikely that the Brihtric of 1009 was reconciled to Godwine, and even less likely that it was through the agency of King Cnut.[46] Napier and Stevenson plausibly suggested that the Godwine of the two charters was probably a Kentish thegn,[47] one of those mentioned who acted as security for the bridegroom in the marriage agreement, and probably the same person as the thegn Godwine Brytael whose name appears as a witness to charters from 1018 until 1035. Also, a Brihtric attested from 1018 until 1042; he may have been the bride's father.[48]

Godwine first witnessed as an earl in 1018 when his signature appears sixth in order of seniority to Thorkell, Eirikr, Eilifr, Hrani and Æthelweard. This charter purports to be the confirmation of a grant previously made by King Edmund of land at Landulf in Cornwall in exchange for land in Devon. The charter has been regarded as doubtful,[49] although containing genuine material, and there is no reason to doubt that the witness list is genuine.[50]

---

[46] 'The Norman Conquest; It's Setting and Impact', Introduction pp.6-7.
[47] 'The Crawford Collection of Early charters and Documents' p.150 for Godwine Brytael, p.151 for Byrtric.
[48] Godwine Brytael who witnessed S 950 in AD 1018, S 958 in AD 1022, S 959 in AD 1023, S 962 in AD 1026, S 968 in AD 1033 and S 975 in AD 1035. A. Brihtric witnessed from AD 1018 until AD 1026 and then from 1038 until 1042 'Atlas' Table LXX 1 of 2.
[49] Chaplais, 'The Authenticity of the Royal Anglo-Saxon Diplomas of Exeter' No 21-2; 'not as a whole authentic and it is impossible to say how much genuine material it may contain.'
[50] S 951 P.Sawyer 'charters' p.286

The Danish Royal Family

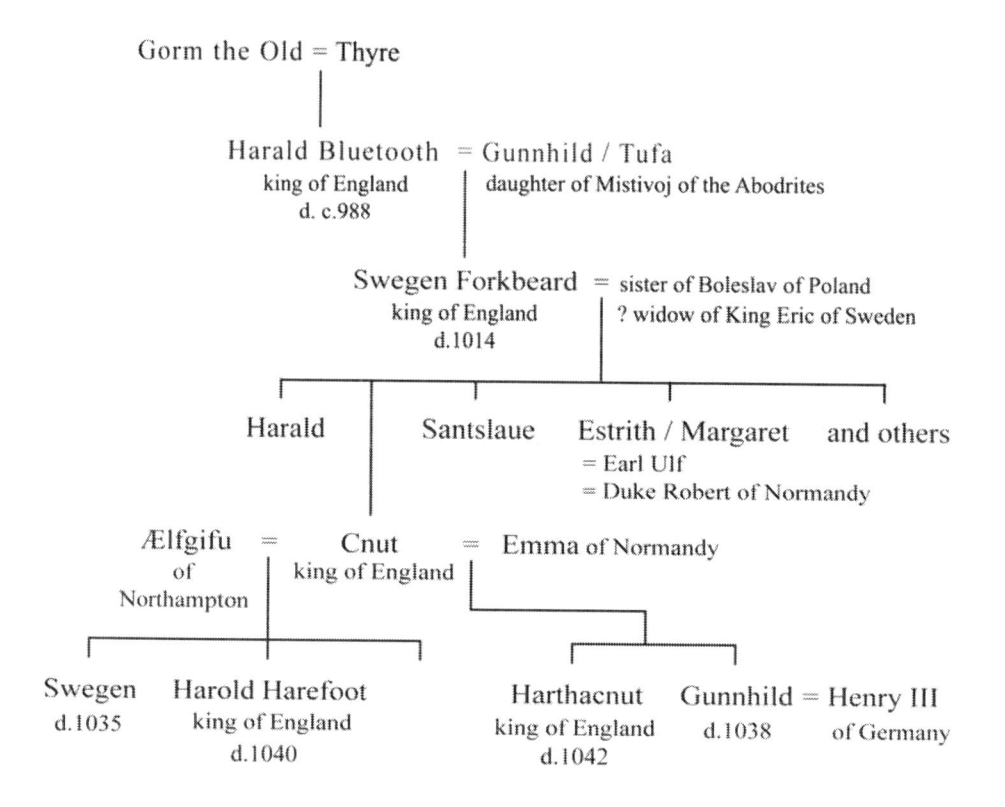

```
Gorm the Old = Thyre
        |
Harald Bluetooth = Gunnhild / Tufa
king of England    daughter of Mistivoj of the Abodrites
d. c.988
        |
Swegen Forkbeard = sister of Boleslav of Poland
king of England    ? widow of King Eric of Sweden
d.1014
        |
   ┌────────────┬──────────────┬──────────────────┬─────────────┐
Harald      Santslaue      Estrith / Margaret    and others
                           = Earl Ulf
                           = Duke Robert of Normandy

Ælfgifu = Cnut = Emma of Normandy
   of    king of England
Northampton
   |                        |
┌──────┬───────────┐      ┌──────────┬─────────┐
Swegen  Harold Harefoot   Harthacnut  Gunnhild = Henry III
d.1035  king of England   king of England  d.1038  of Germany
        d.1040            d.1042
```

From M.K. Lawson,
Cnut: The Danes in England in the Early Eleventh Century, p.273
Longman Group Ltd 1995

All dates are approximate

Stenkil 1060 – 1066
Halsten 1079 – 1099. Son of Stenkil?
Inge 1086 – 1100
Blotsven 1090 – 1099
Philip and Inge brothers 1112 – 1122
Sverker 1st 1132 – 1156
Saint Erik 1150 – 1160
Karl 1161 – 1167
Knut 1170 – 1196
Sverker 2nd 1196 – 1208 died 1210 in Battle of Gestilren
Jon 1216 – 1222 son of Sverker 2nd. Without issue.
Erikkson 1220 – 1250

Table 2. Sequence of Events 986 to 1018

c 986?	King Æthelred's marriage to Ælfgifu.
c 987 – 8	Birth of Ætheling Æthelstan.
c 992 – 3?	Birth of Godwine.
1005	Birth of Edward. Retirement of Æthelmaer and Ordulf.
1006	Murder of Ælfhelm and blinding of Wulfheah and his brother Ufegeat.
1007	Eadric appointed ealdorman of Mercia. Uhtred appointed ealdorman of all Northumbria.
1009	Wulfnoth exiled. Thorkell arrives with immense raiding army.
1012	Thorkell enters Æthelred's service.
1013	Swein Forkbeard arrives in England. Æthelred flees to Normandy.
1014	Swein dies 8 February: Æthelred returns. 25 June Death of the Ætheling Æthelstan.
1015	Murder of Sigeferth and Morcar. Eadric joins Cnut.
1016	23 April Death of King Æthelred. Edmund elected King. 30 November Death of Edmund. Cnut King of England.
1017	Eadric executed. Cnut marries Emma
1018	Godwine appointed an earl

Genealogy of the Kings of Denmark

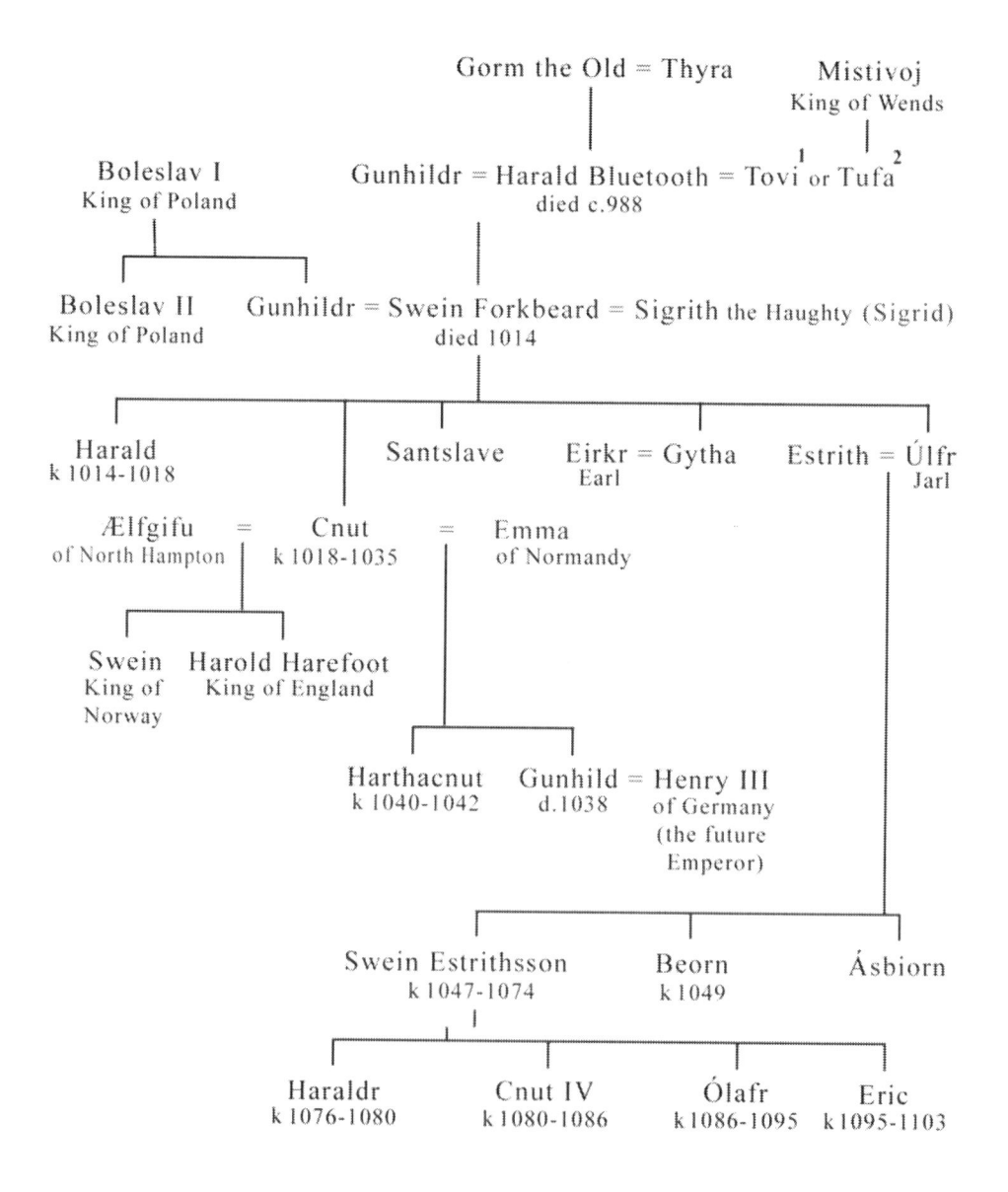

```
                                    Gorm the Old = Thyra      Mistivoj
                                                |              King of Wends
                                                |              
    Boleslav I           Gunhildr = Harald Bluetooth =¹ Tovi or Tufa²
    King of Poland                   died c.988
          |
    ┌─────┴─────┐
 Boleslav II   Gunhildr = Swein Forkbeard = Sigrith the Haughty (Sigrid)
 King of Poland            died 1014
                                 |
   ┌─────────────┬──────────┬──────────┬────────────┐
 Harald      Santslave   Eirkr = Gytha  Estrith = Úlfr
 k 1014-1018                Earl                    Jarl

  Ælfgifu    =    Cnut    =   Emma
  of North Hampton k 1018-1035  of Normandy
         |
    ┌────┴────┐
  Swein   Harold Harefoot
  King of  King of England
  Norway

              Harthacnut   Gunhild = Henry III
              k 1040-1042  d.1038    of Germany
                                     (the future
                                      Emperor)

         ┌──────────────┬──────────┬─────────┐
    Swein Estrithsson  Beorn     Ásbiorn
    k 1047-1074        k 1049
         |
    ┌────────┬────────┬────────┐
  Haraldr  Cnut IV   Ólafr    Eric
  k 1076-1080 k 1080-1086 k 1086-1095 k 1095-1103
```

Note 1 M.K. Lawson, p.273, 1993, *Cnut*, Longman
Note 2 Gwyn Jones, *A History of the Vikings*, p.127, Oxford University Press 1990

3. Godwine's Rise To Power

Cnut's Reign and Godwine's Favour

In August 1013, when King Swein Forkbeard's fleet set sail for England, he left his eldest son, Haraldr, as his regent in Denmark. When Swein died five months later, Haraldr was proclaimed king. Little is known of his reign; within four years he too was dead. His passing was followed by months in which the Danish war-lords jostled for power, and the resumption of Viking activity. Cnut sailed for Denmark in 1019 to lay claim to the Danish throne, leaving Thorkell Hávi as his regent in England.[1] We can form a picture of the England Cnut left from two charters, one of 1018, the other of the following year.[2] Although the authenticity of the first charter may be doubtful, the witness list itself has been generally accepted as being 'copied from a genuine' list of attestations.

The charter of 1019 was witnessed by Thorkell the earl of East Anglia, Eirikr of Northumbria, Godwine of Central Wessex, Eilifr with an earldom based on Gloucestershire and Leofwine of the Hwicce.[3] The earlier charter completes the overall picture with the addition of Hrani earl of Herefordshire and Æthelweard of the western provinces. One other earl whose name appears during 1019 and again in 1023 is Sired of Kent.[4] The year after Cnut's return from Denmark, Thorkell was outlawed on 11 November. No reason is given for this act, either in the different versions of the *Chronicle* or by John of Worcester, who adds that Eadgyth his wife was also expelled. This was the reason for Cnut's second visit to his homeland. As the king of England as well as of Denmark he was faced with the problem of reconciling the more influential and aggressive war-lords, whose sphere of influence lay in his own native country. Foremost among these were the sons of Strút Haraldsson, Thorkell and Hemmingr, and the sons of Thorgils Sprakalegg, Úlfr and Eilifr. It may be that the cause of Thorkell's expulsion in 1021 was that Cnut distrusted him; like Eadric Streona he had changed sides when it suited his own interests. According to Norse tradition Thorkell had been present with his brother Sigvaldi at the great sea battle of Svöld when King Ólafr was defeated, being the commander of the legendary Jómsvikings. He had been the leader of the vast host of Vikings recruited from all over the Scandinavian world which plundered and devastated England from 1009 until 1012. Although Thorkell was probably acting independently of either Swein Forkbeard or of his son Cnut the havoc caused during those years sapped the country of wealth and manpower to such an extent that when, in 1013, Swein made his final assault England was an easy prey. By that time, though, Thorkell, sickened by the brutal

---

[1] A.S.C 'D' 1019/1020; 'E' 1019/1020; Cnut's letter 1019-1020.
[2] S 953 AD 1018.
[3] S 956 AD 1019.
[4] S 954 AD 1019; S 960 AD 1023; Cnut's Earls, S. Keynes p.76

murder of Archbishop Ælfheah, which he had tried his utmost to prevent, paid off his mercenary army with the tribute levied and hired himself with the remaining crew of forty five ships to the service of King Æthelred. It has been suggested that Thorkell remained loyal to the English King until the latter's death, but there is some reason to think that he may have defected with Eadric Streona in 1015.[5] He seemed, at any rate, to be fighting for Cnut against Edmund at Ashingdon, and according to the author of the *Encomium Emmae Regina* also earlier at Sherston.[6]

That Thorkell was very powerful - powerful enough for Cnut to overlook the original cause for his banishment - is evidenced by the reconciliation which was effected the following year, and by the agreement reached that Thorkell should be appointed the regent of Denmark and the foster-father of the young Harthacnut. As a safeguard for Thorkell's good behaviour, his son Haraldr was to be brought up at the English court. It is very doubtful that Harthacnut was ever entrusted to Thorkell, but the boy Haraldr would have been valuable as a guarantee of his father's future loyalty. In any case, the Danish magnate disappears from the pages of recorded history in 1023.

Cnut's third visit to his homeland was in 1026 in response to the threat posed by the alliance of Norway and Sweden, and the ensuing battle of the Holy River in which Cnut suffered a defeat. On one of these three expeditions Godwine accompanied him and distinguished himself to the extent that on their return to England he was promoted from being the Earl of Hampshire and Central Wessex to be the Earl of all Wessex from the rugged coast of Cornwall to the Western borders of Kent.

Henry of Huntingdon placed Godwine's presence in Denmark during the first visit of 1019/1020. 'In the third year of his reign Canute with an army composed both of English and Danes went over to Denmark to war with the '*Wandali*'. He had come up with the enemy and was prepared to give battle the day following, when Godwine who commanded the English troops made a night attack on the enemy's camp without the king's knowledge. Taking them by surprise he made great slaughter and entirely routed them. At daybreak, the king, finding the English gone, supposed that they had either taken flight or deserted to the enemy. However, he marshalled his own force for the attack, but when he reached the camp, he found there only the corpses of the slain, blood and booty, whereupon he ever afterwards held the English in the highest honour, considering them not inferior to the Danes. After that he returned to England.'[7] Henry of Huntingdon's '*Wandali*' was a reference to the Wends, a Slavic people living on the southern shores of the Baltic, who were making themselves a thorn in the flesh to their neighbours.[8]

---

[5] S. Keynes, 'Cnut's Earls,' p.55; R. Fletcher, 'Who's Who', p.200.
[6] EER pp.20-23 ch 6-7
[7] Henry of Huntingdon, 'Historia Anglorum', BK vi p.197
[8] M. K. Lawson, 'Cnut' p.91.

Against this, William of Malmesbury imagined that Godwine accompanied Cnut on his third visit. '... for his valour [Cnut], incapable of rest, and not contented with Denmark, which he held paternally, and England, which he possessed by right of conquest, transferred its rage against the Swedes. These people are contiguous to the Danes, and had excited the displeasure of Cnut by their ceaseless hostility. At first he fell into an ambush, and lost many of his people, but afterwards recruiting his strength, he routed his opponents, and brought the kings of that nation, Ulf and Eiglaf, to terms of peace. The English, at the instance of Earl Godwin, behaved nobly in this conflict; he exhorted them not to forget their ancestors' fame but clearly to display their valour to their new lord, telling them that it must be imputed to fortune that they had formerly been conquered by him, but it would be ascribed to their courage, if they overcame those who had overcome him. In consequence, the English exerted all their strength, and gained the victory, obtained an earldom for their commander, and honour for themselves.'[9]

Of course there is always the possibility that Godwine accompanied Cnut on more than one occasion in the capacity of commander of the English forces, but we are concerned here with the particular visit when, on the return to England he was created Earl of Wessex, and whether this coincided with his marriage to the King's sister-in-law. It seems reasonable to reject William of Malmesbury's story in this context. If Godwine's marriage to Gytha followed the battle of the Holy River, then their first born son, Swegn, would have been no older than sixteen, possibly less, when he was appointed to the difficult task of administering an earldom bordering on Wales.

That Godwine did accompany Cnut on one of his journeys is confirmed by the author of the *Vita Ædwardi Regis*. Writing of the earl, he says 'when, however, some fitting business of the kingdom called Cnut to his own people – for in his absence some unbridled men, putting off his authority from their necks, had prepared to rebel – Godwine was his inseparable companion on the whole journey.'[10] Freeman linked this with the 1019/1020 expedition.[11] Larson, on the other hand, claimed 'that a visit to Denmark earlier than 1022 is quite unlikely.'[12] This is in line with the suggestion, advanced by Professor Keynes, that the excursion of 1022/1023 suited the description of the *Vita* better than that of the earlier voyage. He quotes the evidence of the charters which shows that it was from 1023 onwards that Godwine started to witness in the premier position amongst the earls,[13] although in the first of the three charters of 1022 he signs after Eirikr and Eilifr, and in the other two of that year after Eirikr. In view of the fact that the latter was Cnut's brother-in-law and his most loyal supporter during the campaigns that won England for Cnut – this evidence oncerning Godwine's status

---

[9] GR chs 181-186 pp 322-325
[10] 'Vita' pp 5-6
[11] F.N.C.i pp.419-420; ; A. Williams et al, 'Dark Age Britain,' p.144.
[12] 'Canute the Great,' p.159.
[13] 'S. Keynes, 'Cnut's Earls', pp.73,84-86

may not necessarily be conclusive. Also, after King Haraldr's death in 1018, it would seem that Denmark was in a state of temporary chaos which could apply equally to Cnut's remarks in his letter of 1019 as much as to 1022.

It was, however, at the time of Cnut's second expedition that, according to T. D. Kendrick, 'the mighty Cnut … came sailing into the Baltic, and there conquered Samland [the Könisberg Peninsula on the east side of the Gulf of Danzig],'[14] which could have been the occasion of Godwine's night attack. When Cnut first returned to England in the spring of 1020 one of his first acts was to convene a council at Cirencester, and one of the main reasons for the gathering was to investigate the activities of Æthelweard, the Earl of the western provinces.

Three years earlier, Cnut had to deal with a similar threat to his kingship. On that occasion, the ring leaders – Eadric Streona, Northman, Æthelweard, son of Æthelmaer the Stout, and Beorhtric, son of Ælfheah - were executed. An exception was made of the Ætheling Eadwig and his namesake, known to the annalist as 'the king of the peasants', who were banished from the kingdom.

According to William of Malmesbury, 'Edwi [Eadwig] was driven from England by Edric, at the command of Cnut and 'suffering extremely for a considerable time both by sea and land, his body, as is often the case, became affected by the anxiety of his mind, and he died in England, where he lay concealed after a clandestine return, and lies buried at Tavistock. His sons, Edwy and Edward, were sent to the King of Sweden to be put to death; but, being preserved by his pity, they went to the King of Hungary.'[15] William of Malmesbury's account bristles with inaccuracies; but in spite of the confusion in names he probably preserves a germ of truth in recording that Eadwig did return to England during Cnut's absence to lead the insurrection in 1019/1020, and was eventually buried at Tavistock. Eadwig had strong links with the West Country and his name appeared in a list of founders of Tavistock Abbey. It is recorded that he owned a manor at Plymstock which he bequeathed to the Abbey.[16]

It seems probable that the purge of 1017 was the result of a previous attempt to place Eadwig on the throne, and that those who had been executed with Eadric Streona were his henchmen.[17] Perhaps Cnut had been content to banish the two Eadwigs with the idea that such an action would placate some of the English nobility who still retained strong feelings of loyalty towards the god-descended House of Cerdic, and to win over the peasant classes which had suffered so terribly from the poverty and devastation caused by the three years of raiding by Thorkell's host.[18] Cnut's absence had presented an opportunity to renew the attempt to overthrow him. This time

---

[14] A History of the Vikings', p.131.
[15] GR BK ii, ch 180 pp.318-319.
[16] H.P.R. Finberg, 'Tavistock Abbey', p.3. Among the benefactors of the Abbey were Ordulf, the brother of Queen Ælthryth, his wife Ælfwynn, Lyfing and the Aetheling Eadwig. p.226
[17] N. J. Higham, 'The Death of A.S. England' p.85.
[18] M.K. Lawson, 'Cnut' p.84

support for Eadwig was given by Æthelweard the Earl of the western provinces. The uprising was centred on the shires of his earldom where the Ætheling's cause was strongest. However, it seems that the king returned in time to prevent the rebellion gaining momentum. The Easter council at Cirencester decreed that Æthelweard should be banished from the Kingdom, and according to the 'C' version of the *Chronicle*, Prince Eadwig was executed.

If Godwine succeeded Ælfric as the Earl of Hampshire and Central Wessex in 1018 he was (if not in 1020 then soon afterwards) appointed to the western provinces vacated by Æthelweard. Sired, who held some authority in Kent, is last heard of in 1023 when he witnessed Cnut's charter granting the water dues from the port of Sandwich to Christ Church, Canterbury. It seems that from that time on Godwine was earl of all Wessex, encompassing all England south of the Thames. From that year until his death, his signature always heads the lists of earls. Nevertheless there are reasons to believe that Archbishop Æthelnoth may have held some residual jurisdiction over Kent. Dr Ann Williams has pointed out the earl's share – 'the third penny' – was paid to him and not to Godwine until his death.[19] On the other hand it is doubtful that Cnut would have entrusted such a key shire with its vulnerable coastline to an ecclesiastic, however high he was held in the king's esteem. There remains the possibility that Æthelnoth and Godwine shared the responsibility between them.

Godwine and Gytha

It was then, sometime between 1020 and 1023 that the Earl and Gytha were married. If the marriage was linked to his appointment to all Wessex, it could hardly have been before 1021 or 1022; on the other hand some authorities have put it as early as 1019.[20] Adam of Bremen who was almost a contemporary authority wrote, 'For as we have said before Canute, the King of the Danes gave his sister in-law to Godwine, the duke of the English…'[21] Adam tells us that he gained much of his information from Gytha's nephew, King Swein Estrithsson. As Swein died in April 1074, Adam could well have been gathering details for his work while Gytha was still alive. Saxo Grammaticus says of King Cnut: 'In addition, he gave [Sveno's] sister in marriage to Godwine, a satrap of the English in the hope of bringing the two nations together in love and kinship.'[22] Saxo here errs in calling Gytha Swein Estrithsson's sister instead of his aunt.

Eric Christiansen points out that the word 'sororum' or 'sister' could refer to either Úlfr's sister or Cnut's.[23] Also Gytha was referred to as Cnut's sister in the *Vita* which was commissioned by her eldest daughter Eadgyth. The anonymous author

---

[19] A. Williams, 'Kingship and Government' p.212 note 108.
[20] F.N.C.i Note E E E, p 723-725; A. Williams 'Dark Age Britain' p.144, S. Keynes 'Cnut's Earls' p.73; R. Fletcher, Who's Who p.215
[21] Adam BK 3 schol 65 pp.124-125
[22] Saxo Bk 10 ch XVII p.35.
[23] Eric Christiansen, Note to Saxo, Note 125 pp.197-198.

writes 'Consequently he [Cnut] admitted the man whom he had tested in this way to his counsel and gave him his sister as wife.'[24] The confusion between Cnut's sister and sister-in-law can be explained by the two terms being inter-changeable. It was this confusion which presumably caused William of Malmesbury to invent two wives for Godwine.

Gytha is mentioned by name as Godwine's wife in the *Chronicle of John of Worcester* and as King Harold's mother in the 'D' version of the *Anglo-Saxon Chronicle*.[25] She had two brothers, Eilifr and Úlfr. The former came to England in or soon after 1009 to join Thorkell's Viking host in the company of Hemmingr, Thorkell's brother. When their army disbanded after the murder of Archibishop Ælfheah, Eilifr's movements become uncertain. When Swein Forkbeard invaded England the following year and the whole country submitted to him, he established – according to the 'Supplement to the Jomsviking Saga' – two garrisons in England. One was stationed at 'Slésvik' under Jarl Hemmingr, the other with its headquarters in London commanded by Jarl Elifr. The editors of the *Crawford Charters* identified Slésvik with Hemmingborough, on the Ouse near York.[26] After King Swein's death, Ulfkell was, according to the 'Supplement', responsible for ordering the massacre of the two Danish garrisons. Eilifr was warned of his danger by one of his henchmen, Thorth, who learnt of the plot from his mistress. Eilifr (or Eglaf as he was known in England) made good his escape together with three ship's crews of his house earls. Although the authority of the Supplement is doubtful, Napier and Stevenson point out that Hemmingr is not heard of again.[27] Eilifr witnessed Cnut's charters from 1018 until 1024, so obviously survived. It is also true that Thorkell defected from the English cause soon after, presumably to avenge his brother's death.

The identity of Eilifr's informant Thord or Thorth (Þorðr), is also interesting. The name Thorth appears unusually high in the witness lists from 1018 until 1035. (The man of that name who signed a grant of land in Hampshire seven years later is probably unconnected.) It is noticeable that each time Thorth witnesses a charter Eilifr is present among the signatories until 1024 thus – list of seven charters -

AD 1018	Thorthr S 951	1st	Eilifr	3rd
AD 1018	Thorthr S 953	1st	Eilifr	4th
AD 1019	Thorthr S 956	4th	Eilifr	4th
AD 1022	Thorthr S 980	2nd	Eilifr	4th
AD 1023	Thorthr S 960	4th	Eilifr	2nd
AD 1023	Thorthr S 959	1st	Eilifr	2nd
AD 1024	Thorthr S 961	2nd	Eilifr	2nd [28]

---

[24] 'Vita' p.6.
[25] J.w pp.560-561; A.SC 'D' 1067.
[26] 'Crawford Charters' pp 140-141,32; S. Keynes 'Cnut's Earls' p.52
[27] The Legendary Life of Ólafr Heli' claimed to be one of the oldest Norse Sagas
[28] Robertson, A.S Charters' No LXXXV pp.168-169, 410.

Thorth witnesses as thegn, Eilifr as earl. Thorth continued to sign charters in 1026, 1032 and 1035.[29] In view of the link between the two and the corresponding dates of the earlier signatures, this Thorth could well have been the same man who had warned Eilifr of his danger back in 1014. He might be the Thored or Thorth who made a grant of land to Christ Church in 1036. If so, this grant to Christ Church by Thored or Thorth would have been made some twenty one years after he and Eilifr escaped from the garrison headquarters in London, and about the same time when, according to the *Brut y Tywysogyon* Eilifr was leaving England for the last time, maybe in the company of his henchmen.[30]

From 1018 until 1024 Eilifr consistently witnessed Cnut's charters as Earl, originally in third position of seniority after Thorkell and Eirikr. By 1023 and 1024 he was witnessing second to Godwine. After that his name disappears from the charter lists. It would be a mistake to place too much emphasis on this because, with the exception of the year 1026, there are no extant charters until 1032.[31]

Cnut's Brothers-in-Law

The *Chronicle* records that in 1017 King Cnut 'succeeded to the whole kingdom of the English race, and divided it in four; Wessex for himself, and East Anglia for Thurkil and Mercia for Eadric and Northumbria for Eric'. It is probable that Eilifr, Hrani and Leofwine were already holding subordinate positions under Eadric. After the execution of the latter, Mercia could well have been subdivided under the overlordship of Leofwine. Three Danish earls held office in south-west Mercia. Eilifr was appointed to an earldom that included Gloucestershire; Earl Hakon, the King's nephew and the son of Eirikr had jurisdiction over Worcestershire and to Hrani was entrusted an area centred on Herefordshire.[32]

Eilifr

The Welsh remembered Eilifr as the leader of an army composed of Danes and Englishmen who invaded Wales, penetrated into South Wales, ravaging Dyfed and destroying St David's. The *Annales Cambriae* in the annal for 1022 records 'After that Eiled came to the Isle of Britain, and Dyved was devastated and Meneva was demolished.'[33] After this his name next appears in the entry for 1025 in the 'E' version of the *Chronicle* which reads 'Here King Cnut went to Denmark with ships to the battle-place at the Holy River, and Ulf and Eilaf came against [him], and a very great raiding army; and a ship raiding army from the

---

[29] For Eilifr 'Atlas' Table LXIX; for Thorth/Thored; Table LXX, S 1222
[30] Brut y Tysogyon Red Book of Hergest s.a 1035
[31] S. Keynes, 'Atlas' Table LXIX; 'Cnut's Earls,' pp.53, 58, 66
[32] A. Williams, 'Cockles Amongst the Wheat.'
[33] 'Annales Cambriae,' s.a 1022 quoted from F.N.C.i pp.443 Note 3; see also K.L. Maund, 'Ireland, Wales and England' p.161.

Swedish nation, and there many men perished on Cnut's side, both of Danish men and of English; the Swedes took possession of the place of slaughter.'[34]

This annal has raised a storm of controversy regarding the date, the identity of 'Ulf and Eilaf', and the actual course of the battle. According to Saxo Úlfr [Ulvo] was himself involved against Cnut, advising his followers not to interfere with the bridge the Danes were building to span the two islands occupied by the opposing armies until it was completed. The bridge collapsed under the weight of the Danish forces as they started to cross. 'Then Ulvo, the deceiver, rather than the conquerer of the Danes obtained by the foolhardiness of other men which he could not by his own strength.'[35] Eilifr is not mentioned by Saxo. According to Danish tradition, Saxo and the *Saga of Knútr* Úlfr was involved in the battle and the instigator of a coalition between King Ólafr of Norway and King Ánundr of Sweden. Icelandic sources also make Úlfr present, although according to Snorri Sturluson Úlfr came to Cnut's rescue. The *Saga of St Ólafr* says that the jarl had incurred the king's displeasure by attempting to have the boy Harthacnut nominated as Sovereign of Denmark in his father's place. Úlfr joins the fray in an effort to salvage his position.[36] Freeman thought that 'Ulf and Eilaf' may have been a scribal error for Úlf and Olaf' and that 'Ulf and Eilaf' were doubtless the sons of Rögnvaldr and Ingiborg of whom Snorri speaks in the *Saga of St Olafr*.[37] Freeman concludes 'At any rate the Ulf spoken of cannot be Ulf, the son of Thorgils and brother of Gytha, nor can Eglaf be the Eglaf of whom we have already heard.'[38] It should be noted that he failed to connect Eilifr with the brother of Úlfr and Gytha.

M. K. Lawson refers to the skaldic poetry of Sigvat which alludes to Rögnvaldr the father of Úlfr and an unnamed son whose name was later supplied by Snorri Sturluson as Eglaf. Lawson sums up by saying 'In all, identifying Ulf as the son of Rögenvald seems at least as plausible as believing that he was Cnut's brother-in-law.'[39] Freeman's suggestion that the 'Eilaf' of the *Chronicle* entry may have been an error for Olaf, a reference to King Ólafr of Norway has been supported by Alisdair Campbell, 'Such a slip might very easily have been made by a copyist, owing to the fact that Úlfr was very closely associated with Eilifr in England.' But he disagrees with Freeman, 'that Úlfr and Eilifr mentioned by the E *Chronicle* were not Knútr's earls, but the sons of Earl Rögenvaldr of Gotland, can be dismissed as mere sophistry.'[40] It is doubtful therefore that Eilifr was present at the battle, as he is not mentioned by Saxo while Úlfr is portrayed as one of the prime leaders of the alliance which involved the Kings of Norway and Sweden,

---

[34] A.S.C 'E' s.a 1025.
[35] Saxo ch CXVI p.82f.
[36] Saga of St Olaf ch CLVIII pp 305-307.
[37] F.N.C.i Note MMM pp.742-743; Crawford Charters p.142
[38] F.N.C.i p.743
[39] M.K Lawson 'Cnut' pp.97,98
[40] E.E.R App III p.86.

presumably 'the two princes' mentioned by Ottar the Black in the *Knuts Drapa*.[41] Johannes Brondsted's interpretation was that Ólafr had married Ástridr, the daughter of Ólafr Skotkonung and the sister of Ánundr, which made the two kings not only brothers-in-law but also natural allies in the face of Cnut's growing power.[42] The two kings seized the opportunity afforded by the growing tension between Cnut and his regent Úlfr to make him a potential ally. The confederates chose the estuary of the Holy River to clash with the Danish king's fleet. Three years later, when Ólafr returned from exile in Russia, Ánundr again gave him aid with manpower and equipment.

To sum up; the sources which thought that Úlfr and perhaps Eilifr were present at the confrontation at the Holy River included the 'E' version of the *Anglo-Saxon Chronicle*, Saxo, Danish tradition, the *Saga of Knutr* verified by Snorri in *St Olaf's Saga*.[43] Perhaps the consensus of modern opinion can best be summed up in the words of Professor Keynes 'The most natural assumption, however, must be that the Chronicle's reference was to Cnut's earl Úlfr, and by extension through their association, to Úlfr's brother Eilifr.'[44]

Saxo makes much of 'Ulvo's treachery', but makes no mention of his brother. Jones regards 'Jarl Ulf' as 'playing a decisive role on both sides',[45] as proved by his subsequent murder at Cnut's instigation. Stenton considered that Ólafr and Ánundr, the protagonists, were joined by Úlfr and Eilifr.[46] Snorri, however, makes Úlfr hasten to Cnut's rescue in spite of his earlier misdeeds.[47] On the other hand the *Fagrskinna* makes no mention of Úlfr's part, the Sagas do not allude to the sons of Thorgils in this context, and Ottar the Black's reference to the 'two princes' seem to exclude the presence of the two brothers. Amongst modern authorities who take this view are Freeman, Lund and Lawson.[48]

Another possibility is that there was an earlier encounter which involved King Cnut at the Holy River in which Úlfr and Eilifr did take part. The former may have abused his position as regent of Denmark by using the young Harthacnut – his wife's nephew – to further his own ambitious schemes. It is feasible that Eilifr left England soon after witnessing the charter of 1024 to assist his brother, and that a sea battle was fought in 1025 with help from Sweden. The power-base of the sons of Thorgils Sprakalegg could well have been in Scania. What seemed important to the *Chronicle* annalist involving names of prominent people he knew would have appeared a relatively minor event to Scandinavian writers and skalds in relation to

---

[41] ibid App iii p.86.
[42] J Bronsted, 'The Vikings' p.95.
[43] A.S.C 'E' s.a 1025; St Olaf's Saga, ch CLVII; Saxo BK10, Note 117 pp 196-197
[44] 'Cnut's Earls' p.60.
[45] Gwyn Jones 'History of the Vikings' p.381
[46] F. Stenton 'A.S.E' pp 403, 404.
[47] St Olaf's Saga ch CLVIII p.307.
[48] F.N.C i Note MMM pp 742-743; Niels Lund 'Cnuts Danish Kingdom' p.37; M.K Lawson, 'Cnut' p.98.

the more important clash two years afterwards. P. A. Munch advanced this suggestion in 1874,[49] which the editors of the Crawford charters considered a probability on the basis of the *Chronicle* dating and the apparent corroboration of Saxo. 'It is possible that Jarl Úlf and Eglaf were fighting against Cnut in 1025, and that Úlf had made his peace with Cnut again before 1027.'[50]

In consideration of all this we are left with five different possibilities in connection with the involvement of Gytha's brothers.

1. That the 'Úlf and Eilaf' of the Chronicle were the sons of Rögnvaldr. Supported notably by E. A. Freeman, Ove Moberg, Niels Lund and M. K. Lawson.
2. That 'Úlf and Eilaf' were the sons of Thorgils Sprakalegg; the view favoured by Johannes Brondsted, Eric Christiansen, Simon Keynes, F. Stenton & Ann Williams.[51]
3. That 'Eilaf' might be a scribal error for Ólafr; E. A. Freeman and A. Campbell.[52]
4. That Jarl Úlfr aided Cnut in the battle at the Holy river; Snorri Sturluson.[53] The idea is opposed by the Sagas and Danish tradition; 'Fagrskinna' does not mention Ulfr at the battle.
5. That Úlfr and Eilifr fought an earlier engagement with Cnut in 1025 as already mentioned.

The actual date of the battle at the Holy River may throw some light on this last possibility. Alisdair Campbell considered that it was fought in 1027 and points out that in the *Saga of Ólaf Helgi* the engagement is dated the year before Ólafr's flight to Sweden and thence to the court of Yaroslav in Russia. As his retreat took place two years before his death, a date can be fixed with some certainty by both English and Norse sources which dates the battle in 1027.[54] Campbell further draws attention to the letter Cnut sent to his English subjects when returning from the coronation of Conrad II in Rome which he attended. He wrote '…And therefore I wish to make known to you that returning by the same that I went, I am going to Denmark, to conclude with the council of all the Danes peace and a firm treaty with the nations and peoples who wished, if it had been possible for them, to deprive us of the Kingdom and of life, but could not, since God destroyed their strength.'[55]

---

[49] P.A Munch 'Samlede Af Handlinger' pp 726-727.
[50] 'Crawford Charters' p.142.
[51] F.N.C.i pp 742, 743; Neils Lund, 'Cnut's Danish Kingdom' p.37; M.K Lawson p.98; Ove Moberg, J. Brondsted, 'The Vikings' pp.95, 96; E. Christiansen, 'Saxo' Note 117 pp.195-196; S. Keynes, 'Cnut's Earls' pp.60-64; F. Stenton 'ASE' pp.403, 404; A. Williams, 'Dark Age Britian,' pp.131,231.
[52] F.N.C.i p.745; E.E.R App iii p.86.
[53] St Olaf's Saga, ch CLX p.309. 'After a short time also Earl Ulf came up with his fleet, and then the battle began.'
[54] A. Campbell E.E.R pp.83
[55] Quoted from E.H.D vol i. D. Whitelock. No 53.

Cnut visited Rome in March and April 1027, and the battle of the Holy River has been placed in September of that year. So it is quite likely that Cnut had put down a minor insurrection involving Úlfr and perhaps his brother in 1025, and then faced the major threat from King Ólafr of Norway and King Ánundr of Sweden in the same area two years later. The presence of Eilifr at the Holy River, as far as I am aware, rests solely on the entry of the 'E' recension of the *Chronicle*. According to the *Brut y Tywysogyon* he was in England when Cnut died and left England for *'Germania'*,[56] a term loosely applied to either Germany or to one of the Scandinavian countries.[57] Obviously he must have been reconciled to Cnut – if he had been involved – but seems no longer to have held any office. It may well be, as Ann Williams suggested, that when Earl Leofric succeeded in procuring the nomination of Harold Harefoot to the throne of England in 1035, Eilifr left for pastures new. Perhaps he was jealous of Leofric's increasing influence; possibly, like Godwine, he was in favour of closer unity with Denmark which Harthacnut's succession would have entailed.[58]

Perhaps the passage in the 'Supplement to the Jomsviking Saga' is correct in saying that Eilifr went to Micklegarth or Constantinople, that he became a captain of the Varangian Guard and met his death fighting for the Emperor of Byzantium is possible, although in the Supplement this is mistakenly placed at the time of Cnut's invasion of England twenty years earlier.

Ulfr

Úlfr was to become one of those figures in Danish history about whom a great deal of legendary fantasy accumulated. Yet there is some evidence that he played some part in England also. If we were to place any credence on the late and doubtful authority of the mid-thirteenth century *Knytlinga Saga* Úlfr was in England in 1015 and took part in the battle of Sherston the following year. 'Many Chieftans went with King Knut to England. First of these was his brother-in-law Earl Ulf Strut-Legs son, who was married at the time to Astrid, Sveins' daughter, Knut's sister, ….'[59]

Úlfr was certainly in England about 1022 and there are some grounds for thinking that in some ways he followed in the footsteps of Thorkell. The latter was appointed Earl of East Anglia in 1017 and was outlawed in November 1021. Adam of Bremen calls Úlfr *'dux Angliae'*,[60] which would seem to imply that at some time he held office in England. This tends to be substantiated by the charters to which his name appears as a signatory. Three charters bear his signature. S 981 is regarded as spurious;[61] S 980, which constitutes a grant of

---

[56] 'Brut y Tywysogian, Red Book of Hergest,' s.a 1035.
[57] S. Keynes, 'Cnut's Earls' p.60.
[58] A. Williams, 'Cockles Amongst the Wheat' p.9.
[59] 'Knytlinga Saga', ch 8 p.29.
[60] Adam, Bk 2 LIV (52) page 92.
[61] Robertson, Charters', No LXXXV pp.168-171.

privileges to Bury St Edmund's Abbey is accepted as genuine by Dr Cyril Hart,[62] and the third S 984, King Cnut's grant to the Abbey of St Benet of Holme of land in Norfolk was accepted by Alisdair Campbell, 'although not in its original form.'[63] The importance of this is that the scribes who copied these charters, originating from Canterbury, S981, Bury St Edmunds and St Benet of Holme – even if in two cases there is some room for doubt – were either copying lists of signatures from sources no longer extant, or were aware of Úlfr's presence in England at that time.[64] In view of the provenance of two of the charters concerned, both East Anglian abbeys which can be dated c1023 there is a possibility that Úlfr may have held some office in that earldom, perhaps even have succeeded Thorkell after his expulsion in 1021.

Another pointer to his presence in England can be found in the *Liber Vitae* of Thorney Abbey. Úlfr and some of Cnut's earls and leading thegns had entered into a religious or benevolent fellowships with the Abbey. These included Thorkell, Eirikr, Hákon, Eilifr, as well as Tovi, Osgod Clapa and other Scandinavians. Úlfr is not given the title of Earl in this document, which implies that his appointment as earl, if indeed it ever happened, post-dated Thorkell's exile. When the latter disappeared from the records as the regent of Denmark, either through death or ill health, Jarl Úlfr seems to have been appointed as his successor and Harthacnut put into his care. According to William of Malmesbury, Thorkell was murdered on his return to Denmark, but the account has been disregarded by most authorities.[65]

Úlfr was married to Cnut's sister Ástriðr or Estrith, thus the boy Harthacnut was fostered by his aunt and uncle by marriage. Possibly Swein, later to become King Swein Estrilhsson, was taken to the king's court in London to be reared. As the years passed, relations between Cnut and Úlfr deteriorated; it appears, as we have seen, that the jarl used his nephew to further his schemes, aided - perhaps prompted - by Emma's own ambitions for her son.

Norse/Icelandic tradition of the early thirteenth century tells us that Úlfr succeeded in persuading the Danish 'Thing' or counsel 'that it was Knut's own wish that his son Harthacnut should be crowned in his stead'. This was made to seem more credible because of Emma's theft of the royal seal, and letters she had forged in Cnut's own name. As soon as his suspicions were aroused the king arrived with a fleet in Danish waters. A good deal of the blame lay with Emma: 'The Queen had been the principal promoter of this determination, for she had got the letter to be written, and provided with the seal, having cunningly got hold of the King's signet, but from him it was all concealed.[66]

---

[62] C. Hart, 'The Early Charters of Eastern England,' No 86.
[63] EER p.86.
[64] S. Keynes, 'Cnut's Earls' p.63.
[65] G.R. p.181; also 'Translatio Sancti Ælfegi Cantuariensis.' in 'The Reign of Cnut' p.298; E.E.R p.76 note 1.
[66] 'St Olaf's Saga,' ch CLVIII p.306

Perhaps Úlfr's actions were understandable: facing the threat from a Norwegian–Swedish coalition, he may have thought that the country would be more likely to unite under a boy king in their midst than an absent monarch. At any rate, according to Snorri when the invasion came Úlfr and his forces fell back to Jutland, the heartland of Danish strength. He lays emphasis on the jarl's treachery in the part he played in Harthacnut's election as King' not on any intrigue in connection with the Norwegian-Swedish alliance, and implies that Úlfr like Thorkell had a very strong power-base in Denmark. Cnut must have recognised that it was in his best interests to work with him as long as it was possible. According to Saxo, Úlfr 'carefully worked out a plan for the invasion of Denmark and enlisted the co-operation of Onundus and Olavus.'[67] Ólafr was to invade Zealand with the Norwegian navy, Önund or Ánundr to attack Scania with the Swedish army, and Úlfr was to command the Swedish fleet. Saxo and Snorri describe different characteristics of the jarl: to Saxo he was treacherous, cunning and evil; Snorri says he was 'hasty in temper, stiff, in nothing yielding, but everything he managed went well in his hands: and he was a great warrior about whom there were many stories. He was the most powerful man in Denmark next to the King.'[68] Adam relates that Úlfr's marriage to Cnut's sister occurred after her marriage to Duke Richard of Normandy, who rejected her.[69] He places it at the same time as the king's own marriage to Emma. Adam was mistaken in saying that Estrith married Richard II; she became the wife of Richard's son, Robert I. It is most unlikely that Estrith was wed to the Norman duke prior to her marriage to Úlfr. A clue to the date of the latter may be found in the words of Snorri, 'Jarl Úlfr sent his son Svend who was a sister's son of King Cnut, and the same age as Harthaknut, to the King.'[70] Harthacnut was probably born c1018, so if this is correct it would mean that Úlfr and Estrith would presumably have become man and wife about the same time as Cnut's own wedding to Emma. As this would then have coincided with Cnut's accession to the English throne, the arrangement was probably made to strengthen his position in Denmark, just as he was at a later date to give his sister in wedlock to duke Robert to offset a threat from Normandy. The author of the *Knytlinga Saga* says that Úlfr was already married to Estrith when Cnut invaded England.[71] After she was repudiated by the Norman duke, according to Adam, she married a Russian prince. This is possible, as much of his information was obtained from her son King Swein.[72]

The twelfth century Roskilde tradition believed that Cnut had Úlfr murdered in the church of St Lucius in Roskilde, because of Cnut's disapproval of his marriage to Estrith. This Danish tradition does not associate his murder with treachery at the Holy River, or that it was Cnut himself who endowed the church in order to

---

[67] Saxo Bk 10 ch XVI p.34.
[68] St Olaf's Saga ch CLXII p.312.
[69] Adam, Bk 2 LIV (52) p.92
[70] St Olaf's Saga ch CLVIII p.307.
[71] 'Knytlinga Saga' ch 11
[72] Adam Bk 3 schol 64/65 pp 124,125

expiate his guilt.[73] Norse Sagas connect Úlfr's murder with his part in Harthacnut's election as King of Denmark, Cnut forgives his son – and Emma – but later gives orders to have the jarl assassinated. Snorri elaborates the story by introducing an argument over a game of chess. The murder is not mentioned by Adam or Svenn Aggeson, but it does occur in the *Fagrskinna*, Snorri Sturluson, the *Chronicon Roskildense* and Saxo. According to the latter, in chxvii p36, Úlfr was invited to a feast at Roskilde by King Cnut. Becoming very drunk he began to brag and make up songs relating to the disaster he had engineered at the battle of the Holy River when many of Cnut's army were, according to Saxo, drowned. The king became extremely angry and the jarl paid, 'a just penalty for his over-hasty tongue'. It is probable that Úlfr met his death in 1028, after Ólafr [the future saint] was driven from Norway and Cnut felt secure enough in the North to dispense with his brother-in-law's doubtful loyalty.

Gytha and her Father

William of Malmesbury failed to name the mother of Godwine's children or to reveal her identity. This is surprising in view of the number of references to her in the records. She is mentioned in the *Chronicle*, by John of Worcester and in the near contemporary history of Adam of Bremen who relates 'Duke Ulf who married his sister to Godwine, the duke of the English.'[74] The Worcester version of the *chronicle* calls her by name under the year 1067 as does John of Worcester in writing of Swegn her eldest son. Gytha's kinship to Eilifr is vouched for in the *Liber Vitae of Thorney* which calls him Úlfr's brother. In the relevant charters Eilifr always signs immediately after Úlfr.

Little is know of their father. In the Norse sources he appears only as the father of 'Gyða' or of Úlfr. No deeds of valour or of intrigue are attached to his name. The *Morkinskinna* referring to King Harold II, calls him, 'the son of Godwin and G'yðu, the daughter of Þorgils Sprakaleggr.'[75] This is repeated word for word from the *Fagrskinna*. Snorri, in the *Saga of Magnus the Good* says of Swein Estrithsson,[76] 'a son of Earl Ulf and a grandson of Torgils Sprakalegg'. There are mentions of him also in the *Knytlinga Saga*.

It may be surmised from the status of his sons that Thorgils was a powerful magnate with Danish and Swedish connections. Saxo, writing of Swein Estrithson, says 'But Sveno's affairs were now desperate, and he had set out for Scania, as we said and promised to return to Sweden, where his father's family had originated.'[77] At this point we pass from history into the realms of pure fantasy and romance. John of Worcester under the year 1049 tells us 'Earl Beorn, son of Swein's

---

[73] 'Chronicon Roskildense' vol VII; Saxo Note 113 p.193. A. Campell E.E.R App 3.
[74] Adam Bk 3 Schol 64/65 pp.124-125.
[75] 'Fagrskinna' ch 37 p.163; Morkinskinna p 113.
[76] Saga of 'Magnus, The Good' ch XXII p.143.
[77] Saxo Bk 10 ch XXII p.142 and Note 167 p.214 p.217.

maternal uncle, the Danish Earl Ulf, son of Spracling, son of Urse.'[78] From this J. M. Lappenberg concluded 'Among the followers of Cnut, Jarl Ulf, son of Thorgils Sprakalegg, a son of Styrbjorn was particularly distinguished.'[79] Later in the nineteenth century Freeman wrote 'This Ulf, the son of Thurgils Sprakaleg, is one of the most distinguished characters in the Danish history or romance of the time. Like some other famous heroes his parentage was not wholly human. The father of Thurgils, Bjorn was the offspring of a bear, who had carried off a human damsel.'[80] There are references to Styrbiorn in the *Flateyjarbók*,[81] the *Knytlinga Saga* and a passing mention in Snorri's *St Olaf's Saga*.[82] The relationship between Styrbjorn and Thorgils was originally made by J. Langebek and P. Suhm, followed by other Scandinavian historians such as P. A. Munch and J. Steenstrup.[83] Styrbjörn was allegedly the son of Ólafr and the grandson of Björn the king either of, or in Uppsala, Sweden. Styrbjörn had married Thyra, the daughter of King Haraldr Gormsson of Denmark. The young prince, at the prompting of his father-in-law, attempted to wrest the throne from his uncle Eirikr. At the head of an army he penetrated to the heartland of his uncle's kingdom and gave battle on Fyris Plain. Apparently he was badly let down; either the promises given of help from Denmark failed to materialise, or the Danes who had joined his army had no heart for the struggle. His forces were routed; he was amongst the slain, and his uncle gained the sobriquet *enn sigrsaeli* or 'the victorious'. Styrbjörn and his Vikings were not dishonoured; runestones bear testimony to their valour. One stone in Skane records of Toki 'He did not flee at Uppsala'. Another of Asbjörn says 'He did not flee at Uppsala, but fought as long as he had weapon', and one in memory of Ásmundr who 'fell at Fyris.'[84]

Styrbjörn

Legends accumulated around the name of Styrbjörn. He was credited with being the captain of the Jomsvikings; his turbulent nature gave rise to the story that he had an ursine forebear! After his death his widow was betrothed to Boleslav or Burislief, King of the Wends of Poland. According to Snorri he was old and a pagan, and the young widow found him repugnant; she escaped to Norway where King Ólafr Tryggvason received her kindly and took her in marriage.

Saxo's interpretation of the defeat on Fyris Plain was that the Danish forces were withdrawn owing to the German invasion of Denmark by the German emperor Otto II is incorrect. Otto's campaign took place in AD974. In attempting to establish the

---

[78] J.W. pp.548-549.
[79] 'A History of England Under the A S Kings' p.208.
[80] F.N.C.i p.420.
[81] Flateyjarbók p 96; Flateyjarbók chapter 61 pp 147-149.
[82] 'Knytlinga Saga' ch 2 p.24; St Olaf's Saga ch LXXI p.176.
[83] The relationship between Stybjorn and Thorgils was first made by J. Langebek in 'Scriptores Rerum Danicarum Medii Ævi', vol III pp.281-282.
[84] J. Bronsted, 'The Vikings' p.207.

supposed date of the battle of Fyris Plain it is helpful to remember that Ólafr Tryggvason reigned in Norway from 995 until he was defeated and met his death in the great sea battle of Svöld in 999 or 1000. This would presumably date Ólafr and Thyra's marriage any time between 995 and 998. Haraldr Gormsson died in 987.[85] In 983 he was engaged in an attack on the Germans in alliance with his father-in-law, the Slavic prince Mistivoj. Eirikr the Victorious died some time between 992 and 995.[86] It seems therefore that Styrbjörn's fatal expedition, if it ever happened, took place some time between 983 and 985 when Haraldr Gormsson was at the height of his power. Adam records of Thyra 'After the death of her husband his wife spent her life miserably, in hunger and want, as she deserved.'[87]

Langebek identified Styrbjörn with the bear, Spratling his son with Thorgils Sprakalegg and Beorn Bearsson with a brother of Jarl Úlfr. In 1866 Charles Kingsley, Professor of Modern History at Cambridge and the author of *Hereward the Wake*, at the end of chapter xvii gave Styrbjörn a pedigree based on these lines. W. G. Searle includes a similar genealogy in his book, *Anglo-Saxon Bishops, Kings and Nobles* although he omits Thyra's name. More recently this has found its way into the *Carmen de Bello Hastingae Proelio* translated and edited by Catherine Morton and Hope Muntz, in the genealogy of the Kings of England by John Brookes-Little when he was Richmond Herald, and also in Denis Butler's fine book *1066, The Story of a Year*.

Against all this, Lauritz Weibull started in 1910 to discredit the reliability of the Norse sagas. He ruthlessly questioned all the sources and came to the conclusion that they were worthless as historical evidence. To quote the words of Rolf Arvidson 'In this way he wipes out a whole series of persons and events; there never was a Sigríðr Stórráða; no Jómsborg ever existed: there never was a battle with Jómsvikings on Fyris-fields by Uppsala..' 'Weibeull claimed that his source criticism gave a reappraisal of hitherto accepted values .. it became clear that only scattered events and the crudest outlines of the history of the age are successfully demonstrable .. in short the Jomsvikings, the battle of Fyris Plain are all pure fable.[88] Alisdair Campbell regarded the Styrbjörn-Thorgils connection as a 'strange piece of rationalization originally due to Langebek.'[89] Eric Christiansen has pointed out that Ursus/Biorn is on no account to be identified with Styrbjörn the Strong ... Styrbjörn, Eric the Victorious and the battle of Fyris Plain belong to heroic legend or pure invention ... Thorgils Sprakalegg is merely a name without a clear historical date, personality or setting, ...'[90] However, Tore Nyberg, the editor of *Medieval Scandinavia* of Odense University in 1972 wrote, 'Lauritz Weibull's results do not stand the test of time in various ways.'[91]

---

[85] Niels, 'Cnut's Danish Kingdom' p.27 note 2 in 'The Reign of Cnut.'
[86] Death of Eirkr 'the victorious,' Ólafr Skntkonnung succeeded in 995.
[87] Adam Bk 2 ch XL p.82.
[88] 'Source Criticism', Rolf Arvidson p.97.
[89] EER A pp. III p.86.
[90] A personal correspondence with Eric Christiansen March 18 and April 19 1986.
[91] 'Source Criticism' p.136.

Two questions now emerge. Firstly, was Styrbjörn more than just a myth? And secondly, was he the father of Thorgils? It is obvious that the bear legend of Saxo has to be relegated to its proper place as pure fiction. But is it possible that in view of his supposed link with Haraldr Gormsson and Eirikr the Victorious there may be some small substance of truth in his existence which Saxo and the author of the *Knytlinga Saga* built up and elaborated upon until, like Geoffrey of Monmouth's treatment of King Arthur the end product bore scant resemblance to the original historical person? Whether the link between Styrbjörn and Thorgils can be sustained or not is even more doubtful. What were the reasons for Langebek to first make the connection? There may be some evidence to support this in the careers of Úlfr and Eilifr. A son born to Styrbjörn and Thyra would have been part Swedish, part Danish. The *Chronicle* and Saxo claim Úlfr had Swedish aid at the Holy River. According to Adam, Swein the son of Úlfr fought for King Ánundr for twelve years.[92] Larson observed that the family had close links with both Denmark and Sweden.[93]

Chronologically it would have been possible for Thorgils to have been Styrbjörn's son. It is noticeable that the name *Björn,* or compounds of it, occur with regularity in the family tree. Styrbjörn's grandfather was called Björn, and - if Langebek's assumption was correct - Styrbjörn's grandson Úlfr named two of his sons Björn (or the English equivalent, Beorn) and Ásbjörn.[94] Could it be relevant that the names of two of the heroes commemorated on the rune stones, Ásbjörn and Ásmundr, both crop up, one as the son of Úlfr, the other as his grandson, and were they the brothers or cousin's of Styrbjörn who accompanied him of that fateful expedition? Apart from a Björn who the missionary Ansker met ca. 829 and another who is supposed to have reigned for fifty years, no other of that name is mentioned apart from the immediate family.

The existence of Styrbjörn rests solely on the authority of the sagas, which were written down long after he was supposed to have lived and the evidence of his being the ancestor of Godwine's wife rests on the flimsiest of grounds. We have, therefore, to admit that in the generations preceding Gytha there exists only a name – Thorgils Sprakaleggr. No charters or writs were used to either confirm or disprove his status, or the extent of his influence.

It is sufficient to say that in spite of the turbulent character of her eldest brother Úlfr this in no way influenced the steadfast loyalty of Godwine and Gytha towards King Cnut.

---

[92] Adam Bk 2 ch LXXIII [71] p.106; see also E.Christiansen, Saxo Note 167 p.214.
[93] 'Canute the Great' p.214; Saxo ch CXVI p.32.
[94] J. Bronsted, 'The Vikings' p.207; Morkinskinna pp.237-238. 'The dispute between Ásmundrr and King Swein began when Swegn Godwinson killed Ásmundr's father Beorn'. I am indebted to Eric Christiansen for bringing this to my attention.

Table 3. Sequence of Events 945 – 1035

c945	Accession of Haraldr Gormsson in Denmark
c950	Accession of Eirikr the Victorious in Sweden
971	Accession of Emperor Otto II
983	Haraldr Gormsson and a Slavic prince attack Germany Danes destroy Otto's fortress as Slesvig. Death of Otto II
c984	Styrbjörn invades Sweden: defeated and killed on Fyris Plain?
988	Death of Haraldr Gormsson; Accession of Swein Forkbeard
c994	Death of Eirikr the Victorious; Accession of Ólafr Skotkonung
c995-998	Possible marriage of Ólafr Tryggvason and Thyra
999	Battle of Svöld; Death of Ólafr Tryggvason
1000	Jarl Eirikr ruler of Western Norway under Swein Forkbeard
1009	Eilifr and Hemmingr join Thorkell's raiding host
1017	Cnut crowned King of England; Death of Eadric Streona – Prince Eadwig outlawed
1019/1020	Cnut visits Denmark to claim the Danish throne
1020	Council of Cirencester; Æthelweard outlawed: Godwine appointed to his earldom
1021	Thorkell outlawed
1022/1023	Úlfr in England; possibly Earl of East Anglia?
1023	Cnut's second visit to Denmark; Thorkell appointed regent
after 1023	Úlfr appointed regent of Denmark ; fosters Harthacnut
1025	Úlfr and Eilifr encounter Cnut at the Holy River and are reconciled to him?
1026/1027	The battle of the Holy River; Norwegian and Swedish coalition confront Cnut
1028	Murder of Jarl Úlfr
1035	Death of King Cnut; Eilifr leaves England to join the Varangian Guard

4. Earl Godwine in the Reign Of King Cnut

It is remarkable that the *Chronicle* makes almost no reference to Godwine at all during the reign of King Cnut. There is the one allusion to him in the 'F' version under the year 1009, which mentions Wulfnoth as being the 'father of Earl Godwine', and then nothing more until 1036 in connection with the murder of the Ætheling Alfred. In this the *Chronicle* is followed by John of Worcester, Simeon of Durham and all the other twelfth century chroniclers with the exception of Henry of Huntingdon,[1] William of Malmesbury[2] and, of course, the *Vita Ædwardi Regis*.

As we have seen Henry wrote that Godwine accompanied Cnut on his visit to Denmark in 1019/20 and William of Malmesbury in 1026/27. Keynes suggested good reasons for thinking that the occasion when Godwine distinguished himself was more likely to have been in 1022/23.[3] There does, however, remain the possibility that both the Huntingdon archdeacon and the Malmesbury librarian were relating genuine traditions and that, as commander of the English forces, Godwine may indeed have been with the King on more than one expedition.

Indeed, if it were not for Godwine's prominent position in the list of attestations, purely from the recorded annals, we would have no reason to believe he was the '*dux et baiulus*' of almost all the kingdom.[4] The evidence other than the charters comes from the '*Vita*' which, although likely to be biased, is nearly enough contemporary to be of value, with all the necessary reservations. According to this work, Godwine was renowned 'for loyalty', he was among the new nobles attached to the King's side, judged by the King himself 'the most cautious in counsel and the most active in war'[5]. He is described as of 'equitable temperament', 'incomparable in his tireless application to work'; he was humble, gentle and 'was revered by all the country's sons as a father'[6].

Cnut's reign is poorly documented, apart from records of his visits abroad. As has already been mentioned, in 1019/20 he returned to Denmark after his brother's death to lay claim to the Danish throne. His return in 1022/23 was to effect a reconciliation with the outlawed Thorkell Hávi. Two years later he was in his home country again, this time to confront the first whiff of trouble which

---

[1] 'Historia Anglorum' p.197 [of Cnut, 'In the third year of his reign'].
[2] G.R. Bk 2 ch 181 pp.324-325.
[3] 'Cnut's Earls' p.73.
[4] 'Vita' pp.10-11 and n16.
[5] ibid pp.10-11.
[6] ibid pp.10-11.

culminated in the events of 1026. The year 1027 saw him journeying to Rome, and in 1028/29 he was making good his claim to the Norwegian throne. All these absences from England are reflected in the granting of charters.

Godwine's advancement to the earldom of all Wessex occurred in three stages. He was probably appointed to Hampshire and Central Wessex in or before 1018, following the death of Ealdorman Ælfric at the battle of Ashingdon in 1016.[7] Following Æthelweard's banishment in 1020 the western provinces were added to his sphere of influence, but there is good evidence to show that Kent was not added to his earldom until after Cnut's death.[8] This is in the main the view taken by most authorities including Ann Williams, Simon Keynes, M. K. Lawson and Ian Walker. However, Freeman considered that Godwine's first earldom was probably Kent, to which he may have been appointed in 1018.[9] According to Stenton, Godwine was created earl of most of Wessex in 1018 and married Gytha at that time. Anscombe suggested that Sussex was his first appointment, in which he is followed by Higham.[10]

Godwine's Marriage and Elevation

In connection with the date of Godwine's marriage to Gytha Stenton, Lawson and F. McLynn agree on 1018; Simon Keynes puts it between 1022 and 1023, and suggests they were married in Denmark.[11] The fact that Swegn, Godwine's son, was appointed to an earldom bordering Wales in the year 1043 would seem to indicate that his parents were married prior to 1022-1023. It seems most likely that it was on this Baltic expedition that Godwine excelled with his night attack on the Wends, and it was on his return that he became earl of all Wessex (except Kent) and was promoted to the exalted position of premier earl. If this is correct the author of the *Vita Ædwardi Regis* telescoped the events into one account.

Family Tree of Gytha

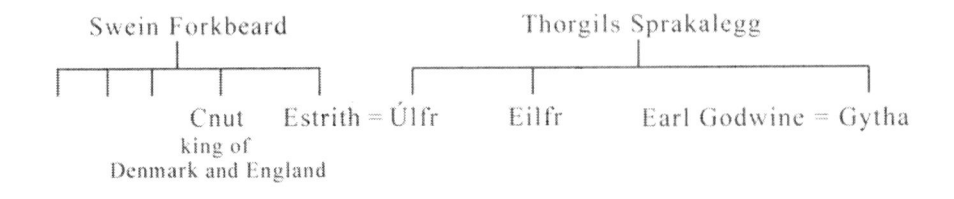

```
         Swein Forkbeard                    Thorgils Sprakalegg
              |                                      |
    ┌────┬────┼────┐                        ┌────────┼────────┐
                                                                
         Cnut    Estrith = Úlfr        Eilfr      Earl Godwine = Gytha
         king of
     Denmark and England
```

---

[7] A. Williams et al, 'Dark Age Britain' p.144.
[8] A. Williams, 'Kingship and Government' p.133 and note 108 p.212.
[9] F.N.C.i p.712.
[10] Anscombe p.138; Higham p.101.
[11] F. Stenton, A.S.E p.417; M. Lawson, 'Cnut' p.188; and F. McLynn for 1018; A. Williams et all 'Dark Age Britain' p.144, I. Walker, 'Harold' p.10; S. Keynes, 'Cnut's Earls' p.73, Professor Barlow, 'The Godwins' p.22 for 1919.

From this point our authorities are divided; on the one hand Freeman and Keynes, on the other Professor L. M. Larson and Miles Campbell. Freeman considered that from 1020 Godwine occupied a place 'second only to royalty', and as regent or 'viceroy' was left in charge of the government of the country when Cnut was abroad.[12] Keynes, with some modification as to the date, takes a similar view.[13] In contrast, Larson's opinion may be summed up briefly in this way: in 1022 Godwine was with the host when Cnut attacked the Slavs on the South Baltic shores; he fought valiantly in the Swedish campaign of 1026; his presence is recorded in Norway, presumably in 1028; and in view of Cnut's doubts about English fighting abilities, 'the presence of Godwine as a chief in Cnut's host may, therefore, be taken as a mark of peculiar confidence on the king's part'.[14] Furthermore Campbell summed up his position thus: 'The extant references to his [Godwine's] activities between 1023 and 1029 suggest that he continued to serve Canute primarily as a soldier, not as a 'viceroy' as Freeman thought', and again, 'Godwin's continued presence in the overseas expeditions of the king belies, however, the theory that he was the king's viceroy'[15]. The basis of this argument is that Godwine was 'closely connected' with the royal housecarls, and as such was necessarily in command of such warlike expeditions as Cnut was engaged in.

The evidence that Godwine was present on such excursions after 1022/3 is provided by William of Malmesbury, Geoffrey Gaimar and a runestone in Norway. William, writing of the 1026 campaign, says 'he routed his opponents, and brought the Kings of that nation [the Swedes] Ulf and Eifel to terms of peace. The English, at the instance of Earl Godwin, behaved nobly...'[16] Gaimar, relating the source of some of Godwine's wealth, writes (presumably of the same expedition) 'gained ... from the King of Sweden whom he killed'[17]. The runestone was a memorial to Bjór Arnsteinson, 'who found his death in Godwin's host when Cnut sailed [back] to England'.

Keynes has shown that William of Malmesbury's entry is a conflation of the 'E' annal in the *Chronicle* for the year 1025 and the words in the *Vita Ædwardi Regis*. He has also, following Musset, pointed out that the wording on the runestone does not refer to Godwine at all, and should read, 'Arnestein raised this stone in memory of Bjór, his son, he was killed in the 'lith' when Cnut attacked England', and the inscription which Larson and Campbell refers to about Godwine was actually a reference to God.[18] Far from being evidence of the earl's presence in Norway, it has rather to do with Cnut's attack on England on his return to contest the throne with King Edmund Ironside in 1015. Gaimar's remarks are apparently related to the same Norwegian Swedish war also; it is difficult to make any sense

---

[12] F.N.C.i pp.422-423, 712.
[13] 'Cnut's Earls' p.73.
[14] 'Canute the Great' p.151.
[15] Miles Campbell, 'The Rise of an Anglo-Saxon Kingmaker' p.23 note 33.
[16] G.R ch 181 pp.322-325.
[17] L'Estoire des Engleis' lines 4891-4894.
[18] 'Cnut's Earls' p.74 and note 170.

of his claim that Godwine was supposed to have killed a 'King of Sweden'[19], when Ólafr Skóttkonung died in 1022, and his son Ánundr was still alive thirty years later. Little credence can be given to him as a reliable historian. Writing in the middle of the twelfth century, his inaccuracies and love of myths - to say nothing of his dislike of Godwine - make him extremely unreliable, except for his preservation of local traditions particularly relating to Lincolnshire.[20]

Clarification of Godwine's role is more reliably afforded by the charters of Cnut's reign. Thorkell signs first in the charters through 1018 and 1019. We know from the letter the king sent from Denmark that he was acting as regent on that occasion during Cnut's absence. Thorkell was banished on 11th November 1021. From then until 1023, when he died, Éirikr was the premier earl,[21] and was, I believe, acting as regent during Cnut's second visit to Denmark in 1022/23. It seems reasonable to suppose that, in view of the fact that from late 1023 until 1038, Godwine always witnessed as the senior earl on all subsequent journeys abroad, he acted as the regent or 'viceroy'. The author of the *Vita Ædwardi Regis* corroborates this when he wrote 'In the reign of King Cnut, Godwin flourished in the royal palace, having the first place among the highest nobles of the kingdom; and, as was just, what he wrote all decreed should be written, and what he erased, erased. And he throve mightily in the seat of authority...', and 'whenever wrongs appeared, right and law were promptly restored there.'[22] Campbell did, however, conclude that, 'If, as seems likely, King Canute was hampered by illness during his last years, it may have been that Earl Godwin, having served his lord well in war, would have been in a position to assume a more significant role in the peace that settled on England.'[23]

After 1023 there were at least three, and possibly five occasions when the King was absent from the country. In 1025 he was confronting Úlfr and Éilifr;[24] the following year the more serious threat from the Norwegian and Swedish coalition had to be faced; in the spring of 1027 Cnut was in Rome; and in 1028 in Norway, driving Ólafr Haraldsson into exile. During these years the King must have been absent from England for long periods, and quite obviously someone must have been left in charge of the administration. These duties commenced when it became necessary to investigate rumours which were reaching the king's ears regarding Úlfr's doubtful loyalty. Éilifr had probably joined his brother in Denmark, initially to assist him in the legitimate business of the country. They seem to have held divided loyalties to both the Danish and Swedish monarchs, and in the spring of 1025 Cnut confronted them. As on his previous visit he found it expedient to

---

[19] But see Miles Campbell p.24.
[20] A. Gransden, 'Historical Writing' pp.209-212. 'It presents Anglo-Saxon history seen through the eyes of romance' p.210.
[21] S. Keynes, 'Cnut's Earls', pp.53, 57, 84.
[22] 'Vita' pp.10-11.
[23] Miles Campbell ibid p.24.
[24] A.S.C 'E' s.a 1025.

Genealogy of the Kings of Sweden

Eirikr *the Victorious* king c.980-995 = Sigrid *the Haughty* (Sigrid)
|
Ólafr Skotkonung king 995-1022 (Onund Jacob)
|
Anundr king 1020-1056
Edmund *the Old* king 1056-1060

The grand-daughter of Ólafr Skotkonung = Stenkil king 1060-?
|
Inge king 1086-1110
|
Katarina — Kristina = Harald Msistislav
|
Kristina = St Erik king 1150-1160
|
Knut king 1170-1195

Sverker I king 1131-1167 = Úlfhildr
|
Kristina = Karl king 1161-1167
|
Sverker II king c.1188-1208 died 1216

Erik king 1210-c.1250 = Rekissa daughter of
defeated Sverker II   Valdimar I King of Denmark
in battle

See - The *Morkinskinna* chapter 66 pp 328, 329
 - The *Fagrskinna* chapter 77 p236 and App II pp301,302
 - Birgit and Peter Sawyer, *Medieval Scandinavia*

I am indebted to Mr Eric Christiansen for his help and telephone conversations which have proved invaluable in compiling this geneology. Any faults which appear are entirely my own.

compromise, as he had with Thorkell; Éilifr returned to England with him as a surety for Úlfr's future allegiance, as before Thorkell's son had been required for the same reason. The sons of Thorgils Sprakalegg were too powerful to risk a showdown, especially since Ólafr Haraldsson and Ánundr had settled the differences which had existed between Ólafr and the latter's father. and were in alliance. Cnut needed all the support he could get in Scandinavia.

The entry in the 'E' version of the *Chronicle* alone records Cnut's expedition against his brother-in-law and Éilifr. The 'D' version jumps from the translation of St Ælfheah's body in 1023 to Bishop Ælfric's journey to Rome to receive the pallium in 1026; 'C' passes from 1023 to Cnut's invasion of Norway in 1028; and John of Worcester, under 1025, merely records the appointment of Edmund to the bishopric of Lindisfarne.[25] So information of the involvement of the brothers rests solely on that one *Chronicle* entry, and it would appear that the annalist confused a minor incident with the more serious conflict the following year.[26] It looks as if Cnut patched up an uneasy peace with Úlfr until such time as Ólafr was expelled from Norway and Hákon had the country under control. Then, with the Norwegian-Swedish pact ended, he could afford to do without his unruly regent.

Cnut was back in England in the summer of 1025, but by 1026 he was again in Scandinavian waters to meet the threat posed by the alliance. Norse sources tell us that Ólafr arrived off the coast of Zealand with a fleet of sixty ships while Ánundr commenced to harry Skane; Cnut had arrived with his English fleet in Limfjord, Jutland, and there he was joined by a Danish contingent. The allies retreated before Cnut's combined forces and took up battle positions at the mouth of the Holy River. The result of the battle, although a defeat for Cnut, must have been inconclusive. There are traditions of a dam built up-river by Ánundr, which when destroyed wrecked a great many of Cnut's ships. However, Ánundr headed for home; Ólafr returned overland to Norway to attempt to quell the growing unrest in his own country, and Cnut overwintered in Denmark.

Cnut and Rome

The following spring Cnut was in Rome to attend the coronation of Conrad II, the German emperor, and visiting churches on his journey as a penitent pilgrim. Germany's relations with Denmark had been strained; a history of German attacks under Otto I and his successor, Otto II, were not forgotten, and it is possible that one reason for Cnut's presence was to offer allegiance to the emperor. There is the further possibility that the future marriage of the emperor's son, Henry, then a boy of ten years, to Cnut's daughter, Gunnhildr, perhaps a year or so younger, may have been discussed. However, some conversations were already in progress regarding a possible match for the boy; ambassadors were even then in Constantinople endeavouring to arrange for his betrothal to the daughter of the Byzantine emperor, Constantine VIII. This came to nothing

---

[25] J.W. pp.508-509.
[26] Plummer and Earle, 'Two of the Saxon Chronicles Parallel' vol ii p.205.

when Constantine died the following year. One of his daughters, Zoe, had the forethought to marry Romanus Argyrus on her father's death bed and her newly acquired husband became the next Byzantine emperor as Romanus III,[27] so the prospect of the two empires becoming united came to nothing.

Negotiations then went ahead for Henry's union with Gunnhildr. A new atmosphere of friendship commenced between Germany and Denmark. Schleswig and land north of the river Eider was ceded to Denmark. The couple were not married until June 1036; their only child, Beatrice, was later to become Abbess of Quedlingberg. Gunnhildr died two years after the marriage while on a visit to Italy with her husband and his mother. The intolerable heat of the Italian summer, with its attendant pestilence, were too much for her delicate constitution. (All Cnut's children died young: Swein was probably little more than twenty two, if that, when he died; Harold and Harthacnut perhaps twenty four, and Gunnhildr a little over nineteen.) Henry then married Agnes, the daughter of William the Count of Poitiou.

While in Rome Cnut was able to obtain concessions for English pilgrims; to arrange aid for English traders by the removal of trade barriers, and to obtain the Pope's permission to allow English bishops to waive the need to undertake the arduous, often dangerous journey to Rome to obtain the pallium. All this he proudly put into the letter which he sent to his English subjects in the keeping of Abbot Lyfing of Tavistock.

Conrad II became king on the death of Henry II. His claim to the title was derived from his great grandmother, Liutgard, who had married Conrad the Red, duke of Lorraine. She was the daughter of Otto I who had reigned as emperor from 936 to 973. Conrad had married Gisela, the duchess of Swabia. He came to the throne in 1024, but opposition prevented him being crowned as emperor of the Holy Roman Empire by Pope John XIX until Easter Sunday 1027.[28] The following year he had his son Henry crowned as his successor and, about the same time, Cnut proclaimed Harthacnut as his heir with the title of King of Denmark.

According to the 'D' recension of the *Chronicle*, on his return from Rome Cnut attacked Scotland and forced King Malcolm to become his vassal. The 'E' version under the same year, 1031, adds that two other kings, Maelbeth and Ichmare, also submitted. Both versions place the visit to Rome in 1031, but make no mention of the Emperor's coronation. 'D' and 'E' have no entry for 1026 or 1027; 'C' jumps from 1023 to 1028. Like the *Chronicle*, most English annalists record Cnut's visit to Rome under the year 1031. William of Malmesbury says: 'In the fifteenth year of his reign Cnut went to Rome, and after remaining there some time, and atoning for his crimes by giving alms to the several churches, he sailed back to England.'[29] However, the letter he sent back to his English subjects expressly states the presence of Pope John, Conrad, Rodolfe of Burgundy and 'all the princes' which surely links the visit to Conrad's coronation in 1027.

---

[27] T. Tout, 'The Empire and the Papacy' pp.165-167; F. McLynn p.47.
[28] T. Tout, ibid pp.53-59.
[29] G.R. 182 pp.324-5.

All of the above tends to prove that Cnut made two visits to Rome, one in 1027 and a second in 1031, and it was after the second that he led an expedition into Scotland. It is most unlikely that he would have engaged in a military operation against the Scots between the Norwegian-Swedish offensive and settling his score with Ólafr in 1028. It seems, therefore, that Cnut was in Rome in the spring of 1027, returned by way of Denmark and the following year invaded Norway. This is substantiated by the letter written on his way to Denmark, in which he says: 'And therefore I wish to make known to you, that, returning by the same way I went, I am going to Denmark, to conclude with the counsel of all the Danes peace and a firm treaty with those nations and peoples who wished, if it had been possible for them, to deprive us both of the kingdom and of life, but could not, since God indeed destroyed their strength.'[30] This was obviously an allusion to Cnut's defeat at the Holy River.

To understand the position in Norway in 1028 it is necessary to go back to the death of Háraldr Fairhair, the first King of all Norway. He lived until he was over eighty and had many wives and concubines. Snorri mentions seven wives by name, and in another passage records: 'for it is told that King Háraldr put away nine wives when he married Rognhild the Mighty.'[31] She was the daughter of King Eirikr of Jutland and of Gunnhildr, the daughter of King Gorm of Denmark. Because of the importance of his maternal relations, the son born of this union, later to be known as Eirikr Bloodaxe, was given pride of place among his many half-brothers who were all ready to claim their right to be their father's successor. Surprisingly, although nominated by his father as his heir, after four years Eirikr threw up his claim to Norway and established himself as Lord of Orkney, and later was to become King of York for two brief spells. Among his half brothers, three were to have some bearing on the future of Norway. Hákon, who had been fostered by King Æthelstan, became King of Norway from 934 until 960. Another son, Ólafr, became king of the district of Viken; his grandson was the famour Ólafr Tryggvason. A third, Bjorn, was the great-grandfather of Ólafr, the future king and saint.

In his day Tryggvi's son, Ólafr, had to contend with an alliance of Sweden and Denmark in the persons of Ólafr Skóttkonung and Swein Forkbeard, supported by the discontented magnates whose authority had been eroded when Ólafr established his kingship; most notable of these was Jarl Eirikr of Hlathir. Activated by the hope of gain, and perhaps envy of the charismatic personality of the Norwegian king, the confederates waylaid Ólafr on his return journey from a meeting with Boleslav, king of Wendland. The opportunity came when the Norwegian fleet became separated - according to Snorri through the treachery of Sigvaldi, Thorkell Havi's brother. In the sea-battle that ensued, when all was lost Ólafr, wounded, leapt to his death, rather than be taken captive.[32]

---

[30] 'English Historical Documents' vol i ed. D. Whitelock no 53.
[31] 'Saga of Harald the Fair' ch XX p.65.
[32] King Olaf Trygvasson's Saga' ch CXXI p.97.

Norway Divided

Norway was divided between the protagonists - Swein Forkbeard, Ólafr Skóttkonung and Jarl Eirikr. The battle of Svöld resulted in the Danish king's overlordship of Norway, with Eirikr and his brother Swein having authority under him. According to Snorri, this Swein married Holmfrid, Ólafr Skóttkonung's daughter,[33] and therefore Ánundr's sister, and the Swedish king gave his share of the spoils into Jarl Swein's care. This was the pattern which existed in 1015 when another Ólafr appeared in Norway, a descendant of Harald Fairhair through Bjorn. His father, Haraldr Grenske, died before he was born and his mother, Aasta, married Sigurd Sýr, one of the petty kings of Opland. When Ólafr Haraldson was twelve years old he was given the command of a ship captained by Hrani 'the foster father of kings'. Under Hrani's tutelage they harried in Denmark, Sweden, Finland and Friesland. He is next heard of with Thorkell, fighting against Ulfkell at the battle of Ringmere and present at the siege of Canterbury in September 1011. When Thorkell's army was disbanded, Ólafr went on fresh Viking adventures along the coasts of France and Spain. Hiring himself into the service of Duke Robert of Normandy, he met King Æthelred in Rouen when the latter was in exile, and returned with the king to England. Ólafr siezed the opportunity afforded by Cnut's return to England accompanied by Éirikr of Hláthir, leaving Norway to be governed by Eirikr's brother Swein and his son Hákon. Landing in the west of the country he recruited his father-in-law, along with two other Opland kings, and travelling through the districts bordering the Oslo Fiord gathered support from a region which was traditionally pro-Danish. He defeated Swein Hakonson in the sea battle of Nesjar; tricked Hákon into taking an oath that he would never take up arms against him, and at a Thing in Throndheim - with Jarl Swein defeated and in exile in Sweden, where he died two years later, and with Eirkir and Hákon in England - Ólafr was proclaimed King of Norway.

One of his first priorities was to attempt to form an alliance with the Swedish king, Ólafr Skóttkonung, who was himself far from popular with his subjects due to his fanatical zeal to convert Sweden to Christianity. The Swedes clung stubbornly to the old religion and eventually he was forced to share the rule of his realm with his son, Ánundr.

Ólafr Haraldson too made many enemies amongst his own countrymen. His enthusiasm to Christianise Norway forcibly made many enemies for him; the aristocracy which had initially supported him saw their authority taken from them, and the final straw was the murder of Erling Skalgsson after offering him his peace. for Erling was 'loved and respected even by his enemies'.[34]

Cnut was hailed as king and deliverer wherever he landed as his fleet sailed up the Norwegian coast. At Nidaros he received the acclamation of the men of Trondheim, and Ólafr fled the country shortly after. Cnut summoned a Thing at

---

[33] ibid ch CXXIII p.98.
[34] Saint Olaf's Saga' ch CLXXXVI pp.329-331.

Genealogy of the Norwegian Royal Family
After F. Barlow, *Edward the Confessor*, Scandinavian Dynasties

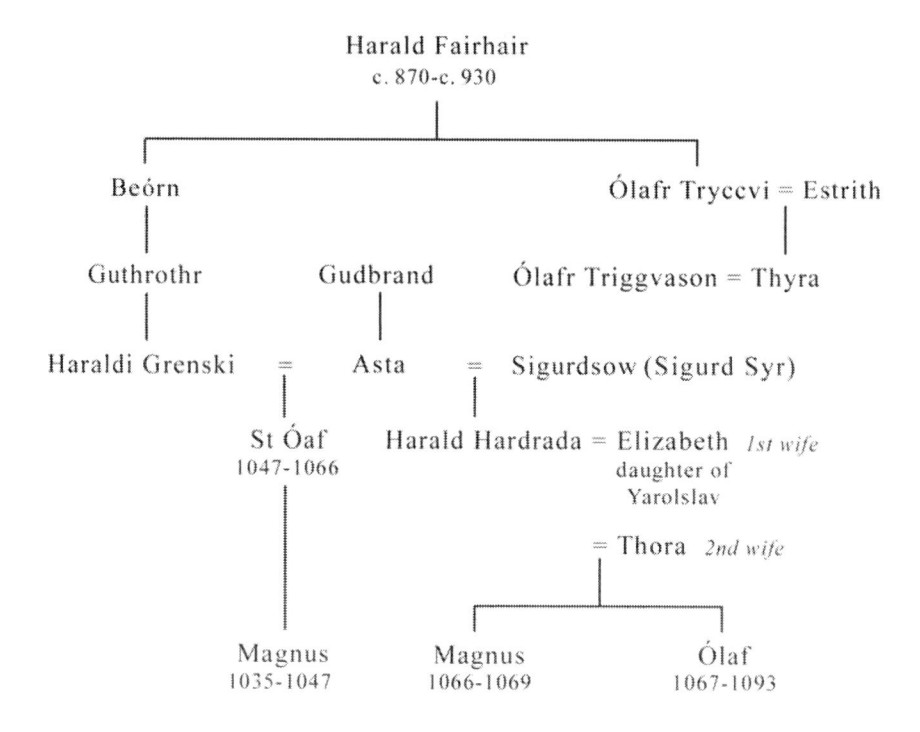

```
                        Harald Fairhair
                         c. 870-c. 930
        ┌──────────────────────┴──────────────────────┐
      Beórn                                   Ólafr Tryccvi = Estrith
        │                                              │
    Guthrothr          Gudbrand              Ólafr Triggvason = Thyra
        │                 │                             │
  Haraldi Grenski    =    Asta    =    Sigurdsow (Sigurd Syr)
                          │              │
                       St Óaf       Harald Hardrada = Elizabeth  1st wife
                     1047-1066                       daughter of
                          │                           Yarolslav
                          │                      = Thora  2nd wife
                          │                             │
                          │                    ┌────────┴────────┐
                       Magnus               Magnus             Ólaf
                     1035-1047             1066-1069         1067-1093
```

Nidaros; he appointed Hákon Eirksson, who had accompanied him from England as his regent in Norway and took hostages from all the *lendermen* and *bonders* as a guarantee of their good behaviour. The jarls of Hlathir, who had exercised authority under the Danish overlords since Swein Forkbeard's time, were more acceptable to the fiercely independent Norwegian aristocracy than a foreigner and Cnut's arrangement would, no doubt, have worked well. But within a year Hákon was drowned when his ship sank in the Pentland Firth. Apparently he was coming to England to fetch his wife, Gunnhildr, the daughter of Cnut's sister and Wyrtgeorn, a King of the Wends. The news of Hákon's death reached Ólafr at the court of Yaroslav in Kiev and this prompted him to make a bid to regain his throne. Recruiting men from Sweden and gathering whomever would join him, he led his motley army across the Kjolen mountain and journeyed on to Trondelagen and to his death at Stiklestad.

In Hákon's place Cnut appointed his eldest son, Swein, as king of Norway with his mother, Ælfgifu, acting as his regent. Their enterprise was doomed to failure from the start. The Norwegian nobility were hardly likely to accept an Englishwoman and her Anglo-Danish son when they had rejected both Ólafr Tryggvason and Ólafr Haraldson. Kalv Arnesson and Einar Tambarskjelver had both supported Cnut and looked for their reward; neither relished being passed over for a foreign youngster and his mother. Two other factors played a part: a succession of bad harvests - for which they were not to blame - brought hardship and hunger in their wake; and a growing sense of Norwegian nationalism was being fostered by tales of miracles which were reported at the dead monarch's tomb in St Clement's church in Nidaros. Ólafr the saint bore little relation to Ólafr the man; he was rather a reflection of what his countrymen nostalgically liked to imagine he had been, and his posthumous popularity owed much to his son Magnus's military prowess and ability to throw off the Danish yoke which his father had been unable to accomplish.

Cnut's last absence from England when Godwine was called upon to act as his regent would have been, as mentioned earlier, the second pilgrimage to Rome and the invasion of Scotland following it. Professor A. A. M. Duncan, a leading authority on Scottish history, placed the campaign in 1031, which he suggested may have been linked with Scotland providing sanctuary for Cnut's opponents from Scandinavia.[35] W.Kappelle remarked that 'sometime between 1027 and 1031 the King came north, and received the submission of Malcolm II and two northern sub-kings'.[36] Confirmation of the date of the invasion of Scotland - and therefore the likelihood of a second visit to Rome - is given by Dr Alfred Smyth who stated that Cnut's excursion took place in 1031-2.[37] I think that in view of this it can be assumed that the king went to Rome for a second time and was in Scotland in 1031 and 1032; and that Godwine was again acting as his regent at this time.

Leofric

At this point it is necessary to examine the family which more than any other was destined to play a part in the future of Earl Godwine and his children. It was in the year 1032 that the name Leofric first makes an appearance in the charter witness lists as an earl. From that point, he almost always witnessed second in order of seniority after Godwine; except in a charter of Harthacnut's which constitutes a grant of privilege to the abbey of Bury St Edmunds, dated by Sawyer as 1036 x 1039[38] (and which is in any case regarded as spurious).

---

[35] 'Scotland; The Making of the Kingdom' p.99.
[36] Kapelle, 'The Norman Conquest of the North' pp.25-26.
[37] 'Dark Age Britain' p.178; M.K. Lawson, 'Cnut' p.104.
[38] S 995.

Family of Leofric Earl of Mercia

After Ann Williams, *The English and Norman Conquest,*
The Earls of Mercia, p.52, The Boydell Press 1997

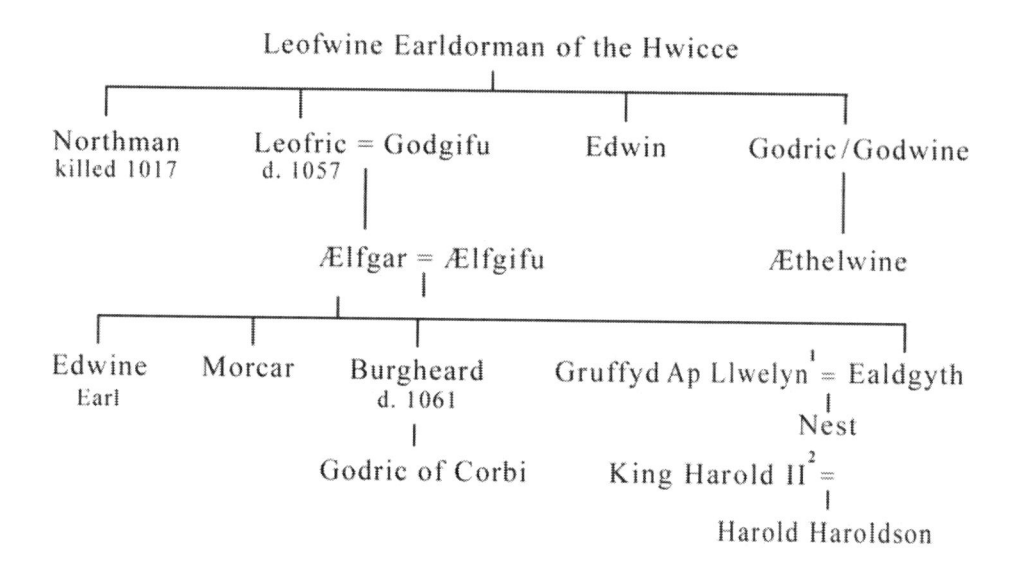

```
                    Leofwine Earldorman of the Hwicce
     ┌──────────────┬──────────────┬──────────────┐
  Northman      Leofric = Godgifu   Edwin     Godric/Godwine
  killed 1017   d. 1057
                       │                           │
                 Ælfgar = Ælfgifu              Æthelwine
                       │
   ┌──────────┬────────┼─────────────────┐
  Edwine   Morcar   Burgheard      Gruffyd Ap Llwelyn¹ = Ealdgyth
  Earl               d. 1061                              │
                       │                                 Nest
                 Godric of Corbi              King Harold II² =
                                                          │
                                                  Harold Haroldson
```

Leofric was the son of Ealdormen Leofwine, and the brother of Northman, Edwin and Godric or Godwine. A charter of 1017 recording a lease of land in Worcestershire made by Archbishop Wulfstan of York to his brother Ælfric was witnessed by Eadric Streona as the Earl of Mercia, by Leofwine and three of his sons, Northman, Edwin and Leofric. Before that year ended, both Eadric and Northman were executed. John of Worcester mistakenly styled Northman as '*dux*' and thought that on his death Leofric succeeded to his ealdormanry.[39] A Leofric, who may be Leofwine's son, witnessed as a thegn during the years 1019-1026.[40] It seems that he may have held the office of sheriff of Worcestershire - the evidence for this is found in the abbot of Evesham's lease to Æthelmaer of land in Worcestershire with the provision that it reverted to the abbey after three lives. This charter A. J. Robertson dates as 'not later than 28 May 1023, the date of Archbishop Wulfstan's death. It was probably not much earlier'.[41] It records that the land leased was lying waste when it was bought

---

[39] J.W. pp.504-505.
[40] S. Keynes, 'Atlas' Table LXX 1 of 2
[41] S 1423; Robertson 'Charters', No LXXXI pp.156-157 and p.405; Leofric witnessed with Eadwine as first amongst the thegns after Leofwine as ealdorman.

from Hákon, the Earl of Worcestershire and Leofric (presumably the sheriff) and the whole shire. This was witnessed by Hákon and Eilifr as earls, Leofwine as ealdorman, and then by Leofric and Edwin. Whitelock suggested that Leofric may have succeeded Eilifr in Western Mercia.[42] Williams stated that, in her opinion, Leofric started his public life as the sheriff of Worcestershire under Earl Hákon and was promoted to the Earldom of Mercia after his father's death c1023.[43] A charter recording King Cnut's grant of land to Æthelwine, the Abbot of Athelney, and the community there has been cited as evidence that Leofric was attesting charters as early as 1023/4 by Miss F. Harmer, which led her to assume that 'Leofric may have held some subordinate earldom as early as 1017'.[44] In support of this contention she pointed out that John of Worcester stated that Cnut appointed him to fill the vacancy caused by Northman's execution in 1017.[45] Freeman thought that, if Leofric was appointed to a subordinate earldom at that time, it was probably based on Chester.[46]

Like Ealdormen Æthelmaer, Leofwine ealdorman of the Hwicce[47] submitted to Swein in 1013; like Æthelmaer - and Godwine - Leofwine had little cause to trust Eadric Streona. His son Northman's mistaken involvement with the latter would be an added reason for his hatred of the man.[48] It is also probable that both Leofwine and Godwine were supporters of the Ætheling Æthelstan, and had on his death given their support to King Edmund.

King Æthelred granted Leofwine land at Southam, Ladbroke and Redbourne in Warwickshire in 998, and in 1014, perhaps in the hope of regaining his loyalty - by now given to the Æthelings Æthelstan and Edmund, - land at Mathon in Herefordshire.[49] The last time his name appears on a charter was a grant by Cnut to a monk, Ælfric of Evesham, which is dated by Sawyer as 1021/23. It is presumed that he died soon after this, as his period in office spanned thirty years, from 994 to 1024.[50]

According to the chronicle of Hugh Candidus, Leofwine's father was called Ælfwine.[51] It has been suggested that Ælfwine might be identified with a son of Ælfric, the ealdorman of Mercia from 993 until 995; the Ælfric 'Cild' who appears in a list of magnates acting as surety in connection with the estate of Warmington for Bishop Æthelwold.[52] Ælfric succeeded Ælfhere as ealdorman of Mercia and was

---

[42] 'Saga Book of the Viking Society' XII 1940 p.135.
[43] 'Dark Age Britain' pp.169-170.
[44] S 979, 'A.S. Writs' p.565.
[45] J.W. pp.504-505.
[46] F.N.C.i p.719.
[47] S. Keynes, 'Cnut's Earls' pp.74-75; and notes 173, 174 on p.74.
[48] N Higham, 'Death of A.S. England' pp.84-85.
[49] S 892, S 932, S 1503 'A.S. Wills' D. Whitelock No 20 pp.56-63.
[50] S. Keynes, 'Cnut's Earls' pp.74-75; A. Williams, 'Dark Age Britain' pp.170-171.
[51] 'The Chronicle of Hugh Candidus' p.68 'Leofuuinus Alderman filius Elfuuine'.
[52] A. J. Robertson, 'A.S. Charters' No XL pp.74-83, particularly pp.76, 77 and 369-370.

banished, according to the *Chronicle* two years later. John of Worcester tells us that Ælfric was Ælfhere's son,[53] although it has also been suggested that he was his brother-in-law. His son, Ælfwine, was killed in the battle of Maldon, Essex in 991.

An interesting theory advanced by P. Stafford identifies Æthelwine with the youngest son of Æthelstan 'Half-King', called Æthelwine 'amicus Dei' who had sons named Leofwine and Eadwine[54]. In spite of many similarities, this seems very doubtful. Leofwine had four sons who are known to history. Northman was probably implicated with Eadric in Eadwig's attempt to gain the throne after King Edmund's death. Northman *'minister'* received land at Hampton and Evesham in Worcestershire in 988. In 1016 he witnessed King Æthelred's charter restoring land in Gloucestershire to Evesham Abbey, which may have been one of the King's last charters. In 1013 a Northman *'miles'* was granted land at Twywell in Northamptonshire and in 1017, when his death was drawing near, he witnessed Archbishop Wulfstan's lease to his brother Ælfwig, as already mentioned.[55]

Another brother, Edwin, was probably younger than Leofric. He signs after his brother in a document concerning a lease of some land by Abbot Ælfweard to one Æthelmaer. There is evidence to show that Edwin acted as sheriff in Herefordshire. A charter which records a dispute between Æthelstan, the bishop of Hereford, and Wulfstan and his son over some land in Worcestershire and of another family dispute involving a mother and her son concerning land in Herefordshire would seem to establish a link between Edwin and that shire. Attending the shire-moot where the case was heard were Bishop Æthelstan, Earl Hrani of Hereford 'and Edwin, the Earl's [son]'. An Edwin witnessed Æthelred's charters intermittently from 1005 until 1016, but there is nothing to connect him definitely as Leofwine's son.[56]

Edwin, son of Leofwine, was killed in the battle of Rhyd Y Groes in 1039. According to J. E. Lloyd, he was possibly acting as Earl Hrani's deputy which would be natural if he were the Sheriff of Hereford. Gruffydd ap Llewelyn, King of Gwynedd, ambushed a Mercian army led by Edwin at a ford near Welshpool on the Severn, near the Welsh border. Taking the English army by surprise, he inflicted a crushing defeat on them. The Mercian leaders Edwin, Thorkell and Ælfgeat were slain and Gruffydd established a reputation for himself. Hemming, the monk of Worcester, asserted that Edwin held land at Bickmarsh in Warwickshire which rightfully belonged to his community.[57]

Leofwine's remaining son was named Godric (or possibly Godwine), perhaps the same Godric who witnessed from 1003-1013. He too, according to Hemming, stood condemned of illegally withholding lands which belonged to the monks of

---

[53] J.W. pp.434-435; A. Williams 'Dark Age Britian' pp.10-11, Ælfhere p.147 note 21.
[54] P. Stafford, 'Limitations of Royal Policy' p.43 note 71.
[55] S 873, 872, 935 and 1384.
[56] A.J. Robertson, 'A.S. Charters', No LXXVIII pp.150-151.
[57] 'A History of Wales' pp.359-360; Hemming pp.278-279.

Coventry, an accusation repeated by William of Malmesbury.[58] Apparently when Godric lay on his death-bed he relented, and with a little persuasion from Prior Wulfstan, who was in attendance to perform the last rites, agreed to restore the land at Salwarpe in Worcestershire to the Abbey. Unfortunately for the church, his son, Æthelwine, refused to honour his father's last request and did so with the support of his uncle Leofric. This Æthelwine was given as a hostage to Swein Forkbeard, probably when Leofwine submitted to him in 1013, and was perhaps among the hostages who were mutilated by Cnut before his flight back to Denmark the following year. Although his hands were cut off, the Domesday Book shows that he was alive at the time of the Conquest, and was still in possession of Salwarpe. By this time he must have been in his sixties. According to one story, Æthelwine died dishonoured and poverty-stricken in a herdsman's cottage which is not surprising when it is remembered how the English were treated after the Norman Conquest.[59]

Leofric himself is not exempt from the critical pen of Hemming. The Earl used his influence to force the Prior of Worcester to grant land belonging to the monks of Worcester to one of his thegns in return for military service. Hemming also accuses Leofric - although he returned two estates wrongly possessed by his father - of keeping the others himself. He also asserted his authority in order to have his nephew and namesake appointed to the abbeys of Burton-upon-Trent, Peterborough, Coventry, Grayland and Thorney, which constitutes pluralism of excessive proportions.[60] In his nephew's favour it must be recorded that he was well loved at Peterborough. There is no evidence to show who his father was, or whether his mother was perhaps Leofric's sister.

To return to Earl Leofric; his generosity to the abbey of Coventry, which he founded, and his gifts to other monastic foundations contrast strangely with his recorded dealings with the ecclesiastical establishment at Worcester. He is accused of transferring an estate from Worcester to Coventry. Evesham, Leominster, Wenlock, Stow St Mary's in Lincolnshire and the monastery of St John's and St Mary's in Chester all remembered him as a benefactor. The estate that Northman received at Hampton from King Æthelred passed to Leofric, and at a later date he restored it to the Abbey of Evesham. Hemming states that the two estates at Wolverly and Blackwell, both in Worcestershire, were held unjustly, but at a later date were returned to the monastery of St Mary during the last few years of his life. Other estates which rightfully belonged to the church Leofric promised would be restored at his death, but instead were still in his wife's possession, and

---

[58] Hemming, 'Chartularium', i pp.259-260.
[59] Hemming ibid, F.Barlow, 'The English Church' pp.57; A. Williams, 'Cockles Amongst the Wheat' p.7, p.18 note 33.
[60] Hemming i pp.261-262; 264-265. It is only fair to say that Leofric as Abbot of Peterborough may only have exercised a responsibility for the small Fenland monasteries of Crowland and Thorney and a natural interest in Coventry and Burton, the two houses closely linked to his family. I am indebted to Dr Ann Williams for this correction.

eventually were appropriated by her grandsons.[61] His wife, Godgifu, was noted for her piety and generosity to the Church. In this respect it must also be remembered that Godwine's wife, Gytha, was celebrated for her gifts to religious foundations. From the commencement of King Edward's reign, Leofric and Godgifu started on a veritable frenzy of good works and church-building.

The legend of Lady Godiva's (Godgifu's) ride through the streets of Coventry naked may contain a grain of truth. According to Osbert of Clere in his *Vita Beati Edwardi* Leofric, when in the company of King Edward at Westminster, saw a vision of Christ. Perhaps because of this experience he repented of his unjust seizure of church property and the high taxes he had levied, and sought to make amends. Through the good influence of his wife he devoted much of his wealth for the benefit of the Church. The 'D' version of the *Chronicle* in recording his death s.a. 1057 says, 'He was very wise in all matters, both religious and secular, that benefited all this nation', and the *Evesham Chronicle* vouches for the high esteem in which King Cnut held him.[62]

Many historians have sought to show that a rivalry existed between the two earls; comparing Leofric's moderation and piety with Godwine's lack of such finer qualities. Stenton writes of the 'rivalry of the families which ... fatally weakened the possibility of a united English resistance to the Norman invasion of 1066,' and again, 'Leofric of Mercia and Siward of Northumbria regarded Godwine, if not with jealousy, at least with complete detachment.'[63] It would seem that Leofric was a peaceful man with an insular policy, whereas Godwine favoured closer links with Denmark. This led to their different attitudes to the succession question in 1035/36 and their different opinions regarding the advisability of sending naval aid to King Swein Estrithson in 1047 and 1048. But in 1036, when it became obvious that Harthacnut was unable to leave Denmark, Godwine recognised that Leofric's championship of Harald Harefoot was the only solution in the circumstances, and once convinced, supported him wholeheartedly.

Nor is there any evidence of personal enmity between Godwine and Leofric. It is significant that one of King Harold's supporters, who was in attendance on him when he lay gravely ill at Oxford, was Bishop Lyfing who was one of Godwine's close friends. In 1040 when Harthacnut arraigned Godwine for complicity in the murder of Alfred, his half brother, according to the testimony of John of Worcester, he was required to clear himself by taking an oath to prove his innocence. In this he was supported by 'almost all the chief men and most important thegns'.[64] During the crisis of 1051 Leofric and Siward initially brought with them only token support to Gloucester. The *Chronicle* says: 'at first they came with only moderate reinforcements'. It was only when King Edward demanded it that the two earls sent for more reserves. Even then, the earls

---

[61] Hemming i pp.261-262. A. Williams, 'The Spoliation of Worcester' pp.386-387.
[62] 'A.S.C' 'D' s.a 1057; F. Barlow, 'Edward' p.274.
[63] 'A.S.E' pp.416, 561.
[64] J.W. ii pp.530-533.

pointed out the stupidity of armed conflict. They thought 'it would be great folly if they joined battle, between well nigh all the noblest in England were present in those two companies'. The annalist adds: 'and they were convinced they would be leaving the country open to the invasion of our enemies'.[65] This may have been true of the 1040's also, but on October 25th 1047 King Magnus died, and in 1051 Hárald Harðráða was too busily engaged with Swein Estrithson to constitute a threat at the time.

It is more likely that Leofric, although he may not have agreed with Godwine's foreign policy, did appreciate that basically they were both patriots with the good of their country at heart. To substantiate this John of Worcester expressly says that it was Earl Leofric who endeavoured to act as peacemaker at Gloucester.[66] Again in 1052, on Godwine's return from exile, there was the same reluctance to take up arms in support of the king against Godwine and in the *Vita*' especially commissioned by Godwine's own daughter Queen Eadgyth, Leofric is spoken of as 'an excellent man, very devoted to God'. This hardly supports the idea that personal ill feeling existed between the two earls. After Godwine's death, Leofric, Godwine's son Earl Harold and Bishop Ealdred were working together to establish peace between the Welsh king, Gruffydd ap Llewelyn, and his English overlord, King Edward. During the last years of Cnut's life Godwine and Leofric were his closest advisers, and it was not until Godwine's son, Tostig, and Leofric's grandsons, Edwin and Morcar, became bitter enemies that hostility actually existed between the two families. In 1055 Harold persuaded the King to pardon Earl Ælfgar after the sacking of Hereford and ten years later as the representative of Edward he negotiated with the Northumbrians to accept Morcar as their earl.

Archbishop Æthelnoth

One of the most influential men with whom Godwine had to work closely was Æthelnoth, who became the Archbishop of Canterbury in 1020. He was the son of Ealdorman Æthelmaer.[67] As a monk and then prior of Christ Church, Canterbury, Cnut was following his policy of promoting members of the Anglo-Saxon nobility into prominent positions. He had tried to do this with Ealdorman Æthelmaer's son-in-law, Æthelweard, but failed when the latter became involved in the plot to place Eadwig the Ætheling on the throne. Cnut did the same with more success with Godwine, Leofwine and Leofric.

Æthelnoth was consecrated by Wulfstan, the Archbishop of York, on 30th November, 1020. John of Worcester tells us that he was known as 'the Good', and the 'D' version of the *Chronicle* introduces the moving story of the grief of Bishop Æthelwine of Selsey at Æthelnoth's death. On the authority of Osbert of Clere he was held in high esteem by King Cnut because he had anointed him with

---

[65] 'A.S.C' 'D' s.a 1052/1051; trans G. N. Garmonsway p.175.
[66] J.W. ii pp.560-561.
[67] J. W. calls him 'nobilis viri Ægelmari filius' p.506.

the Holy Chrism.[68] The charter shows that the king was a generous patron of Christ Church. In 1023 he officiated at the removal of the body of St Ælfheah - who had been brutally murdered by the Danes eleven years before - from St Paul's in London to Canterbury, by order of Cnut as a token of reconciliation. It is recorded that Æthelnoth had bought land at Godmersham in Kent from Earl Sired, and towards the end of this life gave it to Christ Church.[69] For a few years before his death in 1038 he suffered from ill-health, and Eadsige, who eventually succeeded him as Archbishop of Canterbury, took over many of his official duties.

Lyfing

The other ecclesiastic with whom Godwine worked in close harmony was Lyfing. His reputation was not good. William of Malmesbury thought him ambitious and summed up his character by saying, 'he valued nothing that did not suit his purpose'.[70] However John of Worcester spoke of him as being 'a most prudent man', and the *Chronicle* speaks of his eloquence.[71] It is true that he was a pluralist but the monks of Tavistock Abbey remembered him with reverence and affection. He was buried at Tavistock and William of Malmesbury does, in spite of his critical remarks, state that the monks were still singing and reciting psalms in reverent remembrance. The Reverend Alford, Vicar of Tavistock at the end of the nineteenth century, wrote that Lyfing did so much for the Abbey that he was almost regarded as its founder, and H. P. R. Finberg the author of '*Tavistock Abbey*' and numerous other historical studies says 'Lyfing who was abbot in 1027 raised it [the Abbey] to a new height of prosperity.'[72]

Normandy

Cnut's last years were clouded by deteriorating relations with Normandy. The Norman duke, Richard II, had maintained friendly relations with him, which had been cemented by Cnut's marriage to his sister, Emma. On his death in 1026 he was succeeded briefly by his lacklustre son, Richard III, who, it is reliably said, was poisoned by his younger brother, Robert, who followed him as the duke of Normandy in 1027. During his time of office he did his utmost to live up to one of his nicknames, 'the Devil'. Normandy was torn by internal strife for Robert was headstrong, ruthless and cruel. He rejected his father's policy towards Cnut and used the English Æthelings, Edward and Alfred, to foment trouble. Their sister, Godgifu, was married to Count Dreux of the Vexin, Robert's close friend. Robert treated the brothers as princes, posing a threat to Cnut's kingship. In an effort to renew Anglo-Norman friendly relations Cnut gave his sister, the

---

[68] F. Harmer, 'A.S Writs' nos 27-31 pp.182-185; M. Lawson 'Cnut' pp.148-149; 'Atlas' Table LXVI; witnessing from 1022-1038.
[69] S 1389; A. J. Robertson, 'A.S. Charters' No LXXXIX pp.174-175.
[70] 'Gesta Pontificum' ch 94 pp.133-134.
[71] J. W. pp.512-513; A.S.C 'D' s.a 1047/1046.
[72] 'Tavistock Abbey' p.3; Rev. Alford, 'The Abbots of Tavistock' ch VI pp.23-27.

recently widowed Estrith, in marriage to Robert in the hope that a further marital alliance would serve to avert the threat.

Prior to this Robert had discarded his mistress, Herleve, who had given birth to a son, William, and married her off to Herluin, Vicomte de Conteville. However, Robert was not smitten with Estrith and, according to Ralph Glaber, soon divorced her. She later, according to one story, married a Russian prince, but was at one time living on Úlfr's estates in Scania when her son Swein joined her after one of his many defeats. Consequently Cnut's efforts to renew the alliance were thwarted.

In the witness lists of one of Robert's charters 'granting properties and rights to the Abbey of Fécamp' dated 1031 x 1035, immediately after Robert's name, his young son William's and the ecclesiastics, and before the counts or viscounts of Normandy comes the signature of Edward as *'Eduardi regis'*. In another charter Edward prematurely grants to the monks of Mont Saint-Michel the land and estates of St Michael's Mount in Cornwall together with the land and estates of Vennesire - identified by Keynes as the Lizard Peninsula and an unidentified port. In this charter he styles himself as 'Edwardus, King of the English' in anticipation of his obtaining the English throne.[73]

These two charters and Edward's titles have been accepted by Keynes as genuine, and there can be little doubt that Robert encouraged Edward in the belief that Norman support would be forthcoming when the time came. Indeed, if William of Jumièges is to be believed, Robert sent envoys to King Cnut demanding that the Æthelings be restored to what was rightfully theirs. The envoys returned empty-handed and in a great rage the duke gained the assent of his magnates to launch a naval expedition against England. But, setting sail from Fécamp, the fleet encountered a violent storm and was forced to take refuge on the island of Jersey. Robert then abandoned the attempt, but at a later date emissaries were supposed to have arrived from Cnut, then seriously ill, saying that he wished for peace during his lifetime and agreeing that 'the sons of Æthelred should be granted half of the English kingdom'. However, Robert decided to leave the matter until after his return from the pilgrimage to Jerusalem. William of Jumièges is the only author to mention Robert's threat to the English king, his intended invasion or Cnut's reply, but the Æthelings' descent on the shores of England so quickly after Cnut's death suggests that Normandy had previously entertained designs on the English throne.[74]

---

[73] For these and the remaining details regarding the relations with Normandy see S. Keynes, 'The Æthelings in Normandy' pp.173-204 and notes to pp.191-194.

[74] G.N.D. ii Bk VI 9/10 pp.76-79.

Descendents of Richard, duke of Normandy

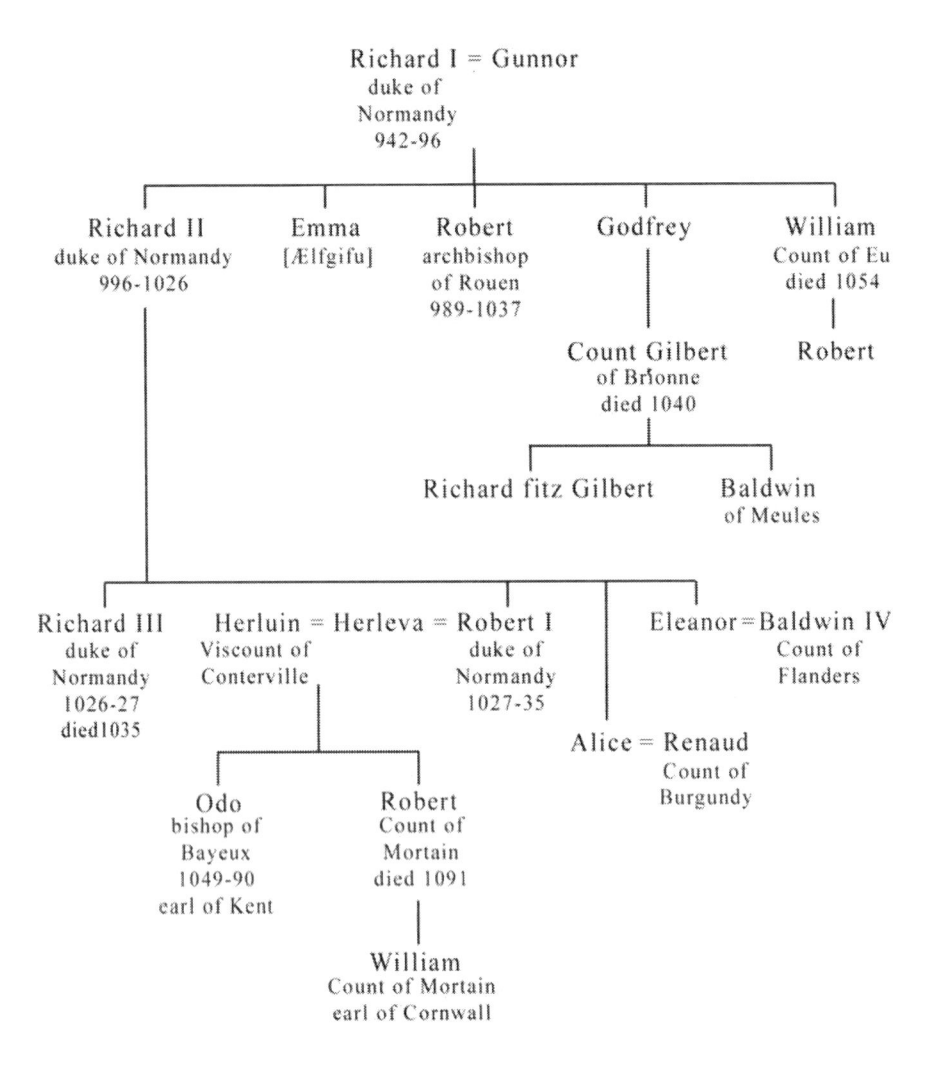

```
Richard I = Gunnor
duke of
Normandy
942-96
```

- **Richard II** — duke of Normandy 996-1026
- **Emma** [Ælfgifu]
- **Robert** — archbishop of Rouen 989-1037
- **Godfrey**
  - **Count Gilbert** of Brionne, died 1040
    - **Richard fitz Gilbert**
    - **Baldwin** of Meules
- **William** — Count of Eu, died 1054
  - **Robert**

Children of Richard II:

- **Richard III** — duke of Normandy 1026-27, died 1035
- **Herleva** = **Herluin** (Viscount of Conterville)
  - **Odo** — bishop of Bayeux 1049-90, earl of Kent
  - **Robert** — Count of Mortain, died 1091
    - **William** — Count of Mortain, earl of Cornwall
- **Herleva** = **Robert I** — duke of Normandy 1027-35
- **Eleanor** = **Baldwin IV** — Count of Flanders
  - **Alice** = **Renaud** — Count of Burgundy

Cnut's Death

Little is known of the remaining years of Cnut's life. From 1032 until his death, ten charters have survived which can be dated; two from 1032; five from 1033, and three from 1035. In each of these Godwine and Leofric witness in first and second place, with only an occasional signature from Ælfwine, and one, a York charter which bears Siward's name. Of these M. K. Lawson singles out S 975 as of special interest. This charter is dated 1035, the year of Cnut's death, and concerns a grant of land at Corscombe in Dorset to the monks of Sherborne Abbey. This document, regarded as authentic by Finberg, gives clear indications that Cnut was terminally ill and resigned to imminent death when it was drawn up. In addition to the usual expressions of hope for spiritual salvation there is the earnest wish that the monks of Sherborne will diligently and continually pray to Almighty God and beseech Him by the singing of psalms and the observance of mass that at the last Cnut will - in spite of his sins - enter into the kingdom of heaven.[75] This, no doubt, explains why Cnut was unable to go to the aid of his son Swein when Magnus returned to Norway and he and his mother were forced to flee to Denmark.

According to the *Knytlinga Saga* he died of an illness related to jaundice. It said: 'on returning to his realm of England, King Cnut contracted an illness which first showed itself in the form of what is called jaundice. He lay in bed over the summer and in the autumn he died, on November thirteenth in a great town called 'Merst'. He was thirty seven years of age, having ruled for twenty-four years in England and seven in Norway'. Apart from the length of his reign in England being several years adrift there is no reason to doubt the other statements.[76] According to the *Chronicle* 'C' and 'D' Cnut died at Shaftesbury on 12 November, and he was conveyed to Winchester and there buried; John of Worcester adds 'with due honours'. His corpse was laid alongside those of earlier English kings such as Ecgberht, Æthelwulf, Ælfred, Edward the Elder, Eadred and Eadwig; and later when their time came his son Harthacnut, his nephew Beorn and his widow Emma. Cnut had requested to be buried at Winchester. In choosing Winchester, he was endeavouring to establishing himself in the tradition of an Anglo-Saxon King.

Perhaps one of the finest tributes to Cnut's memory may be summed up in the words of T. Kendrick: 'a dignified monarch whose reign is an honourable page in the history of the two realms he governed'.[77]

The question arises whether Emma may have acted as regent during Cnut's absences, as she seems to have for her son Harthacnut in 1035, or as Ælfgifu of Northampton did for Swein in Norway. When Cnut was in Denmark in 1019/20 he left Thorkell as his regent; in his letter the king singles out Thorkell and entrusts him with the peace of the realm. In neither letter does he mention Emma as being in control of the kingdom. Professor Stafford points out that 'All the

---

[75] M. K. Lawson, 'Cnut' p.113; H.P.R. Finberg, 'The Early charters of Wessex' No 623; S 975.
[76] 'Knytlinga Saga' ch 18.
[77] 'A History of the Vikings' p.118

contemporary evidence points to the regency of earldormen or bishops, in the case of royal absences ... the case for female regency during the absence of an adult king in late Anglo-Saxon England is unproven, and on the balance of evidence unlikely, unless as is possible, 1040-1042 was a period of regency'.[78] In view of the words quoted from the *Vita Ædwardi Regis* and the evidence supplied by the charter witness lists it would appear obvious that during Cnut's many absences from the realm during the years 1025 and 1031, and when illness prevented him from governing the Kingdom, Godwine acted as his regent. Higham points out that Cnut's frequent journeys in Scandinavia and Rome 'arguably required that England be left in the charge of a royal council which looked to a single executive Chairman, and Godwine is by far the likeliest candidate for that role'.[79]

Once Cnut's reign had become established he gave England a period of peace; freedom from Viking raids, improved trading opportunities and the opportunity for increased prosperity. Unlike the Norman, William, he ruled as soon as possible mainly through English earls; he had no need to build castles to hold down the local population in subservience; nor did he devastate a large area of the country and leave its people to starve or freeze to death, and unlike William he was able to understand his English subjects in both speech and in custom.

English Earldoms

In an effort to trace the earldoms during Cnut's reign, as mentioned earlier, it seems a reasonable assumption that Godwine was appointed to Central Wessex in succession to Ælfric in or before 1018; that he succeeded the banished Æthelweard in 1020, and that Kent was added after the death of Archbishop Æthelnoth and the retirement of Earl Sired.

East Anglia

The earldom of East Anglia was originally given to Thorkell in 1017. After his banishment in 1021 it is possible that Úlfr held the earldom until some time after 1023/24 when he succeeded Thorkell as regent in Denmark. After this Osgod Clapa had the authority if not the title of earldorman, as Ulfkell 'Snilling' had done before his death at the battle of Ashingdon.[80]

Northumbria

Northumbria can best be treated as two separate provinces: the northern part based on Bamburgh and roughly the ancient kingdom of *Bernicia*; the southern based on York approximating the kingdom of *Deira*. The two provinces were united under Uhtred, scion of the house of Bamburgh in succession to his father Waltheof.

---

[78] 'Queen Emma and Queen Edith' pp.188-189; N. Higham p.109-110.
[79] N. Higham p.104.
[80] C. Hart, 'The Danelaw' p.195.

After Uhtred's murder in 1016 he was succeeded in the northern sector by his brother, Eadulf, until 1019. For the next nineteen years Eadred, a son of Uhtred's by his first wife Ecgfrida, became the earl and in 1038 he was followed by his younger half brother Eadulf whose mother was Uhtred's second wife, Sige, the daughter of Styr Ulfson. He was murdered in 1041 by Earl Siward.

In southern Northumbria, Cnut promoted Eirikr of Hlathir in 1016 and he governed it as earl and perhaps overlord of the north until 1023 when he ceases to witness and presumably died soon after. There is then a ten year gap until Earl Siward witnesses a charter of that year. Whitelock suggested that 'Eadulf may have been earl of all Northumbria' and 'that Siward may have been his immediate successor.'[81] An intriguing suggestion put forward tentatively by Keynes is that Eirikr's son, Hákon, may have succeeded his father.[82] If this were correct he would presumably have held the earldom until he accompanied Cnut to Norway in 1028. Another possibility is that Karl, Thorbrand's son, may, like Osgod Clapa, have had the authority of an earl without the title. Kapelle draws attention to the fact that Karl starts to witness as *'minister'* in 1024, which corresponds with the time when Eirikr's name ceases to appear. Kapelle assumes that, like his father, he held the title of *'hold'* or king's high reeve and sums up by saying, 'Carl probably did defend Cnut's interest in the North between 1023-1033'.[83] Karl (or Carl) witnessed charters from 1019 until 1042; during Cnut's reign his name appears once in each year. In none of these does he witness higher than sixth in order of seniority amongst the thegns.[84]

Mercia

The position in Mercia is more complicated. The *Chronicle* records that in 1017 Eadric Streona was the senior earl. There is evidence that Hrani or Ranig had the authority and title of an earl based on Herefordshire as early as 1016. Soon after this Eilifr was appointed as earl to a domain centred on Gloucestershire and Hákon elected to one on Worcestershire. Thuri was acting in the same capacity for the 'middle Angles' in 1038 but was, no doubt appointed after Cnut's death. Leofwine had been ealdorman of the Hwicce, the name given to a people who had settled in an area which originally took in Gloucestershire, Worcestershire and the western half of Warwickshire in the seventh century.[85] As Eilifr's responsibility was for Gloucester and Hákon's for Worcestershire by 1018 and 1019, it would seem that Leofwine may have been given authority over the whole of Mercia by that time, or even immediately after Eadric's execution, and that on his death ca. 1023 Leofric succeeded him. This could depend on the date assigned to the charter S979 which

---

[81] D. Whitelock, 'The Dealings of the Kings of England with Northumbria' pp.70-88.
[82] 'Cnut's Earls' p.61.
[83] 'The Norman conquest of the North' ch I pp.22-26.
[84] S. Keynes, 'Atlas of Attestations', Table LXX 2 of 2.
[85] F. Stenton, 'A.S.E' pp.44-48; A. J. Robertson 'A.S. Charters' p.260; M. Swanton, A.S Chronicles p.58 Note 1.

is a grant of land by Cnut to Abbot Æthelwine and the bretheren of Athelney in Somerset. Robertson suggested a date of 1023 with which Harmer was in agreement, both with the proviso, 'if genuine'.[86] Finberg considered the charter to be genuine.[87] Williams placed Leofwine's promotion to the earldom of Mercia after Eadric's execution, which he held until his death in c1023 'after which he was succeeded by his son'. However, Keynes casts doubts on the dating of this charter, and Sawyer provides dates of 1027 x 1032.[88]

But with Leofwine probably dead c1023, Eilifr ceasing to witness after 1024, and, if Hákon did succeed his father in Northumbria, it would seem as though Leofric may have been elevated to the earldom in the mid 1020s. One other possibility remains, which it must be admitted does seem doubtful: that Hákon may have been Earl of Mercia during the years 1023 and 1028. He was attesting charters third in 1024 after Godwine and Elifr and then second. As the next charter which can be dated is not until 1032 there does seem to be a possibility that Hákon may have succeeded Leofwine in 1023 or 1024, and that when he left England for Norway in 1028 Leofric was appointed in his place.[89]

---

[86] F. Harmer, 'A.S. Writs' p.565; A. J. Robertson, 'A.S. Charters' LXXXIII p.412-413; S. Keynes, 'Cnut's Earls' p.77.

[87] 'The Early Charters of Wessex' No 527; Sawyer, 'charters' p.293.

[88] A. Williams, 'Cockles Amongst the Wheat' p.7; S. Keynes, 'Cnut's Earls' p.51 note 44; P. Sawyer, 'Charters' p.293.

[89] 'Cnut's Earls' p.61. A wholly fictitious genealogy of Leofric's antecedents was included in one of the manuscripts of John of Worcesters' chronicle. The MS is late; no earlier than the thirteenth century. Freeman drew attention to this in the first volume of his 'History of the Norman Conquest' vol i APP, note ccc pp. 717-720. The pedigree appeared in Searle's 'Anglo Saxon bishops, Kings and Nobles' no 87 pp.450-451.

- It traces Leofric's ancestry from a Leofric who flourished, according to the doubtful chronicle of Ingulf from 716-727. His son Ælfgar is supposed to have been the Ælfgar who witnessed as 'Comes' S 1189, which constituted a gift of land which he gave to Siward the abbot of Crowland dated 810. His son, another Ælfgar'Comes', was killed, according to Ingulf, in 870. He witnessed a very doubtful charter, S 200 in 851, another gift of land to Abbot Siward by King Beorht Wulf of Mercia. This Ælfgar's son, another Leofric received a mention in Dugdale's, 'Monasticon Anglicarum.'

- According to this family tree he was the father of Ealdorman Leofwine, who according to this version, had a brother called Leofric and of course Leofwine fathered Leofric, Northman, Eadwine and Godric or Godwine. E.A Freeman pointed out the absurdity of Ealdorman Leofwine having a grandfather who was witnessing charters in 851 and being killed in 870.

- Charles Kingsley dismissed the pedigree as mythical and summed up by saying. 'The monks of Crowland were perhaps trying to work on the Norman kings when they invented those charters of the eighth and ninth centuries with the names of Saxon kings and nobles of Leofric and Godiva's house. 'Hereward the Wake' p 21.

Table 4. Sequence of Events 1017 - 1035

Year	Event
1017	Cnut crowned King. Cnut marries Emma. Eadric and Northmen executed.
c1018	Godwine appointed earl of Central Wessex in succession to Ælfric.
1020-1022	Godwine's marriage to Gytha.
1019/20	Godwine accompanies Cnut to Denmark.
1020	Godwine appointed Earl of the Western Provinces in succession to Æthelweard.
1021	Outlawry of Thorkell
1022/3	Godwine with Cnut in Denmark; Reconciliation with Thorkell.
1023	Death of Thorkell; Úlfr regent of Denmark.
1025	Cnut's expedition against Úlfr and Éilifr; Godwine acting as regent.
1026	Cnut's campaign against Norwegian Swedish coalition; Godwine left in charge of England.
1027	Cnut's visit to Rome. Coronation of Conrad II. Godwine left in charge of England.
1028	Cnut's invasion of Norway; Ólafr driven into exile. Godwine left in charge of England.
1030	Ólafr returns and killed at Sticklestad. Hákon drowned. Swein, Cnutsson King of Norway.
1031	Cnut's second visit to Rome and expedition to Scotland.
1032	Leofric starts to witness charters second to Godwine.
1033	Cnut grants 'five' charters.
1035	Death of Cnut.

5. Godwine, Loyalty and the Royal Succession

Cnut's successors

King Cnut's death was neither sudden nor unexpected. The accumulated evidence of the Sherborne charter, the Sandwich Writ, the *Knytlinga Saga* and of the Norman chronicler William of Jumièges all bear witness to the fact. However, a great deal of confusion exists regarding the exact order of events that followed. This applies particularly to the meeting of the Witan and the seizure of the royal treasury. According to Plummer and Professor Stafford, Harold's men took it from Emma immediately afterwards; Sir Frank Stenton says: 'for soon after the agreement at Oxford, if not indeed before it had been concluded, Harold sent a force to the city and took possession'.[1] This confusion has been caused by the 'C' and 'D' versions of the *Chronicle* which record the seizure of the treasury immediately after Cnut's death and Emma taking up residence in Winchester under the year 1036, which implies immediate action. These versions have no mention of the meeting of the Witan at Oxford; on the other hand 'E' omits all mention of the seizure of the treasury and relates that 'soon after his [Cnut's] passing there was a meeting of all the councillors at Oxford.' Surely if Harold had ordered the confiscation of the King's valuables before the mid winter meeting of the *Witenagemot*, Godwine and Emma would have been in no position to bargain for retaining Wessex for Harthacnut. It would only have been after the council had agreed that Harold should be elected as regent, that he was in a position to do this.

When the Witan did meet, the outcome was a temporary compromise. Earl Leofric and the thegns of almost all Mercia and Northumbria, together with the naval crews in London, were all for electing Harold, the son of Cnut and Ælfgifu. He was two years older than his rival claimant for the throne, connected with the nobility of Mercia, and probably related by marriage to Leofric himself.[2] He would have been well known north of the Thames where his kinsmen's estates extended over vast areas of the Midlands and the North. Moreover he was partly English whereas Harthacnut was partly Norman.

The role of the rivals' respective mothers must also be significant. Harthacnut's mother, Emma, could have inspired little affection in English hearts when, in her thirst for power, she had been willing to wed the young king who had been

---

[1] P. Stafford, 'Queen Emma and Queen Edith', p.237; F. Stenton 'ASE' p.420.
[2] P. Sawyer, 'Charters of Burton Abbey' pXLII.

responsible for her first husband's downfall. Ælfgifu, the mother of Harold Harefoot, had powerful connections with those families that had suffered at the hands of King Æthelred and his advisers in the same manner as many other Englishmen who were gathered in the council chamber that day.

Of Cnut's three sons, Harthacnut had been proclaimed King of Denmark in 1028; Swein, Harold's brother, appointed King of Norway in 1030; surely it would have seemed logical to the third son, Harold, that the throne of England should be his. Indeed, Simeon of Durham wrote that Cnut 'before his death appointed his son Harold, born of Elgive, King of the Angles'[3] and Adam of Bremen states that after Cnut's death he was succeeded by 'Harold in England, Swein in Norway, Harthacnut in Denmark, as he had determined'[4].

But there were powerful magnates in opposition to Harold's election. Foremost of these was of course the dead king's widow, then in residence on her dower lands in Winchester with the royal treasures in her keeping. Speaking eloquently in the Witan, Earl Godwine endeavoured to sway the assembly in favour of Harthacnut. In this he had the support of Æthelnoth, the Archbishop of Canterbury, and 'all the most prominent men of Wessex'. Some modern historians have seen this as an example of a personal rivalry between Godwine and Leofric, or of the desire of Wessex to dominate the Midlands and the North. But it is possible that Godwine and his supporters believed that continued union with Denmark would lead to a continuation of the prosperity which had been enjoyed under Cnut, while the northern representatives could have feared that if Harthacnut became the King of England as well as Denmark, English money and resources would be used to fight a prolonged and exhausting war with Magnus of Norway. It is also possible, however, that Earl Godwine had mixed feelings in spite of his strenuous efforts to thwart Harold's candidature. As one of the Ætheling Æthelstan's associates, he had shared the same loyalties and misgivings as Sigeferth and Morcar, Ælfgifu's cousins and Leofwine, Leofric's father. His family fortunes had suffered, as had Ælfgifu's. Like her family, he had thrown in his lot with King Cnut on the deaths of Æthelstan and Edmund. The phrase used by the *Chronicle* 'E' annalist that Godwine was Emma's 'most loyal man' has, I believe, been misconstrued, and has led to a great deal of misunderstanding of Godwine's actions. Godwine's loyalty was not to Emma, but to what he considered were Cnut's wishes, as subsequent events were to prove.

It is possible that, with Harthacnut in Denmark and Swein in Norway, their father had intended at one point that Harold should succeed him in England. It is also possible that with Ælfgifu and her son in Norway, and with illness clouding Cnut's last months, Emma may have seized her chance to press the claims of her absent son. She could have reminded him of his promise, made in 1017, that any son of hers would take precedence over those of any previous union; this could only

---

[3] Simeon of Durham, 'A History of the Kings of England', s.a 1035 p.114.
[4] Adam Bk II LXXIV [72] p.107.

mean a son of her rival Ælfgifu.[5] At that time this applied only to England, as in 1017 Cnut had yet to inherit Denmark or to conquer Norway. At the Oxford Witan, therefore, Godwine may have taken his stance because he believed that the dying king had promised Emma to honour that oath, even though that left Harold with nothing and his half-brother with Denmark and England. To Emma it meant that, in her son's absence in Scandinavia, she would be acting as his regent. Whatever plans Cnut had previously made for the English succession, Emma would not have scrupled to turn to her own and to her favourite son's advantage.

After a great deal of argument the Witan eventually decided on a compromise. Harold was to act as regent for himself and his brother; Emma and Godwine with the King's housecarls were to control Wessex, with Harold exercising authority north of the Thames. Similar examples of a division of the country had occurred back in AD957 when Eadwig was King of Wessex and his brother Edgar King of Mercia and Northumbria. In 1016 the Treaty of Alney made a similar division with Edmund ruling south of the Thames and Cnut north of it.

In his capacity as regent Harold was justified in obtaining possession of the royal treasury. It is noteworthy that there is no recorded opposition to his action; no mention of the housecarls who were to protect Wessex in Harthacnut's interest opposing the treasury raid. We have to conclude that what Harold did was his legitimate right to do, and occurred after the decision at Oxford. It is also obvious that what was taken from Emma was not hers by the King's bequest. John of Worcester, although hostile to Harold, admits that he only took possession of 'the bigger and better part of the treasures which King Cnut had left her'.[6] She was apparently left enough to give alms generously during her stay in Bruges, and to be wealthy enough for King Edward seven years later to act as Harold had done. On that occasion according to the *Chronicle* 'an indescribable number of things of gold and silver' were taken from her.[7]

Presumably amongst the royal treasurs taken from Emma were the coronation insignia, the crown and sceptre, and as Stafford suggested[8] it may have been at this time that Harold urged Archbishop Æthelnoth to consecrate and crown him King. If this were the case, it is obvious that the primate was in no position to do so; the Witan had not at that point nominated him as his father's successor. The Encomiast recounts that Harold summoned the Archbishop and prayed to be consecrated and crowned as King. According to the same source, the Archbishop refused and with a dramatic gesture placed the crown and sceptre upon the holy altar and forbade any bishop to remove them or to consecrate Harold. He is further supposed to have declared that Cnut had entrusted the royal insignia to him and that while the sons of Emma lived he would approve no other man as King.[9] In his introduction to the *Encomium Emmae*

---

[5] E.E.R Bk II ch 16 p.33.
[6] JW pp.520, 521.
[7] A.S.C 'C'/'D' s.a 1043; 'E' 1042/3; A.S.C 'C', 'E' trans G.N. Garmonsway.
[8] 'Queen Emma and Queen Edith' p.237.
[9] EER Bk 3 ch I pp.40-41.

Reginae, Campbell points out that the Archbishop was not able to crown Harold or anyone else who had not been elected by the Witan and adds that there was no reason to think that he would have refused to crown him if he had been elected.[10]

In any case Harold and his supporters, if indeed there was any truth in the story, realised that the right course was to set about gaining the support necessary to secure election. There are some reasons for believing that Harold was duly crowned when the right time came. The Encomiast claimed that, on account of the Archbishop's refusal to crown him, Harold came to despise the Christian religion and its observances. When mass was being celebrated in church on Sunday mornings he would be hunting or indulging in other trivial pasttimes.[11] In addition to this, he was supposedly guilty of forging a letter to the two Æthelings in Normandy in order to 'kill the children of his lady'. He is further described as 'the most abominable tyrant' and as, 'an unjust usurper'.[12] The author of the *Vita Ædwardi Regis* calls him 'an arrogant fellow of bad character'.[13]

It is certain, however, that this opinion was not shared by all ecclesiastics. Bishop Ælfric, in his will dated AD1035 x 1040, leaves bequests to 'my royal lord Harold I grant two marks of gold and I grant to my Lady one mark of gold...'[14] Although the will is undated, the British Museum regards it as in a contemporary hand.[15] Ælfric was the bishop of Elmham and according to the *Chronicle* he died in 1038[16]. John of Worcester speaks of two Ælfrics who were both bishops of Elmham or of East Anglia, and records the death of the first.[17] Both appear in the list of Popes and bishops prefixed to his *Chronicle*.[18] According to the *Anglo-Saxon Chronicle* Stigand was consecrated bishop of East Anglia in 1043, so evidently the second Ælfric was bishop from 1038 until 1043. This second Ælfric is mentioned by William of Malmesbury.[19] It would seem that the first Ælfric held the see from sometime after 1022 until his death in 1038, which would mean that the bequests to Harold and the 'Lady' were almost certainly made by the first Bishop Ælfric.

The *History* of Ingulf which was written by a monk of Crowland to promote the welfare of his monastery has largely been regarded as at best doubtful. It does, however, contain a very interesting allusion to King Harold, and it is difficult to see why this should be false because the monastery stood little to gain when other writers were slandering him. The monk wrote: 'This prince presented to our monastery his coronation robe of silk with golden flowers, which our sacrist

---

[10] EER 'Introduction' pLXIV.
[11] ibid Bk 3 ch 1 pp.40-41.
[12] ibid, Bk 3 ch 3 pp.42-43; ch 2 pp.40-41.
[13] Vita pp.32-33.
[14] S 1489; D. Whitelock, 'Wills' No 26 pp.70-73, 181-184.
[15] Quoted from 'An Alleged Son of Harold Harefoot' p.115 and note 16.
[16] A.S.C 'C' 'E' s.a 1038.
[17] JW pp.142-3; 526-527.
[18] 'Florence of Worcester, Chronicon ex Chronicis', trans T. Forester.
[19] 'Gesta Pontificum' ch 74 p.98.

afterwards converted into a hood, and [such was the favour which the lord abbot Brihtmaer found with him] would have conferred many more advantages upon us if he had not been snatched away by a sudden and premature death.'[20] In Cnut's charter to Christ Church, Canterbury dated 1023, judged by A. J. Robertson to be authentic, Abbot Brihtmaer witnesses second among the abbots.[21] In Earl Leofric and Godgifu's endowment of Stow St Mary dated 1053 x 1055 he witnesses again;[22] a span of thirty years. He is mentioned in a confirmation of land to Crowland Abbey dated 1032 as a beneficiary. If Ingulf was correct, Harold was eventually consecrated and crowned.[23]

A point in Harold's favour is the magnanimity he showed to those who opposed his election in 1035, as noted by Freeman. We hear of no executions during his reign other than that of Alfred; Godwine and Æthelnoth continued to hold their appointments, and, other than Emma, there is no evidence that anyone was banished. It is obvious that the story of his loathing for religious leaders was quite unfounded. During his last illness at Oxford, Harold was attended by Bishop Lyfing and the monk Thancred.[24] According to William of Malmesbury Harold gave a shrine to Glastonbury Abbey, and he was remembered favourably at Ramsey.[25] This belies the Encomiasts' claim that Harold 'so despised the apostolic benediction, that he hated not only the benediction itself, but indeed turned from the whole Christian religion.'[26]

Meanwhile in Norway King Swein and his mother were compelled to accept the inevitable. The swelling tide of nationalism engendered by the dynamic young Magnus eroded their support and they took refuge in Denmark. According to Snorri Sturluson, Harthacnut received his half brother kindly and offered to divide the kingdom with him; without Emma's influence Harthacnut displayed a more generous spirit towards Swein than he did towards Harold's memory when his mother was with him in England. Or did he have some other motive?

Shortly after this Cnut died, and within weeks Swein was dead also; Snorri says, 'the same winter'.[27] No doubt by February or March Ælfgifu was back in England to help her other son. For the next year the campaigns for the two half-brothers were orchestrated by their mothers.

---

[20] Ingulf pp.654-655.
[21] A. J. Robertson, 'A.S. Charters' No LXXXII pp.158-61; 'Cnut's Charter to Christchurch' p.160.
[22] ibid no CXV, 'Endowment of Stow St Mary by Earl Leofric and Godgifu' pp.212-217 date 1053-1055; Keynes 'Atlas' Table LXXIII; A. J. Robertson, 'A.S. Charters' p.468.
[23] E.E.R, Introduction pLXIV; Ingulf pp.654-655.
[24] A.J. Robertson, 'A.S. Charters' No XCI pp.174-179, particularly pp.176-177.
[25] 'De Antique Ecclesiae' i p.89; 'Chronicon Abbatiae Ramesiensis'; for both Glastonbury and Ramsey I am indebted to Professor F. Barlow, 'The English Church', p.41 Note 6.
[26] E.E.R Bk 3 ch1 pp.40-41.
[27] 'Saga of Magnus the Good' ch V p.131.

According to a letter written by Immo to Azeko the bishop of Worms in late July or the first week of August Ælfgifu was 'scheming' to influence the great men to deprive Harthacnut of his realm. This letter was written from the court of Conrad II and mentions Gunnhildr, Cnut and Emma's daughter, who had been married to Conrad's son, Henry, barely two months before. In the strange surroundings of the German imperial court she was lonely and miserable and missed the kindly friendship of Immo who had probably left the court in order to take up his appointment as bishop of Arezzo. Apparently Gunnhildr had heard this news from England just before the letter was written, which would have done nothing to improve her spirits. According to her information Ælfgifu was attempting to win support by getting the 'great folk' to take oaths to support her and her son.[28] In the supposedly forged letter that Emma sent to her sons in Normandy she wrote of Harold '... for he goes round hamlets and cities ceaselessly, and makes the chief men his friends by gifts, threats and prayers.'[29] While Ælfgifu and Harold were canvassing for support in this way Emma was endeavouring to maintain her position by stooping to the use of propaganda in its most malevolent form. She spread rumours about Harold's scorn for religious observances and, as her rival's support was growing, even stooped to inventing stories to the effect that Harold was not Cnut's son. In this she was probably helped by the fact that Harold was brought up on his mother's establishment in Northampton - hence her name, 'Ælfgifu of Northampton' - and was perhaps a stranger at court.[30]

No doubt once Cnut had appointed Harold's brother Swein as King of Norway and his mother as regent, Emma would have done all in her power to ensure that the absent Harthacnut's claim to the throne of England was kept alive at all costs. The thought must have entered her mind that with three sons and three kingdoms and with Harold the only son still in England, she would need all her powers of influence to ensure that he was expected to stay in his part of the country. She would have reminded Cnut of his promise with regard to a son of hers succeeding to the English throne.[31]

That the rumours regarding Harold's parentage were being spread early is evidenced by the fact that the *Chronicle* reported them in all the three extant versions; 'C' says 'Harold, who claimed to be Cnut's son by the other Ælfgifu, although it was quite untrue...'. 'D' records virtually the same, and 'E' adds 'some said of Harold that he was the son of Cnut by Ælfgifu, daughter of Ealdorman Ælfhelm, but many thought this quite incredible'. Further additions to the scandal were added as and when needed to ensure that the message was having the desired effect. The Encomiast added: 'Haraldr, who is declared, owing to a false estimation of the matter, to be the son of a certain concubine of the above mentioned King Knutr, as a matter of fact, the assertion of a great many people has it that the same Haraldr was secretly taken from a servant who was in childbed, and put in the chamber of the concubine who

---

[28] 'An Alleged son of Harold Harefoot' pp.115-116.
[29] E.E.R Bk 3 ch 3 pp.42-43.
[30] A.S.C 'D' s.a 1035; M. K. Lawson, 'Cnut' p.131.
[31] 'Queen Emma and Queen Edith' p.234.

was indisposed; and this can be believed as the more truthful account'.[32] This is from the work commissioned by Emma herself. Further additions to the story were yet to come: John of Worcester writing in the early twelfth century provided further details. Recording Swein's appointment as King of the Norwegians he wrote: 'He is said to be his [Cnut's] son by Ælfgifu of Northampton... However, several asserted that he was not the son of the king and that same Ælfgifu, but that Ælfgifu wanted to have a son by the king and could not, and therefore ordered the new born child of some priest's concubine to be brought to her, and made the king fully believe that she had just borne him a son... But Harold claimed to be the son of King Cnut by Ælfgifu of Northampson, but that is quite untrue, for some say that he was the son of a certain cobbler, but that Ælfgifu had acted in the same way with him as she is said to have done with Swein'. However, John does add that as the matter was open to doubt, 'we have been unable to make a firm statement about the parentage of either'.[33] John's testimony is late, but there is some evidence that his reference to a 'certain cobbler' may have been current at a much earlier date.[34] Where John got his additional information from is questionable, unless Emma and her friends were making slanderous accusations that contemporary writers shrank from committing to vellum. It must be remembered that all the chroniclers were writing from religious houses and would have looked with disfavour on Cnut's first marriage, a union after the Danish custom, and would be inclined to look more favourably on the wedding with Emma which was consecrated with the full blessings of the church.

A further smear on Ælfgifu's reputation was made by Saxo Grammaticus, the Danish historian, writing about two centuries later. According to the *Gesta Danorum* Ælfgifu had, before her marriage to Cnut, been the mistress of Ólafr Haraldsson, the future King and saint of Norway. Ólafr was in England fighting under the command of Thorkell Hávi and his presence is recorded in AD1010 at the battle of Ringmere. When Thorkell's raiding party was disbanded in 1012 he hired out his services to Duke Richard of Normandy where he met King Æthelred II, then an exile at Rouen. He returned with the king to England the following year. In 1015 he was back in Norway making a bid for the crown. Ælfgifu's attachment to Cnut probably commenced in 1013 when he was left in charge of the Danish fleet at Gainsborough.[35] No other Norse or English source mentions a relationship with Ólafr, not even the Sagas devoted to Saint Ólafr, and the story has been generally regarded as groundless by authorities on Scandinavian history.[36]

In Norway Ælfgifu was chiefly remembered for the years when, with her as regent, the country suffered a succession of bad harvests and discontentment. As the years went by, men looked back on those years as 'Alfiva's time'. One Norse chronicler wrote of the misery and tyranny endured when 'the people lived more off cattle

---

[32] E.E.R Bk 3 ch I page 40-41.
[33] J.W. ii pages 520-521.
[34] 'The Lady Ælfgyva in the Bayeux Tapestry' pages 666-667.
[35] A. Williams et al, 'Dark Age Britain' p.81.
[36] Eric Christiansen in 'Saxo' Note 96 Bk 10 p.188; Miles Campbell, 'Cnut the Great's Women' p.69.

The Earls of Mercia

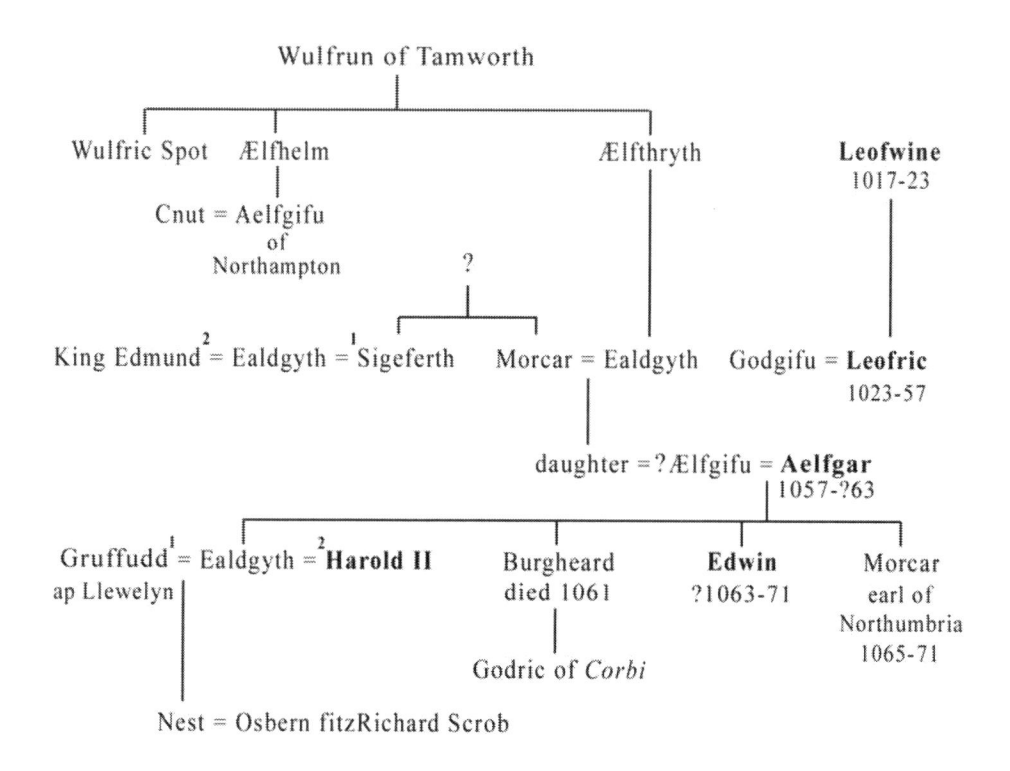

```
                        Wulfrun of Tamworth
    ┌──────────────────────┬──────────────────┬─────────────────┐
Wulfric Spot   Ælfhelm                    Ælfthryth          Leofwine
                  │                                           1017-23
              Cnut = Aelfgifu
                     of
                  Northampton
                           ?
                           ┌──────────────┐
King Edmund² = Ealdgyth ¹= Sigeferth    Morcar = Ealdgyth   Godgifu = Leofric
                                                                      1023-57
                                              │
                              daughter =? Ælfgifu = Aelfgar
                                                   1057-?63
        ┌──────────────────┬────────────┬──────────┬─────────┐
Gruffudd¹= Ealdgyth ²= Harold II    Burgheard    Edwin      Morcar
ap Llewelyn│                        died 1061   ?1063-71    earl of
           │                            │                   Northumbria
           │                       Godric of Corbi          1065-71
  Nest = Osbern fitzRichard Scrob
```

Ann Williams, *The English and the Norman Conquest*
'The Earls of Mercia', p.52, The Boydell Press 1997

fodder than the food of men, because the seasons were never good in their time'.[37] Another chronicler spoke of being 'unable to bear the tyranny of Swein's mother, Álfifa'.[38] Snorri tells us of new laws based on Danish legislature, taxes and the rising cult of Ólafr's sanctity.[39] But there is another side to the story: the Norwegians had rejected the living Ólafr and, had Jarl Hákon Eiriksson lived, all might have been well. Ælfgifu was viewed as a foreigner imposed on them by a Danish conqueror. In Norway she and Swein had not only to contend with this drawback but with the growing belief in Ólafr's saintliness. Ólafr dead was a far more potent

---

[37] 'Agrip A F Noregs Konunga Sogum' ch XXXII pp.44-45.
[38] 'Theodoricus Monachus', ch 21 p.33.
[39] 'St Olaf's Saga' ch CCLIII pp.385-386; ch CCLIX pp.389-390.

force than Ólafr alive had ever been.[40] It must also be remembered that almost all the details of Ælfgifu's life are recorded by hostile writers. To the ecclesiastical historians she was viewed not as Cnut's wife but as a concubine; to them Emma's slanders fell on fertile soil.[41] Also, it has to be taken into account that when she was a child her father was murdered and her two brothers were blinded by order of Æthelred, so it is hardly surprising that she welcomed Cnut's advances.[42]

Numismatic evidence shows that the compromise reached at Oxford was shortlived. Coins were initially being struck in the name of both kings; mints were producing coins recognising Harold north of the Thames, and Harthacnut in Wessex. This did not last long; even in the Winchester mint, where Emma's influence was at its strongest, it soon ceased.[43]

Genealogy of Ælfgar & Ælfgifu of Northampton
From P. Sawyer *Charters of Burton Abbey*, 1979

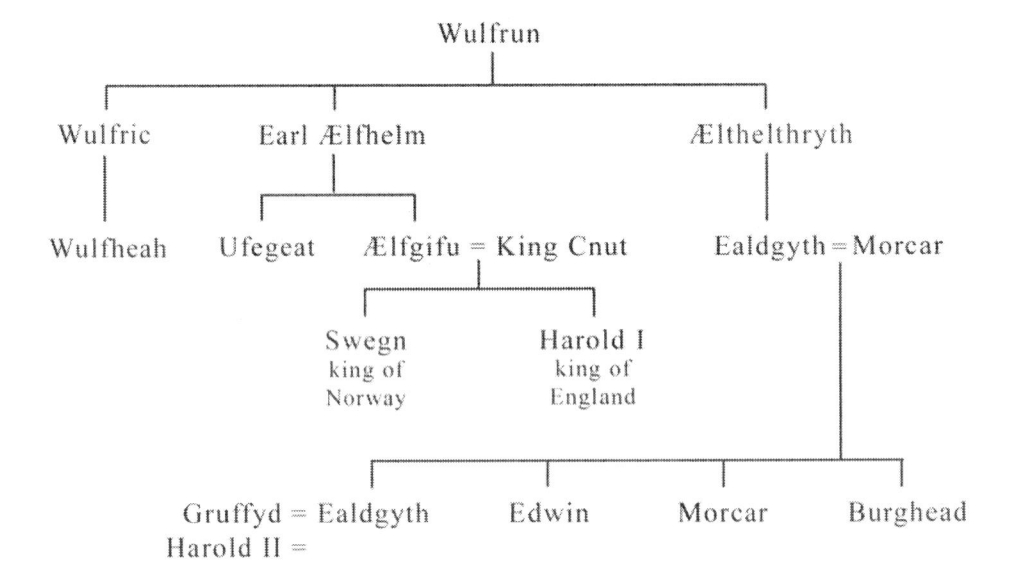

```
                            Wulfrun
           ┌───────────────────┼───────────────────┐
        Wulfric          Earl Ælfhelm         Ælthelthryth
           │                   │                   │
           │         ┌─────────┴─────────┐         │
        Wulfheah   Ufegeat    Ælfgifu = King Cnut    Ealdgyth = Morcar
                              ┌────────┴────────┐
                           Swegn              Harold I
                          king of             king of
                          Norway              England

           ┌─────────────────┬─────────────┬─────────────┐
       Gruffyd = Ealdgyth   Edwin       Morcar       Burghead
       Harold II =
```

---

[40] Gwyn Jones, 'History of the Vikings' p.385.
[41] 'Their muletings are recorded, their acts of oppression noted in detail, taxes, legal diabilities, enforced services, but there is no good reason for believing any of it', p.385.
[42] A.S.C s.a 1006; JW ii pp.456-459, 520-521.
[43] P. Stafford, 'Unification and Conquest', p.79.

Æthelred's sons

The events of 1036 can be dated with reasonable certainty by the letter previously mentioned written by Immo at the German court. It has been dated with accuracy by W. H. Stevenson to the last week of July or the first few days of August, 1036.[44] It seems obvious from the contents that at that stage Emma was still hoping that Harthacnut would come shortly to claim the throne; she may even have been hoping that Gunnhildr would have been able to use some influence or add her own entreaties to alert her brother to the urgency of the situation.

It must have been sometime after this that Emma in desperation called on her sons by Æthelred in the hope of retrieving her deteriorating position. If Edward had made his attempt first, as the Norman writers asserted, no doubt correctly, this would have meant that it would have been in the autumn of 1036 when Alfred left Flanders for Dover. This ties in with the date when the monks of Ely commemorated his death on February 5 [obviously in 1037].[45] By the autumn of 1036 Harold was sufficiently in control to make it most unlikely that Emma was correct in thinking that Harthacnut was still going to be accepted as king or king-elect of Wessex; that she still had authority as his regent, or that Godwine was their chief supporter.[46]

Those who had supported Harthacnut at Oxford had waited for eight or nine months and had begun to realise that he might be delayed indefinitely. Nor is it possible to understand the reasoning which prompts David Raraty to conclude that 'Godwine had always been her [Emma's] man, had never gone over to Harold, and could subsequently not be distanced from her with regard to the murder of Alfred Ætheling'.[47] He uses the *Encomium Emmae Reginae* as evidence of this, but it seems likely that the overwhelming hatred Emma harboured for her rival induced her to pin all the blame on Harold - a hatred which superseded all other considerations. Raraty's theory is in contradiction to the words of the Abingdon recension of the *Chronicle* which distinctly says: 'Earl Godwine would not permit him [Alfred], neither would other men who wielded great power, because the popular cry was greatly in favour of Harold'[48]. Nor is it in agreement with the way Godwine was treated when Harthacnut and Emma were at last in power.

Rarity was not alone in believing that the earl was still Emma's 'most loyal man'. Sir Charles Oman wrote that in the autumn of 1036 the Earl 'was still the leader of Harthacnut's faction'.[49] This does not allow for the fact that by this time Emma had decided that her youngest son had let her down and was prepared to retrieve her position in any way possible. Godwine was still supporting Emma up to that point, but when he knew that she was prepared to invite one or both of the

---

[44] 'An Alleged Son of Harold Harefoot', pp.113-114.
[45] F. Barlow, 'Edward', pp.44-45 and note 4.
[46] F. N.C.i p.484.
[47] D. Raraty, 'Earl Godwine of Wssex', p.14.
[48] A.S.C 'C' s.a 1036.
[49] 'England Before the Norman Conquest' pp.603-604.

Æthelings to England it became obvious that Emma's loyalty was to herself and to maintaining her own position.[50]

It has to be stressed that Earl Godwine's allegiance was not to Cnut's widow but rather to Cnut, and to the sons of Cnut. Any further support from him came to an end when Edward arrived in Southampton Water with forty ships, 'filled with armed men'.[51] He had sailed from a Norman port accompanied by Norman supporters, and according to the Norman sources the local populace opposed him. A battle was fought and the casualties on the English side were heavy. In spite of this, Edward was forced to withdraw with what booty he had been able to capture; William of Poitiers is definite that Edward's object was to wrest the throne from Harold.[52]

This attempted invasion by Edward is mentioned only by the two Norman sources; both were writing over thirty years later. No reference to it is made by the *Chronicle*. It is true that both Norman authors were endeavouring to portray Edward as being indebted to the Norman court as much as possible. It is understandable that English sources would be likely to gloss over an attempt which failed, as Edward's did. It seems logical to conclude, with Professor Barlow, that 'it is plausible, and one that William of Jumièges, followed by William of Poitiers is unlikely to have invented.'[53] John of Worcester makes Edward and Alfred come together; Edward reaches his mother at Winchester and Alfred is waylaid in the attempt. The important point here is that both of the Æthelings were acting in concert with their mother.

Shortly after Edward's failure, Alfred decided to make an attempt himself. It is possible that he had a more spirited temperament and viewed Edward's discouragement with impatience. Encouraged by his mother's letter, Alfred was led to believe that once he had succeeded to make good a landing on English soil the men of Wessex would flock to his standard out of the old traditional loyalty to the ancient god-descended line of Cerdic. Emma, in her desperation, had obviously overestimated the support her sons were likely to attract, or Alfred himself completely misjudged the situation. He attempted to land at Dover to make his bid for the crown.[54] The interpretation given in the 'C' and 'D' versions of the *Chronicle* is that he was simply going to visit his mother, presumably on a purely filial basis. If that was his sole purpose, it seems strange that he came with an armed escort.[55]

---

[50] Eric John in 'The Anglo-Saxons' ed. J. Campbell ch 9 p.216, 'Presumably Godwin and Emma were still in alliance when the invitation was sent'.
[51] G.N.D. vol ii pp.104-107 Bk VII 5[8].
[52] W.P. Part One pp.4-5.
[53] F. Barlow, 'Edward' p.45 and note 1.
[54] E.E.R Bk 3, ch 4, pp. 42-43.
[55] A.S.C 'C', 'D'; G.N.D. volume ii pp.106-107; Bk VII 6 [9]; W.P. Part One ch ii pp.2-5; ch iii pp.4-5, 'He also sought his father's septre'; 'Vita'. 'A few armed Frenchmen'; J.W. speaks of 600 knights', pp.522-523.

It is probable, as has been suggested, that Alfred drew his support from Flanders and the Vexin.[56] Alfred's sister, Godgifu, had been married to Drogo, Count of the Vexin, through the good offices of his friend Duke Robert while she was staying at the Norman Court with her brothers. Drogo accompanied the duke on his pilgrimage to Jerusalem and both died on the return journey in 1035. On the count's death he was succeeded by his son, Walter. His eldest son, Fulk, became the bishop of Amiens and Ralph, the third son, was in due course to play a part in English history. On the death of her first husband, Godgifu married Eustace sometime in 1036; eleven years later he was to succeed as Count of Boulogne.[57]

According to the Norman writers 'Alfred went with a considerable force'. William of Poitiers says that Edward had a fleet in excess of forty ships and that Alfred was even better prepared. The Encomiast writes of Alfred that he 'selected companions with his brother's approval, and beginning the journey came into the country of Flanders; where he lingered for a little while.'[58] This implies that he took some Norman companions and then recruited others from Flanders – possibly, as has been said, from his brother-in-law and his nephew. On the other hand, John of Worcester speaks of Edward and Alfred coming together and continues: 'They brought with them many Norman Knights.' Referring to Alfred's supporters only, he says that Godwine 'put 600 men to various pitiable deaths at Guildford.'[59]

At this point some uncertainty creeps in with regard to Alfred's intended destination. The *Chronicle* distinctly says that Alfred 'came hither to this country in order to visit his mother who was then residing in Winchester.'[60] This purpose is supported by the *Encomium Emmae Regina*, although it does say his destination was London.[61] John of Worcester relates that both Æthelings 'went to hold discussions with their mother, who was living at Winchester'. A few sentences later he seems to contradict this by adding that Godwine detained Alfred when he was hastening towards London to confer with King Harold as he had commanded.[62] This seems extremely unlikely, especially in view of what eventually happened. One possible solution is that Edward was indeed with his mother, as John of Worcester claims, and that Harold may have been willing to meet Alfred in order to create a rift between the two brothers and their mother.[63] However, this would only apply if the sons of Æthelred and Emma were believed to be in a much stronger position than they actually were. As this depends solely on the late testimony of John of Worcester, it may be dismissed as doubtful.

---

[56] I. Walker, 'Harold' p.14.
[57] For the history of the family see D. Bates, 'Lord Sudeley's Ancestors; The Sudeleys, Lords of Toddington', pp.34-48, 1987.
[58] E.E.R Bk 3 ch 4 pp.42-43; W.P. Part One ch 2 pp.4-5, ch 3 pp.4-5.
[59] J.W. ii pp.522-523.
[60] A.S.C 'C', 'D' s.a 1036.
[61] E.E.R Bk 3 ch 4 pp.42-43.
[62] J.W. pp.522-523.
[63] P. Stafford, 'Queen Emma and Queen Edith' p.240.

Travelling through Kent and Surrey, avoiding the risk of capture as he and his escort went, Alfred at last met Godwine. By this time the earl was aware that Emma had given up on Harthacnut. Godwine intercepted the ætheling when he was nearing Winchester. The Encomiast relates: 'But when he was already near his goal, Earl Godwine met him and took him under his protection. Diverting him from London, he took him into the town of Guildford.'[64] This reference to London has no connection with the Worcester chronicler's supposed meeting with the king. The Encomiast destinctly says earlier: 'He landed, however, at another port, and attempted to go to his mother ...' William of Jumièges, agreeing with the *Chronicle*, records that Alfred landed at Dover and 'advancing into the interior of the kingdom he came up against Earl Godwin. The earl took him into his protection, but the same night played the role of Judas by betraying his trust.'[65] The *Chronicle* entries more or less confirm this: 'he came hither to this country in order to visit his mother who was residing in Winchester, but Earl Godwine would not permit him, neither would other men who wielded great power ...' Of the later writers, John follows the Encomiast in mentioning Alfred's destination as London and being diverted to Guildford, but is alone in introducing a proposed meeting with King Harold. Henry of Huntingdon places Alfred's death after Harthacnut's, and William of Malmesbury puts it between Harold's death and Harthacnut's arrival in England.[66]

It is obvious that when Godwine diverted Alfred and his companions to Guildford he was acting in cooperation with Harold. It was, however, Emma who had changed her loyalties, not Godwine who had been committed to a son of Cnut from the beginning. He and 'the other great men' could remember the strife and misery of the years before Cnut had established his kingship; the evils perpetrated in those days when Eadric Streona became predominant at Æthelred's court; the internal strife and treachery which caused Englishmen actually to welcome Swein Forkbeard's invasion in 1013.

John of Worcester records that at the time of Alfred's arrival in England the leading men 'were much more devoted to Harold .. especially, they say, Earl Godwine'.[67] It seem likely that Harold was well liked, and had he lived longer could well have been a good king; he might even have established a lasting Danish dynasty in England. The bye-name 'Harefoot' by which he was known, and was probably contemporary, seems to have been due to a reputation he had acquired in his youth for his athletic ability.

Having diverted Alfred to Guildford the question is what part Godwine actually played in the events which followed. Stenton considered that 'since without his consent the Ætheling could never have been given to his tormentors, Godwine was justly held responsible for his death by Harthacnut'.[68] There is no doubt that the

---

[64] E.E.R Bk 3 ch 4 pp.42-43.
[65] G.N.D vol ii Bk VII 6[9] pp.106-107.
[66] 'Historia Anglorum', s.a 1040 p.201; G.R. ch 188.
[67] J.W. ii pp.522-523.
[68] A.S.E p.421.

Abingdon annalist placed all the blame on Godwine for the treatment of Alfred's followers at Guildford, although the Worcester version would, by omission of his name, seem to imply that Harold was responsible. Both Freeman and Plummer pointed out that the Abingdon version was the original and version 'D' may possibly have contained a scribal error. Both the Norman writers blame Godwine for the fate of Alfred's followers; John goes even further and blames him for Alfred's blinding, and in fact omits mention of King Harold in this respect.[69]

In contrast the *Encomium Emmae Reginae* exonerates Godwine and places all the blame for both the treatment of Alfred's followers and of his blinding and death on 'men leagued with the most abominable tyrant Haraldr'. After describing his horrendous torture the Encomiast is alone in recording that the unfortunate prince died during this process and then his lifeless body was left with the monks of Ely. It differs from all the other authorities in mentioning a trial of sorts.[70]

As well as the inconsistencies noted as to date and other details, there still remains a certain amount of doubt about this tragedy. For instance, William of Malmesbury, after describing Alfred's death, says: 'I have mentioned these circumstances because such is the common report; but as the chronicles are silent I do not assert them as fact.'[71] Presumably he was referring to the 'E' recension of the *Chronicle*. As this was compiled at St Augustine's, Canterbury during this period, the annalist would have been in a good position to know exactly what happened. It can only be assumed that he omitted any mention of the invasions of both Æthelings out of respect and esteem for Godwine.

Modern historians have in general taken the view that the earl was guilty of complicity in Harold's interest. However, the great pioneer into the history of the Norman Conquest, E. A. Freeman, believed that he was still the leader of Harthacnut's supporters[72] and in this he was followed by C. Plummer and P. Stafford.[73] Freeman pointed out that Alfred was not a lawful king, driven from his throne, and that Harold was not a usurper, which is undeniably true. At the meeting of the Witan, Harold had been elected as regent of all England on behalf of himself and his half brother Harthacnut. In the Worcester version of the *Chronicle* under the entry for 1035, it records: 'In this year King Cnut passed away, and his son succeeded to the Kingdom.' The Abingdon passage omits this, which highlights the hostility of that ecclesiastical centre which becomes evident in other entries.

The fact remains that pretenders who threatened an established government were invariably punished by death. However sad Alfred's fate was, it is difficult to understand the outcry which accompanied it in the *Chronicles* of the time and

---

[69] J.W. volume 2 pp.524-525.

[70] E.E.R Bk 3 ch 6 pp.44-45.

[71] G.R. ch 188 pp.336-337, 'This I have not omitted, because it is a well known story, but, since the Chronicle is silent, I do not affirm it as certain'.

[72] F.N.C.i pp.489-490.

[73] 'Two of the Saxon Chronicles Parallel' vol 2 pp.212-215; P. Stafford, 'Queen Emma and Queen Edith' p.239.

indeed of many later historians. Kings had a way of disposing of rival claimants: a cursory glance at the kings of England will show that pretenders to the throne of an established kingship often met much the same fate. King Æthelstan, according to Simeon of Durham, had his brother Edwin drowned at sea and Stenton suggested that this may have been the result of a rebellion against him.[74] King Æthelred went even further and ordered 'all the Danish people who were in England to be slain on St Brice's Day, because the king had been told that they wished to deprive him of his life by treachery.'[75] This is possibly an exaggeration but there is evidence of a massacre of some proportions. King Cnut, according to the *Chronicle*, was responsible for the death of Eadwig, the last surviving son of Æthelred by his first wife.[76] King John murdered his nephew, Arthur of Brittany; Edward II was assassinated in Berkeley Castle by order of his wife, Queen Isabella, and her paramour, Mortimer. Henry IV did not scruple to have the deposed Richard II killed by ruffians in Pontefract Castle. Edward IV had Henry VI done to death in the Tower and his own brother, the Duke of Clarence, drowned in a butt of Malmsey wine. Nor were the Tudors any different: Henry VII had Peter Warbeck executed; Mary Tudor sent Lady Jane Grey to the block, a martyr to her father's ambition. Thirty three years later Elizabeth Tudor ordered Mary, Queen of Scots, to be beheaded because she had become a focus for rebellion and intrigue. The Duke of Monmouth, unlike Alfred, was able to enlist a following of sorts in the country, but had little chance of success; when the rising was quelled he was beheaded and, like Alfred, his supporters were slaughtered. Nor was it unknown for victims of the Norman kings to have their eyesight destroyed. Henry I ordered two of his granddaughters to be blinded.[77] He had his brother, Robert, imprisoned and 'had his eyes burnt out with a red hot iron as a precaution against a rising in his favour.'[78] He meted out the same fate to his first cousin, William of Mortain. Nor was his father over-squeamish with those who stood in his way: according to Orderic Vitalis he had Walter, the son of Drogo, and his wife, Biota, poisoned when his guests were at Falaise.[79] Conan, the duke of Brittany, also died by poison, arranged by William on the eve of his invasion of England in 1066.[80] With the exception of Lady Jane Grey, the pretenders were themselves all playing for high stakes. However the horror expressed in the 'C' and 'D' versions of the *Chronicle*, the *Encomium Emmae Reginae*, the Norman writers and any of the later chronicles at Alfred's fate is not mirrored in recounting the fates of others in the writings of their own times. We are left to discover the reason for this.

---

[74] Simeon of Durham, 'History of the Kings of England' s.a 933 p.88, A.S.E pp.355-356.

[75] A.S.C 'E' s.a 1002.

[76] A.S.C 'C' s.a 1017; J.W. pp.502-503; Simeon of Durham 'History of the Kings' s.a 1017 p.112.

[77] Christopher Brooke, 'The Saxon and Norman Kings' p.176; Henry of Huntingdon, 'H.A' ch VIII p.261.

[78] T. B. Costain, 'The Three Edwards' p.242; C. Tyerman, 'Who's Who in Medieval England' p.77.

[79] O.V. volume ii Bk iii pp.116-119; Bk iv pp.312-313.

[80] O.V. continuation of William of Jumieges vii p.33.

Abingdon attitudes

All the chronicles of the period were written by monks in religious establishments. The Encomiast's attitude is obvious; Emma commissioned him to blacken Harold as far as possible and to absolve her for the part she played in encouraging Alfred to come to England to his death. The Norman writers were determined to use the incident to blame Godwine and, by extension, his son King Harold II in order to justify the Norman Conquest. The later Anglo-Norman writers were taking their cue from the Abingdon version of the *Chronicle* and the Norman accounts.[81] It is noteworthy that it is the 'C' version of the *Chronicle* compiled at Abingdon that is so hostile to Godwine, while 'D', the Worcester edition, perhaps deliberately, omits his name, and the 'E' compilation emanating from St Augustine's, Canterbury does not even mention Alfred's fate at all. So the *Chronicle's* condemnation of Godwine rests solely on the Abingdon scribe. It is difficult to see why this was so, but it is true that there were two Norman abbots at Abingdon, which may have coloured their attitude to the house of Godwine. Rotulf, a Norman relative of Emma's and Alfred's, had been with Ólafr Haroldson attempting to evangelise Norway.[82] He succeeded Spearhafoc when the latter fled the country in 1050 and died the following year. The second Norman abbot was at Abingdon after the Conquest; he bore the English name of Athelhelm and had come from Jumièges.

In a list of charters purporting to be grants to Abingdon, fifteen have been listed as spurious; thirteen as genuine and twelve as either doubtful or with no comment.[83] Admittedly, in comparison to Evesham, Chertsey, Crowland and Westminster Abbey the number of dubious charters compiled for the enrichment of Abingdon's Abbey was no worse, in some cases slightly better. The monks were not averse to claiming land and revenues to enrich their monasteries, and perhaps the words of the Abingdon annal for the year 1052 provide a clue to the hostility Abingdon had for the earl. The entry reads: 'Godwine was taken ill soon after he landed, and afterwards recovered, but he made far too few amends regarding church property which he had taken from many holy places.' Both 'D' and 'E' have no such comment; it seems likely that the hostility was engendered because of greed, and perhaps the culprit may not necessarily have been the earl.

Dr Keynes points out that King Cnut's grant of land at Lyford in Berkshire and of property in Oxford in 1032, and of land in Warwickshire to Abingdon Abbey the following year were perhaps forgeries.[84] It may well have been the cause of friction between the Earl and the Abbey.

---

[81] William of Malmesbury, Henry of Huntingdon etc.
[82] J W Appendix A. p.615; F Stenton 'A.S.E' p.463.
[83] P. Sawyer, Anglo-Saxon charters'.
[84] S. Kenyes, 'Cnut's Earls, p.51 and note 48, S 964 and S 967.

Scots and Welsh

It was after the failure of the Æthelings' attempts that Harold 'was chosen everywhere as King and Harthacnut repudiated because he remained too long in Denmark.'[85] One of the King's first acts was to exile Emma and it is recorded that she 'was driven from the country without any mercy to face the raging winter.' The 'D' version has no mention of this and 'E' merely says, 'she was driven from the country'. The Encomiast tells a different story: 'And so, having enjoyed favourable winds, they crossed the sea.'[86] He may, as Campbell suggested, have wished to gloss over Emma's forced departure and to represent her as always acting on her own volition.

Harold could scarcely be blamed for wanting Emma out of the country as soon as possible. A woman capable of inventing the scurrilous stories about his parentage and the insults to his mother could hardly be expected to be treated leniently. She was also a focal point for sedition. If the *Annals of St Mildred* can have any reliance placed upon them, they depict a woman who was capable of 'inciting Magnus, King of Norway, to invade England, and it was said that she had given countless treasures to Magnus', and was prepared to stoop to anything. Even if it was only an idea she toyed with and nothing more, it still revealed a character that was both scheming and unscrupulous. The scribe who penned the Annals summed her up as, 'this traitor to the Kingdom, this enemy of the country, the betrayer of her own son...'[87]

If Emma was exiled in the 'raging winter' and Alfred's death occurred in early February, it would seem that she left England in late February or early March 1037. She was received kindly by Count Baldwin of Flanders who gave her a house in Bruges where she dwelt until 17 June 1040, when she returned to England with her son Harthacnut after King Harold's death.

We are left to wonder about the character of the man whom the English chose as their king; the man to whom Godwine transferred his allegiance, and whose popularity was such that when Harthacnut eventually was free to leave Denmark he found it necessary to sail with a fleet of sixty ships. He then decided to wait at Bruges until after he heard the news of his half brother's death. Early in the year 1039, Harthacnut and Magnus confronted each other at the Gotha river. Thanks to the efforts of the leading men in both armies, a reconciliation was effected and at last the Danish king was free to obey his mother's urgent summons. Edward had been called on to join her, but he pointed out to his mother that he could do nothing to help. The English leaders had not taken any oaths of loyalty to him, and he advised her to renew the pleas she had been sending to Harthacnut.

---

[85] A.S.C 'C' s.a 1037.
[86] E.E.R Bk 3 ch 7 pp.46-47.
[87] 'Annals of Mildred' ed and trans by T.D. Hardy in 'Catalogue of Materials' quoted from 'E. H. Documents' vol i p.381.

In Wales Gruffydd ap Llewelyn had recently come to the throne of Gwynedd and Powys. His father, Llewelyn ap Seisyll, King of Gwynedd, had died in 1023 and was succeeded by Iago ab Idwal.[88] In 1039 he was slain by Gruffydd, his distant relative. Gruffydd became the only king who could eventually claim kingship of all Wales, and in the years that followed he was to become a formidable enemy of both the other Welsh kings and a thorn in the flesh of the English.[89] Soon after he succeeded to the throne, he gained an overwhelming victory over a Mercian army, which was taken completely by surprise and ambushed at Rhyd y Groes at a ford on the upper Severn near Welshpool.[90] The 'C' version of the *Chronicle* records that 'The Welsh slew Eadwine, the brother of Earl Leofric and Thurkil and Ælfgeat, together with many other good men.'[91] Both Thurkil and Ælfgeat can probably be identified as witnessing charters as thegns. An Ælfgeat witnesses from 1018 to 1035. An Abingdon charter (S 993 of 1042 which is a grant to that Abbey of land at Farnborough by Harthacnut) would seem to indicate that this was not Edwin's companion at Rhyd y Groes. However, as the charter itself is regarded as spurious[92] it is quite possible that the monk was copying from an earlier genuine charter witness list. Thurkil witnessed first in 1019 and continued until Cnut's grant to Fecamp dated by Sawyer as 1028 x 1035.[93] A confirmation of this charter by Harthacnut may provide an explanation for the similar late dating of Ælfgeat's signature of S 993. Edwin, leader of the Mercian army, would have been acting in his capacity as the Sheriff of Hereford.[94]

There was also trouble that year on the northern frontier. Duncan had succeeded his grandfather, Malcolm II, as the King of Scotland in November 1034. His relationship to Malcolm was through the female line which presented difficulties. He was the son of Bethoc, the King's daughter, and of Crinan, the abbot of Dunkeld. Malcolm had ruthlessly eliminated any likely opposition to his grandson's succession because of this irregularity. In retribution for an attack on Cumbria by Eadulf, the earl of Bernician Northumbria, Duncan led an army south and laid siege to Durham city. Issuing forth, the inhabitants inflicted a devastating defeat on the Scots; severed heads stuck on poles on the city walls bore a grisly witness to their victory. This incursion did nothing to bolster Duncan's authority among his subjects and in the following year he was defeated and killed by Macbeth. Neither the events in Wales nor those in Scotland directly affected Earl Godwine, but they were both to have far reaching effects on the subsequent fortunes of his family.

---

[88] K. L. Maund, 'Ireland, Wales and England' pp.59-62 for Iago AB Idwal pp.62-64.
[89] W. Davies, 'Wales in the Early Middle Ages' pp.108-124; J.E. Lloyd, 'A History of Wales' pp.359-371; K. L. Maund pp.64-68.
[90] J.W. p.528-529; A.S.C s.a 1052, M. Swanton p.176; Identified by C. Oman as Crossford 6 miles west of Shrewsbury, 'History of England Before the Norman Conquest' p.606.
[91] A.S.C 'C' 1039.
[92] P. Sawyer 'A.S. Charters' p.297.
[93] S. Keynes, 'Atlas', Table LXX 2 of 2; LXIV 3 of 3.
[94] A. Williams et al, 'Dark Age Britain' p.130.

An appointment made by Harold was that of Thuri as Earl of the East Midlands. His name first appears in the witness lists in 1038, and then in two charters of Harthacnut.[95] He was one of the earls sent by Harthacnut to ravage Worcester, and was succeeded as earl in 1044 by Beorn Estrithson. The most important ecclesiastical appointment was to the archbishopric of Canterbury when Ælthelnoth died and was succeeded by Eadsige. The former had been in poor health for some time during which Eadsige had taken over some of his duties.

Only one charter is extant of Harold's reign, or more accurately a document stating that Ælfstan, the abbot of St Augustine's, had cunningly obtained from the king's steward, Steorra, the right to the third penny of the dues of Sandwich for two whole herring seasons. In 1023 King Cnut had granted the port of Sandwich to Christ Church, Canterbury. When Archbishop Eadsige realised the injustice which had been arranged between Abbot Ælfstan and Steorra he sent the monk, Ælfgar, to make representations to the king; Ælfgar pointed out to the ailing king that he had sinned greatly in taking from Christ Church that which his father had given them. It became obvious that Abbot Ælfstan had been instrumental in perpetrating this great wrong and King Harold sent Ælfgar back to the Archbishop, giving orders to put right the transgression that had been committed.[96]

Harold Harefoot's death

Harold died on 17 March 1040 and was buried at Westminster. After his death, invitations were sent to Harthacnut in Bruges offering him the English throne. Ælfgifu must have known that England was no place for her if Emma and her son returned to power, and that she could expect no mercy from her rival. The article *An Alleged Son of King Harold Harefoot* by W. H. Steveson probably throws some light on her future movements: in a cartulary printed by M. Gustave Desjerdins it relates *'Igitus Alboynus Anglorum terrae, urbis Lundena hortus fuit; pater eius Heraldus rex fuit Anglorum terrae; mater euis nomine Alveva.'* 'This Alboynus came from the city of London in the land of the English; his father was Harold, king of the land of the English; his mother's name was Alveva'.

'Alboynus' Stevenson identifies with the English Ælfwine and 'Alveva' with Ælfgifu. Ælfwine, who claimed to be the son of King Harold, arrived in the county of Rouergue and came to an uninhabited village. He persuaded the lords to rebuild the disused church and became its prior when it was dedicated in 1060.[97] Ælfwine would have been approximately twenty-two or -three at the time and, if this is correct, it would seem likely that Ælfgifu would have been his grandmother's name instead of his mother's.

---

[95] 'Atlas' Table LXIX S 994, 995, 1392.
[96] A. J. Robertson No XCI pp.174-179; S 1467 and Miss Robertson's comments p.422-424; for Cnut's Charter Robertson No LXXXII pp.158-161; S 959.
[97] Printed in E.H. Review XXVIII 1913 pp.112-117.

The name 'Ælfwine' does crop up in the family relationships. Ælfwine was Leofric's grandfather, and a strong possibility exists that the family of Leofric and of Ælfgifu were related, and perhaps not only by marriage.[98] Also, in her uncle's will there is a mention of a '*dux Alwinus*' which could represent the name Ælfwine. No ealdorman of that name has been identified, but is is possible that there was an Ælfwine in Ælgifu's family.[99] In any case, the prefix *Ælf-* appears in the names Ælfhelm, Ælfthryth and Ælfgifu. It is conceivable that Harold had married, was the father of a son, and that in the spring of 1040 Ælfgifu, her grandson and his mother found a refuge in France; as Eadgyth Swannehals was to do twenty six years later.[100]

A review of Harold's reign reveals that the charges that his critics levelled against him contained little or no substance. The doubts concerning his parentage were unfounded; Cnut acknowledged both his sons by Ælfgifu with the royal names he gave them. Harold's alleged disdain for the Christian religion is entirely unsubstantiated; his friendship for the Bishops Lyfing and Ælfric disproves it. The seizure of the royal treasury was justified[101] - as regent of all England, it was necessary for it to be in his keeping. Alfred's blinding and subsequent murder have parallels in all ages for those who challenged recognised authority, and it is difficult to see how he could have acted differently in respect of Emma's banishment. The letters he is supposed to have forged were surely a ploy to excuse Emma; the last thing Harold would have wanted was the presence of other contenders to the throne in England to complicate his chances.

One other offence that Harold has been accused of was the selling of the bishopric of Selsey to Grimketel 'for gold'[102]. In addition there was the charge of simony. This involved Bishop Lyfing's appointment to the see of Worcester in addition to Devon and Cornwall. However, the devastation caused in the see he held already by the Danish attacks must have impoverished the west country. No doubt the wealth of Worcester was expected to offset the poverty of the former. The *Chronicle* bears testimony to the sufferings endured and the havoc caused: Exeter was attacked in 875, 893, and in 1003 'the host utterly laid waste to the borough'; in 981 and 997 the Danes ravaged in Devon and Cornwall and left a trail of devastation through the counties.[103]

In any case, Harold was far from being alone in this respect. Queen Eadgyth is recorded as having received payments from Ramsey, Peterborough and

---

[98] P. Sawyer, 'Charters of Burton Abbey' pp.XLII-XLIII.
[99] D. Whitelock, 'A.S. Wills', No XVII pp.46-47; Sawyer, 'Charters of Burton Abbey' pp.XLII-XLIII; S 1489.
[100] G. Beech, 'England and Aquitaine before the Norman Conquest' pp.81-101, particularly pp.94-95.
[101] P. Stafford, 'Queen Emma and Queen Edith' p.240.
[102] J.W. pp.526-527, 'Grimketel was elected bishop of Sussex for gold'; F. Barlow, 'English Church' p.41 note 7.
[103] A.S.C 'A' AD 875; 893, 894/893, 1001, 'E', 'F' 1003, A.S.C 'C' 981-982, 988; A.S.C 'E' 997, 'E', 'F' 1003.

Evesham;[104] Archbishop Stigand was guilty of selling bishoprics and abbeys, and King Edward was agreeable to some of these transactions;[105] in fact his predecessor Æthelred II, as well as his successors, Harthacnut and Edward the Confessor were all guilty in this way.[106]

Table 5. Sequence of Events 1035 - 1040

1035 Nov 12th	Death of King Cnut.
1035 December	Meeting of the Witan at Oxford; Harold elected regent.
1036 Jan/Feb	Seizure of the treasury at Winchester.
1036 Jan/Feb	Return of Ælfgifu to England.
1036 Spring	Ælfgifu and Harold canvassing for support.
1036 end of July/ 1st week in Aug	Letter confirming Harthacnut's continued absence in spite of continued pleas.
1036 August	Emma sends to Edward and Alfred for their intervention
1036 Summer	Edward's invasion in Southampton area.
1036 Autumn	Alfred's invasion.
1037 February 3rd	Alfred's death at Ely.
1037 Spring	Harold elected King of all England.
1037 Autumn/ Early winter	Emma banished; seeks refuge in Flanders.
1038	Appointment of Thuri as Earl of East Midlands. Grimketel appointed bishop of Selsey. Lyfing appointed to Worcester. Edward summoned to Bruges by Emma. Death of Æthelnoth.
1039	Mercian defeat at Rhyd Y Groes: Duncan defeated at Durham. Peace treaty concluded between Harthacnut and Magnus.
1040 17 March	Death of Harold at Oxford
1040 March	Harold buried at Winchester
1040 March/April	Ælfgifu, her daughter-in-law and grandson seek refuge in France.

---

[104] P. Stafford, 'Queen Emma and Queen Edith' p.145.
[105] F. Barlow, 'English church' p.113-114.
[106] ibid; for Harold I p.108 n 4; for Æthelred ii p.112 n 4; for Edward p.115 n 3.

6. Earl Godwine the Scapegoat

After Harold's death, the English magnates sent to Bruges for Harthacnut, thinking that they were acting wisely, according to the *Chronicle* 'C' 'D' s.a 1040. According to the *Chronicle*, Cnut had married Emma 'before 1 August' in 1017.[107] It would seem therefore that Harthacnut was probably born between the years 1018 and 1020.[108] In 1023 the bones of St Ælfheah were taken from their resting place in London and conveyed across the Thames to Southwark and thence to Rochester. On 11 June the procession led by Archbishop Æthelnoth was joined by Emma and 'her royal child' Harthacnut.[109] That same year King Cnut and Earl Thorkell Hávi were reconciled. The *Chronicle* records that 'Cnut delivered Denmark and his son into Thurkil's keeping and the King took Thurkil's son with him to England'.[110] According to the *Chronicle* the reconciliation took place before the removal of St Ælfheah's body, which means that either 'Cnut's son' was not Harthacnut but one of Ælfgifu's sons[111], or that Cnut only arranged to send Harthacnut to Denmark at a later date[112]. It is doubtful that this was ever done, as far as Thorkell was concerned[113]. M. K. Lawson pointed out that, as Harthacnut was no older than five in 1023, it is far more likely to have been one of his half-brothers who was taken hostage. On the basis of the boys' ages, it seems that Swein could well have been the most likely son as at the time he could have been eight or nine years old. Thorkell's son would have been Haraldr, who was probably brought up in Cnut's household, and who was in due course appointed an English earl. He witnesses as such in Cnut's grant of land to Christ Church, Canterbury where his name appears after Úlfr, Eilifr and Leofwine and before Eirikr. This was dated 1032. Although both A. J. Robertson and F. Harmer regarded this charter as spurious,[114] the witness list may well have been copied from other genuine documents. However, in the same year he witnessed Cnut's grant to Abingdon as a thegn,[115], and another very doubtful one to Crowland Abbey in the same manner.[116] The following year, again in the same capacity, his name appears on a charter in which the king gave a grant of land to Archbishop Ælfric of York.[117] Haraldr did witness as earl a charter of 1042, a Worcester lease of Bishop Lyfing's, and it is possible that the Christ Church charter of 1032

---

[107] A.S.C 'D', 'E' s.a 1017.
[108] 'The Reign of Cnut' p.4 1018; 'Dark Age Britain' p.152 c1020.
[109] 'The Reign of Cnut', June 15th 1023; pp.283-315, particularly p.285; A.S.C 'D' 1023.
[110] A.S.C 'C' s.a 1023.
[111] M.K. Lawson, 'Cnut' p.94, 131.
[112] E.E.R App III pp.75,76; Neils Lund, 'Cnut's Danish Kingdom' p.36.
[113] A. Williams, 'Dark Age Britain', pp.225-226.
[114] A.J. Robertson, 'A.S. Charters' No LXXXV pp.168-171; F. Harmer, 'Writs' pp.168-172; 181-182 'Cnut's Earls' Keynes p.66 n129; S 981.
[115] S 964 Table LXX 2 of 2.
[116] S 965 Table LXX 2 of 2 considered doubtful; P. Sawyer, 'Charters' p.290.
[117] S 968, S. Keynes, 'Cnut's Earls p.66 and notes 129, 131-132.

anticipated his appointment by ten years.[118] Haraldr married Gunnhildr, the daughter of an unnamed sister of King Cnut and of Wyrtgeorn, King of the Wends. Gunnhildr had been widowed in 1030 by the death of her first husband, Hákon Eiríksson. It has been suggested that Haraldr may have succeeded to Hákon's earldom of Worcester[119].

It is possible that the story of Harthacnut's being fostered by Thorkell may have been a confusion with his subsequent fostering by his aunt, Estrith, and her husband, Úlfr, when the latter became regent of Denmark in succession to Thorkell. At any rate it would seem that from 1024 Harthacnut was to spend little or no time in England until his arrival in 1040. Few of the leading men and probably none of the ordinary people in England would have known him. His father had appointed him king of Denmark in 1028 and coins were minted for him as 'Rex' at that time.[120] Harthacnut could only have been nine or ten years old when, at the 'Thing' at Nidaros, Cnut 'led his son to the high seat at his side, gave him the title of King, and therewith the whole Danish dominion.'[121] Jarl Úlfr was probably murdered in 1028 and some regency must have been designated to guide him under his father's instructions. Little is known of Harthacnut's reign in Denmark: Sven Aggeson speaks of him as 'a sort of helper during the time his father had command of the helm of state.'[122] That advisers were set up to guide the young King may be inferred from Snorri's *Saga of Magnus the Good.*[123]

In the spring of 1034 a deputation headed by Einar Tambar-Skelve, Jarl Ragnvaldr and Kálfr Árneson set off from Norway, journeying east through Sweden, and then by ship to Ladoga. Imbued by a growing sense of King Ólafr's holiness, as indicated by the miracles which were happening at his tomb,[124] and embittered by subjugation to Danish rule, they determined to bring back with them Ólafr's son, Magnus. He had been left by his father at the court of Yaroslav in Kiev. They promised on oath that they would proclaim him king and give him every assistance in their power.[125] For them the eleven year old boy was the best hope of gaining Norwegian independence. Before King Cnut's death in November 1035, he had already been proclaimed king of Norway[126]. From then until 1038, Harthacnut was constantly threatened by a developing tide of Norwegian nationalism and wish for revenge. Kalfr Árneson and others repented of the part they had played in Ólafr's downfall.[127] Hostilities between Norway and Denmark continued until a peace treaty was concluded on an island at the mouth

---

[118] S 1396.
[119] A. Williams, 'Dark Age Britain' p.147.
[120] P. Stafford, 'Queen Emma and Queen Edith' p.234 and note 108.
[121] Snorri, 'St Olaf's Saga' ch CLXXXI p.325.
[122] 'The Works of Sven Aggesen' ch 11 p.39 ed and trans E. Christiansen.
[123] 'Saga of Magnus the Good' ch VI pp.131-132.
[124] 'Ágrip' p.100 note 100.
[125] Snorri, 'St Olaf's Saga' ch CCLXV pp.395-396.
[126] Gwyn Jones, 'A History of the Vikings' pp.385-386.
[127] 'Ágrip' ch XXXIV pp.46-47.

of the Götha river between the two young kings,[128] which left Harthacnut free to mobilise a force, assemble a fleet, and sail to join his mother in Flanders. Towards the end of 1039 he left Denmark with ten ships; however a fleet of sixty warships were harboured in an inlet, probably in Denmark, ready for action if required.[129] The Encomiast relates: '... he set out accompanied by not more than ten ships to go to his mother.' The *Chronicle* says he came 'to the country with sixty ships before midsummer'[130]. According to Adam of Bremen, he left Swein Estrithson as his regent in Denmark[131].

Harthacnut in England

It can only be assumed that Emma had heard news from England that King Harold was suffering from the illness from which he was to die in the following March. However, even after a report of the king's death had reached Bruges, Harthacnut and his mother still remained in Flanders until a second delegation arrived from England inviting the former to accept the English crown[132]. It was midsummer before the Danish king crossed to England. No doubt there was a great deal of consternation amongst some of the leading magnates who had supported Harold in 1036 and 1037. The Encomiast claims that the deputation crossed to Flanders, 'reporting that the English nobles did not wish to oppose him, but to rejoice together in jubilations of every kind.'[133] Harthacnut's subjects did not have to wait long before their jubilation evaporated and their worst fears were more than justified.

His first action as king was to give orders to have the late king's body dug up. The *Chronicle* says: 'He had the body disinterred and cast into a ditch.'[134] The St Augustine's version omits the incident altogether; John of Worcester elaborates, recording that Harthacnut ordered Ælfric, the Archbishop of York and Earl Godwine to attend together with 'Stor, master of his household, Eadric, his steward, Thrond, his executioner and other men of great rank to London, and ordered them to dig up Harold's body and throw it into a marsh'. After this, the corpse was pulled out of the marsh and thrown in the River Thames.[135] Fishermen retrieved the body and had it buried reverently in a cemetery of the Danes in London. William of Malmesbury and Ingulf both say that the body was decapitated before being thrown into the Thames and both agree that it was eventually buried in a cemetery of the Danes in London.[136]

---

[128] 'Theodoricus' pp.94-95 note 223; Gwyn Jones, 'A History of the Vikings' p.400.
[129] F. Stenton, 'A.S.E' pp.421-422.
[130] E.E.R Bk 3 ch 9 pp.48-49; A.S.C 'C' s.a 1040.
[131] Adam Bk 2 ch LXXVII [74] pp.107 - 108.
[132] 'Chron of Ramsey Abbey' pp.149-150.
[133] E.E.R Bk 3 ch 10 pp.50-51.
[134] A.S.C 'C' s.a 1040; G.N. Garmonsway; M. Swanton 'a fen' as does D. Whitelock, EHDi p.234.
[135] J.W. pp.530-531. It is possible that Stor may be identified with Steorra who was acting as Harold Harefoot's steward in the Sandwich writ. Robertson 'Charters', XCI pp.174-175.
[136] GR Bk 2 ch 188 pp.336-337; Ingulf p.655.

This disgusting action of Harthacnut's was not only motivated by pure spite but constituted a deliberate attempt to depict his predecessor as a usurper who was not even, according to Harthacnut and Emma, of royal blood. The plan for Emma to act as her son's regent until it was possible for him to leave Denmark had been thwarted - and Godwine was held responsible. In any case, the power and influence the earl wielded made him a target for the King's wrath, and it became one of his main objectives to break him at all costs. Nor was Emma likely to have forgotten Godwine's withdrawal of support when she turned to the Æthelings in Normandy to come to her assistance. Although their reasons were different, both were determined to make Godwine a scapegoat for all that had happened since Cnut's death, and the royal couple found a willing accomplice in the Archbishop of York. It has been suggested that he may have crowned Harold in spite of Æthelnoth's reluctance.[137] This is possible, both because of the latter's unwillingness before the Witan had formally elected him, and also that the heartland of Harold's support lay north of the Thames. If this were so, the need to ingratiate himself with the king is obvious. At any rate, William of Malmesbury says it was Ælfric who incited Harthacnut to have his half-brother's body dug up[138], and it was Ælfric who accused Godwine and Bishop Lyfing of complicity in Alfred's death. His accusation of the earl and the bishop stood him in good stead, as the primate continued to prosper for another fifteen years. Lyfing's see of Worcester, which had been bestowed on him by Harold, was taken from him and given back to York, if only for a short time. Lyfing had presumably incurred the new monarch's displeasure because of his friendship with the late king, and the desire of Ælfric to regain the see of Worcester.

Godwine was arraigned for his part in the death of the Ætheling. A great deal has been made of Harthacnut's fraternal love for Alfred and Edward, and even for Swein when he was driven from Norway. Snorri is our authority for the latter[139] and it may be a confusion with Harthacnut's later invitation to Edward to join him in England. The amount of brotherly love he had for Alfred, and his desire to seek vengeance for his death, was probably prompted more by policy than emotion. In his eyes Godwine's sin was as much the power he had attained as his part in Alfred's death. After all, both Alfred and Edward had made a bid for the throne which he regarded as rightfully his own. The Chronicler's entry 'Furthermore he burnt with great anger because of his brother Alfred's death against Earl Godwine and Lyfing, bishop of Worcester ...'[140] was probably what Harthacnut wanted people to think, rather than his true motive. The fact that Godwine had two sons about his own age, named Swegn and Harold, may not have helped.

Godwine was required to swear on oath that he neither advised nor wished Alfred blinded, but had done what his king had ordered him to do. In this he was assisted as oath-helpers by 'the earls and most important thegns of almost all England'.

---

[137] Ian Walker, 'Harold' p.16.
[138] G.R. Bk 2 ch 188 pp.336-337.
[139] 'Saga of Magnus the good' ch IV p.130.
[140] J.W. pp.530-531.

This whole incident is recorded in none of the versions of the *Chronicle* but appears in John of Worcester, followed by Simeon of Durham and William of Malmesbury.[141] It is, however, too explicit and detailed to be any other than correct and has been accepted by modern historians as true.[142] Harthacnut was not able to ruin Godwine because, in spite of all the supposed jealousy and the smears on his character by Norman and later writers, when it came to the crunch the chief men of England were prepared to stand by him. From this it may be inferred that when Harthacnut realised that he was in no position to destroy the earl, he decided to make the best of the situation. Godwine could be useful, and the gift of a splendidly equipped warship adequately crewed was sufficient for the king's anger to be appeased. It may have been for the same reason that the Encomiast was instructed to obscure Godwine's part in Alfred's death.

Harthacnut had to raise enough tax to pay off the fleet he had retained in preparation for an invasion. One of the *Chronicle* accounts records that this amounted to twenty-one thousand and ninety-nine pounds and a further eleven thousand and forty-eight pounds to maintain a standing fleet of thirty two ships[143] - double the number that had been kept by Cnut and Harold. The other versions, from Abingdon and Worcester, say: 'he came then to this country with sixty two ships before midsummer; and then imposed a severe tax which was borne with difficulty; it was fixed at eight marks a rowlock' and John of Worcester added: 'and twelve [marks] to each steersman'.[144] A steersman was either the pilot or more probably the ship's master. Lawson pointed out that, according to the value of the mark, this would mean somewhere between fifty and eighty men per ship. Godwine's gift of a warship included eighty splendidly equipped warriors, but this need not mean that this was the normal complement.

Taxation loomed large and was reflected in the comments of the annalists. The *heregeld* became all the more unpopular with the realisation that the size of the fleet was doubled in order to assist Harthacnut in his struggle against Magnus of Norway. A century later William of Malmesbury wrote: 'He imposed a rigid and intolerable tribute upon England.'[145] The heavy tax burden was felt even more keenly in the price of wheat, which rose in 1040 to fifty five pence a sester 'and even higher'.[146] The inflation in the price of wheat may be attributed to the terrible weather experienced during the winter of 1039-40. As this is not mentioned in the 'E' version of the *Chronicle* which was compiled at that time at St Augustine's in Canterbury[147] but is noted by the Abingdon and Worcester editions, by John of Worcester and Simeon of Durham, the effects were probably more severe in the

---

[141] Simeon of Durham, 'History of the Kings', s.a 1040; J.W. pp.530-533; G.R. ch 188 pp.336-337.
[142] E. A. Freeman, F. Stenton, F. Barlow, P. Stafford, A. Williams, M.K. Lawson etc.
[143] A.S.C 'E' 1040/1041; A.S.C 'C' 1040.
[144] J.W. pp.528-529.
[145] G.R. Bk 2 ch 188 pp.336-337.
[146] A.S.C 'E' s.a 1039/1040.
[147] G.N. Garmonsway, 'The Anglo-Saxon chronicle' Introduction pp XXVII-XXXVIII.

Midlands and the North. The 'C' and 'D' annals under the year 1039 record 'This was the year of the great gale'; John says: 'In this year the winter was very harsh',[148] and Simeon has: 'There was a very severe winter this year'.[149] It is more than likely that the aged monk, Florence, had vivid memories of the severity of the weather which he passed on to the Chronicler John. An autumn tilled crop, such as wheat, would have suffered badly, perhaps becoming waterlogged and rotting in the ground, or the sowing delayed until spring. The combined effects of the intolerable burden of the *heregeld*, accentuated by the rising price of wheat and other associated commodities, were enough to cause deep resentment - deep enough to make Harthacnut's former enthusiastic supporters turn against him. According to one annalist 'wherefore to all who had greatly desired his coming he became supremely hateful'.[150] The scribe who wrote the 'C' entry for 1040 summed up the feelings of his contemporaries when he said 'He never did anything worthy of a king while he reigned.'[151]

The inevitable outcome occurred the following year: feelings ran so high that Harthacnut had to employ his housecarls to collect the taxes throughout the country. Desperation, engendered by poverty and hunger, erupted at Worcester. It is significant that, in the Abingdon and Worcester recensions of the *Chronicle* and that of John of Worcester, accounts of the rebellion figure prominently whereas the reaction in Worcester and its sequel is not mentioned in the St Augustine's, Canterbury version.

On 4th May 1040 feelings could no longer be restrained. It is possible that, as William of Malmesbury thought, the housecarls were unduly overbearing and exceeded their duty.[152] At any rate two of them, Feader and Thurston, were chased through the streets of the city and forced to seek refuge in a turret in one of the towers of Worcester monastery, whence they were dragged out and slain.[153] The *Chronicle* implies that they were on their own;[154] John suggests that there were other housecarls collecting taxes in the city. When the Danegeld was being collected in former years, those unable to meet their tax demand must have been forced to sell their land or estate to those more affluent in order to meet the demands made of them, and such circumstances recurred here.[155] The King was infuriated at the murder of his men but he waited for six months before he exacted retribution. Possibly he delayed until winter, when the effects of his planned revenge would be felt more severely.

---

[148] J.W. pp.528-529.
[149] Simeon of Durham, 'History of the Kings' s.a 1039 pp.116.
[150] J.W. pp.530-531.
[151] A.S.C 'C' s.a 1040.
[152] G.R. Bk 2 ch 188 pp.336-337.
[153] J.W. pp.532-533.
[154] A.S.C 'C' s.a 1041.
[155] A. Williams, 'Kingship and Government' p.130.

In the meantime the Ætheling, Edward, arrived in England. It seems incredible that only five years earlier he was making a bid for the throne himself and now he should be welcomed intp the country by Harthacnut. There are many explanations put forward by both contemporary and modern writers to explain the underlying implications. According to the *Chronicle*, immediately after narrating the insurrection in Worcester it records: 'And early in the same year came Edward, his brother on his mother's side, from abroad'. Version 'E' adds that he came from France; John of Worcester has 'from Normandy where he had spent many years as an exile'. William of Malmesbury speaks of Edward being 'weary of continued wandering, revisiting his native land in the hope of finding fraternal kindness'.[156] However, the Encomiast distinctly says that Edward came to England by express invitation; that messengers were sent asking for him to come and 'hold the Kingdom together with himself.'[157] The Norman writers agree with this and probably used the *Encomium Emmae Reginae* as the source of their information.[158] Many modern historians such as Freeman, Oman and Stenton agree that Edward came to this country because he was invited by his half-brother.

John of Worcester says he was honourably received by Harthacnut and dwelt in his court. The Abingdon and Worcester versions add that Edward was sworn in as the future king and William of Malmesbury stresses that he was entertained 'most affectionately'.[159] Adam of Bremen agrees that prior to Harthacnut's death the English had already chosen Edward as his heir.[160] Campbell accepts that an invitiation was sent, the warm reception he received, and that he was recognised as the king's heir in view of Harthacnut's failing health.[161] Presumably this is based on William of Poitiers's remarks, although, as he is the only authority to mention it, the story could well have been prompted by the king's early death the following year.

Three reasons emerge for the welcome Edward received, whether an invitiation had been sent to him or not: firstly, Edward arrived in England soon after the Worcester riot; Englishmen were still filled with resentment at the hardship caused by the imposition of the horrendous tax and nauseated by the disinterment of their late king. No doubt many of those in authority were shaken by the attack on Godwine and Lyfing. By acknowledging Edward as joint-king and heir, Harthacnut and his mother were endeavouring to gain for themselves some support and to appeal to those who looked back with nostalgia to the charisma which was once associated with the house of Wessex.[162] A second possible reason was that Harthacnut needed a regent to act for him in England while he returned to Denmark to resume his struggle with Magnus. The Norwegian king was showing every sign of taking advantage of his absence in England to stage an invasion, and this makes sense in so

---

[156] G.R. ch 188 pp.336-337; A.S.C 'C', 'D' s.a 1041, 'E' 1040/1041; J.W. pp.532-533.
[157] E.E.R Bk 3 ch 13 pp.52-53.
[158] W. J. G.N.D Bk 11 6(9) pp.106-107; W. P. Part One ch 5 pp.6-7.
[159] G.R. Bk 2 ch 188 pp.336-337.
[160] Adam Bk 2 LXVIII [74] p.108.
[161] E.E.R, Introduction p LXVIII; E.E.R ch 13-14 p.53.
[162] S. Keynes, 'The Æthelings in Normandy' p.198; F. Barlow, 'Edward' pp.48-49.

much that all the leading men were inherited from his rival and enemy Harold. Godwine, Cnut's regent, he had attempted to ruin, and moreover, all the nobility had shown clearly where their loyalties lay if it came to a choice between the king and the earl. But Edward was as much a stranger in England as Harthacnut; he had no following in the country to constitute a threat when the latter was absent.[163] The third reason advanced is that Harthacnut was prepared to share the government of England with Edward, not because of any brotherly love (as the Encomiast would have his readers believe), but as a matter of policy. Saxo Grammaticus, writing nearly two centuries later, paints a completely different picture: Edward had ambitions for the crown and in order to quell them Harthacnut appointed him joint-king, being afraid of the ill-will of his subjects and the respect which Edward's lineage gave him.[164] Dr Sten Körner put the case that Emma and Harthacnut were forced to accept Edward's return, and pointed to the extraordinary situation whereby a reigning monarch invites a former claimant to share the kingdom with him. Williams went further and suggested tha,t because of the state of unrest and disillusionment in the England of 1041, Edward was encouraged to return and that Harthacnut's position was so insecure that Edward was in a position to force his half-brother to acknowledge him as his heir.[165]

That Edward was adopted as Harthacnut's heir seems ludicrous unless the latter did perhaps have a premonition of impending death. Edward could well have been born sometime between 1003 and 1005, when his name appears on charters, so would have been at least thirty-six in 1041.[166] Harthacnut was probably born between 1018 and 1020,[167] and would then have been only twenty-one or -two. Harthacnut was young and could be expected to marry and have children, while Edward was still unmarried. Either Harthacnut's offer to make Edward his heir was an empty gesture, or it might after all tend to prove that Harthacnut's life-expectancy was suspect.

The charter evidence does little to prove that Edward occupied a very exalted position at the court. One document dated 1042 is a grant of land in Berkshire to Abingdon Abbey. This alone bears the signature of Edward as the brother of the King, and is in any case classified as doubtful or spurious, while other charters of Harthacnut do not even bear his name.[168] This casts some doubts on Edward's standing in 1041 and early 1042, and makes it entirely possible that if Edward was welcomed, perhaps even invited, it was a case of convenience. With Harthacnut's popularity plummeting it was safer to have Edward at the court rather than as a potential threat in Normandy.

---

[163] F. Barlow suggests the aetheling regent, 'Edward' p.49; N. Higham, 'The Death of A.S England' pp.114-115 for Edward's advantages to Harthacnut.
[164] Saxo, Bk 10 note 159 p.209 and chapter XXI pp.46-47; S. Körner, 'Battle of Hastings' pp.64-67.
[165] A. Williams et al, 'Dark Age Britain' p.152; S. Körner, ibid pp.69-71, A.S.C 'C', 'D' s.a 1041, 'E' 1041/1042.
[166] F. Barlow, 'Edward' p.29.
[167] A. Rumble, 'The Reign of Cnut' p.4; A. Williams, 'Dark Age Britain' p.152.
[168] S. Keynes, 'Atlas', Table LXV; the exception being S 993, a doubtful Abingdon charter of 1042.

In November the king gave his attention to taking reprisals against the rioters of Worcester. He gave orders for the earls Godwine, Leofric, Siward, Thuri of the East Midlands and Hrani of Hereford, together with his army of housecarls to kill, plunder and burn the city and to lay waste the surrounding countryside. Commencing on the twelfth, the devastation continued for five days. The townspeople had received a warning in advance and took refuge on the island of Bevere in the river Severn; the inhabitants of the surrounding countryside found safety in the hills and the more remote and inaccessible areas. But Worcester was laid in ruins; the houses were destroyed by fire; cattle were slaughtered or driven off; food supplies and valuables were seized as booty and the whole terrain left a desolate waste. Given the chance to avenge the death of two of their companions, the housecarls did their frightful work with a will. When the inhabitants of Worcester emerged from their hiding places after the withdrawal of the avenging host, they found themselves left to face the rigours of the approaching winter with no homes or food. John of Worcester wrote with obvious feeling and concluded his account by saying: 'On the fifth day accordingly, when the city had been burnt, and all returned home with great booty the king's anger was straightaway slaked'.[169] Worcester was made an example to all who provoked his anger, with the result that he 'sullied his fame and diminished the love of his subjects'.[170] It is true that other Kings of England had used the 'harrying' of a district or city as a means of punishment. In 952 King Eadred had Thetford ravaged as a form of retribution for the murder of Abbot Ealhelm.[171] In 969 King Edgar 'ordered the whole of the Isle of Thanet to be harried',[172] and in 986 King Æthelred 'laid waste the diocese of Rochester' for reasons unknown, except perhaps friction between the King and the bishop.[173] There may well have been other instances. It is perhaps significant that the *Chronicle* compiled at St Augustine's does not mention the Worcester riot. That we know so much of this incident is due to the local traditions preserved in John's *Chronicle*; for the same reason the ravaging of Thetford is mentioned in the former but in no other version.

One of the last and most treacherous actions in Harthacnut's reign involved the last representative of the house of Bamburgh to hold the office of ealdorman of northern Northumbria, albeit in a subordinate capacity. Eadulf's family had been closely linked with the land that stretched from the Tees to the Tweed; the province that corresponded to the former kingdom of Bernicia, from the early tenth Century. Eadulf, the son of Uhtred of Bamburgh and Sige, had perhaps been a supporter of King Harold Harefoot. Elated by his victory over Duncan, King of Scots, he judged the time right to make his peace with Harthacnut. The first lord of Bamburgh of whom we have any record is another Eadulf who, according to

---

[169] J.W. pp.532-533.
[170] William of Malmesbury, GR Bk 2 ch 188 pp.336-337. 'He suffered a slur on his reputation and a loss to his popularity'.
[171] A.S.C 'D'; J.W. pp.402-403.
[172] A.S.C 'E' s.a 969.
[173] A.S.C 'C' 'E' s.a 986; Roger of Wendover, 'Flowers of History' s.a 983, pp.268-269; J.W. pp.434-435.

Asser, was a close friend of King Alfred. On his death he was succeeded by his son Ealdred. Faced with a threat from Ragnall, the Viking king of York, Ealdred obtained assistance from Constantine II of Scotland whose army was twice defeated. After the deaths of Ragnall and his brother Sigtrygg Ceach in 920 and 927, the latter's son Ólafr was expelled by King Athelstan, and Ealdred was able to resume his position as lord of Bamburgh until his death three years later. His son, Osulf, succeeded him, and his name appears in the witness lists of Charters of Athelstan and his half brothers Edmund and Eadred.[174]

When Eirikr Bloodaxe was endeavouring to make his escape at the end of his second period as King of York, it was Osulf who was responsible for his ambush and death on Stainmore in 954, and the next year, King Eadred appointed him ealdorman of all Northumbria; a position he continued to hold until his death nine years later. The relationship between Osulf and his successor Eadulf 'Evilchild' is unclear, although he obviously came from the same family. At Osulf's death Northumbria was again divided by King Edgar, and Oslac was appointed to York, while Eadulf 'Evilchild' retained Bamburgh. Eadulf's successor, Waltheof, would seem to have inherited the hereditary office by marrying into the family: his Scandinavian name would, as Stenton suggested, imply this,[175] and it is possible that he had married perhaps a daughter of Osulf's or of Eadulf's, which may be confirmed by the naming of his children and grandchildren, other than Uhtred, with the family names of Eadulf, Ealdred and Osulf.

Freeman thought that Waltheof may have held the whole of Northumbria at one time.[176] Some doubt exists on the date when his elder son, Uhtred, succeeded him. He was taking the initiative in 995 and by 1006 he was responsible for Malcolm's defeat, when the latter laid siege to Durham. Malcolm, King of Scots, had attempted to establish his authority on the Bamburgh ealdormanny and Waltheof was by this time too old to participate in military actions. The following year Uhtred was created earl of all Northumbria following the murder of ealdorman Ælfhelm. As we have seen, Uhtred was murdered by Thurbrand the Hold with the connivance of King Cnut. However, his brother, Eadulf 'Cudel', did succeed to Bamburgh, probably with Eirikr of southern Northumbria designated as his overlord. After being overcome by Malcolm II in 1018, he was supplanted by Ealdred the son of Uhtred and Ecgfrida, his 'first' wife. His period in office was characterised by tension and conflict between the two northern provinces, which had been precipitated by the murder of Thurbrand in revenge for the death of his father, Uhtred. Ealdred's own life was cut short when he, in turn, was slain by Thurbrand's son, Carl. By his second marriage Uhtred had two sons, Eadulf and Gospatric; Eadulf succeeded to the earldom and proved himself to be a capable warrior. According to Simeon 'he cruelly pillaged the Britons',[177] in his attack on

---

[174] Keynes, 'Atlas', Table XXXVIII; S 407, 425, 434; S 520, 544, 548 as high reeve in a Barking charter of AD 950 in Table XLV for Osulf see 'Dark Age Britain' p.195.
[175] A.S.E p.417.
[176] F.N.C.i note KK p.645.
[177] Simeon of Durham, 'History of the Kings', s.a 1072 p.143.

Cumbria. Duncan retaliated and was defeated and, elated by his success, Eadulf sought and was granted safe conduct to travel south to negotiate with Harthacnut. It is possible, as Freeman suggested,[178] that he and his followers had been amongst King Harold's foremost supporters in 1036, and in view of his successes against the Scots he probably thought the time opportune to secure his position. The fortunes of the house of Bamburgh are evidence that the family had a strong hereditary claim - either as high-reeve or as earl - to the province, whether acknowledging the King of England or of Scotland as overlord.[179]

Harthacnut's pledge of safe conduct was as unreliable and vindictive as his other actions. The *Chronicle* records 'And in this year also Harthacnut betrayed Earl Eadulf, although he had guaranteed his safety, and thereby became a breaker of his pledge'.[180] According to Simeon of Durham, it was Siward the earl of southern Northumbria who killed Eadulf.[181] As a reward he was appointed earl of the whole of Northumbria 'from the Humber to the Tweed'. This is not mentioned by either of the versions of the *Chronicle* or by John of Worcester, but Simeon is a primary authority for Northern affairs.

Earl Siward

Siward was a Dane; the *Vita Ædwardi Regis* says he was 'called in the Danish tongue Digera that is the Strong'.[182] Henry of Huntingdon said of him 'he was a very brave man, a giant in stature.'[183] As Archdeacon of Huntingdon in the early years of the twelfth century, he was in a good position to have heard stories and reminiscences of Siward whose earldom had at one time included Huntingdon. The name Siward was an English form of Sigwarth or the Scandinavian Sigvarðr.[184] The first record of Siward as the earl of the province based on York is in 1033 when he witnesses a charter of King Cnut's granting land at Patrington in Yorkshire to Archbishop Ælfric.[185] When he was appointed to the earldom is doubtful: Earl Eirikr last appears as a charter witness in 1023, which leaves a gap of ten years. Keynes tentatively suggested that his son, Hákon, may have

---

[178] F.N.C.i p.522.
[179] Eadulf d 913; Ealdred 913-930; Osulf 934-963; Eadulf 'Evil Child' 963-? 1038; Waltheof c 965-1006; Uhtred 1006-1016; Eadulf 'Cudel' Uhtred's brother 1016-C 1019; Ealdred, son of Uhtred and Eegfrida 1019-1038; Eadulf son of Uhtred and Sige 1038-1041; Eadulf's brother, Gospatric was killed in 1064. See 'Dark Age Britain' for contributions by Dr Ann Williams and Dr A. P. Smyth; also 'The English and the Norman Conquest' p.28 by A. Williams; and W.E. Kapelle, 'The Norman Conquest of the North' ch 1 pp.3-36.
[180] A.S.C 'C', 'D' s.a 1040 trans G.N. Garmonsway.
[181] Simeon of Durham s.a 1072 'History of the Kings' p.143, 'He was put to death by Siward'.
[182] 'Vita' pp.34-35.
[183] 'Historia Anglorum', Bk VI s.a 1054 p.204.
[184] F. Harmer p.572; S. Keynes, 'Cnut's Earls' pp.65-66.
[185] S 968.

succeeded his father in that capacity.[186] If this were correct, Siward would perhaps have become earl when Hákon took up his position as regent of Norway in 1028. Freeman suggested the possibility that Eadulf may have held the whole of Northumbria for a while during this ten year gap.[187] Unfortunately no charters are extant from 1026, when Hákon could have been the earl of southern Northumbria, until 1032, and there always exists the possibility that Siward may have been appointed to the earldom at any time after Eirikr's death. Alternatively there is a chance that he may have been the 'Siward thegn' who witnessed charters in 1019, 1024, 1033 and 1035 - except that by 1035 he had already taken up his position in the North. Apart from this 1035 charter, they all represent gifts of land by Cnut to his thegns Agemund, Orc and Bovi in Dorset.[188] This last charter of 1035 rules out the identification of this thegn being the future earl.[189] There is, however, a Siward who witnesses first amongst the thegns in a charter of 1032, Cnut's grant of land in Berkshire to Abingdon Abbey, which may be the coming earl.[190] That Siward did have connections with Dorset has been suggested from the lease of land to Edmund the Ætheling by the community of Sherborne.[191]

Myths and legends gathered about this giant of a man. A life of Waltheof, his son, which emanated from Crowland in the late twelfth century, makes Siward the son of Beorn Beresun. According to this romantic biography Beorn's grandfather was called 'Ursus' ('bear') and he came from the world of fantasy as the child of a white bear and woman of noble birth, which ties in with Thorgils Sprakaleggr's mythical ancestry and John of Worcester's genealogy. Apparently Siward was supposed to have furry ears, which lent some colour to a legend with its origin in the Northlands and had been brought to the Danelaw where it flourished.[192] Freeman quoted the mythical pedigree as '*Ursus genuit Spratlingum, Spratlingus Ulsium, Ulsius Biorn, Cognumentum Bereson, hoc est filius Ursi*'.[193] To seriously suggest that Siward was the son of Biorn Ulfsson, Earl Godwine's nephew, as this implies, and as W. G. Searle included in his genealogy of the Northumbrian earls[194] is not only chronologically impossible but also completely uncorroborated by any other evidence. It remains possible that Siward's father was called Biorn (Beorn), especially in view of the fact that he named his first son Ásbiorn or Osbeorn, but other details must remain in doubt. The *Vita et Passio Waldevi* speaks of Siward's sailing from Denmark and making his first landfall in the

---

[186] 'Cnut's Earls' pp.61-62.
[187] F.N.C.i p.646 followed by D. Whitelock in 'The Anglo-Saxons' ed P. Clemoes pp.70-88.
[188] S 955, 961, 969 and 975.
[189] M.K. Lawson, 'Cnut' p.187.
[190] S 964, see 'Cnut's Earls' p.65, 'the Siward minister who heads the list of thegns in S 964 [dated 1032] was perhaps a different person'.
[191] A. J. Robertson, 'A.S. Charters' No LXXIV pp.146-149 where a Siweard 'minister' witnesses second among the thegns, 'and all the chief thegns of Dorset' which Miss Robertson dates AD1012 pp.392-394; S 1422.
[192] Saxo Bk 10 note 102 p.190 and ch XV p.29.
[193] F.N.C. i p.768.
[194] 'Anglo-Saxon Bishops, Kings and Nobles'; J.W. pp.548-549.

Orkneys, where he killed a dragon which had been preying on animals and humans. Journeying on to London, where Edward the Confessor was king, he murdered a purely fictitious Tostig who was married to Earl Godwine's daughter, and in gratitude for this act, King Edward made him the Earl of Huntingdon in succession to the murdered Tostig.[195] In some way Earl Siward was related to Duncan I of Scotland: according to Fordun, Duncan married a kinswoman of Siward's.[196] Searle makes Duncan's wife a daughter of the earl and Ælfflaed named Sybilla, which is also mentioned by Freeman. Anderson considered that the King of Scots had married Siward's sister. A third alternative is that he married another of Ealdred's daughters, which would have made him Siward's brother-in-law.[197] That there was a relationship is substantiated by the fact that Duncan's eldest son took refuge at the court of the Northumbrian earl after his father's death in 1040, and Siward subsequently intervened against Macbeth in Malcolm's interest in 1054. The suggestion that Duncan may have married one of Earl Ealdred's five daughters is possible, as this would have enabled him to strengthen his own position by allying himself both with the Lord of Bamburgh and with the earl of southern Northumbria - as the son-in-law of the former and the brother-in-law of the latter.

Siward himself must have been married three times. His first wife, whose name is not known, was the mother of Ásbiorn or Osbeorn Bulax. As Osbeorn was old enough to be fighting against Macbeth in 1054 it is likely that he was born in the late 1020s or early 1030s. His nickname implies that he had already made a name for himself as a warrior of some repute. Siward may have followed Uhtred's example and put away his first wife when he was appointed earl of all Northumbria. In order to placate his new subjects he married one of Ealdred's daughters, as mentioned above. In addition it has been suggested that he may have given Gospatric, Uhtred's son, and the brother of the murdered Eadulf, some official subordinate position under him.[198] Furthermore, to associate himself more closely to the house of Bamburgh, when a son was born to Ælfflaed the boy was named Waltheof after his mother's grandfather.

His third wife was named Godgifu, who, we are told, was a widow when he married her. She is known to us as the donor of two mansions of Ryhall and Belmesthorpe to Peterborough Abbey.[199] She predeceased Siward, who came to an agreement with the Abbey to retain both manors during his lifetime.[200] There is also a record that 'Lady Godgit' gave land in Bamwell, also in Northamptonshire

---

[195] Printed in 'The Cultivation of Saga', C. Wright, App of Texts 25 pp.267-70 and pp.129-133.

[196] Fordun, 'Chronicle of the Scottish Nation' vol I ch XLIV p.179, 'Now Duncan ... begat of the cousin of Earl Siward two sons' trans W. F. Skene, 'Consanguinea Siwardi Comitas'.

[197] Dorothy Dunnot in her novel, 'King Hereafter', Genealogical Table.

[198] W. E. Kapelle ch 2 p.29.

[199] S 1481.

[200] P. A. Clarke, 'The English Nobility under Edward the confessor' p.69.

to the Abbey, and two manors in Yorkshire of Binnington and Conisbrough.[201] The name Godgifu was a common one in the eleventh century, and it is not easy to disentangle the various ladies who bore it. According to the *Liber Eliensis*, a widow named Godiva or Godgifu gave to the Abbey of Ely three estates in Essex named High Easter, South Fambridge and Terling, all of which had belonged to her late huband; in addition there were gifts to other ecclesiastical foundations. He is styled as an earl but not named. As this was during the time of Leofric's tenure as abbot, these gifts were presumably made in the 1020s. Another entry also states that a lady Godgifu gave to Ely Abbey land that she had inherited at Barking in Suffolk, and this bequest was made when her life was despaired of. All these estates are listed in King Edward's confirmation of privileges to Ely.[202] Joan Lancaster suggested the possibility that the two Godgifu's are identical, and that she may have been Lady Godiva of Coventry, Earl Leofric's wife – and further that she might have recovered from her critical illness. She rejected fifteen of the sixteen earls as likely candidates for the first husband and then advanced the name of Eilifr.[203] However, an entry in the '*Brut y Tywysogyon*' mentions that Eilifr was in England at the time of Cnut's death[204] and then returned to Scandinavia rather than stay in England where his future was in doubt.[205] Another more plausible candidate may be Sired, earl of Kent, whose name appears in Archbishop Æthelnoth's grant of land to Christ Church, Canterbury.[206] Admittedly, Leofric's wife originally came from the Danelaw but it seems more likely to have been the future wife of Earl Siward.

Siward governed all Northumbria for fourteen years. It is possible that Gospatric attempted to succeed his brother as Lord of Bamburgh, and that Siward initially met with some resistance to his appointment, which may have lasted as long as two years before the opposition was broken down.[207] He kept the turbulent north in order and extended the borders of his earldom into Cumbria, as evidenced by Gospatric's writ which speaks of 'the peace which Earl Siward and I have granted him' when speaking of 'the lands which were Cumbrian'.[208] For Siward to be in a position to do this he maintained a body of housecarls, and to meet the expense he was appointed to the earldom of Northamptonshire and later Huntingdonshire.[209] Siward and Leofric were to become Godwine's associates in the government of England during the coming reign of Edward the Confessor.

---

[201] C. Hart, 'The Danelaw' p.157, 165; 'The Early Charters of Northern England and the North Midlands' p.63 note 21; David Roffe, 'Lady Godiva, the Book and Washingborough' p.9, 10 and note 6.

[202] S 1051.

[203] 'Godiva of Coventry' pp.20-21 and particularly notes 6 and 8 on p.10.

[204] 'Brut y Tywysogyon', pp.22-23; 'Eilif fled to Germany'.

[205] S. Keynes, 'Cnut's Earls' pp.58-60 particularly p.60.

[206] A. J. Robertson, 'A.S. Charters' No LXXXIX pp.174-175 and p.422 dated 1036; reference to Godric in 'Cnut's Earls' p.76.

[207] 'Annales Dunelmi' s.a 1043 p.508; W. E. Kapelle ch 1 p.26.

[208] F. Harmer, 'Writs', Gospatric's writ pp.419-424, 531-536.

[209] W. E. Kapelle ch 2 p.29.

Encomium Emmae Reginae

It is clear that by 1041 opinion in England was hardening against Harthacnut. The *Encomium Emmae Reginae* was probably commenced when Emma was in Flanders, after Harthacnut had joined her there while they were waiting for an invitation from the English nobles to accept the throne.[210] It was completed sometime early in 1041 after Edward's arrival in England. The author was probably a monk of St Bertin at St Omer,[211] and was commissioned by Emma who wished him to write her interpretation of the events which culminated in her period of triumph. It was vital for her to distance herself from the invitation which brought Alfred to England and his death, and the author was also instructed to blacken the names of Harold and Ælfgifu; Harold was a 'usurping bastard', 'an apostate', 'a tyrant', his mother an unnamed concubine. The Encomiast's account of English history was hazy to say the least, or completely manipulated to present a picture which suited Emma's purpose. Her marriage to King Æthelred might never have happened; when Cnut married her, she is depicted as a virgin, the sons she had by Æthelred are represented as younger than Harthacnut, instead of living in exile in Normandy where they had been sent to be brought up by a relative.[212] Opinions are varied about the underlying purpose of the work: to Stenton it was 'a panegyric of Cnut';[213] to P. Stafford it was written as 'an apologia necessary because Emma recognised the need to counter alternative views'.[214] Sten Körner considered it political propaganda to assert Harthacnut's right to the throne, and to deny Edward's. He summed up by saying: 'Any political intention behind the propaganda could only be directed against a pretender to the throne'.[215] He pointed out that both Swein and Harold were dead; the sons of Æthelred by his first wife were also deceased. Of his sons by Emma, Alfred had been killed five years before. Only Edward remained, and he was at Harthacnut's court, enjoying some sort of position. The Encomiast had to stress that it was purely due to Harthacnut's generosity and kindness of heart that this was so; that oaths had been taken in support of Harthacnut even before he was born and that Edward himself was supposed to have pointed out to his mother in Bruges that the English nobles had sworn no oath to him.[216] One thing seems obvious: Emma's intense hatred for Ælfgifu and Harold outweighed every other consideration and the Encomiast was instructed to place the entire blame for Alfred's death on Harold, and in doing so allowed his readers to form their own conclusions on the part Godwine played. There is no evidence that Emma was trying to absolve Godwine because he had

---

[210] 'E.E.R' Introduction pXXI.
[211] A. Gransden, 'Historical Writing' pp.56-60; E.E.R, Simon Keynes Introduction to the 1998 reprint ppXXXIX-XLI.
[212] E.E.R Bk 3 ch 1 pp.38-39.
[213] A.S.E p.697.
[214] P. Stafford, 'Queen Emma and Queen Edith' p.249.
[215] Sten Körner p.68.
[216] E.E.R Bk 3 ch 8 pp.48-49.

remained loyal to her, as Raraty thought.[217] The earl had proved his innocence on oath, supported by 'the earldorman of almost all England and the greater thegns'. Harthacnut had tried to ruin Godwine, and had failed. Emma's Encomiast was in no position to question this verdict, and in any case with the king and his mother's popularity plummeting it was better not to antagonise further a subject with the public support and power which Godwine enjoyed. What does emerge is the character of Emma herself, which comes through as a vain, unscrupulous woman who was prepared to stoop to any depths to achieve her ends.[218] Emma had not long to enjoy 'the bond of motherly and brotherly love' - on 8th June Harthacnut died 'as he stood at his drink and fell to the ground with horrible convulsions and he never spoke again'.[219] The *Chronicle* 'E' version adds that it happened at Lambeth, the length of his reign in England, and that he was buried in the Old Minster at Winchester with his father. To this 'F' adds that Emma gave to the New Minster the head of the martyr, St Valentine, 'for his soul's salvation'. Harthacnut could not have been more than twenty two or twenty three years of age; his half-brothers and sister, Gunnhildr, had all died at an early age so perhaps his death was not completely unexpected. By far the most detailed account is to be found in John of Worcester's *Chronicle*[220] which explains that the occasion was the feast provided by Osgod Clapa to celebrate the wedding of his daughter, Gytha, to Tovi the Proud. It adds that the king appeared in good health and spirits as he stood drinking with the bride and other guests, when he suddenly collapsed and died (on 8th June which was a Tuesday) and that he was buried next to his father.

Osgod and Tovi

Osgod and Tovi were powerful landowners and both held the position of 'Staller'. Osgod's lands lay in the Danelaw and he witnessed charters as *'minister'* from 1026, mostly in first or second place in order of seniority. From 1033 until 1042 he always headed the list.[221] His name could be a version of the old Norse Ásgautr or the old Danish Asgot[222] which would imply that he was one of Cnut's Danish followers. However, there are reasons for believing that he may have been related to Theodred, the bishop of London in the second quarter of the tenth century.[223] According to Theodred's will[224] he bequeathed estates in Suffolk to an Osgot whose father, Eadulf, was related to Bishop Theodred. One of these, Pakenham, was later in the possession of Osgod Clapa[225] which would tend to substantiate this

---

[217] 'Earl Godwine of Wessex' p.14.
[218] A. Gransden, 'Historical Writing' p.59.
[219] A.S.C 'C' 'D' s.a 1042 'E' 1041/1042.
[220] J. W. pp.534-575.
[221] 'Atlas' Table LXX 2 of 2.
[222] F. Harmer, 'Writs' p.569.
[223] A. Williams, 'Dark Age Britain' pp.193, 223.
[224] D. Whitelock, 'Wills,' 1930 No 1 pp 2-5; EHD i 1955 no 106 pp.99-103, 510-511; P. Sawyer 'A.S. Charters' S 1526 pp.427-428.
[225] F. Harmer 'Writs' p.569; C. Hart, 'The Danelaw' p.210 note 19.

theory. From 1026 until his exile he seems to have exercised the authority, although without the title, of Earl of East Anglia[226].

While there may be some doubt regarding Osgod's nationality there can be none about Tovi's. John of Worcester calls him, 'Tofi the Proud, a Dane, and a man of influence'.[227] As his first signature to a charter was in 1018[228] it seems likely that he was one of Cnut's hearthtroop and had been with him during the conquest of England. From 1018 onwards he continued to witness regularly until 1042, often as high as among the first three names.[229] According to the *Waltham Chronicle* he acted as the king's standard bearer; he certainly acted on the king's behalf in a Hereford lawsuit.[230] He founded a church at Waltham to house the Black Rood, a cross which was discovered on his estate at Montacute, in Somerset. As told in the *De Inventione S. Crucis apud Waltham Historia*,[231] the finding of the holy treasure and its being conveyed to Waltham was accompanied by a miraculous train of events. (Probably the monks had hurriedly buried the cross and other valuables when a Viking raid was imminent many years earlier and when the community were slaughtered in the ensuing attack the whole incident was forgotten.) Tovi must have been advanced in years at the time of his marriage. He had a grown son named Athelstan who lost his inheritance; possibly he was involved with Osgod in the events which led to the latter's exile in 1046. A grandson, Esgar, who had reached maturity before 1066, had retrieved the family fortunes and was in possession of some of the estates forfeited by his father. There is reason to believe that Athelstan, before his fall from grace, had held the office of 'Staller', and, as Esgar and his grandfather Tovi certainly did, it seems likely that the office was hereditary.[232]

Freeman suggested that Gytha (Osgod's daughter and Tovi's bride) may, after Tovi's death, have married Ralph the Earl of Hereford.[233] Other suggestions have been advanced to rectify this. After Tovi's marriage to Gytha the pair gave generously to the church he had founded at Waltham, and the *Waltham Chronicle* says that they 'showered wealth on the church'.[234] It seems that Tovi did not long survive the wedding; he last witnessed a charter in 1042 and was acting as executor of a will in 1042 or 1043.[235]

---

[226] 'The Danelaw', Table 5.2 p.195.
[227] J.W. pp.534-535.
[228] S 951, 'Atlas' Table LXX 2 of 2.
[229] 'Atlas' Table LXX 2 of 2; S 951, 953, 955, 961, 962, 963, 964, 969, 970, 974, 975, 982, 983. The name Tovi is a common one at that period, but the likelihood is that most of these signatures belong to Gytha's husband.
[230] A. J. Robertson, 'A.S. Charters' No LXXXVIII pp.151-157.
[231] Translated and edited by W. Stubbs p.6; 'The Waltham Chronicle' p.2-23, particularly pp.7-12, 12-21.
[232] 'The Waltham Chronicle', ed 1. Watkiss and M. Chibnall, Introduction pp.12-13.
[233] F.N.C.i p.525, 776; A. Williams, 'The King's Nephew' pp 336-337, Table ii and iii.
[234] 'De Inventione', ch 12 pp.22-23, ch 13 pp.22-23; see also 'The Waltham Chronicle' quoted above.
[235] S 993, an Abingdon charter; S 1537, 'Will of Wulfsige', D. Whitelock, 'Wills' No 27 pp.74, 75, 185; A. J. Robertson, 'A.S. Charters' No LXXVIII pp.151-153, 400.

Harthacnut the King

It is difficult to come to an understanding of Harthacnut's character. Stenton recognised a streak of kindness, evidenced by his treatment of his half-brothers, Swein and Edward, and Harmer noted his grants to monasteries and gifts to the poor.[236] Henry of Huntingdon wrote of his ingenuous disposition and his generosity in providing four meals daily for the whole court, although Henry did say that any food left over from these sumptuous feasts was gathered up rather than allow any uninvited court follower to partake.[237] Yet his attitude towards his half-brothers was probably dictated more by his own deteriorating popularity than by fraternal kindness. His liberality to the church must be set against a charge of simony. Simeon of Durham related that Eadred extracted from the treasures of the church of Durham 'no small sum of money' and bought the bishopric from King Harthacnut.[238] The *Chronicle* scribe says 'He never did anything worthy of a king'.[239] His gifts to the poor seem strange in view of the enormous tax he levied to pay off his fleet and maintain twice the navy kept by Cnut and Harold, which must have made tremendous hardship for his subjects. John of Worcester wrote of a 'tribute so heavy that scarcely anyone could pay it'.[240] Henry of Huntingdon's remark about his amiable temperament seems to contrast strangely with the vindictive streak in his nature which ordered Harold's body to be dug up and thrown into a marsh. Perhaps Freeman summed up Harthacnut's character most aptly when he wrote: 'But all his recorded acts set before us a picture of a rapacious, brutal and bloodthirsty tyrant.'[241]

---

[236] 'A.S.E' p.422; F. Harmer. 'Writs' p.563.
[237] 'Historia Anglorum', s.a 1040 Bk VI pp.200-201.
[238] Simeon, 'History of the Church of Durham', ch XLIV p.680.
[239] A.S.C 'C' s.a 1040.
[240] J.W. pp.530-531.
[241] F.N.C.i p.507.

Table 6. Sequence of Events 1034 - 1042

1034 Autumn	Magnus brought back from Russia; proclaimed King
1039	Peace Treaty between Harthacnut and Magnus at the Götha river.
1039 (Late in year)	Harthacnut joins Emma in Flanders
1040 March 17	Death of King Harold.
1040	Invitation sent to Harthacnut from England.
1040 June 17	Harthacnut and Emma arrive at Sandwich. Proclaimed King. Harold's body disinterred; Godwine and Lyfing accused of complicity in Alfred's death. Lyfing deprived of the see of Worcester. Godwine clears himself on oath. Makes the gift of a warship to the King.
1041	Collection of Heregeld
1041 May 4	Rioting at Worcester; two housecarles killed. Arrival of Edward from Normandy. Encomium Emmae completed. Lyfing restored to the see of Worcester. Eadulf of Bamburgh murdered at Harthacnut's court. Siward appointed to northern Northumbria.
1041 November 12 – 17	Harrying of Worcester.
1042 June 8.	Death of Harthacnut

7. The Premier Earl

Godwine's Offspring

By 1043 it seems likely that all except one or two of Godwine and Gytha's children had been born. Swegn, Harold, Tostig, Gyrth and Gunhild were undoubtedly amongst the earlier members of the family. They were all born during the lifetime of King Cnut while Leofwine, Wulfnoth and Ælfgifu were born later. Swegn and Harold were named after Cnut's sons and Gunnhild after his daughter. Tostig and Gyrth, or their Danish equivalents, Toste and Gyrd, were popular names in Denmark, and Wulfnoth was obviously called after his paternal grandfather. Ælfgifu was a favoured name with the royal house of Wessex: the first wife of King Edmund I and the mother of Eadwig and Edgar was called Ælfgifu, as was Eadwig's wife. It is even possible that Godwine's daughter may have been named after Emma's rival as it must be remembered that their two families had a great deal in common in the closing years of King Æthelred's reign; both had suffered from the same web of treachery and intrigue. Ælfgifu of Northampton was related in some way to Earl Leofric of Mercia and it has been suggested that Leofwine may have been called after Leofric's father[1] - nor is this an unreasonable assumption; Godwine and Leofwine were both adherents of the Ætheling Æthelstan; there is no evidence that hostility existed between Godwine and Leofric, and on several occasions it was the latter who advised moderation when the king and his counsellors were in favour of drastic action against the earl of Wessex.

Freeman considered Eadgyth the eldest of all Godwine's children[2] and the *Vita Ædwardi Regis* also speaks of her as 'the eldest of the daughters'.[3] Eadgyth (or Eadgytha) is an Anglo-Saxon name and it can be objected that this does not agree with the theory that the older children were all given Danish names. On the other hand there is the likelihood that Eadgyth may originally have been called Gytha after her mother. Indeed, Snorri recorded in the *Saga of St Olafr* that 'Gyda was the name of their daughter who was married to the English King';[4] in the *Saga of Harald the Stern* he wrote: 'King Edward's wife was Gyda, a daughter of Earl Godwin, the son of Ulfnad'.[5] It is probable that her original name was Gytha, the English rendering of Gyda, and that it was changed to Eadgyth on her marriage to King Edward. Eadgyth was educated at Wilton, a nunnery closely linked to royalty. It was to Wilton that Wulfthryth, King Edgar's first wife, retired as a nun, and where eventually she became its abbess. Her daughter, St Edith, found sanctuary there as years earlier had Ælfflaed, ealdorman Æthelfrith's sister, when

---

[1] Ian Walker, 'Harold' p.12.
[2] F.N.C. ii App note 'F' 1st ed p 552; 2nd p 555; F.N.C iv, Note R pp 754-757.
[3] Vita pp 22 -23 (Osbert of Clare c4)
[4] St Olaf's Saga, ch CLXII p.312
[5] Saga of Harald the Stern, ch LXXV p.219.

Edward the Elder divorced her.[6] It was at Wilton that Eadgyth learnt to excel at embroidery, spinning, languages, poetry and prose. According to the *Vita Ædwardi*, which it must be remembered was likely to be somewhat biased, Eadgyth was of ineffable beauty, gracious, inferior to none, superior to all.[7]

Godwine's eldest son, and arguably his oldest child, was the first of the family to enter public life: Swegn, of all the earl's children, most closely displayed the wild, irresponsible streak inherited from his Scandinavian forbears, a trait reminiscent of his uncle Úlfr. He must have caused his parents much heartache and sadness. According to the Worcester monk, Hemming, he claimed that his real father was King Cnut. This his mother vigorously denied on oath, supported by many ladies of the nobility.[8] Hemming may have been prejudiced; Swegn had appropriated two manors which rightfully belonged to the church of Worcester. There just may have been some sinister forces at work to explain his subsequent behaviour in connection with Leominster.[9] Even so, it is difficult to escape the conviction that his conduct was both wild and violent.

Another son, Hákon, is known to history as one of the hostages given to King Edward either in 1051, or according to Eadmer in 1052.[10] Dr Lappenberg identified him with the Jarl Hákon who, in the year 1075, entered the Humber with a Danish fleet captained by Cnut Sweinsson. Avoiding conflict, they looted St Peter's Church in York, carried off all the booty they could collect, and made their way back to Flanders.[11] Amongst the slain was Jarl Hakon's son. Freeman rejected this identification, pointing out that if Hákon was born in ca. 1047 he was hardly likely to have a son of an age implied in the *Chronicle* entry.[12] However, this assumes that Hákon was the son of the abbess Eadgifu, but with a distinctly Scandinavian name it is more likely that, as Professor Barlow pointed out, he was the child of an earlier affair.[13] This could mean that Hákon was born as early as c1040-1042, and his participation in the raid of 1075 would at least be chronologically possible. Gaimar mentioned another son of Swegn's, named Tostig, who came with Harold's sons, Godwine and Edmund, to the west country in 1068. The 'D' version of the *Chronicle* records under the years 1067 and 1068, 'Harold's sons came'. John of Worcester named them Godwine, Edmund and Magnus. Geoffrey Gaimer, writing in the third decade of the twelfth century, preserved many traditions unrecorded in other sources but his statement that Swegn had a son called Tostig is not corroborated by any other writer.[14]

---

[6] P. Stafford, 'Queens, Concubines and Dowagers' pp.32, 179, 180.
[7] Vita pp 22 -23 (Osbert of Clare c4)
[8] Hemming pp.275-276; F.N.C ii p xxxiii. It is however only fair to say that this is not mentioned in any other source. A. Williams, 'Spoliation of Worcester' pp 386-406.
[9] P. Stafford, 'Queen Emma and Queen Edith' pp.138-139.
[10] 'Historia Novorum' p.7.
[11] A.S.C 'D' s.a 1076 recte 1075; 'E' s.a 1075.
[12] F.N.C. IV pp.585-586 and note 5.
[13] F. Barlow, 'Edward' p.303.
[14] 'L'Estoire des Engleis', lines 5399-5403.

Genealogy of Godwine's Descendants

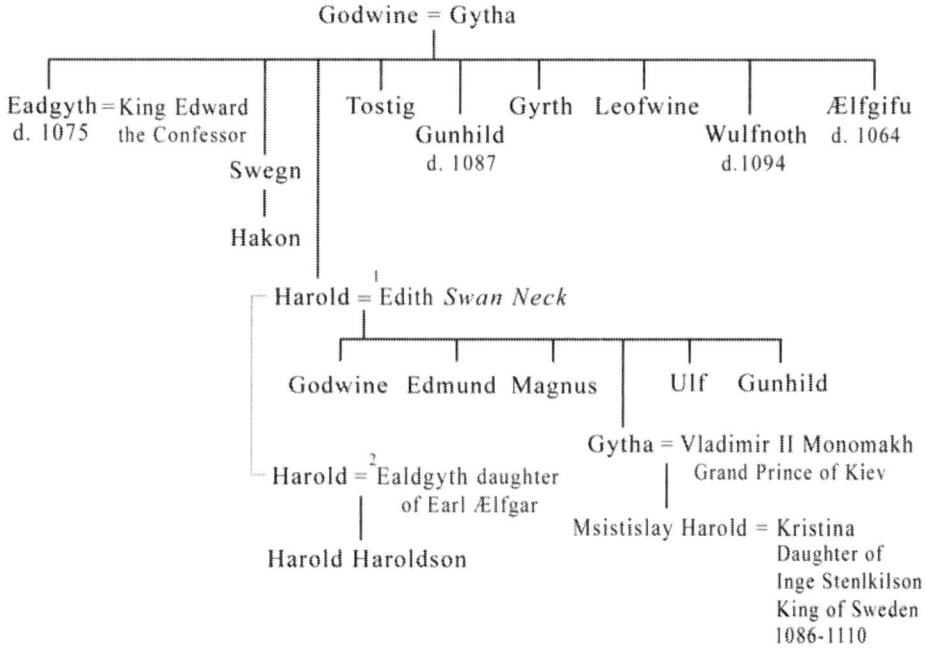

```
                              Godwine = Gytha
    ┌──────────────┬──────────┬─────────┬────────┬─────────┬──────────┐
Eadgyth=King Edward  Tostig   Gyrth  Leofwine           Ælfgifu
d. 1075  the Confessor         Gunhild              Wulfnoth   d. 1064
              │                d. 1087              d. 1094
            Swegn
              │
            Hakon
              │
         Harold = Edith Swan Neck
    ┌────────┬────────┬─────────┬─────────┐
  Godwine  Edmund  Magnus      Ulf    Gunhild
                            Gytha = Vladimir II Monomakh
   Harold =² Ealdgyth daughter        Grand Prince of Kiev
            of Earl Ælfgar                │
              │                   Msistislav Harold = Kristina
         Harold Haroldson                      Daughter of
                                               Inge Stenlkilson
                                               King of Sweden
                                               1086-1110
```

Information from - Ian Walker
The Last Anglo-Saxon King, p. 194-195
Sutton Publishing 1997

Godwine's second son, Harold, was destined to become the most famous member of the family. The author of the *Vita Ædwardi Regis* describes Harold as standing forth among people like a second Judas Maccabeus, a true friend of his race and country, walking in patience and mercy and with kindess to men of goodwill. He was also endowed with mildness of temper, could bear contradiction well, and was generous and brave.[15] He first appears on the witness lists as '*nobilis*' to an Exeter charter of 1044,[16] then as '*minister*' in two Westminster charters of 1045.[17] The earliest dated and authentic royal charter in which Harold witnesses as '*dux*' belongs to 1045,[18] but he does appear with the title of earl as a witness to a will of Thurstan, the son of Wine. Thurstan made bequests of land in Essex, Norfolk,

---

[15] Vita pp 48 -49; F Harmer 'Writs' p 563.
[16] S 1003; F. Harmer, 'Writs' p 563; 'Atlas' Table LXXIV.
[17] S 1007, 1012; F.Harmer, 'Writs' p.563; Atlas Table LXXIV
[18] S 1008, Harmer, 'Writs' p 563; 'Atlas' table LXXIV.

Suffolk and Cambridgeshire to ecclesiastical foundations, to his wife, his heriot to the king, and half a mark of gold to Earl Harold and to Bishop Stigand. Dorothy Whitelock dated the will not later than 1044 when Leofstan, the Dean, a witness to the will, was appointed an Abbot.[19] Professor Stafford associated the Harold who witnessed three charters of 1032 and 1033 as Godwine's son.[20] In view of the fact that his birth has been variously dated from 1022 to 1026, this seems extremely unlikely. The Harold who witnessed in the 1030s was possibly Thorkell's son of the same name, whom Cnut had fostered, and who later became an earl and was witnessing as such in 1042.[21]

Gunhild's existence is verified by the *Exon Domesday* which records '*Gunnhilla, filia comitas Godwini*'. She held land in Somerset and Sussex.[22] Two manors in her possession in Somerset were valued at £22-0-0 and in Sussex Gunhild held 7 hides.[23] She too was educated at Wilton and from her youth dedicated her life to the church. We learn something of her character from an inscription on a leaden plate which was found by workmen doing repairs in the church of St Donatius in Bruges, where she was buried, in 1087. The inscription says that while 'still a young maiden ... she declined the advances of several noble princes'. It records her 'gay, modest disposition towards her servants', 'she was kind and equitable towards strangers', and that she 'denied herself delicacies and meat and wore a hard hair cloth'.[24] After the Conquest of 1066 she had fled from England with her mother, first to the island of Flatholme,[25] and thence to seek sanctuary at St Omer. Later she journeyed to Denmark where her cousin, King Swein, gave her a kindly welcome. Her last years were spent in Bruges where she was remembered for her gifts to the church of St Donatius which included the mantle of St Brigit of Kildare, and a psalter decorated with Anglo Saxon artistry, which became known as *Gunnhild's Psalter*.[26] She died peacefully on 26th August, 1087, a fortnight before the Conqueror lay dying in agony near Rouen.[27]

Tostig, Godwine's third son, first appears as a witness to an Abingdon charter of 1043 where he and his brother, Leofwine, sign low down on the list. The following year they and Harold are styled as '*nobilis*'. Unlike Swegn, Tostig was outwardly pious, liberal in gifts to the church, but hasty and irresponsible. He was courageous, wise, shrewd, but perhaps overzealous in stamping out evil, and

---

[19] S 1531, D. Whitelock, 'Wills' No XXI pp.80-85, 192-197;
[20] Prof Stafford, 'Queen Emma and Queen Edith' pp.256-257 and note 9; S 964, 965, 968, 'Atlas' Table LXX.
[21] Harold Thorkell's son not Godwine's; see S. Keynes, 'Cnut's Earls' p.66
[22] D. B. Somerset, Phillimore No 8 ed Caroline and Frank Thorn; Sussex No 2 ed John Morris.
[23] Somerset 1.24, Hardington 10 hides; Creech 1.18 10½ hides; Claverham 5.17 2 hides; Sussex 13.29 7 hides in Kingston.
[24] H. Ellis, Introduction to D.B. vol ii pp.136-137.
[25] A.S.C 'D' s.a 1067.
[26] I. Walker, 'Harold' p.35.
[27] O.V. IV Bk VII p.100-101.

inclined to be secretive. He was also generous, chaste and devoted to his wife.[28] In 1051, Tostig was married to Judith, the daughter of Baldwin IV, the Count of Flanders, and the half-sister of Baldwin V. Their sons - if Judith was their mother - would not have been more than fourteen and thirteen in 1066, if as old as that. Their names, Skule and Ketel, were distinctly Norse, and the question arises whether Tostig had a previous relationship. According to Scandinavian tradition, Skule and Ketel Krok both accompanied Ólafr Haraldsson back to Norway from the Orkney Isles when the defeated remnants of the Norwegian army returned home after their disastrous defeat at Stamford Bridge, when Ólafr was proclaimed king in succession to his father Haraldr Harðráða. Ketel Krok lived in the north of the country where he married and settled. Skule was adopted by Ólafr, married the king's relative, Gudron, and founded a noble family.[29]

After sketching in the characters of Harold and Tostig the author of the *Vita Ædwardi* remarks: 'Also the king did not suffer their younger brother, Gyrth, of whom we spoke before, to be left out of the honours, but gave him a shire at the extremity of East Anglia, and promised to increase this when he was older and had thrown off his boyhood years'.[30] This implies that before his appointment as earl of East Anglia in 1057, he held a subordinate position, either under Harold during the years 1044-1051 and September 1052-April 1053, or less probably under Ælfgar from 1053 until 1057. His name was attached to the witness list of the doubtful Ghent charter, possibly one of Osbert of Clare's forgeries.[31] His signature does not appear again until 1059. It is surprising that no genuine extant charter includes Gyrth's name either as thegn or '*nobilis*', and there is no evidence of his presence at court or of his public participation until he became earl.

It is possible that as children Tostig, Gyrth and Leofwine may have lived with Eadgyth as members of the royal household.[32] The first mention of Gyrth in the *Chronicle* is in 1051 when he, with his father and brothers, Swegn and Tostig sought refuge in Flanders.[33] John of Worcester recorded that he was with his brothers, Harold and Tostig, when their father collapsed on Easter Monday 1053 and assisted his brothers in carrying Godwine into the King's chamber.[34] In 1061 he accompanied Bishop Ealdred, Tostig and Countess Judith on the journey to Rome.[35] He possessed lands and manors in Bedfordshire, Berkshire, Cambridgeshire, Hampshire, Hertfordshire, Norfolk, Suffolk and Sussex.[36] Even

---

[28] Tostig Vita pp 48 -49, 50-51
[29] 'Saga of Harald The Stern' ch xcviii
[30] Vita pp 50 -51.
[31] Chaplias, 'The Original Charters of Herbert and Gervase, Abbots of Westminster' in 'A Medieval Miscellany' for D. M. Stenton pp.92-95.
[32] F. Barlow, 'Edward' pp.163 - 164.
[33] A.S.C 'C' s.a 1051, 'D' 1052/1051; J.W pp.560-561
[34] J.W. pp.572-573. A.S.C omits Gyrth.
[35] Vita pp 52 – 53.
[36] Ellis, 'Introduction to D.B. vol II pp.133-134; Phillimore, Index to Persons no37.

so, his landed holdings amounted to less than his brother, Leofwine's.[37] Gyrth was the youngest of Godwine's sons with a Danish name and was, no doubt, born before Cnut's death. He certainly did not lack courage, initiative or loyalty when the English army prepared to meet the Norman invaders in October 1066.[38]

Leofwine witnesses for the first time as *'nobilis'* in 1049 - if we disregard the spurious Ghent Charter already mentioned[39] - and as a thegn in 1050 and 1054. His first signature with the style of earl comes in 1059.[40] Leofwine joined Harold when the earl made his escape to Ireland, which would indicate that he was probably born soon after 1035. This tends to bear out the assumption that the boy was named as a sort of declaration of the bond that had existed (and still did) between the families of Godwine and Leofric. It meant a great deal in 1036 when Leofric was championing the cause of Harold Harefoot and Godwine was prepared to do likewise.

The youngest son, Wulfnoth, was given as one of the hostages to the king in 1051 or 1052. According to Eadmer they were sent to Normandy 'to the guardianship of Duke William.'[41] Simeon of Durham, writing of William's dying speech, says: 'Wulfnoth, the king's brother, whom he had detained in captivity from childhood'.[42] Sir Henry Ellis identified 'Ulfnod' with Wulfnoth; this 'Ulfnod' held land in Kent, Sussex and Hampshire.[43] A 'Young Wulfnoth' or 'Wulfnoth Cild' held land in Kent,[44] but whether either of them was Godwine's youngest son is doubtful. William of Malmesbury tells us that in the Conqueror's reign Wulfnoth was kept in chains at Salisbury,[45] and Orderic says that he died an old man there.[46] He could not have been much older than twelve when he was taken to Normandy to languish in a Norman prison. On William's death, he was released for a few weeks and then taken back to England by William Rufus to be cast into prison again.[47] According to Orderic he 'feared God and lived according to His laws, confessing the true faith'. That he became a monk, as Orderic implied, may possibly be true. He died in AD 1094.[48]

Godwine's youngest daughter was Ælfgifu. In the Domesday Survey she is referred to as *'Ælueua soror Haroldi comitis'*.[49] She held land in

---

[37] P.A. Clarke, 'The English Nobility under Edward the confessor'; Leofwine, £588, Gyrth £250.
[38] Wace; Gyrth at Senlac v 68 93-70 50.
[39] S 1003 AD 1044; Atlas LXXIV, LXXV.
[40] S 1027, Atlas, table LXXIV.
[41] 'Historia Novorum' p.7.
[42] 'History of the Kings' s.a 1087 p.154.
[43] 'Introduction to D.B.' vol II p.21 and note 1.
[44] Wulfnoth 'cild' Dom Monachorum 2-31 86.
[45] G.R. ch 200 pp 362-363.
[46] O.V. volume II Bk 3 pp.178-179.
[47] J.W. volume III s.a 1087 pp.46-47; Wulfnoth, 'whom he kept in custody from childhood'.
[48] F. Barlow, 'William Rufus' pp.65, 66; I. Walker, 'Harold' pp.196,197.
[49] D.B i p.309.

Buckinghamshire. Freeman suggested that if Harold's ill-fated stay in Normandy in 1064 had started off as a yachting trip, Ælfgifu might have accompanied him, and was possibly the Ælviva of the Bayeux Tapestry.[50] Simeon of Durham related, on the occasion of Harold's oath, that William stipulated: 'If amongst other things ... that you will give your sister whom I may marry to one of my nobles'.[51] Eadmer, writing of the interchange of messages which are supposed to have taken place before the battle in 1066, has William remind Harold of the promise regarding his sister, and the latter replies, 'My sister, whom according to our pact you ask for, is dead'.[52] From this we may infer that Ælfgifu was of marriagable age in 1066 and that she had died between 1064 and the autumn of 1066.

The Norse writers credited Godwine with other children. Snorri Sturluson thought he was the father of Morkere and Waltheof,[53] as did the author of the *Knytlinga Saga*.[54] These may be regarded as errors; of more interest is the list of his children given by Orderic as Swegn, Tostig, Harold, Gyrth, Ælfgar and Wulfnoth.[55] Orderic refers to Ælfgar as a pilgrim and a monk at Rheims. In fact it was Ælfgar's son, Burgheard, who was connected with Rheims: he died there in 1061, returning from Rome, where he had gone in company with Ealdred, Archbishop of York, to receive his pallium from Pope Nicholas. Ælfgar made a number of gifts to Rheims in his son's memory: he sent a gospel book with an illustration of St Luke from the Gospels. In 1061-2 he gave the church a grant of land at Lapley in Staffordshire, and estates at Meaford and Hamstall Ridware, also in Staffordshire.

Ælfgar himself was the son, not of Godwine, but of Earl Leofric, whom he succeeded as Earl of Mercia in 1057. He disappears from the pages of history in 1062 after a troubled and stormy career. The charter evidence is of little value in recording his activities: he attests the Waltham and a York charter of 1065 but both of them are generally regarded as spurious. His son, Edwin, succeeded him as the Earl of Mercia, but again the charters he witnesses are of doubtful reliability. Two definite dates available are Ælfgar's support, with Harold's, for the appointment of Wulfstan to the bishop of Worcester which was ratified on 29 August 1062, and that Edwin was established as earl by 1065. Ælfgar was probably dead by 1062, after Christmas, when Harold marched his army into Wales and raided Rhuddlan, an expedition which would normally have been the responsibility of Earl of Mercia. It is improbable at all events that Ælfgar was living in 1063 when Harold and his brother Tostig invaded Wales by land and sea, causing Gruffydd ap Llewelyn to be slain by his own followers, for Gruffydd was Ælfgar's son-in-law, having married his daughter Ealdgyth. Had Ælfgar been living, he would surely have attempted to assist his son-in-law and ally.

---

[50] F.N.C iii note S. p 699; B.T. plate 17, D.Wilson, F.N.C.iii note U p.703.
[51] Simeon 'History of the Kings' s.a 1066 p 135.
[52] 'Historia Novorum' pp.7-8.
[53] 'St Olaf's Saga' ch CLXII p.312; 'Saga of Harald the Stern' ch LXXV for Mauro – Kaare; also Walter p.219.
[54] 'Knytlinga Saga' ch II p.34.
[55] O.V. volume 2, Bk iii pp.178-179.

Godwine's favourite son seems to have been the wayward and perverse Swegn. His repeated intercession on his son's behalf, even to the detriment of his family's interest, would seem to show this. Gytha probably favoured Harold; she offered his weight in gold to be able to give his body honourable interment. Eadgyth thought a great deal of her father but her mother is not even mentioned in the work that she commissioned - perhaps she wished to distance herself from her Danish relatives. Her preferred brother was obviously Tostig for whom she was prepared to contrive the murder of Gospatric, the son of Uhtred, Lord of Bamburgh, and his second wife Sige in 1064/1065. Among the brothers Harold and Leofwine seem to have a close bond; Leofwine went to Ireland with Harold when the rest of the family took refuge in Flanders; Gyrth accompanied Tostig and Judith on the journey to Rome. It is possible that Gunhild was Harold's best loved sister. He called one of his daughters after her, and the other after his mother.

It is necessary, at this stage to recognise that there is no evidence of any discord between Harold and Tostig - or Harold and Eadgyth - prior to 1064; the two brothers were co-operating in 1063 in the invasion of Wales. It is possible that the first signs of family strife came as a result of the murder of Gospatric at the king's court on 28 December 1064,[56] when Tostig and Eadgyth were guilty of co-operating in the crime. It was perhaps then that Harold realised that it was no longer possible to countenance behaviour every bit as treacherous as that of King Æthelred's henchmen.

The approximate ages of Godwine's children can be calculated to some extent by the dates when the sons were appointed to earldoms, to the names given them, and to the references in the contemporary chronicles. Freeman summed this up by saying that in 1043 Swegn and Harold were old enough to hold office; Eadgyth and Gunhild were young women; Tostig approaching manhood; Gyrth and Leofwine boys; Ælfgifu and Wulfnoth were babies. Professor Barlow, assuming that their parents were married in 1019, suggested the dates of birth as Eadgyth c1021, Swegn c1023, Harold c1026, Tostig c1029, Gyrth c1032 and Leofwine c1035.[57] If, however, we allow that Godwine's marriage took place in 1022-3 an alternative set of dates could well have been Swegn c1023, Eadgyth c1024, Harold c1026, Gunhild c 1027/8, Tostig c1029, Gyrth c1032/3, Leofwine c1036, Ælfgifu c1039/40 and Wulfnoth c1042.

The family home was Godwine's manor at Bosham, Sussex. The lordship had belonged to Cnut and was probably gifted to the earl. Situated in a creek in Chichester harbour, Bosham lay in the fertile coastal plain with the rolling Sussex Downs stretching back to the forest of *Andredesweald*. According to the *Chronicle* 'This forest from east to west is a hundred and twenty miles broad'.[58] The Romans had built two roads through the forest to link their city of Noviomagus, the

---

[56] J.W 598 - 599
[57] Vita p 4, 1st Edition
[58] A.S.C 'A' s.a 893/892; actually 90 miles according to P. Seaward, 'Pimlico County History,' Sussex p 76.

forerunner of Chichester, with London and Winchester, and these conveniently connected the manor of Bosham with the king's court. Christianity had come to the settlement, according to Bede's *Ecclesiastical History*, in the seventh century through the efforts of an Irish monk, Di'cul, who 'had a very small monastery, at the place called *Bosenham*, encompassed with the sea and wood, and in it five or six brothers'. St Wilfrid found the Irish monks there when he visited Bosham in AD681.[59] It was here that Cnut founded a church and here the king's eight year old daughter lies buried: she had, it is believed, been drowned in the mill-stream which runs alongside the church. Bosham was liable to flooding and Godwine had a stone hall built above the harbour.[60] It was in Cnut's church that Harold prayed for a safe journey before his ill-starred voyage in 1064; it was the manor house at Bosham where Harold feasted while waiting for a favourable wind.[61] Swegn took the hapless Beorn to Bosham in 1049; Godwine and members of his family left from Bosham in 1051 when they went into exile. Today, the harbour is silted up but the church where the Godwinesons worshipped is still there and is now the parish church of the Holy Trinity.[62] Walter Map relates the absurd story of how Godwine tricked Archbishop Æthelnoth with a play on the words 'Bosium', a kiss of blessing, and 'Bosium' or 'Bosenham', to which the archbishop replied in surprise, 'Me give you Bosium?'[63] Godwine had other manors in his vast earldom where the family dwelt when his official duties took him there. In Exeter the street named *Frierhay* had been called '*Irles Byri*' before the Conquest. This was probably such a residence for the earl and his family when in the southwest.[64] This is more likely due to its nearness to the church of St Olave of which the Earl's wife, Gytha, was a benefactor. We hear also about Gytha's reluctance, when the earl was in Gloucestershire, at eating any produce from the manor in Berkeley because of the destruction of the Abbey there, and Godwine's connection with it. Owing to her scruples, the earl bought an estate at nearby Woodchester from Azor when business took him to the shire.[65]

Edward the King

On Easter Day the third of April, 1043, Edward was crowned by Archbishop Eadsige with Ælfric of York assisting. Harthacnut had died almost ten months before. Although it was not unusual for some delay between the death of one king and the coronation of his successor, in this case it seems strange in view of Edward's position at his half brother's court. According to the *Chronicle* he had

---

[59] Quoted from 'A History of Sussex' by J.R Armstrong p 37.
[60] 'Harold and his England,' by Michael Phillips p 5
[61] BT Plate 3.
[62] 'The Norman Conquest, Sandlacu' p 10 by C.F. Barrs; 'Harold Rex' by J. Pollock p 2.
[63] 'De Nugis Curralum' V ch 3 pp 418-421 and p 418-419 note 5.
[64] J. Haslam, 'Saxon Exeter' in 'Anglo Saxon Towns in Southern England, Chichester 1984' pp.402-404; I am indebted to Ann Williams for this reference, 'The English and the Norman Conquest' p.20 and notes 91, 92.
[65] F. Barlow, 'The English Church,' p 58 note 5; DB Gloucestershire.

been sworn in as the future king.⁶⁶ Adam of Bremen wrote that the English had chosen Edward as Harthacnut's successor, and the Encomiast implied that he was recognised at the court as the heir to the throne.⁶⁷ Yet if William of Malmesbury is to be believed, Edward actually contemplated returning to Normandy and was only persuaded to accept the kingship by Earl Godwine.⁶⁸ That there was some opposition to his election is shown by John of Worcester who wrote that Edward's acceptance was 'mainly by the exertions of Earl Godwine and Lyfing, bishop of Worcester'.⁶⁹ The author of the *Vita Ædwardi Regis* corroborated this, stating that Godwine 'took the lead in urging that they should admit their king to the throne that was his by right of birth ...'⁷⁰

The delay in the coronation may have been due to claims put forward by others. There must have been many with Danish sympathies who looked to Swein Estrithson, one of Cnut's nearest surviving relatives: as Cnut's nephew and Harthacnut's cousin it would be natural to regard him as the successor to his two cousins. It could be, however, that Harthacnut had intended, if indeed he made any preparations for the succession, for Edward to succeed him in England and Swein in Denmark. He had appointed the latter as commander of the Danish fleet.⁷¹ Adam of Bremen stated that Edward suspected that Swein would claim the English throne and to appease him Edward promised to make him his heir even if he had sons of his own.⁷² In any case Swein's brother, Beorn, remained in England and in due course he was given an earldom, perhaps another attempt to mollify Swein. According to Adam, Ásbiorn (or Osbeorn), their brother, was also in England.⁷³ Freeman considered he also held an earldom in England.⁷⁴ He was banished, perhaps at the same time as the other expulsions, or as Adam thought, later after Beorn's murder.⁷⁵

Swein had returned to England after being defeated by Magnus Ólafsson to find Harthacnut dead and Edward chosen by the people as their future King. That Swein had a following in England is shown by the number of people who were banished after Edward's coronation. The following year Gunnhildr and her sons were exiled. Gunnhildr was Cnut's niece and her second husband, Haraldr Thorkellsson, had been brought up in England at Cnut's court. He had left England after Harthacnut's death to go on a pilgrimage to Rome and been murdered on the return journey by Duke Ordulf of Saxony, who had married the sister of Magnus - who desired his death presumably because of his relationship to

---

⁶⁶ A.S.C s.a 1041 'C' 'D'
⁶⁷ Adam of Bremen BK 2 ch lxxviii (74) p.108
⁶⁸ E.E.R BK iii ch 13-14 pp 52-53.
⁶⁹ G.R BK ii ch 196 pp 350-351
⁷⁰ Vita pp 14 -15
⁷¹ Adam Bk 2 ch LXXVII [74] pp 108 EER p.53.
⁷² ibid BK 2 ch LXXVIII (74) p 108
⁷³ ibid Bk 3 ch XIV [13] p.125.
⁷⁴ F.N.C. ii, p 63, 521
⁷⁵ Adam Bk 3 ch XIV [13] pp 125.

the Danish royal family. Osgod Clapa was another likely supporter of Swein's claim and with him Athelstan, the son of Tovi. Osgod was exiled and Athelstan's lands were confiscated. Thuri, earl of the Mid-Angles disappeared in 1044, but whether he was exiled, died or retired from public life history does not tell us.[76] The fact that Swein was engaged in a deadly struggle with Magnus may have influenced Godwine against the candidature of his wife's nephew: he may have considered it more expedient to send him aid when possible rather than to embroil England in a war with the energetic young Norwegian King.

Another possible claimant to the English throne, but one who had the disadvantage of being far away and out of close touch with events in England, was Edward, known to history as 'the Exile'. As babies he and his brother, Edmund, had been taken from the land of their birth. These sons of Edmund Ironside, the hero king, were either sent to Sweden with Cnut's instructions to have them murdered or taken abroad after their father's death in November 1016 by their mother.[77] Edward could not have been more than six months old when his father died; it is possible that he and Edmund were twins. Ólafr Skötkonung, to whom they were sent, had no relish for carrying out his ally's wishes, and according to John of Worcester 'sent them to the King of Hungary to be reared and kept alive'.[78] With three exceptions the Anglo-Norman chroniclers all followed John's version of the tale, and the *Chronicle* itself in a reference to the return of Edward simply says: 'This prince Cnut had banished into Hungary'. Orderic and Gaimer both thought the Æthelings were first taken to Denmark; the latter imagined that there had been a conspiracy to re-instate them.[79] It is difficult to detect any logic in this, unless it had been advocated by one of the Danish king's more turbulent magnates. Gaimer goes on to say that 'they passed Russia and came to the land of Hungary', but Adam of Bremen claimed that the princes were 'condemned to exile in Russia'.[80] In this version the Swedish king, reluctant to have the babies put to death, sent them for safety to the court of Yaroslav who was then the Grand Duke of Novgorod. He had married Ingigerd, the daughter of Ólafr Skötkonung and Ástrithr his queen, and had a reputation for providing sanctuary to refugees. Within two years he became the Prince of Kiev; the Kievan court was to be a haven for Ólafr Haroldsson when he fled from Norway in 1028, and for his young son Magnus. To Yaroslav, the English princes may have seemed like pawns in the chess board of European politics - useful if Cnut were defeated by the Swedish-Norwegian coalition. Yaroslav was a far-seeing monarch who saw the possibilities of marital alliances. He was to marry three of his daughters into royal families:

---

[76] A.S.C 'C' 1046 'D' 1047/ 1046, 'E' 1044/ 1046 for Osgod's outlawry; Thurri witnessed charters from 1033 until 1042, 'Atlas' Table LXIX and S 1228 Table LXXIV which constituted Æthelwine the Black's grant of land to St Alban's which is dated AD 1042-1049. If as Freeman suggested Beorn succeeded Thurri this would mean that the latter dropped out in 1044 or 1045. F.N.C.ii p.557, S1228; Atlas Table LXXIV.

[77] F. Barlow, 'Edward' p.217 note 1.

[78] J.W. pp.502-503.

[79] O.V. volume 1 Bk 1 ch XXIV; Gaimar lines 4497-4664.

[80] Adam Bk 2 ch LIII (51) p.92.

Elizabeth to Haraldr Sigurdsson, Anna to Henry I of France and Anastasia to Andrew of Hungary. He had a sister married to the king of Poland; three of his sons were married into German royal families and another, Vsevolod, to the daughter of the Emperor Monomakhus of Byzantium.[81]

It was at the court of Yaroslav that Edward and Edmund would have met Andrew, who was destined to marry Anastasia and to become the King of Hungary. In his country Stephen, the Duke of Hungary, had been recognised as king by Pope Sylvester III. The former married Henry II's sister, Gisela, which paved the way for closer ties with the Empire. Stephen was succeeded by his nephew, Peter, a weak and ineffective monarch who paid homage to the Emperor, Henry III, and Hungary became a fief of the Empire. A resurgence of national pride led to Peter's downfall; Andrew was recalled and acclaimed king.[82] Ronay conjectures that the English Æthelings met Andrew when he too was an exile at the Kieven court, and together they returned to Hungary in 1046.[83] Edmund, according to Lappenberg ,married Hedwig; the second daughter of the saint and King Stephen of Hungary.[84] He subsequently died and was buried in Hungary. Edward married Agatha, a daughter of Emperor Henry II's brother.[85] The Æthelings' sojourn in Russia and the time when they went to Hungary is pure conjecture: all that can be said is that it would fit in with what is known of European political history.

In the thoughts of all the English leaders must have been the threat hanging over the country, like a dark and angry cloud, of Magnus of Norway. His claim to the English throne was based on the alleged treaty he had made with Harthacnut in 1039 at the Gotha river. That the threat was a serious one is shown by Edward's presence with the fleet at Sandwich the year following his coronation in anticipation of the expected danger. The next year the fleet was mobilised again in readiness. It was thanks to Swein Estrithson, in furtherance of his own interests, that England was saved from invasion. Magnus was fully occupied in Denmark in 1043, although in 1045 and 1046 King Edward again thought it necessary to station the fleet at Sandwich. Apart from the hostility which the Danish element in England must have felt for Magnus, it is surprising that his cause may have had some support in this country, and from no less a person that Emma herself. According to the '*Annals of St Mildred*', speaking of Edward the Confessor it said: 'While he was reigning in peace like unto Solomon his own mother was accused of inciting Magnus, King of Norway, to invade England, and it was said that she had given countless treasure to Magnus'.[86] Ridiculous as the story seems, there are some reasons for believing that the charge may not be entirely without foundation.

---

[81] Gwyn Jones, 'A History of the Vikings' p 263.
[82] 'The Empire and the Papacy,' T.F. Tout pp 45, 61.
[83] 'The Lost King of England' p.71.
[84] J.M Lappenberg , AS. Kings volume 1
[85] F.Barlow, 'Edward' p.215.
[86] T.D Hardy, Catalogue of Materials' vol 1 p 381.

The most convincing proof that she was guilty of some doubtful design is to be found in Edward's first recorded action after his consecration as King. The *Chronicle* records: 'And in the same year, a fortnight before St Andrews' day, the king was advised to ride from Gloucester, and with Earl Leofric, and Earl Godwine and Earl Siward and their band came to Winchester and took the lady unawares'.[87] The 'C' and 'E' annals says it was because she had been too tight-fisted with him; 'D' says it was 'because she had been too strict with the king, her son, in that she had done less for him than he wished, both before his accession and afterwards ...', with which John of Worcester agrees.[88] It has been suggested that Emma may have been backing Magnus against Swein in Denmark to spite Godwine, Swein's uncle.[89] An alternative hypothesis is that the shock and disappointment of Harthacnut's death - and the irony of Edward's good fortune - was sufficient to induce her to toy with the idea of encouraging 'northern pretenders', without actually doing more, in order to provoke Edward. Other charges were to be brought against her.[90] On 15th November Edward found it necessary to ride from the meeting of the Witan at Gloucester, to Winchester. He was accompanied by his three most powerful earls with their followers; surely evidence of the gravity of the situation and the power that the dowager queen still retained. This contrasts strangely with the happy atmosphere portrayed in the *Encomium Emmae Reginae* of 'the bond of motherly and brotherly love of the mother and both sons'.[91] The most reasonable conclusion is that rumours had reached the Witan which were sufficiently grave to cause alarm and consternation; information which required immediate and drastic action. Later writers were to accuse Emma of having a sexual relationship with Ælfwine, the bishop of Winchester, and, as a result of her infatuation, she was unmoved by the death of Alfred and uninterested in Edward's welfare. According to Richard of Devizes, writing towards the end of the twelfth century, she was consenting to the death of Alfred and was even party to a plot to poison Edward. On account of this she was forced to clear herself by walking barefoot over red-hot plough shares to establish her innocence.[92] With Alisdair Campbell, it is advisable to regard these later accusations as 'mere foolish stories'.[93]

Three possibilities exist in connection with the accusation regarding Emma's involvement with the Norwegian King. Firstly, that there was no foundation in the charge at all; secondly, that she was prepared to use the vast wealth she had amassed to give Magnus financial aid in order to invade and conquer England in order to score against the son she despised and the earl she hated.[94] Thirdly, that in

---

[87] Quoted from E.H.D vol ii p.112
[88] A.S.C 'D' and 'C' s.a 1043; 'E' 1042/1043; translations from G.N.Garmonsway.
[89] J.W. pp.534-535.
[90] P. Stafford, 'Queen Emma and Queen Edith' p 251
[91] E.E.R ch 14 p 53.
[92] 'Church Historians' iv part 1 p 354; Annals of Winchester; P. Stafford, 'Queen Emma and Queen Edith' pp.19-22.
[93] E.E.R L, page cxxxii
[94] P. Stafford, 'Queen Emma and Queen Edith' p.251.

her fury and frustration she had indeed toyed with the idea, and that words spoken unguardedly had reached unsympathetic ears, and were then reported to the meeting of the Witan in Gloucester. If we accept John of Worcester's statement that Edward became king, 'mainly by the exertions of Earl Godwine and Lyfing, bishop of Worcester', it seems likely that being a stranger to the English nobility he was glad to avail himself of the support of the most powerful magnate in the country. There are good grounds for believing that Edward's marriage to Godwine's daughter, Eadgyth, was agreed at this time. To Emma, this spelt the end of her importance at court: she would be relegated to relative retirement in order to make way for a daughter of Godwine! It also meant that the earl, whom she and Harthacnut had attempted to destroy two years before, would become even more powerful and also a member of the royal family. She must have reflected on Edward's disinclination to help her when she had appealed to him in Bruges in 1039. Now, far from being reliant on her for guidance, he would be advised by the man who had withdrawn his support from her cause in 1036. What were the thoughts passing through Emma's mind that November? Emma had come to England in her early teens, the youngest daughter of Richard I of Normandy and the duchess Gunnor. At the time of their marriage King Æthelred must have been in his mid-thirties and had already fathered seven or eight sons and five or six daughters by one or more wives. Emma had come to a country hostile to the Danes from a duchy which made its ports and harbours available to Danish pirates. English people understandably looked on Æthelred's girl bride with ill-will. Within eleven years she was back in Normandy again, this time as an exile, with her husband and two sons. Months later the royal family returned to England, and Æthelred to his death.

Just over a year elapsed before Emma had married her husband's enemy, King Cnut. There followed a period in which she was Cnut's queen, her happiness marred only by the existence of Ælfgifu and her sons. After his death, there had followed a period of humiliation and exile until she returned in triumph with Harthacnut. Life had taken on a euphoric aspect then, like a cruel jest, her favourite son died in less than two years. Visions of a return to power faded. She could have been like another Eadgifu, presiding over the reigns of her sons, Edmund and Eadred, as the driving force behind the throne, with even more authority than she had enjoyed while her second husband lived. Thanks to Harthacnut's harsh taxation policy she had been able to amass a fortune which might still enable her to influence the tide of affairs. By supplying Magnus with financial support she would be in a position to assist him in the overthrow of Godwine's nephew in Denmark, humiliate the earl and his daughter, and teach Edward that she was still a force to be reckoned with.[95] Nevertheless, she must have realised that any hope of such a scheme was gone when the clatter of horses' hooves signalled the approach of a considerable company and she recognised her son, the king, with the three earls in the lead. Edward accused her of treasonable

---

[95] F. Barlow, 'Edward' p 76

conduct.[96] Her wealth, which constituted her bargaining power, was confiscated, her lands taken from her. Although her position was somewhat ameliorated the following year, for the last ten years of her life she lived in relative retirement.

Sharing in her downfall was Stigand, her confidant and adviser. His had been one of Edward's earliest appointments as bishop of East Anglia. It is possible that he was Emma's chaplain; he was witnessing charters as a royal priest possibly as early as 1027.[97] This continued until 1042 when he was assigned to the East Anglian see of Elmham.[98] The *Chronicle* records that in 1020 Cnut had a church built at Ashingdon in memory of the slain, both English and Danish, and gave it into the charge of 'his own priest, whose name was Stigand'.[99] Conflicting stories exist about Stigand: on the one hand he was accused of simony and of blatant pluralism; on the other, no scandal was attached to his private life. He was remembered by the churches of Ely and Winchester for his generosity. Some ecclesiastical foundations thought highly of him, others gave him a poor character. In this respect, the same could be said of Earl Leofric and many others. William of Malmesbury considered Stigand illiterate, but this is obviously not correct;[100] for years he was at the head of the country's administration and the Conqueror was glad to avail himself of Stigand's expertise until it suited him to dispense with it in 1070. His usefulness is demonstrated by the fact that King Edward reinstated him to the bishopric in 1044 and Stigand then went on from strength to strength.[101] Emma too was forgiven, up to the point that she was witnessing charters as the king's mother from 1043 until 1045, but this ceased completely after Edward's marriage.

During the next four years there is every reason to believe that the king and Godwine worked amicably together. The first instance of this occurs in the year following Edward's coronation, when Archbishop Eadsige became incapacitated and was unable to fulfil his ecclesiastical duties.[102] On this account he was forced to resign many of the responsibilities of his office. He is first heard of in 1024 when he witnessed as 'priest' King Cnut's grant of land in Dorset to his thegn, Orc.[103] The 'F' version of the *Chronicle* calls him a 'king's priest'.[104] In 1032 his name appears in a charter of an agreement concerning land and Christ Church, again styled as priest,[105] but by 1035 he had become the bishop of St Martin's,

---

[96] ASC 'C' 1043; 'D' 1043 'E' 1042/1043. 'The translation of St Mildred' in 'Catalogue of Materials' 1 pp 380 – 382; F.Barlow, 'Edward' p 58

[97] Stigand witnessing as royal priest as parly as 1027; ASC 'F' s.a 1026; Atlas LXVIII; S 979

[98] Stigand bishop of Elmham ASC 'E' s.a 1042/ 1043; J.W pp 526 -527.

[99] A.S.C 'F' p.155 note 9 s.a 1020, Swanton, 'Anglo Saxon Chronicles.

[100] F. Barlow, 'English Church' pp.79-80 I W.M. Gesta Pontificum' chapter 23 pp 25-26.

[101] A.S.C 'C' s.a 1044; 'E' 1043 / 1044 N 116 A.S.C s.a 1044 'E' s.a 1043.

[102] Eadsige incapacitated ASC 'C' 1044 'E' 1043 / 1044

[103] S 961; Atlas Table LXVIII

[104] A.S.C 'F' s.a 1038; see M. Swanton A.S.C p.161 note 15.

[105] Eadsige witnessing as priest S 961; Robertson, AS charter p 417 no LXXXVI,'To Eadsige their priest' pp 170 – 171.

near Canterbury.[106] It seems that Cnut had him earmarked as a successor to Æthelnoth, and with this in view Eadsige became a monk at Christ Church to prepare himself for the appointment.[107] When Æthelnoth died in November 1038 he was duly elected as his successor and in 1040 he went to Rome to obtain his pallium.[108] From 1038 he witnessed as Archbishop,[109] and once in 1045, but by this time he was already in ill-health. In the previous year he had appealed to the king and Earl Godwine to nominate Siward, the Abbot of Abingdon, as his co-adjutor rather than go through the normal procedure of a nomination by the Witan. It must be assumed that there was a special reason for this - either that the Archbishop felt that he could work more easily with Siward, or that there was someone who he feared might secure the position by bribery or by unfair lobbying of members of the Witan.[110] Siward started his ecclesiastical career as a monk at Glastonbury; in 1030 he was appointed abbot of Abingdon and witnessed charters as such in 1042 and 1044; from 1045 until 1048 as co-adjutor.[111] In this respect it is interesting to note that on one occasion both Eadsige and Siward affirmed the same document.[112] Eadsige resumed his position as Archbishop in 1048 when Siward retired in ill health, and died two months later.[113] In his frail condition Eadsige needed the powerful support of Earl Godwine to ensure that the rights of the church would be protected. In this capacity Godwine was rewarded with grants of church property which at the time were right and proper, but were to have repercussions in later years as a means of blackening his character.[114] It was at this time that the 'Third Penny', the earl's share in the revenues of Kent, which had been received by Archbishop Æthelnoth, was transferred to Godwine.[115] An instance of Godwine acting as an arbitrator involving the church is revealed in a charter of 1044 or 1045 which records an agreement between the abbot of St Augustine's, Canterbury, called Ælfstan,[116] and a priest called Leofwine in connection with the property of St Mildred's. Leofwine claimed that he had bought the land from King Cnut.[117] Earl Godwine settled the matter by arranging that Leofwine was to have two ploughlands and to receive 5 pounds of pennies at six monthly intervals during his lifetime, but at his death the estates and the money

---

[106] M.K Lawson, 'Cnut' p.149

[107] A.S.C 'A' s.a 1040.

[108] 'Atlas', Table LXVI, LXVII.

[109] A.S.C 'C' s.a 1044; 'E' 1043/1044.

[110] Eadmer 'Historia Novorum' pp 6-8, 'a bitter enemy of the church of Canterbury 'for he stole from that church the manor of Folkstone having first bribed Archbishop Eadsige.' The Early History of Canterbury' by Nichalas Brooks p 301.

[111] S 998, 999, 1001 and 1006 Atlas Table lxxiii and from 1045 until 1048 as co adjutor S 1011, 1471, 1010, 1012, 1007, 1008, 1009, Table lxxii.

[112] 'Alas' Table LXXII, S 1010 in AD 1045, S 1014

[113] For Siward see F.Harmer, 'As Writs' pp.571-572.

[114] A.J Robertson, 'Charters,' No cii pp.190-191, 438, 439 and p 420

[115] For Ælfstan see also F. Harmer 'Writs' p 550; S 1472

[116] A.J. Robertson, 'Charters' pp.190-191.

[117] A.J. Robertson charters cii pp 190 -191; S 1472

were to revert to St Augustine's. This was witnessed by Archbishop Eadsige, Bishop Siward and Earl Godwine.[118]

There can be little doubt that in return for Godwine's support, Edward promised that he would provide earldoms for the older members of the earl's family and agreed to marry his daughter Eadgyth. The opportunity came to carry out part of the agreement within the year. Hrani, who had been witnessing Cnut's charters since 1018,[119] had been invested with an earldom based on Herefordshire. His last signature on a charter was in 1026 or 1027 but he was still in office in 1041, which is proved by John of Worcester when recording the harrying of Worcester. He wrote that the earls ordered to take part were Thored, Leofric, Godwine, Siward and 'Hrani of the Magonsæte'. It is logical to assume that he either died or retired from office a short time later,[120] and that Edward availed himself of the vacancy to appoint Swegn as the successor in 1043. During the years 1043 to 1046 Swegn witnessed regularly, proof that he must have been frequently at court. Evidence for his authority in Herefordshire is provided by a charter recording the purchase of an estate in that shire by a Leofwine of land at Mansel from his kinsman, Eadric, with the 'cognisance of Earl Swegn, Bishop Athelstan and all the thegns of Herefordshire'.[121] According to John of Worcester his earldom in 1051 included Oxfordshire, Gloucestershire, Herefordshire, Somerset and Berkshire,[122] but his original appointment was probably confined to Hrani's area of jurisdiction only.[123]

Soon afterwards Harold received the earldom of East Anglia. There is no record of any earl for the province after the exile of Thorkell in 1021, although as mentioned earlier, Úlfr may have succeeded him as the earl of East Anglia and then as regent of Denmark.[124] It has been suggested that Osgod Clapa exercised the authority - but not the title - of earl from ca. 1026 until 1044.[125] It may well have been that Osgod's sympathies were already regarded with the suspicions that led to his exile less than two years later. Harold first appears with the title of earl as a witness to the will of Thurstan, son of Wine, dated 1044.[126] From 1045 onwards he witnesses as such; his first signature on a charter is to a Winchester document of that year.[127] His earldom comprised Norfolk, Suffolk, Essex and possibly Cambridgeshire. Beorn, the son of Úlfr and Estrith and the nephew of Godwine and Gytha, was assigned to an earldom sometime in 1045. He may have been taken as a surety of his father's loyalty in 1025 as Thorkell's son had been in 1023. It is possible that

---

[118] S 1472.

[119] For Hrani see A Williams, 'Cockles Amongst the Wheat' pp 6 -7: S Keynes 'Cnut's Earls' pp 60 -61

[120] J.W pp.532,533.

[121] Robertson charter No XCIX pp 186 187

[122] J.W. pp.558-559.

[123] Walker, 'Harold' pp 205, 213, 235 note 11

[124] Adam Bk 2 ch LIV [52] p.92. Adam refers to Úlfr as 'dux Angliae'

[125] C. Hart, 'the Danelaw', Table 5.2 p.195; F.N.C ii p.556

[126] D. Whitelock 'wills' No xxxi pp 80-85, 192-197; S 1531

[127] S 1008; others; for authentic charters he witnessed Atlas, table LXXIV.

he had been fostered by Godwine and brought up in the earl's household, which would explain why Saxo thought that he was Godwine's son.[128] He is not mentioned in the *Heimskringla* or the *Knytlinga Saga*, and this could be the reason that he is relatively unknown to Norse writers. His brother, Ásbiorn, was in England at some time: Adam says that he was exiled after Beorn's death and implies that he also held the rank of earl, the locale of which, if correct, cannot be established.[129] Freeman considered this correct.[130]

On 23 January 1045 Edward and Eadgyth were married.[131] William of Malmesbury, following Osbert of Clare, goes into raptures in extolling the purity of Eadgyth's mind and the beauty of her features.[132] It is likely that the other earls were in agreement regarding her suitability: Edward was a comparative stranger in England and he was imbued with Norman ideas and culture. He came to England accompanied by Norman friends. To wean him from his upbringing it was necessary that he take an English wife. As far as is known Leofric had no daughters - and Siward's (if he had a daughter) was possibly already married (and widowed) to Duncan of Scotland.[133] Godwine was no doubt anxious for the marriage, apart from any other reason, in order to curb the growing influence of Robert Champart who had been one of those who accompanied Edward from Normandy, and was his particular friend and intimate.[134] Eventually some jealousy may have developed due to Godwine's position as the king's father-in-law, but the fact remains that Edward was expected to marry into the English nobility in order to provide an heir to the throne and Eadgyth was the most suitable choice.

Reasons for Edward's hesitation and delay have been advanced. William of Malmesbury suggested that it was Edward's dislike of Eadgyth's family: the fact that Eadgyth was half-Danish and her father's advancement was due to King Cnut, who had defeated his own father, would have contributed to this.[135] He would also have harboured feelings of mistrust towards Godwine for what he considered the earl's part in Alfred's death, which must have been the more galling because of their mutual involvement, but that Edward did nurse such feelings is proved by his intransigent attitude in 1051.[136] However, at this stage Edward needed Godwine, and it seems that his dislike for the earl became more pronounced as Robert Champart's influence over him became more absolute.

---

[128] Saxo BK 10 ch xvii p 35 and note 125 on page 197

[129] Adam BK3 ch XIV (13) pp.124-125

[130] F.N.C.ii p.63

[131] A.S.C 'E' s.a 1043 for 1045; A.S.C 'C' 1044 for 1045. Not mentioned by A.S.C 'D' or JW.

[132] GR Bk 2 ch 197 pp 352-353;'Vita' pp.22-23.

[133] K. Cutler p.223; for Duncan 'Dark Age Britain', D. Alfred Smyth pp.106-107; for Duncan's wife 'Chronicle of Fordun' ch XLIV p.179.

[134] F.N.C.ii pp.69-70; P. Stafford, 'Queen Emma and Queen Edith' pp.259-262.

[135] GR ch 197; P. Stafford, 'Queen Emma and Queen Edith' pp 259-262

[136] F. Stenton, A.S.E p.425.

Delay of the marriage because of Eadgyth's age is a possibility, but Osbert spoke of her as the 'eldest of the daughters of the most illustrious Earl Godwin'.[137] It seems likely that she was born between Swegn and Harold, and would have been between twenty and twenty-three in 1045, although of course she could have been much younger. The most obvious reason for the delay was caused by the domineering influence of the dowager queen.[138] Until Emma had been relegated to relative retirement, the thought of the clash of personalities involved was a prospect Edward shrank from. Stories of Edward's celibacy and saintly chastity belong to a later date when the royal couple failed to provide an heir.[139]

Table 7. Sequence of Events 1041 - 1045

1041	Edward arrives in England.
1042 June 8	Death of Harthacnut.
1043 April 23	Edward consecrated King.
1043 November 16	Confiscation of Emma's property; Stigand's fall.
1043	Swegn appointed earl of Herefordshire.
1044	Eadsige resigns because of ill health; Siward appointed co-adjutor.
1044 late	Harold appointed Earl of East Anglia.
1045 January 23	Marriage of Edward and Eadgyth.
1045	Beorn appointed to earldom of the East Midlands.

---

[137] 'Vita' pp.22-23.
[138] K. Cutler 'Edith, Queen of England'. p.224
[139] F. Barlow, 'Edward' pp.82-83.

8. The Gathering Shadows

At the beginning of the year 1046 Earl Godwine was undoubtedly the foremost nobleman in England. His daughter, Eadgyth, was the queen; he had two sons and a nephew holding earldoms, and he held sway over the most prosperous province in the country. Yet in just over five years one of the annalists of the *Chronicle* was to write: 'It would have seemed remarkable to everyone who was in England, if anyone earlier told them that it should turn out thus, because he was formerly so very much raised up, as if he ruled the king and all England.'[1]

Two men were largely responsible for Godwine's humiliation: his wayward eldest son, Swegn, and the Norman abbot who accompanied Edward to England, the ambitious Robert Champart.

On 23 March 1046 the earl's old friend, Bishop Lyfing, died. Both Godwine and Lyfing had been charged with having been involved in the death of the Ætheling Alfred and had been acquitted. Both had worked for the accession of Edward in 1042, and both were renowned for their eloquence in the Witenagemot.[2] Lyfing had commenced his ecclesiastical life as a monk at Winchester. In 1024 he became the Abbot of Tavistock and witnessed an Abingdon grant as such in that year.[3] His uncle, Brihtwold, who had been the bishop of Cornwall from 1019[4] either died or retired in 1026 and was succeeded by his nephew. By then the diocese of Crediton included both Devon and Cornwall. He was promoted to the bishopric after he had accompanied King Cnut on his visit to Rome and been entrusted with the king's letter to his subjects while he travelled on to Denmark.[5] In 1038 King Harold Harefoot appointed him bishop of Worcester after the death of Britheah who died on 20th December 1037. After his reinstatement to the see of Worcester in 1041, the bishop leased to the thegn, Æthelric, land in Armscot in Worcestershire.[6] This was witnessed by Harthacnut, his mother and also Earl Leofric. During the years 1038 and 1046 Lyfing was responsible for leasing at least nine lots of land (and possibly as many more which had incomplete texts).[7] At Tavistock he was well liked and it is possible that the uprising of the people of Worcester in 1041 was partly due to a protest at the removal of Lyfing as their bishop.[8]

---

[1] A.S.C 'D' 1052/1051 M. Swanton p.176.
[2] A.S.C 'D' 1047/1046 for Lyfing; 'Vita' pp.10-11 for Godwine.
[3] S 961; Atlas, Table LXVIII.
[4] A.J. Robertson, A.S Charters' p.409; Atlas, Table LXVI.
[5] J.W. pp.512-513.
[6] A. J. Robertson, 'A.S Charters' XCIV pp.180-181 and p.427; S 1394.
[7] P. Sawyer, 'Charters' pp.393, 394 and pp.480-481.
[8] A. Williams et al, 'Dark Age Britain' p.173.

Later in 1046, Osgod Clapa was banished, who had been the leading magnate in East Anglia for twenty years.[9] The *Chronicle* gives him the rank of staller.[10] His signatures as a thegn, often in first place in order of seniority, continued until the year of his expulsion.[11] He held vast estates in East Anglia. Various reasons have been advanced for his exile, and it is possible that Edward suspected him of being a supporter of Swein Estrithsson's claim to the English throne. Freeman considered that Osgod may have entered Swein's service in his fight against Háraldr Harðráða, which would certainly agree with the reason for his exile and is substantiated by John of Worcester when he says of 1049: 'However, Osgod, having taken back his wife, whom he had left at Bruges, *returned* to Denmark' (emphasis mine). It is also possible that he may have resented Harold's appointment to the earldom the previous year and have acted unwisely.[12] He seems to have taken refuge in Flanders[13] where he was soon to be joined by Earl Swegn, Godwine's son.

Earl Swegn

Earl Swegn, after adminstering his earldom with apparent dignity and efficiency for three years, joined forces with the Welsh King of Gwynedd, Gruffydd ap Llewelyn, to carry out a raid in south Wales on the kingdom of Gruffydd ap Rhydderch of Deheubarth. On Swegn's part it may have been in retaliation for an incursion of the latter - they shared a common boundary - or in the hope of preventing a Welsh raid by a show of strength. Both the northern Welsh king and the English earl must have viewed with apprehension the growing power of Gruffydd ap Rhydderch. Swegn's alliance with Gruffydd ap Llewelyn has been regarded as an insult to Earl Leofric in view of the death of his brother, Edwin, at the hands of his ally at Rhyd Y Groes.[14] Further then, the Earl of Mercia would have been already annoyed that a Godwineson should have encroached on his sphere of influence. This does not take into account the practice of English magnates allying themselves with Welsh princes when it suited them. Leofric's son, Ælfgar, became not only Gruffydd ap Llewelyn's ally but also his father-in-law.

Gruffyd ap Llewelyn became King of Gwynedd (and possibly of Powys) in 1039. Almost immediately he secured his notable victory over a Mercian army in the vicinity of Welshpool which must have established his prestige as a formidable warrior. He next turned his attention to Hywel ab Edwin, the King of Deheubarth, whom he defeated and slew at the battle of Ystrad Tywi five years later, after a previous engagement in 1041, which Gruffydd had won. The battle at the mouth of the river Tywi left Gruffydd King of Deheubarth, but this was short-lived. The

---

[9] C. Hart, 'The Danelaw' p.195.
[10] A.S.C 'D' 1047/1046.
[11] S. Keynes, 'Atlas' Table LXXV 1 of 2.
[12] F. Barlow, 'Edward' p.88; F.N.C.ii p.90.
[13] F. Harmer, 'Writs' p.569; A. Williams, 'Dark Age Britain' p.193.
[14] N.J.Higham, 'Death of A.S. England' p.126.

following year the southern Gruffydd was successful in defeating his namesake and maintaining his hold over Dehaubarth for the next ten years.[15]

On Swegn's return from the successful raid in south Wales, laden with captured booty and elated with victory, he broke his homeward journey at the abbey of Leominster in Herefordshire and it was here that the young earl was captivated by the beauty of the abbess, who, according to John of Worcester, was called Eadgifu.[16] It has been suggested that Eadgifu, like many other abbesses, came of a noble family and that Swegn hoped to consolidate his position in the earldom by allying himself with her family and gaining control of her lands.[17] The Domesday returns for Herefordshire prove that Eadgifu and the abbey of Leominster owned a vast estate in the northern part of the shire.[18] However, this cynical view may not be justified: it is also conceivable that Swegn fell in love with her. The *Chronicle* says of Swegn: 'on his way home, he commanded the abbess in Leominster to be fetched to him, and kept her as long as it suited him, and afterwards let her travel home'.[19] It must be admitted that there is no hint of romance in this account, nor for that matter is there any suggestion of the earl hoping to gain any material reward from his actions. On the contrary, surely from a practical viewpoint his behaviour would have been calculated to bring down the wrath of the ecclesiastical establishment and of the king, but if he had fallen deeply in love with the lady perhaps he would have been blind to the consequences of his behaviour.

None of the other versions of the *Chronicle* mentions either Swegn's attack on south Wales or his abduction of the abbess. However, John of Worcester puts a different complexion on the incident: he relates that the young Swegn threw up his earldom in despair because he had been refused permission to marry Eadgifu 'whom he had seduced'.[20] Hemming, the monk of Worcester, wrote that Eadgifu was abducted by force, and that she was kept against her will for a whole year and was only returned because of the threats of excommunication made by both Archbishop Eadsige and Bishop Lyfing. He further stated that in retaliation for Lyfing's condemnation, Swegn appropriated some Shropshire estates. The manors of Cleobury North and Hopton Wafers with Maerbroc were claimed back by the church of Worcester.[21] As the attack on Gruffydd ap Rydderch occurred in the spring of 1046 and Bishop Lyfing died on 23 March 1046 it is difficult to reconcile Hemming's statement with the facts. In addition to this, Eadsige was incapacitated from 1044 until 1048. Barlow suggests the possibility that the earl and the abbess may have been related.[22]

---

[15] J.E. Lloyd pp.360-361; K. Maund, 'Ireland, Wales and England' pp.64-68.
[16] J.W. pp.548-549.
[17] A. Williams, 'Kingship and Government' p.104 and note 51; I. Walker, 'Harold' p.22.
[18] 'The Herefordshire Domesday', ed. A. Williams and R.W.H. Erskine.
[19] A.S.C 'C' s.a 1046 trans. M. Swanton.
[20] J.W. pp.548-549.
[21] Hemming pp.275-276; A. Williams, 'The English and the Norman Conquest' p.94.
[22] F. Barlow, 'Edward' p.91.

Another and more sinister aspect to the whole affair may exist. Leominster had been the home of a religious establishment which had its origin back in the seventh century. The charter which confirms a grant of land to the thegn, Ealstan, by King Edgar in 958 contains a reference to the boundaries of this ecclesiastical foundation.[23] The possibility exists that Swegn's disgrace may have been engineered in some way by Queen Eadgyth and the king in order to gain possession of the abbey and its estates.[24] The queen took over an existing sisterhood in addition to several others she possessed in the West Midlands. It is possible that Swegn and Eadgifu may have been manipulated by his sister and the king, and that the earl was at least in part the victim rather than the culprit. Hemming of Worcester presents a more malign picture of Swegn than does John, another monk of Worcester, or Ealdred, the bishop of the diocese, as later events will reveal.

In any case Swegn was not alone in this respect. In 899 King Æthelred's younger son Æthelwold had abducted a nun 'without the king's leave, and against the command of the bishops'. The lady had been a professed nun from Wimborne Minster in Dorset, and the prince had married her.[25] King Edgar, when visiting the abbey of Wherwell, became infatuated with one of the nuns named Wulfhilde; the abbess, who was Wulfhilde's aunt, actually encouraged the king's advances. To avoid the royal's unwelcome attentions she was forced to escape through the underground sewers of the abbey and King Edgar reluctantly transferred his affections to Wulfhilde's cousin, Wulfthryth, who became his second wife.[26]

It is true that these cases caused censure from the ecclesiastical leaders, but Swegn's actions were not unique and his desire to marry Eadgifu, coupled with the way that he left his earldom and possessions in England to fight in the Scandinavian war, seem to indicate that he had formed a real attachment for her. Leominster monastery was dissolved at a later date. In the reign of Henry I the foundation charter of Reading refers to Leominster's fate 'owing to its sins'.[27] At the time of the Domesday Survey there is a reference to an abbess who held that position in King Edward's time who was still in possession of Fencote, part of Leominster's estate, which was for her maintenance. The possibility that this may have been Eadgifu has been suggested by both Freeman and Barlow.[28] Domesday Book also records that the needs of the nuns were provided for.[29] It seems that the convent was suppressed soon after 1066; obviously it had been by

---

[23] P. Stafford, 'Queen Emma and Queen Edith', pp.137-139; S 677.
[24] ibid p.139.
[25] A.S.C 'A', 'D' s.a 901/899.
[26] P. Stafford, 'Queens, Concubines and Dowagers' p.32.
[27] ibid, 'Queen Emma and Queen Edith' p.138 note 217.
[28] F. Barlow, 'Edward' p.91 and note 2.
[29] For the nuns 1-10b belonging to the manor of Leominster; for the abbess 1-14, 1 free hide Fencote. The abbess held it herself before 1066. Queen Eadgyth held the manor of Leominster of 80 hides.

the time of the Reading foundation charters.[30] On the other hand, the survey seems to imply that it was still in existence in 1086.

After spending the winter in Flanders Swegn set sail for Denmark[31] in the early summer of 1047. Atrocious weather at the beginning of February of that year no doubt hindered his departure, and the *Chronicle* bears ample testimony to its severity. A hard frost had set in with the ground frozen solid; streams and waterways were a sheet of thick ice causing the deaths from the bitter conditions of cattle, birds and fish. Men and women died of cold and hunger. The wind veered north, bringing falls of snow heavy enough to break down trees that had not already been torn out by the roots by tempestuous gales.[32] Conditions were perhaps even more appalling across the Channel on the coastline bordering the North Sea. Meanwhile Swegn was enlisting mercenary crews with his father's encouragement and financial assistance, to offset the refusal of the Witan to send assistance to Swein Estrithson in his struggle for Danish independence.[33] When the thaw set in, Swegn Godwineson was able to set sail at last to aid his beleaguered cousin. At the same time it seems likely that the other refugee from England, Osgod Clapa, was preparing to gather a fleet of Flemish volunteers also bound for Denmark.

To understand the Danish King's predicament it is necessary to go back to the year 1042. After Harthacnut's death Swein Estrithson had made a claim to the Danish throne as King Cnut's rightful heir. As the son of Jarl Úlfr and Estrith, Cnut's sister, he was the next in line of succession. As far as is known Cnut had only one brother in addition to Estrith, and two or possibly three other sisters. His brother Háraldr was presumably the king of Denmark from the death of Swein Forkbeard in February 1014 until 1018 when Cnut travelled to his homeland the following year to claim the throne. According to the author of the '*Encomium Emmae Reginæ*' Háraldr was the younger brother.[34] However, this seems hardly likely: Cnut would not have agreed to his younger brother retaining the throne of his father while he was left to fight for England. There seems no doubt that Háraldr died without issue.[35]

Úlfr and Estrith had three sons: Swein himself, Beorn and Asbjorn. Of Cnut's sisters, Gytha married Jarl Eirikr of Hlathir who became the Earl of Northumbria; they were the parents of Hákon. An unnamed sister married Wyrtgeorn, King of the Wends. Their only child, according to the Norse sources, was a daughter named Gunnhildr who married first her cousin Hákon and, after his death, Háraldr, the son of Thorkell Hávi. She had two sons by her second

---

[30] 'Reading Abbey Cartularies' note 1; P. Stafford, 'Queen Emma and Queen Edith' p.138 note 217.
[31] A.S.C 'C' s.a 1046; J.W. pp.542-543.
[32] A.S.C 'C' s.a 1046 and J.W. pp.542-543.; A.S.C 'C' s.a 1046, 'D' 1048/1047
[33] A.S.C 'D' 1048/1047; J.W. pp.544-555.
[34] E.E.R Bk1 ch 3 pp.10-11.
[35] Niels Lund, 'Cnut's Danish Kingdom' p.28 in A. Rumble, 'The Reign of Cnut'.

marriage, Thorkell and Hemming, who would have been Cnut's great nephews. Another sister, Sanslave, is known only on the evidence of the *Liber Vitae of New Minster, Winchester*. Keynes suggested with great plausibility that she may be the unnamed sister who married Wyrtgeorn.[36]

Of the first generation after Cnut there was his nephew, Hákon, who was drowned in 1030; the daughter, Gunnhildr, whose second husband, Haraldr Thorkelsson, was killed by Ordulf, the duke of Saxony in 1042; and Cnut's own sons. Swein and Harold had died in 1036 and 1040 respectively, and Harthacnut in 1042. This left only the three children born of his sister, Estrith, and her husband, Ulfr Thorgillsson, of whom Swein was the eldest.

At the time of Harthacnut's death Swein was probably in his early twenties and had been acting as his cousins' naval commander against Magnus. According to Adam of Bremen the Norwegian king had, in spite of their treaty, invaded Denmark while Harthacnut was still alive.[37] The latter retaliated by sending the fleet which he had retained in England and the ships that could be assembled in Danish waters under Swein, who was defeated in a sea battle. By the time that he got back to England, Harthacnut was already dead. It seems from Adam's evidence that Swein and his two brothers were all in England during Harthacnut's reign, and that on his death Swein or his supporters urged his right to succeed to the throne of England. Following Edward's nomination, he left England determined to uphold his right as Cnut's heir to the kingdom of Denmark. Magnus, we are told, seized the Danish throne in 1042. One Norse source says that the Danes chose Magnus out of loyalty to the treaty made between him and Harthacnut at the Gotha river in 1039.[38] The *Morkinskinna* recounts that Swein, forced to dissemble, took service with Magnus who created him a jarl and left him as his regent when he returned to Nidaros. Swein used his position of trust to win the affections of his fellow countrymen. Having done so, he was in a position to have himself crowned at a 'Thing' at Viborg. With the arrival of the campaigning season, an angry Magnus came from Norway and forced Swein to flee for safety to Sweden where his cousin, Ánundr, was king. A year later, taking the opportunity afforded when Magnus was engaged in warring against the Slavs, who had invaded Jutland, he returned with a fleet raised there but again he was overcome in battle. In retribution the Norwegian king punished the Danes for their disloyalty by ravaging widely over their territory.[39] A pattern emerges of Swein being defeated again and again, but always returning from his haven of safety to resume the struggle. He retained the love of his countrymen and in the face of adversity his dauntless spirit was unconquerable.

---

[36] 'Cnut's Earls' pp.64-65.
[37] Adam Bk 2 LXXVIII [74] pp.107-108.
[38] Saxo Bk 10 ch XXI p.47.
[39] J.W. pp.544-545.

On one of his visits to the Swedish court he met Háraldr Sigurdsson, fresh from his exploits in Byzantium.[40] According to Snorri Sturluson Swein and Haraldr entered into an alliance against Magnus; Swein, with the object of securing Denmark for himself, Háraldr to force Magnus to accept him as joint King of Norway. With the stepping stone to power which this alliance afforded him, Háraldr tried to bargain with his nephew. When these negotiations broke down the allies raided in Funen and Zealand.

By this time Magnus realised that it was to his advantage to break up the alliance, and eventually it was agreed that uncle and nephew should rule Norway as joint-kings. For Magnus this left the way open for renewing his war with Swein. It was in 1046 that the Norwegian Kings eventually ironed out their difficulties. This spelt disaster for Swein who saw his chances of ever becoming the king of his country evaporate. In vain he appealed to England for naval assistance; Godwine indeed gave wholehearted support to his nephew's plea. It was surely in England's interest to give him aid, for it had been due indirectly to Swein's warring with Magnus that this country was saved from a Norwegian invasion during the previous four years. It would have been well for England if Godwine's advice had been heeded: an Anglo-Danish alliance might have averted the battle of Stamford Bridge which in turn would have avoided a defeat at Hastings. Swein's request was however opposed by Earl Leofric who acted as the spokesman for the remainder of the Witan, 'and so the King refused to send aid'.[41] It may be that Edward and Leofric thought it prudent to keep a strictly neutral attitude to the Scandinavian conflict in fear of eventual reprisals.

The following year Swein again sent messengers to King Edward repeating his petition, this time for help urgently in view of his rapidly worsening situation. Again Godwine did his utmost to convince the council, and again to no avail. By this time Magnus had joined battle with Swein with a vastly superior fleet, and drove his rival out of Denmark. It seems that there were isolationists in the debating chamber who took the view that the best policy was to let the forces of Norway and Denmark exhaust each other; it is possible that some thought that, if victorious, Swein might have constituted as great a threat to England as did Magnus. Magnus and Háraldr had in the spring of 1047 assembled all the manpower of Norway, determined to effect Swein's final overthrow. By the summer he had been forced back to Skane, the Danish territory in Southern Sweden. It was at that point that his cousin, Swegn Godwineson, arrived with his Flemish mercenaries - too little and too late to prevent his cousin from being driven from his kingdom for ever (for the Danish contender had been defeated by Magnus in a furious sea battle.) Heavily outnumbered by the Norwegian fleet, Swein put up a desperate struggle; casualties had been heavy on both sides.[42]

---

[40] Saxo, note 167 p.214, Eric Christiansen.
[41] A.S.C 'D' s.a 1049/1048; I.W. pp.544-545.
[42] J.W. pp.544-545; Saxo, Eric Christiansen, note 164 pp.211-213; Snorri, 'Saga of Magnus the Good' ch XXXV p.157; Morkinskinna ch7 pp.125-126.

Within months the situation changed dramatically, for in October news reached Sweden that Magnus was dead; killed (according to some) when his horse bolted and dashed him against a tree, while other sources said he was drowned, or that he died of some mysterious illness.[43] Whatever may have been the cause, it gave the irrepressible Swein fresh hope at the very time when his fortunes seemed at their lowest ebb. He immediately returned to Denmark, where he was rapturously received by his countrymen and at a 'Thing' in Zealand and again at Viborg in Jutland, was proclaimed their king. It seems that Magnus had a high regard for Swein and on his deathbed confided in his stepbrother, Thor, that while he could do no other than leave Norway to Háraldr he wished Swein to succeed him in Denmark.[44] This did not discourage the former, who had no intention of respecting his nephew's dying wishes: he immediately renewed hostilities, mobilizing his fleet in readiness for an all-out offensive. In the face of this renewed attack and England's refusal of aid, Swein put himself under the protection of the Emperor and became his vassal: King Edward had accepted Háraldr's overtures of peace and friendship, in effect acknowledging neutrality as far as the Scandinavian war was concerned. It is true that Swein had been encouraged by the support afforded him by the unofficial crews that had been raised by both Swegn and Osgod Clapa, which probably amounted to a fleet as great as he had asked for from the English Witan.[45] But now another factor came into play: European alliances were taking on a completely different outlook. The Empire, England, Denmark and Anjou with the wholehearted support of Pope Leo IX, were ranged against the Count of Flanders (Baldwin V), Henry I, King of France (the Count's brother-in-law), and Gottfried, the Count of Upper Lorraine. In that year, 1049, the Emperor sought naval assistance from both England and Denmark to provide a naval blockade in the eventuality of Baldwin attempting to escape by sea.[46] For Godwine, with his long-standing friendship with the Flemish Count, this meant that he was finding himself more and more at odds with the official policy of the king.

This turn of events had its origin two years earlier in Lotharingia. The state took its name from Lothar, the grandson of the Emperor Charlemagne. Lothar's father, Louis the Pious, had inherited the empire from Charlemagne in 814 and his four sons badgered him to divide his dominions among them. When Lothar succeeded his father in 840, his brothers took it badly. One brother, Pipin, predeceased his father. The other two, Charles the Bald and Louis the German, defeated Lothar at the battle of Fontenay and in 843 by the Treaty of Verdun, Lothar was left with the diminished state which stretched from the Italian Alps in the South, including the City of Rome to the North Sea and the city of Aachen. To Louis went the territory to the east, the German peoples, and to

---

[43] Ágrip ch XL pp.54-55; Snorri, 'Saga of Harald the Stern' ch XXVIII, pp.181-182; Saxo Bk 10, ch XXII p.51 and note 168 p.215.
[44] Theodoricus Monachus ch 27 p.44; Morkinskinna ch 26 pp.182-183.
[45] A.S.C 'C' s.a 1046, 'D' 1047/1046, 'E' 1044/1046 for Osgod; F.N.C.ii p.90,
[46] A.S.C 'D' 1050/1049 for Earl Swegn who returned from Denmark having 'ruined himself with the Danes'. For King Swein J.W pp.548-549; for King Edward A.S.C 'D' s.a 1050/1049

Charles that to the west, the Franks. Within thirty years the Empire, as it had been, was virtualy at an end: later Lotharingia became known as Lorraine.

The Lotharingian rebellion was caused by the death of Gazella I, the duke of Lorraine, in 1046. The emperor, Henry III, decreed that the duchy should be divided between his two sons: Gottfried, the older brother, was given Upper Lorraine and Gazella II, Lower Lorraine. The elder brother was unwilling to accept this division of the territory which he considered rightfully his, and allied himself with his cousin, Baldwin V.[47] The rebellion attracted other magnates of the Low Countries and had the moral support of King Henry I of France, whose sister Baldwin had married.

Emperor Henry had been instrumental in having his cousin Bruno appointed to the Papal throne as Leo IX in the same year. As an act of defiance Baldwin had the Emperor's magnificent palace at Nymegen destroyed by fire and, according to the words of the *Chronicle*, 'caused him many other offences'.[48] The French king led his army along the northern boundary of his kingdom as a gesture of solidarity. Baldwin and Gottfried were defeated by the emperor's army and ordered to appear at Aachen. Gottfried who, we are told, was as much in fear of the Pope's threat of excommunication as of the imperial army, made his peace with the emperor and the pope, but Baldwin's surrender was only a temporary one.

The emperor was related to both King Edward and to King Swein. His first wife was Gunnhildr, the daughter of Cnut and Emma, and thus Edward's half-sister and Swein's first cousin. Henry had, after Gunnhildr's early death in 1038, married Agnes, a daughter of William the Pious, the duke of Aquitaine seven years later. Baldwin V was the son of Baldwin IV and Ogiva, the daughter of Count Frederick of Ardenne. Godwine and Baldwin had formed a lasting friendship which could have originated back in the days when Wulfnoth, Godwine's father, may have been forced to seek sanctuary in Flanders. It has been suggested that when he was wrongly exiled in 1009, Wulfnoth may have been forced to take to piracy, and would have used Flemish ports to sell his plunder.[49]

The naval blockade meant that technically Denmark and Flanders were now at war, and the crews which Swegn Godwineson and Osgod Clapa had enlisted during the winter of 1047-8 were put in a difficult position, because they would have been reluctant to fight for the forces guarding against their count's escape by sea. It is possible that they refused to fight for Swein, who needed all the fighting men he could get in preparation for Harðráða's threatened invasion. Swein Estrithsson's naval blockade came into operation in the spring of 1049 and by the summer Swegn was back in England. Significantly, so too was Osgod Clapa.

---

[47] Lynn Thorndyke, 'Medieval Europe' pp.204-205; S. Körner pp.181-189.
[48] A.S.C 'C' 1049; J.W. pp.548-549.
[49] A.S.C 'C' s.a 1049; ASC 'D' 1050/1049; JW pp 548 -549

The *Chronicle* says of Swegn Godwineson that he had 'ruined himself with the Danes'.[50] This is not mentioned by the Abingdon or St Augustine's versions, nor by John of Worcester. It has been inferred that Swegn may have switched his allegiance to the Norwegian king on the strength of a passage in Adam of Bremen, but his words cannot support this interpretation by any stretch of the imagination. Osgod and his fleet lay anchored in a bay of the island of Wulpe. A substantial number then raided in Essex and on their way homeward were for the most part drowned when they were overtaken by a violent storm. Osgod crossed to the mainland and, leaving his wife at Bruges, returned to Denmark with the six crews who remained loyal to him. Swegn, however, was determined to regain the position he had held in England. Relying on his relationship with the king and his father's influence at court, he gained an audience with Edward who was still with the fleet stationed at Sandwich. He was able to make his peace with his royal brother-in-law, who promised him full restitution of all that he had owned before abandoning his earldom in his hour of despair.[51] To Godwine's dismay, both Harold and Beorn refused to co-operate by giving up the extra authority and possessions which had been granted to them when Swegn fled to Flanders. It is possible also that they both feared that his volatile temperament would further damage the family's prospects, feelings which his father was prepared to overlook. Heartened by this division in the earl's family and encouraged by his Norman adviser, the king saw the chance he had been waiting for: he immediately took decisive action - Swegn was given four days to rejoin his ships and leave the country.[52]

What followed must have caused Earl Godwine and his mother deep hurt and concern, involving as it did strained relationships with Denmark, and cut across the very hopes that he held most dear, the welfare of both his family and his wife's. Swegn harboured the eight ships with which he returned in Bosham Creek and joined his father and Beorn at Pevensey where the fleet lay -weather bound. He begged his cousin to accompany him to the king at Sandwich, saying he wished to renew his allegiance. Beorn agreed to assist him to achieve this.[53] By this time the naval blockade had ceased to be needed. Peace had been restored, at least temporarily, and Edward had dismissed the Mercian squadron. Harold and Tostig had been with the fleet at Pevensey but for some reason Beorn had taken over Harold's command - this may have been because news had been received that the larger part of Osgod's contingent had left their leader with the intention of harrying along the east coast.[54] Doubtless Harold was required to make preparations to repulse such an attack. Edward in alarm had tried to recall the Mercian detachment which was then anchored in the Kentish River Stour.

---

[50] A.S.C 'D' s.a 1050, trans. M. Swanton p.169; D. Raraty p.17 n44, p.5.
[51] A.S.C 'E' s.a 1046/1049.
[52] ibid; A.S.C 'F', Latin version, '3 days or put in custody'.
[53] A.S.C 'C' 1049; 'D' 1050/1049; 'E' 1046/1049; J.W. pp.550-551.
[54] J.W. pp.550-551.

All the sources agree that Swegn begged Beorn to help him to 'make his peace with the King'. Three of the annalists stress that Beorn agreed to accompany his cousin, taking only three companions because he relied on the bond of their kinship.[55] The St Augustine's version introduces a variation saying that, on the journey to see the king, Swegn begged Beorn to turn aside and go to Bosham. He explained that the rest of his ships were likely to desert unless he visited them. It is more likely that Professor Garmonsway was correct when he suggested that the route the cousins would take from Pevensey was to travel west and then north around the Weald, to join the Pilgrim's Way, passing Canterbury and thence on to Sandwich.[56] In any case the coastal road would only have taken them to the point where the Romney Marshes reached inland as far as the forest of the *Andredesweald*:[57] If this is correct then they would have had to pass Bosham manor or very close to it. The question arises: at what point and for what reason did Swegn alter his mind, or did he intend all along to make his cousin a captive? Or was it Beorn who altered his mind about pleading for Swegn's reinstatement, and refused to go any further? At any rate, leaving Pevensey behind them they arrived at Bosham. Had Swegn intended to kill his cousin he could have done so as easily at Bosham as at Dartmouth. It would seem that at one point he intended to use Beorn as a hostage, and then for some reason changed his mind, and off the Devonshire coast the hapless earl was murdered. According to some versions he had been bound at Bosham and forced on board ship.[58] Alternatively, Swegn begged him to go on board and, when he refused, Swegn's sailors seized him and, throwing him into a boat, bound him and rowed him to one of their ships.[59]

It has been suggested that Godwine was implicated in Beorn's murder.[60] Presumably this theory is based on the entry in the St Augustine recension which reads: 'Then within two days Earl Swegn came there, and spoke with his father, and with Earl Beorn'. There are also some comments of Adam of Bremen's, but I do not see how either can be construed as involving Godwine in any part of his nephew's murder. As far as I am aware, no other historian has blamed him for it. Far from being likely, this accusation runs directly against the advancement of the earl's most cherished ambitions, an Anglo-Danish alliance.

Beorn's lifeless body was buried in a church in one version, or in a deep ditch covered with earth in another.[61] Harold, with some of his cousin's friends, recovered the corpse and with fitting reverence had it buried in the Old Minster at Winchester beside his uncle, King Cnut. Surely in doing so Harold was acting as his parent's representative, and as a gesture of distancing himself - and them -

---

[55] A.S.C 'C' 1049; 'D' 1050/1049; J.W. pp.550-551.
[56] A.S.C 'C' trans. G.N. Garmonsway p.168 note 2.
[57] M. Swanton, 'The Anglo-Saxon Chronicles', 'Areas of Swamp and Forest' p.274.
[58] A.S.C 'C' 1049; 'D' 1050/1049; J.W. pp.550-551.
[59] A.S.C 'E' s.a 1046/1049.
[60] N.J. Higham, 'The Death of A.S. England' p.127.
[61] A.S.C 'E' s.a 1046/1049; 'F' Latin, 'a little church'; A.S.C 'C' 'D' 'and buried deep'; Adam Bk 3, ch XIV [13] pp.124-125.

from his brother's crime. The Abingdon scribe also records that the king and the whole army pronounced Swegn to be 'nithing', worthless, a man without honour.[62] Three sources stress that Beorn had been wary of accompanying Swegn, but allayed his doubts by trusting in their kinship. The crime was completely at variance with the principles of the ties of relationship held sacred by both Anglo-Saxon and Scandinavian communities. On this was based the *'wergeld'*, the very foundation of their legal codes. Their laws laid down that the kinsmen of a culprit, whether murderer, thief or practicer of witchcraft should be held as liable as the perpetrator to pay the appropriate wergeld. Conversely the same principle applied to the victim and his relatives: if a man was murdered, his family were the recipients of his blood money. This principle was embodied in the law codes of both English and all Scandinavian peoples; it was the obligation of the kin to avenge the death of their relative and to demand justice. A good illustration of the importance of this appears in the *'Heimskringla'*.[63] Hákon Ivarsson had murdered King Swein Estrithsson's nephew. The King dismissed him from his service, declaring 'I will do you no harm, but I cannot keep watch over all our relatives'. Hákon fled for safety to Norway. The murdered young man had been a thorn in the flesh of his uncle owing to his unruly behaviour. His name was Ásmundr who, according to Snorri, was 'said to have been King Swein's sister's son and his foster son'. But in the *Morkinskinna* he is called Ásmundr Bjornsson and he appears as such in the *Saga of Hákon Ivarsson*.[64] If this is correct, Beorn left a son who was fostered by his uncle King Swein.

Of the eight ships which had accompanied Swegn when he returned to England, six forsook him, disgusted with a crime which shook their ideas of what was acceptable. The men of Hastings captured two of them, killed the crews, and left the ships with the king at Sandwich.[65] Swegn then sailed east to Flanders and stayed all that winter in Bruges under Count Baldwin's full protection.[66] This perhaps refers to Beorn's relatives, presumably in Denmark, attempting to get revenge for the death of the earl.

In 1048 a Viking host, sailing from a Flemish port, raided the Isle of Wight, Sandwich, Thanet and Essex until they were driven off by a fleet commanded by the king and the earls, but whether this was connected with Beorn's murder or merely a fortuitous raid is unknown. The following year in late July England suffered another Viking attack, this time in the west: a fleet of Irish Vikings sailed from Ireland up the river Usk. Gruffydd ap Rhydderch, making a virtue of necessity, joined the marauders, thereby saving Deheubarth from devastation. Instead he directed their energies towards raiding the territory of his enemy,

---

[62] A.S.C 'C' 1049.

[63] 'Saga of Harald the Stern', ch XLIX pp.196-197; I am indebted to Mr Eric Christiansen for these references.

[64] Morkinskinna pp 237-238. for the ties of kinship, H.R Loyn, 'Anglo-Saxon England and the N conquest' pp.292-298; F Stenton 'A.S.E' p.315-318.

[65] A.S.C 'C', 'D' 1049; J.W pp 550-551, for giving the ships to the king.

[66] A.S.C 'C' s.a 1049; 'E' 1046/1049; J.W pp.550-551.

Meurig ap Hywe,l in Gwent. The host then sailed up the Severn, crossed the River Wye and destroyed the manor of Tidenham, inflicting enormous slaughter and destruction in the region.[67] The point has been made that the main forces of Herefordshire and Gloucestershire would have been stationed at Sandwich participating in the naval blockade.[68] Bishop Ealdred hastily enlisted any man capable of bearing arms, together with some Welshmen of the border who had promised their loyalty. Secretly they sent a warning to Gruffydd and the English camp was attacked at dawn. Those who were unable to escape were massacred.[69]

Beorn's murder must have caused strained relations between England and Denmark; it must also have been a severe blow for Godwine. It cannot have helped that, at the time, the Norman duke was seeking closer ties with his other ally, Count Baldwin, by asking for his daughter's hand in marriage. It is quite possible that during the winter of 1049/1050 the earl did his utmost to secure his son's return; it is likely that in the Mid-Lent meeting of the Witan in London he was prepared to acquiesce in Leofric's proposal that the size of the fleet be reduced from fourteen ships to five. The presence of a strong naval fleet, he argued, was no longer necessary. Swein and Haraldr were fully occupied fighting each other and in any case, the Norwegian king had secured an alliance with England. The *heregeld* to pay for a standing navy had been a burden borne for over thirty years since Edward's father had imposed it in 1014. Possibly if Beorn had been the commander of the naval fleet his death might have been a contributing factor.[70]

In providing Swegn with sanctuary, Baldwin was prepared to risk the displeasure of the English king, Emperor Henry III and Pope Leo IX. Perhaps Baldwin was prepared to do this as a direct statement of renewed rebellion. which is substantiated by the Flemish Count re-opening hostilities the following year. The year 1050 saw the bishops Ealdred of Worcester and Herman of neighbouring Ramsbury travelling to Rome on a mission for King Edward to attend the Pope's Easter Synod. It was at this meeting that Ealdred obtained the Pope's permission for the removal of the see of Devon and Cornwall from Crediton to Exeter.[71] On the return journey from Rome, they passed through Flanders and met the outlawed Swegn in the city of Bruges. Ealdred was instrumental in bringing him back and effecting a reconciliation with the King. What arguments Ealdred used to obtain Swegn's pardon can only be surmised. It is unknown whether the bishop had met him in Bruges and brought him back to England, or pleaded the earl's case to the king and, with an encouraging response, sent word to Swegn. Ealdred must have been convinced that his remorse was genuine; he probably acted as his confessor. The details we have of Beorn's murder were probably given by Swegn himself there in Bruges to the bishop. As a proof of his repentance he may have declared

---

[67] F. Barlow, 'Edward' p.99.
[68] A.S.C 'D' 1050/1049; J.W pp.550-553, J.E Lloyd ii p 362.
[69] A.S.C 'C' 1049; 'E' 1047/1050; F. Barlow, 'Edward' p 102 and note 3.
[70] A.S.C 'E' 1047/1050; F. Barlow, 'Edward' p.102 note 3.
[71] A.S.C 'C' 1049, 'E' 1047/1050; F. Barlow, 'Edward' p.102 note 3.

his intention of making a pilgrimage to the Holy City. Ealdred may also have been given reasons, unknown to us, of some extenuating circumstances. It is also possible that the good bishop's championship of Swegn's reinstatement was tempered by the humiliating defeat he had suffered the previous year at the hands of Gruffydd ap Rhydderch. It is understandable that he would want to see an able military earl installed in the area as a safeguard against further Welsh incursions. His travelling companion, Herman, would also have had an interest in the appointment of an earl with the military ability to safeguard the border.

Other considerations may have entered into Swegn's reinstatement. Edward may have thought that by doing so he was giving him free rein to further ruin himself and his family.[72] On the other hand, with new developments in Europe and at home, the possibility exists that in the summer of 1050 the king and his in-laws were making a final effort to pull together against a swelling tide of dissension. At all events, Swegn is found witnessing a charter in the same order of seniority that he held back in 1044 and had maintained until his disgrace in 1046, behind his father and Earls Leofric and Siward.[73]

Another indication that the family was endeavouring to unite against the opposition is Harold's willingness to accept his brother's return. At the same time King Edward made a grant of land to Godwine, 'his faithful earl' of land at Sandford-on-Thames, Oxon.[74] Presumably this had been ratified prior to Swegn's re-instatement to his earldom, as it does not bear his signature. The grant may have been made at the same meeting of the Witan in London at Mid-Lent 1050 when his son's outlawry was reversed. It was at this same Witenagemot that no fewer than three new ecclesiastical appointments were made, which heralded the crisis which was shortly to shake the country and spell ruin to the house of Godwine.

On 29th October 1050 Archbishop Eadsige died. On 22nd January 1051, Ælfric archbishop of York also passed away. They had been predeceased by Eadnoth, the good bishop of Dorchester. It was the King's prerogative to make ecclesiastical appointments, but usually the wishes of the brethren of the community concerned were given serious consideration. The monks of Canterbury were all in favour of electing one of their own fraternity, Ælric, a relative of Earl Godwine's, possibly a cousin or nephew.[75] According to the *Vita Ædwardi*, Ælric had grown up in Christ Church from childhood and had been educated in the rules of their monastery. He is described as wise in the ways of the world and loved by the community of the church. By general assent and according to canon law, the clergy elected him to the office of Archbishop.[76] They approached Godwine as the earl to uphold their choice with the king. Owing to Eadsige's failing health, Godwine had been closely involved in the secular welfare of Christ Church, but Edward rode roughshod over

---

[72] F. Barlow, 'Edward' p.103 and note 2.
[73] S 1021; Atlas, Table LXXIV witnessing after Leofric and Siward.
[74] S 1022; Atlas Table LXXIV.
[75] 'Vita' pp.30-31; I. Walker, 'Harold', App1 pp.203, 204.
[76] 'Vita' pp.30,31.

the wishes of both the earl and the monks.[77] He was determined to have the plum office for his friend and confidant, Robert Champart, the bishop of London. The vacancy thus caused was filled by Spearhafoc, the abbot of Abingdon, who is supposed to have purchased the metropolitan see from Stigand. Abingdon was given to the king's elderley relative, Rothulf, a Norman cleric who had recently returned from helping to evangelize Norway.

As a further snub to Godwine, York was given to Cynesige, the king's chaplain,[78] rather than to Ealdred who had become a close associate and friend of the earl's, in spite of the fact that it had become almost traditional for the bishop of Worcester to succeed in due course to the archbishopric of York as had Oswald, Ealdwulf and Wulfstan Lupus. Eadnoth's death allowed Edward to promote another Norman, Ulf, who was also one of the king's chaplains, to the see of Dorchester. The Worcester version of the *Chronicle* says of him that he did nothing worthy of a bishop, so much so that the annalist declines to enlarge on more shameful reasons than he wished to discuss.[79] These were not happy appointments and within the year they were instrumental in bringing the country to the verge of civil war.

Robert Champart, Edward's favourite

Robert Champart had been schooled in the monestery of St Ouen in Rouen where he became a prior. In 1037 he was appointed Abbot of Jumieges and during his tenure of office started an ambitious programme of re-building the church. In 1041 he accompanied Edward to England and, on the death of Ælfweard, was promoted to the bishopric of London in 1044.[80] The fact that Robert's name does not appear on the witness lists until two years later may indicate that there had been some initial opposition to his appointment.[81] William of Malmesbury stated that Robert had a magnetic influence over Edward which may have had its origin in the friendship and support which he was given while in exile in Normandy. Indeed, according to one chronicler, Robert's hold over the King was so absolute that if he said that a black crow was white the king would believe him.[82]

As soon as he was appointed to the archbishopric, Robert set about poisoning Edward's mind against Godwine. This developed into a bitter personal vendetta which the earl endured with patience and tolerance as far as was humanly possible.[83] Robert first accused Godwine of being in possession of lands which

---

[77] ibid
[78] J.W. pp.556-557.
[79] A.S.C 'D' s.a 1050/1049 for Ulf of Dorchester.
[80] J.W. pp.552-553; A.S.C 'E' 1048/1051; A.S.C 'C' 1051; A.S.C 'D' 1051/1050.
[81] A. Williams, 'Kingship and Government' p.138.
[82] 'Annales de Wintonia' in 'Annales Monastici' ed. H. R. Lloyd, quoted from F.N.C.ii p.70 note 2.
[83] 'Vita' pp.30-31.

rightfully belonged to Christ Church.[84] According to Eadmer, a monk of Christ Church writing after the conquest, Godwine, whom he calls a bitter enemy of the Church of Canterbury, stole the manor of Folkestone from the church, having bribed Archbishop Eadsige.[85] This seems in part to be corroborated by the words of the Abingdon annalist when he records that Godwine 'made all too little reparation for God's property which he had from many holy places'.[86] First it must be remembered that both Eadmer and the Abingdon scribe were churchmen, and ecclesiastical writers were ready to believe the worst of any supposed encroachment of church property. In this respect many leading magnates had been similarly charged, including even Leofric and his wife, his brothers Godwine and Edwin, his nephew, Ælfwine, and his grandsons ,Edwin and Morcar.[87] So too was Siward, the earl of Northumbria, and his son Waltheof, who were accused of wronging the Abbey of Peterborough. The saintly Edward was not above reproach, nor was his queen, in that they had made Leominster and Berkeley their property.[88] There is evidence also that in some cases the monastic scribes were guilty of forgery in their enthusiasm to establish the rights of their ecclesiastical foundations.

When Archbishop Eadsige, because of his infirmity, enlisted the support of the king and Godwine to nominate Siward as his coadjutor, it is possible that, in return for the earl's assistance and his championing of Christ Church's interests in secular matters, Godwine was rewarded with some church lands. Eadsige would have viewed these grants as justified and Godwine as earned. It was not only laymen who wrongfully took from the church: witness St Augustine's encroachment on Christ Church's fishing rights at Sandwich as an example of one church vying with another, as Bishop Ælfstan did when he bribed Steorra, the king's steward, to obtain the rights for St Augustine's.[89]

The author of the *Vita Ædwardi*, himself a monk, admitted that in respect of Robert's claims justice was on the archbishop's side.[90] However, if Folkestone was one of these properties, as Eadmer claimed, then it is by no means certain whether justice was on Robert's side. In a charter published by Miss Robertson, King Cnut is recorded as having granted the estate at Folkestone to Christ Church, Canterbury, 'when his priest Eadsige became a monk there'.[91] Previously in the year AD927 King Æthelstan is supposed to have made a similar grant of land at Folkestone to Christ Church when Oda was the Archbishop of Canterbury. Both

---

[84] ibid pp.32-33.
[85] 'Historia Novorum' p.6.
[86] A.S.C 'C' s.a 1052.
[87] F.N.C.ii note E pp.542-552 particularly p.551; A. Williams, 'Spoliation of Worcester' pp.386-388; 'Cockles Amongst the Wheat' p.13-14.
[88] P. Stafford, 'Queen Emma and Queen Edith' pp.139, 145 for King Edward and Eadgyth; for Siward and Waltheof the chronicle of Hugh Candidus.
[89] A.J. Robertson, 'A.S. Charters' No XCI pp.174-179.
[90] 'Vita' pp.32-33.
[91] A.J. Robertson, 'A.S. Charters', No LXXXV pp.168-170; S 981.

of the witness lists to these grants are suspect and it seems reasonable to conclude, with Miss Robertson: 'As both are of doubtful authenticity, it is uncertain whether Christ Church's claim to Folkestone was justly founded or not.'[92] Suspicions are further aroused by another charter, this time of a grant which King Edward is supposed to have made to Christ Church granting numerous estates in Kent, Surrey, Sussex, Essex, Suffolk and Oxfordshire which included Chartham and Folkestone. According to Dr C. Hart only the grant of Chartham in Kent is genuine, all the others being post-Conquest additions.[93] Folkestone is entered in the Domesday survey as in Godwine's possession and as there is no mention of any link with Christ Church it would seem that Eadmer's account is false. Archbishop Æthelnoth had been receiving the 'third penny' of the revenues of Kent and it could have been at this time that, in gratitude for his help, Eadsige surrendered them to Godwine.

Failing to stir up enough trouble for the earl in this way, Robert next started a rumour that he was plotting to murder the king, and then to add fuel to the fire again stirred up the rumours which had been circulating back in 1036 about Alfred's death and Godwine's alleged involvement in it, in spite of the fact that he had been cleared of the charge in a trial in Harthacnut's judicial court. In any case Edward himself had been glad to accept Godwine's support in 1042, and it is unlikely that he would have married the earl's daughter or promoted her brothers if he had felt that there was justification for the charge. The inference is plain: Robert's mesmeric influence over the king had cultivated the seeds of suspicion in his mind which had not been there in 1042.

Finally the archbishop did his utmost to poison his royal master against Eadgyth, using every device to ensure that even the queen herself should be separated from the king 'against the laws of the Christian religion'.[94] According to the laws of Cnut, divorce was unacceptable. Divorce was only tolerated by the church for non-consummation of the marriage, incest and failure to produce an heir. It is thus obvious that the childlessness of the royal couple was the grounds on which Robert was urging Edward to divorce Eadgyth. His father had possibly divorced Ælfgifu, Thored's daughter;[95] his grandfather, King Edgar, had perhaps divorced Æthelflaed, his first wife, who retired from the cares of this world to Wilton Abbey in Dorset.[96] His second wife, Wulfthryth, was certainly repudiated, and taking the veil became an abbess at Wilton.[97] Going back even further, Edward's great grandfather, Edward the Elder, divorced his second wife, Ælfflaed, the

---

[92] ibid p.417.
[93] S 1047; A. J. Robertson No XCV pp.180-182; C. Hart, 'Early charters of Eastern England' no 117.
[94] Vita p.23.
[95] There seems good reason to believe that Æthelred II was married 3 times and that an earlier wife was repudiated before his marriage to Ælfgifu the daughter of Thored. A Williams, 'Æthelred the Unready'. pp.24,25.
[96] ibid pp.3-6
[97] P. Stafford, 'Queens, Concubines and Dowagers' p.197.

daughter of Ealdorman Æthelhelm, presumably on the grounds of their close relationship, although this had only occurred to him after the birth of their eight children and when he wished to marry his third wife, Eadgifu. Ælfflaed also found sanctuary at Wilton where she eventually died.[98]

It is uncertain whether Robert was urging divorce on the grounds of failing to produce an heir to the throne, or on the more serious charge of adultery on Eadgyth's part. One of our leading authorities has suggested that the story of Queen Emma's adultery with the bishop of Winchester, and of her being required to walk barefoot on red hot plough shares to prove her innocence, could have referred, not to Emma, but to her daughter-in-law Eadgyth. According to William of Malmesbury the latter cleared herself of Robert's base accusation by taking an oath on her death bed years later to prove her innocence.[99] Perhaps Edward did intend to divorce Eadgyth in 1051 and marry again; she was sent to Wherwell in 1052. Nunneries were the usual places for divorced queens to spend the rest of their lives. Ælfwine was the bishop of Winchester from 1032 until 1047 and it is chronologically possible that he could have been involved with either queen. The *Chronicle* describes him as a king's priest.[100] The story is told by Richard of Devizes in the *Annals of Winchester* and by William of Malmesbury.

The author of the *Vita Ædwardi* was in no doubt that Archbishop Robert set out to bring about Godwine's downfall. He says of Robert: 'His ambition satisfied at last in the high honour he had obtained, began to provoke and oppose the earl with all his strength and might adding madness to madness [he] tried to turn the king's mind against him.' After Robert's appointment in Mid-Lent 1051 he lost no time in travelling to Rome to obtain his pallium from Pope Leo IX and was back in England by 27th June. According to the Norman sources, Edward sent Robert to Normandy on his way to Rome in order to convey to William, the Norman duke, a promise to make him his heir. Robert would have passed through northern France on his journey to Rome and could well have visited William, but there is no real evidence that he was empowered to make any promises concerning the succession. William of Poitiers would have us believe that Robert made another, later visit to Normandy when he could have conveyed some offer of Edward's. At any rate, on his return in June[101] he wasted no time in stamping his authority on the English church. His first act was to refuse to consecrate Edward's choice for the bishopric of London, Spearhafoc. His reason for this high-handed action was that the Pope had ordered him not to do so because Spearhafoc was guilty of the sin of simony. This knowledge could only have come from Robert himself and by his wish, for the Pope never interfered with English internal episcopal affairs.[102] The king's prerogative had been ignored and Edward was justifiably angered by the actions of his friend. Spearhafoc was permitted to remain in office for some months. He

---

[98] B. Yorke, 'Æthlwold and the politics of the Tenth Century' in 'Æthelwold' pp.70–72.
[99] G.R. Bk 2 ch 197.
[100] A.S.C 'E' s.a 1032.
[101] A.S.C 'E' 1048/1051, pp 172 and 177. As Chronicles, M Swanton.
[102] F. Barlow, 'Edward' p.106.

further showed his displeasure by pointedly staying away on 29th June from Robert's enthronement at Canterbury.[103]

The Mid-Lent council also dismissed the last five mercenary ships, which allowed for a time the suspension of the collection of the *heregeld* and, according to some authorities, addressed the idea of a treaty with Normandy. No doubt there were those who argued that such an alliance would do away with the necessity of maintaining a standing fleet. Such an alliance would have been strongly urged by Robert: Norman friendship had been a key factor in King Æthelred's foreign policy in 1002, as it had been of Cnut's in 1017 and Edward was Norman in outlook, in manners and in culture. But this treaty is only mentioned by the two Norman sources: the archdeacon of Lisieux was writing twenty or possibly twenty five years after the event,[104] and was prepared to distort or fabricate in his attempt to prove the justice of William's claim to the English throne. He attempted to do this by asserting that negotiations for this treaty were drafted at this meeting of the Witan and signed by the three leading earls, Godwine, Leofric and Siward, as well as Archbishop Stigand. No mention was made of Harold, the earl of East Anglia or that Stigand was in 1051 only the bishop of Winchester. Neither was Cynesige included, who was the Archbishop of York. We can only conclude that William of Poitiers knew little of the facts. In the words of Professor Barlow: 'the list was fabricated by the archdeacon himself in order to provide circumstantial detail.'[105] William of Poitiers explained the omission of Harold's name by claiming that he was required to visit Normandy to rectify this omission shortly afterwards. Körner pointed out the incongruous nature of this explanation: Harold's visit occurred in the mid 1060s. By this time all three of the leading earls had been dead several years.[106]

It is most unlikely that Godwine ever signed such a treaty in early 1051. In view of the hostility which existed between him and Robert Champart, the earl was hardly likely to support any scheme of the archbishop's. At the time Godwine's family were about to be united with that of Count Baldwin's by the marriage of Tostig, his third son, to Baldwin's half-sister Judith. She was the daughter of Baldwin IV and his second wife, Eleanor of Normandy. Nor is there evidence either in the *Chronicle*, John of Worcester or in the *Vita Ædwardi* that such a treaty was ever made. Freeman suggested the possibility that Edward's nephew, Ralph, may have been regarded as his heir.[107] It seems unreasonable that the king should consider the Norman duke - whose sole claim to relationship was that Emma was his great aunt - and should have been preferred to his own nephew, who moreover was living in England with the status of an earl.

---

[103] ibid.
[104] 'The Norman Conquest of England,' by R. Allen Brown p.15 and note 1
[105] F. Barlow, 'Edward' p.108.
[106] Sten Körner, 'The Battle of Hastings' p.126.
[107] F.N.C.ii pp.367, 415.

It has been pointed out that it was William's victory at Val-és-Dunes in 1047 which prompted Edward to think of William as a capable warrior and ruler, and a suitable successor to the English throne. Eric John claimed that Robert conveyed the offer of succession to William on his way to Rome and that both Leofric and Siward would have been in agreement with this. He backed up his argument by stating that when the opportunity came in the autumn they were willing to assist in destroying Godwine and his family. But it was surely the French king who was instrumental in overcoming the Norman rebels and William was supporting him only in a subordinate capacity.[108]

William moreover had problems of his own in the years 1049-1051. In the year 1049 Pope Leo and his entourage arrived in the city of Rheims to dedicate the monastery there to Saint Rémy, the apostle to the Franks in the early sixth century. Rémy, or Remigius, had been appointed bishop of Rheims at the early age of twenty two and had been instrumental in baptizing King Clovis.[109] The Pope's visit was combined with a synod of ecclesiastics which was attended by the abbots of Ramsey, St Augustine's and by Bishop Dudoc of Wells.[110] At this synod the Pope prohibited the intended marriage of the Norman duke and Matilda, Baldwin's daughter. The reason for the Pope's edict, according to the testimony of Anselm, himself a monk at the St Rémy monastery and writing within a few years of the synod, was incest. Others included in the prohibition for the same reason were Count Enguerrand II of Ponthiu and Eustace of Boulogne. The pope issued instructions forbidding Baldwin from giving his daughter in marriage to William, and to the latter receiving her in marriage. One story claimed that the impediment was that Matilda was already married, another that there was consanguity in their families. Richard II, duke of Normandy until 1016, was the father of Richard III, Robert I and Eleanor. Robert I was William's father and Eleanor married Baldwin IV, Matilda's grandfather. In addition to this, there had been a betrothal between Richard III and Adela, Countess of Flanders. But the real reason for the Pope's opposition was far more likely to have been political: both he and his cousin, the emperor, would have been anxious to prevent any alliance between Flanders and Normandy and to boycott Baldwin as far as possible.[111]

Eustace married King Edward's sister, Godgifu, after the death in 1035 of her first husband Dreux, Count of the Vexin. There is some evidence that in the following year when the Ætheling Alfred sailed for England from Boulogne, either Godgifu was already married to the Count or soon would be.[112] It seems that Godgifu was dead by 1049 and that Eustace had then married Ida of Boillon and at the synod at Rheims he was excommunicated for an incestuous marriage. Ida was the sister of Gottfried, the duke of Lower Lorraine.[113] The reason for the pope's censure

---

[108] Eric John, 'Edward the Confessor and the Norman Succession' p.255.
[109] 'Dictionary of Saints', by D. Attwater revised by C.R. John p.286.
[110] A.S.C 'E' 1046/1049.
[111] Sten Körner, 'Battle of Hastings', p.182-185 note 13.
[112] E.E.R Bk 3 ch 4 pp.42-43; F. Barlow, 'Edward' p.45 note 3.
[113] 'The Empire and the Papacy', by T.F. Tout, Period ii p.181.

becomes obvious: like the prohibition of William's marriage, the motive owed its origin to the Lotharingian rebellion and the need to isolate Baldwin from Normandy and Gottfried from Boulogne.

By 1051 a realignment of alliances was in process in Europe. At that time Háraldr Sigurdsson was still waging war against Denmark. He had either killed or driven off the more rebellious of the Norwegian magnates. In 1049 he harrried far and wide in Swein's kingdom and in the spring of 1050 he took his fleet to the Gotha river where he was expecting to meet his enemy. With no Swein in sight he set out to create as much havoc as possible, leaving the city of Hedeby razed to the ground. Swein was waiting for him as he sailed homeward, his ships laden with booty and captives. The Norwegians were forced to jettison their spoil and prisoners to effect an escape. Even so, the Danes were able to capture seven of his vessels.

King Edward's sympathies for his allies in the Lotharingian rebellion must have been sorely tried when the Emperor and the Pope saw fit to excommunicate his friend and brother-in-law Eustace. It is also certain that Swein would have viewed England with distrust after Edward had taken no steps to punish his brother's murderer and then reinstated him. Nor would the Danish king have felt anything but anger for Baldwin who had given Swegn full protection during the winter of 1049/1050. To Edward it must have been a further blow when William 'whom he loved as a brother or a son'[114] made overtures of friendship to his enemy, Baldwin, and then in the summer of 1051 came the marriage of Tostig and Judith. Tostig was the King's favourite brother-in-law, and it must have been a bitter pill for him to swallow. This may well have caused the quarrel which erupted in the weeks which followed.

William's future had seemed secure in 1050. His rebels had been disposed of: Guy of Burgundy had surrendered the castle of Brionne after a three year siege. The French king had supported William in quelling the rebellion of Guy of Burgundy and Geoffrey Martel, the Count of Anjou. But in 1051, alarmed at the growing military might of the Norman duke, he switched his support to Geoffrey. With both Henry of France and the formidable Angevin duke aligned against him, by March 1051 the whole situation had changed for him. William found himself engaged in a deadly struggle and was forced to face a powerful attack by Geoffrey who captured Tours. Also the Norman duke had to face a rebellion from William of Arques which involved Enguerrand II, Count of Ponthieu in the hostilities.[115]

Godwine at this time would have viewed the future with growing mistrust. It is true that the re-instatement of his eldest son must have given him cause for satisfaction, as did the closer links through marriage with his friend, the powerful Count Baldwin. Both of these could have repercussions in his relationship with the English king, however, who could hardly have been less than hostile to the Flemish count. The West Saxon earl must also have been alarmed at the growing

---

[114] W.P. i ch 41 pp.68,69.
[115] F. McLynn, 'Three Battles' pp.87-89.

influence of the Normans over the king. Apart from Robert Champart installed at Canterbury, there was William the bishop of London, Ulf of Rochester and the appearance in the witness lists of the priest, Peter, who was to become the bishop of Lichfield after the Conquest.[116] In ecclesiastical appointments Godwine's protégé, Ælfric, had been ignored at Canterbury and Ealdred at York.[117]

Perhaps even more alarming was the establishment of Norman castles which were springing up in the earldoms held by himself and his sons. The King's nephew, Ralph, had been given authority in some part of Swegn's earldom during his exile in 1049/1050. During this time it seems that three castles were built and garrisoned in Herefordshire. Richard Fitz Scrob was in charge of one, Osbern Pentecost another, and the third (which was known as Ewias Harold) was named after Ralph's own son.[118] There is evidence that from their castles the Norman soldiery sallied forth to terrorise the neighbourhood and inflict insults on the English.[119] In Harold's earldom of East Anglia large domains were granted to two Bretons, Robert fitz Wimarc and Ralph the Staller.[120] The former was in possession of a castle at Clavering in Essex which was certainly in existance in 1052. In Godwine's own earldom of Wessex there were at least plans to build a castle at Dover, which it has been suggested may have been put in the keeping of Eustace of Boulogne.[121]

By the end of the summer of 1051 it had become obvious to Godwine that his enemies were gaining the ascendancy. The atmosphere at Edward's court must have resembled the first rumbling of thunder and the flash of lightning which presaged the coming storm. Then in September Eustace landed with his following at Dover.[122]

---

[116] Peter, S 1021 AD 1050; Atlas, Table LXVIII.
[117] J.W. pp.556-557; F. Barlow, 'Edward' p.105.
[118] A. Williams, 'Kingship and Government' p.140. F. Barlow, 'Edward,' p.94.
[119] A. Williams, 'Kingship and Government' p.140.
[120] F. Barlow, 'The Feudal Kingdom of England' p.62.
[121] A. Williams, 'Kingship and Government' p.140 and note 29 p.215
[122] A.S.C 'D' 1052/1051 for Dover; J.W. pp.558-559 for September.

Genealogy of Eustace of Boulogne

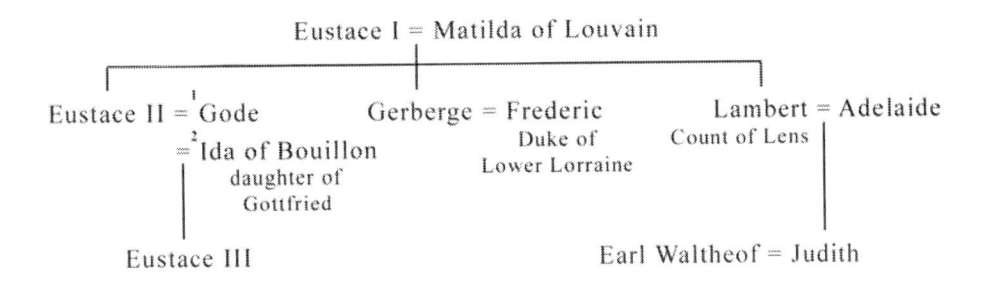

```
                    Eustace I = Matilda of Louvain
        ┌──────────────────────┼──────────────────────┐
Eustace II =¹ Gode      Gerberge = Frederic     Lambert = Adelaide
           =² Ida of Bouillon    Duke of        Count of Lens
              daughter of        Lower Lorraine
              Gottfried
              │                                     │
           Eustace III                    Earl Waltheof = Judith
```

The Expansion of Power & Influence of the Counts of Brulogne under Eustace II 1990
Seminar Paper 3-18 by Heather Tanner. Unpublished. Anglo-Saxon Studies xiv 1992 p.251-286

Table 8. Sequence of Events 1019 - 1051

1019	Lyfing abbot of Tavistock
1027	Lyfing appointed bishop of Crediton
1038	Lyfing installed as bishop of Worcester
1040	Lyfing and Godwine accused by Archbishop Ælfric
1046 March 23	Death of Bishop Lyfing
1046	Ealdred succeeds Lyfing at Worcester
1046 Spring	Swegn and Gruffydd ap Llewelyn raid in South Wales
1046 Winter	Osgod Clapa outlawed and goes to Flanders
1046 Winter	Swegn throws up earldom and spends the winter in Flanders
1047 Feb 2	Severe weather sets in
1047	Haraldr Sigurdsson joint King with Magnus of Norway Battle of Val-és-Dunes Swein appeals for naval aid from King Edward

Continued next page

1047 Summer	Swegn and Osgod sail for Denmark to assist Swein
1047 Oct 25	Death of Magnus
1047/1049	Lotharingian rebellion
1048	Help for Swein refused again
	Raid on Southern England
	Peace concluded with Haraldr of Norway
1048 May 1	Earth tremors in the Midlands, followed by pestilence among men and cattle
1048	Swein returns to Denmark to claim the throne
1049	Leo IX becomes Pope Baldwin V and Gottfried rebel against the Emperor Naval blockade set up by Edward and Swein
1049 Summer	Swegn seeks reconciliation; Osgod also returns
1049 July 29	Bishop Ealdred defeated by Gruffydd ap Rhydderch
1049 Autumn	Swegn murders Beorn; seeks asylum in Flanders
1049 October	Leo IX council at Rheims
1050 Mid-Lent	Witan meet in London; nine ships paid off
1050 Easter	Leo IX's council in Rome
1050 Summer	Earl Swegn pardoned
1050 Oct 29	Death of Archbishop Easige; Ælfric elected by Christ Church
1051 Mid-Lent	Meeting of Witan in London
1051	Robert appointed to Canterbury; Spearhafoc to London; Rothulf to Abingdon; Ælfric succeeded by Cynsige at York Last of mercenary fleet dismissed
1051 Spring	Robert to Rome to receive his pallium Possible negotiations for treaty with Normandy
1051 June 29	Return of Robert from Rome; refuses to consecrate Spearhafoe
1051 August	Marriage of Tostig and Judith of Flanders
1051 September	Arrival of Eustace of Boulogne at Dover

9. Exile of the Godwinesons

The events leading up to Godwine's exile are covered by the Worcester *Chronicle* ['D'], the Canterbury versions ['E' and 'F'], and the *Vita Ædwardi Regis*. The *Chronicle* compiled at Abingdon ['C'] is silent except for merely recording that 'Godwine and his family were put to flight from England'.[1] John of Worcester follows 'D' closely, as does Simeon of Durham and most of the later Anglo-Norman writers. Each of the three contemporary accounts give paramount consideration to their own sphere of interest. Thus the 'E' annals are naturally more detailed and vivid for the events pertaining to Kent, and to Dover in particular. In the same way when the scene of action was transferred to Gloucester, it is only to be expected that the scribe responsible for 'D' should be better informed. Finally, when the Witan was convened in London, the views expressed by the author of the *Vita* are of great significance for they are the views of Queen Eadgyth, of Godwine, and of the court.

Eustace's mission

It seems that during the last week of August or the beginning of September 1051 Eustace II, the Count of Boulogne landed at Dover with a few ships.[2] He travelled with his companions to Gloucester, where King Edward was then in residence, and, according to the Canterbury *Chronicle* 'spoke with him about what he wanted'. The reason for the visit is perhaps the key to the ensuing events, and various explanations have been advanced. One suggestion is that Eustace came to negotiate William of Normandy's nomination as Edward's successor to the throne of England. Another possibility is that Edward had plans to install a castle on the cliffs of Dover and to place Eustace in charge of it.[3] Thirdly, that Eustace and Godgifu had a daughter or a grandson of marriageable age, and that the count was there to promote the interests of his own family.[4] Lastly, he may have come to ensure the continued support of his brother-in-law, King Edward, for the alliance that existed between the English king and the counts of Boulogne, Ponthieu and the Vexin.[5]

That Eustace had come as an emissary for William is most unlikely and certainly does not agree with any known details of their relationship. The second reason is a distinct likelihood in view of the fact that there already existed castles in Hereford

---

[1] A.S.C 'C' s.a 1051.
[2] J.W. pp.558-559 for ships; records in error that he landed at Canterbury; A.S.C 'D' s.a 1052/1051 for Dover; A.S.C 'E' s.a 1048/51; see also J.W. for September.
[3] A. Williams, 'Kingship and Government' p.140 and p.215 note 29.
[4] F. Barlow, 'Edward' pp.109 and Appendix pp.307, 308.
[5] ibid p.97.

in Earl Swegn's earldom and a castle at Clavering in Essex in Harold's East Anglian earldom.[6] It would go far to explain Godwine's hostility, if there were now plans for a fortress manned by Eustace to be built in his own territory.

To assess the importance of the alliance for the Counts of Boulogne, Ponthieu and the Vexin it is necessary to go back and follow the fortunes of the Counts of Boulogne from the early years of the eleventh century. Eustace I had built up the prestige of his inheritance by a series of alliances and strategic marriages; before that his predecessors were of no more than of local importance. Eustace I had married Matilda the daughter of Lambert I, the Count of Louvain. His son, Eustace II, married Godgifu, the daughter of Æthelred I and Emma of Normandy. After her death in 1049 he took as his second wife Ida of Bouillon, whose father, Godfrey (Gottfried), had been the cause of the Lotharingian rebellion. Through these marriages Eustace was thus the brother-in-law of the King of England, the step-father of Earl Ralph, of Walter III, Count of the Vexin, of Fulk the bishop of Amiens, and the brother-in-law of Frederic, the duke of Upper Lorraine on the latter's marriage to Gerberge, Eustace's sister.

Eustace was probably born in the mid 1020s, the eldest of three brothers and a sister. On his father's death in 1046 he succeeded as the Count of Boulogne and his brother, Lambert, became the Count of Lens. His marriage to Godgifu began a friendship with the Æthelings, Edward and Alfred. When the younger brother made his attempt on the English throne, his support was largely drawn from Boulogne and it is likely that Eustace married their sister either in 1036 or soon afterwards. Her first husband, Drogo, had died in 1035.

Godgifu must have been dead in 1049, as it was in that year that the council of Rheims was held in which Pope Leo IX excommunicated Eustace for contracting an incestuous union. Eustace's second wife was Ida, the daughter of Gottfreid, also known as Godfrey 'the Bearded'. As already mentioned he harboured the ambition of bringing Lorraine under his own jurisdiction, which had been the original cause of the Lotharingian rebellion. Eustace and Ida shared a common ancestor, Charles the Bald, some seven generations earlier, but the charge of incest was obviously a political pretext aimed by the emperor and his cousin the Pope to weaken the alliance between Boulogne and Lorraine. Similarly, William's and Matilda's proposed wedding was prohibited in the hope of forestalling co-operation between Normandy and Flanders. Enguerrand of Ponthieu and Adelaide, William's sister, were also excommunicated for incest, because of the danger of Ponthieu becoming allied to the Norman duke. In the cases of Eustace and William, this is substantiated by the requirement that, to appease the papal displeasure, they and their wives were instructed to found monasteries as atonement for their offences.[7] The interdicts laid down at Rheims are readily understandable as a prelude to the Lotharingian rebellion and means of isolating those in revolt.

---

[6] J. W. pp.560-561; A.S.C 'D' s.a 1052/1051, 'and also the French who were in the castle' p.175; M. Swanton. This probably refers to the castle in Herefordshire; see F. Barlow, 'Edward' p.94 note 3.

[7] O.V. IV pp.76-77 and XXXII for Drogo and Godgifu; for Engeurrand pp.84-85.

The threat to Eustace, to his step-son, Walter, and to Enguerrand was the very real danger of losing their independence, squeezed as they were between their two far more powerful neighbours – Flanders to the east and Normandy on the west. To safeguard themselves the three counts had formed an alliance, bound together by the ties of wedlock and common interest. Eustace was distantly related to Enguerrand through Hugh II and Hugh I. The other member of the alliance, also linked by relationship and common interest, was King Edward. His distrust of Baldwin was the main platform of his foreign policy, engendered by the refuge afforded to English outlaws and allowing Flemish ports to be used as a springboard for pirates preying on English shores. The fears of Eustace for the future independence of the alliance were well founded. By October 1053 Enguerrand lay dead on the battlefield of Aubin-sur-Scie, cut down by a Norman sword. His brother, Guy, spent the next two years in one of William's dungeons, and was then released to act as a vassal count of the Norman duke. By 1056 Eustace found it expedient to renew his friendship with his overlord, Baldwin, which had waned somewhat, in order to safeguard his position.[8] In that year he was again a witness to the Flemish count's charters after a lapse of seven years. The third member of the alliance, Walter III, was captured by William in 1063 and, with his wife, Biota, was imprisoned at Falaise. Both died in circumstances which gave rise to the accusation of Orderic Vitalis that they were poisoned one night by the duke's orders.[9]

The three counts had been alarmed by the marriage of Baldwin's daughter to William, thus causing a bond between the two greatest powers in Northern France. To add to their fears was the news of the future marriage ties that were being arranged between Baldwin's half-sister Judith and Godwine's third son, Tostig. This immediately caused shock waves of consternation: what support were they likely to receive from England when the most powerful earl in the land was to become even more closely linked to the Flemish count? What effect was this going to have on the decisions of the English Witan? This concern was surely the main reason for the presence of Eustace in England and the purpose of the conversation which transpired between the Boulonnais count and his royal brother-in-law. It is quite likely, even probable, that Eustace also broached the subject of his own family's interest in relation to the succession.[10] There could be only one way to nullify the damaging effects of Tostig's marriage – Godwine's power must be broken. This would have the added advantage of freeing Edward from the earl's irksome influence, of making divorce from his queen possible, and thus pleasing his confidant and friend, Archbishop Robert.

A plan was evolved which, it was hoped, would provoke Godwine into open rebellion, or at least cause him to lose prestige in the south-east where his support

---

[8] For Eustace and Baldwin see H. Tanner, 'Expansion of Power and Influence of the counts of Boulogne', pp.264f.
[9] O.V. vol ii pp.116-118; 312-313.
[10] F. Barlow, 'Edward'; Appendix I pp.307-308; but see H. Tanner p.266 note 26.

was strongest.[11] So when Eustace and his company arrived at Canterbury on their way to the coast they stopped for a meal, and to finalise their course of action. Some miles from Dover they halted and donned their coats of mail before entering the town. It is obvious that, as had been agreed in Gloucester, Eustace meant to cause trouble and it is hardly likely that the Boulonnais escort would have been riding clad in full armour unless he did.[12]

The Abingdon version of the *Chronicle* passes over the affray at Dover. The author of the *Vita Ædwardi Regis* too is silent. The Worcester annalist is less graphic than the Canterbury scribe, but with little essential variation to alter the main facts.[13] It seems that, when Eustace and his retainers entered the town, they did so in such a cavalier fashion that it was calculated to cause offence. One of their number insolently demanded hospitality from a burgher, who refused. This provided the required pretext for the foreigner to strike him down with his sword. The deed proved too much for his neighbour, who avenged the death of his friend.[14] Tempers flared, and Eustace, mounting his horse, gave the signal to his companions to do likewise; the company charged through the streets trampling women and children under foot. In spite of having to fight armed horsemen, the citizens of Dover swarmed to the attack and nineteen of the foreigners were killed. In the face of their retaliation Eustace and his men took to 'shameful flight'.[15] According to the Canterbury writer, he escaped with a few men,[16] but left the town with twenty of the burghers dead, to say nothing of women and children. In recounting these events, it is apparent that the two versions of the *Chronicle* which emanated from Canterbury were relating vivid memories of the atrocities which happened on their own doorsteps, events which were very real to them, and which find echoes in the writing of John of Worcester.

Eustace had done what he had set out to do and returned to Gloucester to report to King Edward. For the benefit of those with the king he gave a very biased account of what had transpired, placing the entire blame on the men of Dover. Edward put their pre-arranged plan into effect, immediately sent for Godwine and ordered him to invade Kent with an army and to lay waste the countryside with fire and sword, concentrating their most savage attack on the town of Dover itself.[17] Godwine refused, as was anticipated, even though by his refusal he laid himself open to a charge of rebellion. The earl was not prepared to accept the story as Eustace recounted it and refused to act unless the citizens were allowed to give their side of the incident. It must be remembered that it was only ten

---

[11] A.S.C 'D' 1052/1051; 'E' 1048/1051; A. Williams, 'Kingship and government' p.140.
[12] ibid.
[13] F. Barlow, 'Edward' p.110.
[14] A.S.C 'E' s.a 1048/1051; M. Swanton pp.172-173; A.S.C 'D' 1052/1051 pp.173-175; J.W. pp.558-559.
[15] J.W. pp.558-559.
[16] A.S.C 'E' 1048/1051 M. Swanton p.173.
[17] A.S.C 'F' Latin version; '...ordered Godwine Count of Kent to gather an army and invade Kent despoiling all of it, and especially Dover...' M. Swanton p.173.

years earlier that Godwine and his fellow earls had been ordered by an irate Harthacnut to visit Worcester, charged with the command to slay the inhabitants, to burn and lay waste the surrounding neighbourhood.[18] At that time the inhabitants had been given prior warning but in the atmosphere which existed in 1051 this would have been unlikely. Robert and his Norman colleagues were only too anxious to see Godwine's popularity in the shire ruined.

The earl flatly refused. It may be that he was completely unaware of the plot that had been hatched in Gloucester. To his lasting credit, he rejected the King's orders. He was not prepared to countenance the trauma which such a raid would entail for the people of his own earldom. Possibly he realized that the time had come to take a stand: he had been forced to endure the snubs and setbacks from the king and his foreign friends for too long, and enough was enough. Edward had now to represent Godwine in as bad a light as possible if he was to win the support and loyalty of the northern earls. In order to convey this impression, rumours were circulated of intended treachery towards his royal personage. The Archbishop rekindled the charge of the earl's responsibility for Alfred's death fifteen years before and that now he planned to kill his monarch as well.

Godwine and his sons Swegn and Harold gathered the forces from their earldoms and assembled at Beverstone, some three miles distance from Longtree[19] and fourteen and a half miles from Edward's palace. According to the Worcester annalist the Earl's followers were prepared for war. The same authority stated that a message was sent to King Edward demanding that Eustace, his followers and the Frenchmen who held the castles in Herefordshire should be handed over. The 'E' version merely says that Godwine asked that he and his sons be allowed to attend the king to state their side of the case. This was prevented by the false accusations of the 'foreigners', and Edward, as was to be expected, refused their request.[20]

We have here two completely different versions of events. Canterbury presents as sympathetic a picture of the earls as possible; Worcester is almost hostile. The St Augustine's writer would understandably be pro-Godwine for having saved Kent from the horrors attendant on the harrying of his own district: to him, Godwine was the champion of his people who had defied the commands of a king dominated by a Norman archbishop. All that we know of Harold and his father shows that they were both averse to hasty actions. The demands for the surrender of the Normans who were manning the castles in Herefordshire probably came from Swegn and this may have been one of the reasons he was outlawed before the king would even consider treating with his father and brother.

Thoroughly alarmed, Edward sent for support from Earl Leofric and north to Earl Siward. The fact that, when they arrived in Gloucester, they were only accompanied by a small following seems to show that they had some reservations

---

[18] J.W. pp.532-533; I. Walker, 'Harold', pp.32, 36, 38.
[19] A.S.C 'D' 1052/1051.
[20] A.S.C 'E' 1048/1051.

about the justice of the case against their fellow earl. It was only after listening to the king's interpretation of events that they sent for reinforcements. According to the Worcester version, Earl Ralph only gathered support for his uncle and stepfather after the senior earls had called for further assistance.[21]

Heather Tanner has argued that there was enmity between Earl Swegn and Ralph, based on the king's nephew being appointed to the earldom of Hereford when Swegn was outlawed in 1049 after the murder of Beorn. This would have meant that Ralph was responsible for the French colony in Hereford and the castles which had been built in his former earldom, which Swegn found so humiliating on his return. Consequently, she asserts that Ralph, Osbern Pentecost and Hugh the Castellan were among the first to come to Edward's assistance. This is not corroborated by the *Chronicle* - indeed the 'E' annalist does not mention Ralph in this connection at all and 'D' definitely says that Ralph came only after Leofric and Siward had sent for further reinforcements. The theory of hostility existing between the Godwinesons and Ralph depends on the location of Ralph's earldom from his appointment until September 1051. It is true that he held Herefordshire in 1055 and it is quite likely that the shire was under his jurisdiction after September 1052, but John of Worcester lists Herefordshire in Swegn's earldom and his raising troops there in 1051. The question then resolves itself on the locale of Ralph's earldom in the months prior to Godwine's outlawry. Williams has plausibly suggested that he may have succeeded Beorn to the earldom which Thuri held in 1041, that of the East Midlands. After Beorn's murder the position fell vacant; the next year Ralph starts to witness as '*dux*' Williams also points out that the earl of the East Midlands would be in a subordinate capacity, and that Harold and Ralph were working amicably together. Some corroboration for this may be found in the name the latter chose for his son, Harold, and it is even possible that the earl acted as the boy's godfather.[22] There is also evidence that Beorn had been in command of the royal fleet.[23] As Middlesex was included in his earldom and the fleet was stationed in London, this seems likely. Ralph and Odda were joint-commanders of the forty vessels charged with guarding the coast. This would suggest that Ralph did in fact succeed Beorn as earl of the East Midlands and, if this is correct, then the supposed enmity between Ralph and the Godwinesons evaporates.[24]

When reinforcements from Mercia and Northumbria eventually arrived, the king felt in a position to challenge Godwine. He summoned a meeting at Gloucester for 8th September. Meanwhile, according to the Canterbury annal, Godwine sent a message to Edward, requesting or demanding the right to appear before the council 'so that they may have the king's advice and his help, and of all the council, as to how they might avenge the insult to the king and the whole nation'.

---

[21] A.S.C 'D' 1052/1051. Not as Heather Tanner suggests, 'Ralph and his men, Osbern Pentecost and Hugh the Castellan were among the first to come to Gloucester after Edward had heard Eustace's complaint' p.267 and note 30.
[22] A. Williams, 'The King's Nephew' p.330-331 and note 26; F. Barlow, 'Edward' pp.93, 94.
[23] A.S.C 'E' 1046/1049.
[24] ibid s.a 1052.

Stenton suggested that this may well have formed part of the manifesto which Godwine sent to his son-in-law. However, it came to nothing because the king was surrounded by 'foreigners' - no doubt Robert Champart, Eustace, Osbern Pentecost and the other Normans. On the other hand John of Worcester, following 'D', claims that Godwine sent envoys to the king demanding that Eustace and his comrades be surrendered to him under the threat of war.[25]

At this point the mood in both camps was charged with tension; those with Edward 'were resolutely willing to attack Godwine's army if the king asked', while Godwine's followers were 'firmly arrayed in opposition'. Hot-heads in both camps were eager to resolve the suspense by armed conflict.[26] Then, suddenly, the mood changed. Accusations of treachery towards the king were brushed aside. To Godwine's followers it was abhorrent to take a stand against their royal lord. Amongst those with Edward, saner counsels prevailed. The argument used was that it would lay the country open to its enemies. According to John of Worcester, it was Earl Leofric 'and others' who pointed out the folly of civil war.[27] There is no doubt that Edward still commanded respect from the nobility of England and it is unlikely that both Leofric and Siward had sent for larger contingents because of the accusations which had been flying thick and fast that Godwine and his sons had come to Beverstone with treachery planned. What Edward needed was a good reason to make sure that the northern earls would remain loyal to him. They could have considered that Godwine was being harshly treated; it certainly does not appear that they were anxious to assist in his overthrow. The *Vita Ædwardi Regis* gives some grounds for thinking that they had misgivings about where Edward's Norman advisers were leading him. The work Eadgyth commissioned speaks of Leofric as 'an excellent man, very devoted to God', and goes on to say that the earls, Siward and Ælfgar, 'struggled in vain in the royal palace at Gloucester to get the foul charge put to the ordeal'.[28] The inference is obvious: it was only after the arrival of the northern earls that a less bellicose mood triumphed, although it is probably true that before this Swegn had been doing his utmost to urge his father into hostile action. The Witan then advised moderation and suggested that hostages be exchanged on either side.[29] A meeting of the Witan was arranged for 24th September in London, to which Godwine was to appear to plead his cause. The king then, in what must have been utter hypocrisy, is recorded as giving 'his complete friendship to both sides'.[30]

---

[25] J.W. pp.560-561; A.S.C 'D' 1052/1051, 'unless Eustace and his men were given into their hands, and also the French who were in the castle' p.175.

[26] A.S.C 'E' 1048/1051; A.S.C 'D' 1052/1051.

[27] J.W. pp.560-561; William of Malmesbury's strange story of Godwine and his sons claiming to have come to Beverstone with an army to restrain the Welsh must have arisen from a mistranslation of the word 'waelisce' – 'foreign'. G.R. Bk 2 ch 199 pp.358-359.

[28] 'Vita' pp.34-35.

[29] A.S.C 'D' 1052/1051; A.S.C 'E' 1048/1051; J.W. pp.560-561.

[30] A.S.C 'E' 1048/1051.

From Beverstone, Godwine and his adherents trudged down from the Cotswolds to his manor at Southwark on the southern bank of the Thames.[31] He was joined by a 'multitude' of enthusiastic supporters from all over his earldom. As the weeks passed, however, his followers became dispirited and the reasons for their disenchantment were threefold. The king's first move was to call up the militia from north and south of the Thames, thus effectively denying Godwine the support of many of his thegns, who were holding land from the king. Secondly, he demanded the loyalty of all the thegns who were with Earl Harold. Thirdly, he outlawed Swegn, without offering him a chance to vindicate himself, in spite of the fact that he had received a pardon for his previous sins. The reason seems obvious; with Swegn outside the law, the able-bodied men of his earldom were also liable to join the king's muster. By this time Edward was showing that he had not the slightest intention of giving either Godwine or Harold a fair hearing. With his confidence completely restored by these inroads into the earl's supporters, he brusquely ordered them to appear before the Witan accompanied by only twelve men. Godwine's reply – a perfectly reasonable one in the circumstances – was for a guarantee of safe conduct and for hostages as an assurance of good faith. The order for their attendance at the Gemot was repeated again, and once more the earl's request was refused. When it became obvious that Edward had no intention of giving any promises of safe conduct, it must have been apparent that betrayal rather than a fair trial was planned.

Here the *Vita Ædwardi Regis* becomes invaluable in giving an insight into Eadgyth's own opinions of the intrigues taking place at the court during that fateful fortnight. It was at that point that her father appealed to Stigand, the bishop of Winchester, to act as a mediator. As bishop of East Anglia from 1043 until 1047, except for a brief spell, he would have been well acquainted with Harold. He had started his ecclesiastical career as one of Cnut's priests in 1020, so his life in public office spanned the same years as Godwine's. Stigand would have been no friend of Archbishop Robert, if for no other reason than that he coveted the archbishopric for himself. Stigand pleaded with the king in vain: Edward was set on being rid of his father-in-law, and in Robert he found a zealous supporter. Crossing the river, the bishop broke down and cried as he repeated the answer he had been told to deliver: Godwine could only hope for forgiveness if and when he was able to restore his dead brother Alfred to him alive and accompanied by all his companions killed in 1036, together with all their possessions. This message clearly shows the vindictive malice of the king who would revive a charge of which Godwine had been exonerated fifteen years earlier.[32] The king, whose saintliness was to become legendary in later years, had availed himself of the earl's assistance when he came to the throne and had worked amicably with him for several years, did not scruple to resurrect an accusation which he himself had accepted as false in 1042. The very impossibility of Edward's answer was proof enough that he and Harold would

---

[31] A.S.C 'D' 1052/1051; J.W. pp.560-561.
[32] Vita pp.36-37.

be lucky to escape with their lives. In Gloucester the King had promised, according to the Canterbury tradition, that the earls had his complete friendship and the promise to abide by the result of a fair hearing in the Witan.[33] Whether the change in his attitude was all part of the plan concocted at Gloucester, or whether Archbishop Robert was responsible, it is difficult to judge. Queen Eadgyth harboured no doubts about the part played by the ecclesiastic.

The earl sprang to his feet, thrust the table out of his way and had his fastest horse saddled. With him on his manor were his sons Swegn, Harold and Leofwine; Tostig, Gyrth and the women had gone to Bosham, preparing for the worst eventuality. Godwine and Swegn, aware of imminent danger rode hard, stopping only to change horses, until they reached the comparative safety of Bosham. Harold and Leofwine rode west on the Bristol road, for Harold was intent on enlisting help from Ireland.[34] The following morning it was discovered that the earls had fled from Southwark, and Edward had no hesitation in declaring Godwine and his sons outlaws at the meeting which had been previously arranged of the Witan.

Both Canterbury versions of the *Chronicle* confirm that the fugitives were granted five days protection in which to leave the country. In spite of this, Bishop Ealdred was ordered to take a force in order to intercept the brothers before they reached Bristol, as the town lay within the Bishop's diocese. Its port carried on regular commerce with Ireland, some of which was the notorious slave trade. Bishop Ealdred had no enthusiasm for the task and saw to it that Harold and Leofwine arrived safely at their destination. A ship had been made ready, which Swegn had provisioned for his own use and this they were able to commandeer.

Godwine and Swegn had a more determined pursuit to avoid. Instead of honouring the five days which had been granted them, the malicious Archbishop left the king's palace with a troop of soldiers, presumably with the king's knowledge. In hot pursuit they rode day and night in an effort to overtake the earls, in the hope of murdering them if overtaken.[35] But this was Godwine's heartland and those in pursuit were unable to reach their quarry before the family had embarked at Thorney Island in Chichester Creek on ships laden with treasure. Both these actions were in direct contravention of the period of grace sanctioned by the Assembly and indicated direct treachery permitted by the king. Apart from the hostages in Edward's keeping, only one member of Godwine's family remained, Queen Eadgyth. The *Vita* puts the blame for what followed squarely on the shoulders of Robert, exonerating her husband as much as possible. It is only fair to say that the different versions of the *Chronicle* do not agree in some details. According to the brief reference in the Worcester *Chronicle* Eadgyth was brought to Wherwell and 'committed' to the abbess. Wherwell was a nunnery in

---

[33] A.S.C 'E' 1048/1051; 'The King gave the peace of God and his complete friendship to both sides'.
[34] A.S.C 'E' for Harold; A.S.C 'D' for Harold and Leofwine also J.W. pp.562-563.
[35] 'Vita' pp.36-37.

Hampshire presided over by Edward's half-sister, a daughter of King Æthelred II and his first wife, Ælfgifu. The Canterbury account enlarges on this: the king 'abandoned' the lady who was consecrated his queen, confiscated all her possessions in land, treasures, 'and in everything'. It repeats that she was committed to his sister at Wherwell. John of Worcester says that Edward 'repudiated the queen because of his hostility to Godwine and that she was sent to Wherwell with only one servant'.[36] In contradiction to the *Chronicle*, in what was surely Eadgyth's own reminiscences, the author of the *Vita* states that owing to the frenzied prompting of Robert, the king consented reluctantly to divorce his queen. Without actually opposing the prelate, Eadgyth was sent to Wilton convent where she had been educated, with 'royal honours and an imperial retinue'. The king then softened the fact that she had been sent from court by announcing that the queen had been sent to the convent until the kingdom was restored to peace and tranquillity.[37]

Our foremost authorities have taken different views on the apparent discrepancy which appears in the contemporary accounts. Freeman thought Eadgyth was sent to Wherwell with no lack of respect. Plummer regarded Wilton as only a 'slip'. Barlow preferred the *Vita*'s interpretation, Körner accepted this as does Harold's most recent biographer.[38] However, it is certainly conceivable that, in the euphoria of the moment, when Edward realized that he was at last free of the Godwine family, he did send his queen to Wherwell until the divorce could be finalised. Many royal consorts had been set aside to end their days in a nunnery. But as time went on he began to have doubts about the wisdom of his action. Edward may have felt that the Archbishop was alienating many of the English nobility. Leofric and Siward could have entertained misgivings about the path along which Robert's influence was leading and in the summer of 1052 it must have been common knowledge that Godwine was in the country and that the men of Kent, Sussex and Surrey were prepared 'to live and die with him'. It was then that Edward had Eadgyth transferred with due ceremony to Wilton. If the worst happened, all thoughts of divorce could be forgotten and she could be restored to her former honours.[39]

The Worcester version of the *Chronicle* states that the peacemakers at Gloucester 'advised that hostages be exchanged, and a summons issued to London'.[40] John adds that hostages were 'given by both parties'.[41] It has been suggested that Godwine fulfilled his part of the bargain, but was not given any in return.[42] William of Poitiers confirms that the Norman duke was holding a 'son and

---

[36] A.S.C 'D' 1052/1051; 'E' 1048/1051; J.W. pp.562-563.
[37] 'Vita' pp.36-37.
[38] Plummer and Earle, 'Saxon Chronicles Parallel' vol ii p.238; F. Barlow, 'Edward' pp.115-116; S. Körner, 'Battle of Hastings' pp.193, 194 note 12; I. Walker, 'Harold' p.36.
[39] P. Stafford, 'Queen Emma and Queen Edith' p.265.
[40] A.S.C 'D' s.a 1052/1051.
[41] J.W. pp.560-561, "hostages' were given by both sides'.
[42] F. Barlow, 'Edward' p.112.

grandson' of Earl Godwine - according to him as confirmation of Edward's naming William as his successor to the English throne.[43] Professor Barlow clarifies this: the word Poitiers used is *'nepos'* which could mean 'grandson' or 'nephew'. Eadmer, the monk of Christ Church, supplied the names of the two hostages as Wulfnoth and Hákon, the son of Swegn.[44] It is surprising that Harold was not required to provide a son. If his connection with Eadgyth Swan-Neck commenced soon after his appointment to the East Anglian earldom, he probably had a son old enough. Walker suggests that it may have been because Harold was considered more trustworthy, yet he certainly received the same treatment as his father when summoned to attend the Witan in London.[45] It is possible that, in spite of the lack of any confirming evidence, Harold did give a son, and that it was Ulf the son of Harold who was released on William's death-bed in 1087.[46] The only other time when the hostages might have been given was in September 1052. The *Chronicle* says that on Godwine's return 'the wise men both inside the town and outside' [London] 'advised that hostages be fixed on either side, and so it was done';[47] Eadmer thought that this was the occasion and Trggvie Oleson argued strongly for this later date.[48] However, in 1052 there would have been no point in taking Hákon as a hostage because his father was an outlaw far away in a distant land. In any case Godwine was in a far stronger position in 1052 than in 1051, and Oleson's argument was based on Edward's need for Godwine to accept William as heir to the throne as part of the reconciliation process. Subsequent events proved that this was not the case. When the *Vita* was written in about 1065/1066, Eadgyth wanted to soften the details of her disgrace and to present her royal husband in as good a light as possible; to gloss over the ignominy she had suffered in 1051 and to ignore the part played in the plan to divorce her. In order to do this, her intense dislike for the Archbishop is evident everywhere. In an attempt to conceal Edward's part, she chose to denigrate his chief advisor.[49]

The king was now free to follow his own inclinations regarding the foreign policy. The possible repercussions that the marriage of Tostig and Judith might have incurred had been nullified by the family's exile. There remained the threat created by William of Normandy's marriage to Count Baldwin's daughter. Edward had always regarded the Count of Flanders with hostility and a Flemish-Norman coalition was to be avoided at all costs. It was imperative to wean the Norman duke from too close a union between them, and this was also obviously very much in the interests of Eustace, Enguerrand and Walter.

---

[43] W.P. Part I ch 14 pp.20, 21; Part 2 ch 12 pp.120, 121.
[44] 'Historia Novorum' p.6; F. Barlow, 'Edward', App B pp.301-302.
[45] I. Walker, 'Harold' p.33.
[46] J.W. vol iii pp.48,49.
[47] A.S.C 'E' 1052.
[48] 'Edward the Confessor's Promise of the Throne to Duke William', E.H.R LXXII pp.221-228
[49] 'Vita' pp.29f

Genealogy of Baldwin V Count of Flanders

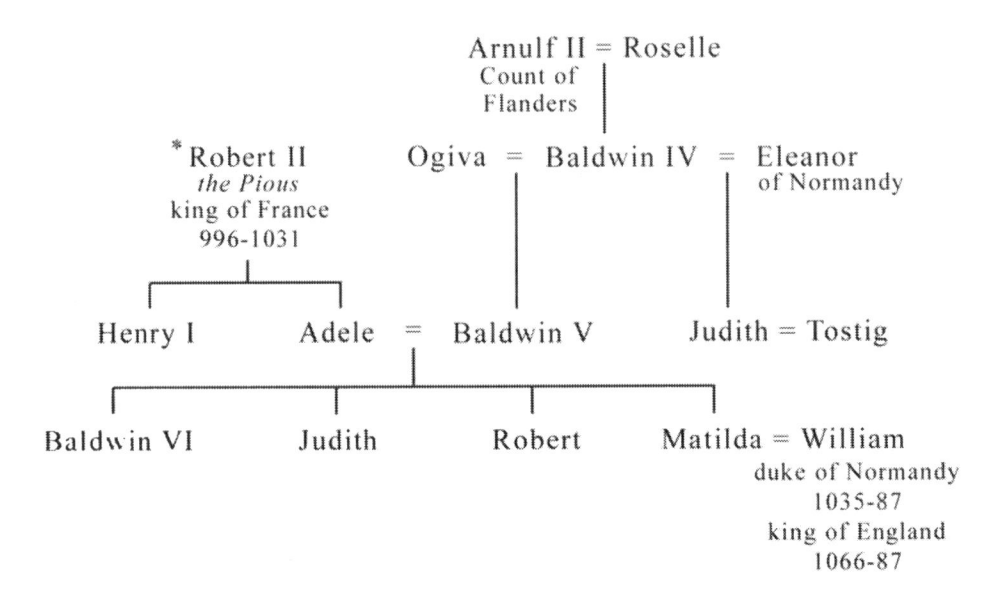

```
                    Arnulf II = Roselle
                    Count of
                    Flanders

 *Robert II        Ogiva = Baldwin IV = Eleanor
  the Pious                              of Normandy
  king of France
  996-1031
     |
  ___|___
 |       |
Henry I  Adele = Baldwin V        Judith = Tostig
                   |
      _____|_____
     |        |        |        |
 Baldwin VI  Judith  Robert   Matilda = William
                                       duke of Normandy
                                       1035-87
                                       king of England
                                       1066-87
```

* Robert the Pious, King of France 996-1031, was married three times
1. Roselle - widow of Arnulf II Count of Flanders
2. Bertha - widow of Eudes of Blois
3. Constance of Anjou

With acknowledgement to
M. Swanton, (edited & translated) *Anglo-Saxon Chronicles*

We do not know Edward's feelings towards William of Normandy at the time. He had spent twenty five years as an exile, presumably most of that time had been spent at the Norman court and he had been encouraged, particularly prior to 1035, to think of himself as the rightful heir to the English throne. But whether he had received the assistance he wished for towards that aim is questionable.[50] The claim made by William of Poitiers that Edward loved William as a brother or a son[51] must surely be pure propaganda included for the purpose of justifying the Norman

---

[50] S. Keynes, 'The Æthelings in Normandy' pp.173-205; F. McLynn, 'The Year of Three Battles' p.14.
[51] W. P. Part 1 ch 41 pp.68, 69.

conquest and the carnage it entailed. William was no more than fourteen when Edward, a man of thirty six or more, left Normandy for England in 1041, and there is no reason to believe that they had further personal contact for the next ten years. It is true that Edward's mother was born into the Norman ducal family, but the relationship between mother and son was anything but cordial. However, with Archbishop Robert acting as the intermediary, Edward started to negotiate with the duke with a view to encouraging William to look to England rather than Flanders.

Meanwhile Godwine and his family found a hearty welcome with Baldwin in Flanders. They stayed in Bruges all that winter under the Count's full protection. Judith, Tostig's wife, was the daughter of Baldwin IV and his second wife Eleanor, and thus the granddaughter of Richard II, which made her the half-sister of Baldwin V and the cousin of Duke William.[52] During the time that the Godwine family were in Flanders, Count Baldwin was preparing to renew hostilities with Emperor Henry III.[53] At some point soon after their arrival, Swegn set off on a pilgrimage to the Holy Land to make atonement for his crimes. This is recorded only in the *Abingdon Chronicle* and in John of Worcester, who adds that he was moved by remorse for the murder of his cousin, Beorn, and that he undertook the journey barefoot.[54] It seems that at one point the Earl intended going to Ireland himself and had a ship provisioned and in readiness but, at the last minute, he changed his mind, deciding instead to make penance for his irresponsible actions. He must have set out on his hazardous and lonely journey in October against the oncoming winter. It has been suggested that his father was instrumental in persuading him to make the journey in order that, as a penitent pilgrim, on his return to England – when and if that time came – he would be more readily acceptable.[55] This may well be true, or possibly Bishop Ealdred, who had close contacts with Swegn - for his diocese lay in Swegn's earldom - succeeded in persuading him that if he were to have a future in England then he must be able to prove the sincerity of his remorse.[56]

Ireland

Harold and Leofwine, having reached Bristol in safety, found the ship already prepared, weighed anchor and set sail from the mouth of the River Avon into the Bristol Channel. A tempestuous storm sprang up with high winds and tumultuous waves lashing the vessel as they entered the Irish Sea. Some of the crew were swept overboard and it was only with the greatest difficulty that the brothers were eventually able to reach the coast of Ireland. They received a hospitable welcome

---

[52] See the Genealogies in H. Tanner's article, 'The Expansion of the Power and Influence of the Counts of Boulogne', and the Genealogies in 'The Carmen' of C. Moreton and H. Muntz.
[53] H. Tanner, 'Expansion of Power' p.264.
[54] J.W. pp.570-571; A.S.C 'C' s.a 1052.
[55] I. Walker, 'Harold' p.43.
[56] It is noticeable that J.W. is more sympathetic to Earl Swegn; he mentions his walking barefoot to Jerusalem, and his desire to marry Eadgifu, the abbess of Leominster.

at the court of King Diarmait Mac Máel Na Mbo who, according to the *'Brut y Tywysogyon'*, had developed a reputation for his kindness to strangers.[57]

Swegn would have been acquainted with Ireland – Bristol being under his jurisdiction - for the town had a regular trade passing through its port to Dublin and east Ireland. It is likely too that Earl Godwine knew Diarmait, which might explain the friendly reception extended to his sons. When Godwine's earldom was extended after the banishment of Æthelweard in 1020 to include the western provinces it is probable that he was granted possession of land in Cornwall. Admittedly, the Domesday Survey does not mention the earl, but it does record twelve estates held by Earl Harold *T.R.E.* (in the time of King Edward) of which Winnianton in West Cornwall was the largest with land for sixty ploughs. At the time of the Survey they were all held by the king. According to the *Chronicle* on Godwine's death Harold succeeded to his father's earldom, 'and to all that his father owned'. Harold also held two estates at Halton and Philliegh and his mother, the Lady Gytha, was in possession of two estates in northeast Cornwall, Poundstock and windswept St Gennys. All this tends to prove that Godwine had connections with the county. That there was a close link between Cornwall and South-eastern Ireland may be inferred from the *De Gestis Herewardi Saxonis* which tells how Hereward came to the rescue of the daughter of Alef, Prince of Cornwall, and her intended bridegroom, the son of a king in Ireland. Legend it may be, but it may hold the germ of an historical association.[58]

Godwine would, no doubt, be conversant with the prowess of a rising star such as Diarmait. Further - and perhaps more reliable - evidence of Godwine's knowledge of Irish affairs is afforded by an entry in the *Annals of Tigernach* which records that in the year 1030 Cnut had used Scandinavian mercenaries from Ireland in an attack on Wales with the words: 'Plundering of Wales by the English and the Foreigners of Dublin'.[59] Two years after this, Diarmait emerges into the pages of Irish history. The kingship of Leinster had been shared by the descendants of Marchad Mac Brian, who died early in the eighth century, until the early eleventh century. In 1037 Donnchad Mac Gilla Patriac, the leader of the Osraige, succeeded in establishing himself as its king and Diarmait, the head of the Úl Chennselaig, allied himself with Donnchad in order to consolidate his own position. By that time he was powerful enough to plunder the Danish occupied city of Waterford. In 1039 Donnchad died and his successor, Domnall Mac Donnchada, carried on the friendship which had existed between his father and Diarmait. Together they contended with Marchad Mac Dunlaig for the latter's right to the kingship of Leinster from 1040 until 1042, the year in which Marchad was slain. By 1046 Diarmait had become the most powerful king in the island. In the same year Echmarcash Mac Rafhnall succeeded Harald, obviously

---

[57] 'Brut y Tywysogyon, Red book of Hergest' pp.28-29 s.a 1072.
[58] I am indebted to Ben Hudson for this line of thought, 'The Family of Harold Godwineson' pp.94, 95; 'De Gestis Hereward Saxonis' trans. M. Swanton in 'The Three Last Englishmen' pp.45-88 particularly pp.48-54.
[59] 'Annals of Tigernach' vol 2 s.a 1030 p.370 MI.

a Dane, to the kingship of Dublin. Some years later, while Earl Harold and Leofwine were the guests of Diarmait, the king cast longing eyes on the Viking city of Dublin and the territory of the Fine Gall and according to the *Annals of Tigernach*: 'the son of Mael Na Mbo took the kingship of Dublin by force'. This was after some desperate fighting around the fortress of the city in which many on either side were slain and Echmarcash fled overseas.

It is very likely that the sons of Godwine took part in the attack, and it is feasible that, because of their help in this campaign, Diarmait gave them every assistance in recruiting mercenaries from the Danish population of Dublin, and years later was to extend the same hospitality to Harold's sons in the wake of the battle of Hastings. The following year Diarmait was victorious against the king of Munster, but it was not until 1054 that he was fully established as the undisputed king of Dublin and Leinster.[60]

Godwine in exile

With the earl and his family in exile Robert renewed his efforts to have Spearhafoc expelled. King Edward had permitted the bishop to retain his office as bishop of London in spite of the Archbishop's remonstrances. From the moment of his elevation to Canterbury, Robert had schemed to have a fellow Norman in the see of London and to that end, on his return from Rome with his pallium, he claimed that the Pope had forbidden him to consecrate Spearhafoc on the grounds of his unsuitability. Whatever the reason for this charge, it can only have been Robert himself who supplied this information. According to the *Chronicle* of Abingdon, when their former bishop was expelled he disappeared with any valuables he could take from his diocese.[61]

King Edward now had several earldoms to confer on his relatives and supporters. His nephew, Ralph, who had, it is suggested, been earl of the East Midlands in succession to Beorn, now received part of the earldom vacated by Swegn, which certainly included Herefordshire and Gloucestershire, although Earl Siward may have been given the shires of Northampton and Huntingdon in a bid to secure his allegiance. The western provinces, which included Cornwall, Devon, Somerset and Dorset, were bestowed on Odda, Edward's kinsman. This Odda witnessed charters of King Æthelred II, Cnut, Harthacnut and Edward from 1013 until 1050, and Worcester leases from 1038 until 1053 or later. He signs as '*dux*' in three charters, witnessing grants made by bishop Ealdred of Worcester, two during Godwine's exile and the third in 1053 or later. All the *Chronicles* speak well of

---

[60] ibid, p.392 MILII; 'Brut' pp.26-29 s.a 1070-1072; For Diarmait see 'The Annals of Tigernach' vol 2 pp.376-409; 'Annals of Ulster' p.474 s.a 1036 – pp.508-509 s.a 1072; 'Annals of Inisfallen' p.217 s.a 1055-1057 – p.228 s.a 1072. See D. Ó-Corrain, 'Ireland Before the Normans' and the 'Career of Diarmart' pp.13-17 in 'The Old Wexford Journal' pp.27-31 and K. L. Maund, 'Ireland, Wales and England in the eleventh Century' pp.163-167.

[61] 'Chronicon Monasterii de Abingdon' vol 1; F. Barlow, 'Edward' p.115 and note 3.

him and he seems to have been a pious, sincere man. William of Malmesbury refers to him as '*regnis cognate*' 'royal kinsman'. His relationship to the royal family, it has been suggested, may have been through Æthelweard the chronicler. Williams persuasively suggests that Odda's parent could have been either Ælfweard or Ælfwaru, the siblings of King Eadwig's queen, Ælfgifu, and of Æthelweard - and thus a distant cousin of Edward's.[62] Known to history as 'Odda of Deerhurst' because of his connections with the town, he founded a church there (still standing in the present day) dedicated to the Holy Trinity in memory of his brother, Ælfric, who predeceased him by three years. Their sister, Eadgyth, is mentioned in the *Domesday* Book as holding land in Herefordshire. In the witness lists Odda's name is always found in close proximity to the brothers, Ordgar and Ælfgar, his own brother, Ælfric, and with Brihtric, all of whom had probably some relationship with the royal family.[63]

As for the other earldoms, it is possible that the Archbishop may have secured lay jurisdiction over Kent as Æthelnoth seems to have done.[64] There were the shires of Wiltshire, Hampshire, Surrey and Sussex still to be disposed of south of the Thames which Edward may have retained himself. It is, however, just possible that he may have had some idea of appointing the Norman duke to some as a surety for his support if Godwine and his sons did try to stage a comeback.[65] To Harold's earldom of East Anglia he assigned Ælfgar to retain his father's loyalty. The son of Earl Leofric and Godgifu is first recorded as a witness to a writ recording a bequest by Thurstan of an estate at Wimbish in Essex to Christ Church, in order that prayers be said for the souls of his mother Leofwaru, his wife Æthelgyth, and his own. This, according to the list of witnesses, must have been drawn up in 1042 or 1043. Amongst those who attested the writ were Earls Godwine, Leofric and 'the earl's son Ælfgar' - this last phrase was apparently added later.[66] However Thurstan's will, which was drawn up one or two years later, includes Ælfgar as the principal witness in Essex.[67] There is an Ælfgar, styled as '*nobilis*', who witnessed King Edward's grant of land to a thegn named Eadulf in St Dennis, Cornwall, but this is almost certainly Ordgar's brother of that name.[68] The only other record of Ælfgar Leofricsson before his appointment as earl is made by the author of the *Vita Ædwardi Regis* who mentions that he was with his father and Earl Siward at Gloucester.[69] It would seem from this that before then he was rarely at court. It is difficult to assess Ælfgar's age at this time. If his daughter, Ealdgyth, was married to Gruffydd ap Llewlyn some time between

---

[62] A. Williams, 'Odda of Deerhurst' pp.4-6.
[63] ibid pp 16-17.
[64] A. Williams, 'Kingship and Government' p.133, 212 and note108.
[65] P. Stafford, 'Unification' p.91.
[66] S 1530; D. Whitelock, 'Wills' No 30 p.78, 189-192.
[67] ibid S 1531 'Wills' No 31 pp.80, 85, 192-197; There is an Ælfgar who witnessed twice as 'nobilis', S 1003 in AD 1044 and S1019 in AD 1049 who was the brother of Ordgar. For this and his other attestations see S. Keynes, 'Atlas'.
[68] S 1033, 1034, 1036, 1042; Atlas, Table LXXV 1 of 2.
[69] 'Vita' pp.34, 35.

1055 and 1057, she must have been born in 1040 or perhaps earlier, which would mean that Ælfgar must have been at least thirty at the time, and possibly older. Legend made him the father of a daughter called Lucy who became the wife of Ivo Taille Bois, which is entirely without foundation.[70] His wife, Ælfgifu, came from the East Midlands or East Anglia and held lands in Derbyshire, Essex, Hertfordshire, Leicestershire, Northants, Nottingham and Suffolk.[71] A mythical pedigree made her a sister of William Malet de Graville.[72] In 1979, Ælfgifu's relationships were rescued from the realms of fantasy by Professor Sawyer in his book, 'Charters of Burton Abbey'. He advanced the convincing theory that Ælfgar's wife was the daughter of Ealdgyth and of Morcar, the thegn of the Five Boroughs who, with his brother, Sigeferth, was murdered by Eadric Streona in 1015. She would thus have been the great niece of Ælfhelm, the ealdorman of Northumbria, and of Wulfric Spot, which would make her the cousin of the other Ælfgifu 'of Northampton', the first wife of King Cnut.[73] This explanation, if accepted, goes far to account for the way her kinsman, Leofric, championed the cause of Harold Harefoot. The families of Leofric and Wulfric may have been closely connected for a long time: it is even chronologically possible that Ælfgar and Ælfgifu were already married in 1035. One of their children would have been called after his grandfather, Morcar, and the girl after her grandmother, Ealdgyth.

The 'D' version of the *Chronicle* records that, soon after Queen Eadgyth was sent to Wherwell, Duke William came to England with a great troop of Frenchmen 'and the King received him…'.[74] This entry has been the cause of a great deal of controversy and raises many questions. Perhaps the most convincing reason for accepting the historicity of the entry is its timing. The Godwinesons were all in exile; the Norman faction was dominant, and Edward was anxious to offer inducements to William to coax him away from Baldwin's influence. There are, however, a number of problems. If he landed at any of the ports in Kent or Sussex and met the king at Winchester or London, it is difficult to understand the silence of the Canterbury or Abingdon chroniclers. If, however, as Professor Barlow suggests, he landed at Southampton and met the king at Gloucester, this might provide an explanation.[75]

That William's visit is not mentioned by either William of Jumièges or William of Poitiers has been explained by some authorities as the reluctance of the Norman writers to represent their duke as a 'petitioner', and as always being in charge of every situation.[76] But surely this would have been a wonderful opportunity for the occasion to be used to prove Edward's intention of nominating William as his intended heir. There is also the possibility that the entry in the *Chronicle* may have

---

[70] F.N.C.iv p.472; Ingulf p.661.
[71] A. Williams, 'Cockles Amongst the Wheat', pp.8, 19 note 44; 'Dark Age Britain', pp.169-170.
[72] See note 70 above.
[73] 'Charters of Burton Abbey' pp XLII, XLIII, and XIX.
[74] A.S.C 'D' s.a 1052/1051; J.W. pp.562-563.
[75] F. Barlow, 'Edward' p.116.
[76] ibid.

been inserted at a later date: David Douglas argued that the visit was a figment of the scribes' imagination, but this has been rejected by both Tryggvie Oleson and Sten Körner.[77] William's presence in England in 1051 was accepted by such leading historians as E. A. Freeman, Frank Stenton and by most other writers on the subject until David Douglas - showing the need to take into consideration conditions in Normandy in 1051/1052 - pointed out that from March 1051 until August 1052, the duke was in no position to leave his duchy, and was struggling to maintain his authority in Normandy. Against this, Körner argued that the coalition between the King of France and the Count of Anjou against Normandy did not actually come into effect until 1054. He then concluded: 'there are, therefore, no sound arguments for rejecting the statement that William visited England in 1051'.[78] However, although William was not threatened by the transfer of support by the French King from Normandy to Anjou until a later date, it is certain that in late 1051 he was in no position to find the time for a visit to England 'with a great troop of Frenchmen'. At the time implied by the Worcester *Chronicle*, William was in the far south of Normandy contesting with Geoffrey Martell for the control of Belleme county and of Maine. The towns of Domfront and Alençon were on the southern borders of the duchy and it is difficult to see how the duke could have been conducting a siege of the former and striking terror into the hearts of the latter, and still have found the time for a foreign visit.[79]

As winter passed into spring the Queen Mother's failing health became apparent and on 6th March she died.[80] Emma had come to England fifty years earlier as King Æthelred's child bride. During those years she had devoted her abundant energies into amassing and retaining all the power and wealth she could accumulate. Apart from the last few years, she had been a guiding force in the kingdom except while in exile. She was buried in the Old Minster in Winchester by the side of her second husband, Cnut, and her son, Harthacnut, who was probably the only person she ever actually loved. Emma had outlived her two husbands and four of her five children. In the last years of her life she must have had cause to reflect on the irony of fate: the son she detested, who had humiliated her in the presence of the senior earls, alone had outlived her other children.

As soon as the campaigning season commenced, Gruffydd ap Llewelyn launched a vicious attack against Herefordshire, reaching the outskirts of Leominster, ravaging far and wide. Englishmen and the Normans of the castles rallied to oppose him. Losses were severe on both sides, but the Welsh had the victory and made off with a great deal of booty.[81] It has been suggested that his raid on Earl

---

[77] Körner, 'Battle of Hastings' pp.158-163; T. Oleson, 'Edward's Promise of the Throne' p.221f.
[78] ibid, 'Battle of Hastings' pp.162-163.
[79] N. J. Higham, 'The Death of A.S. England', pp.133-134.
[80] A.S.C 'C' 1051/1052; 'D' 1052, 'E' 1052, 'F' 1051; J.W. pp.566-567: for Emma's career see P. Stafford,'Queen Emma and Queen Edith' and S. Keynes, 'E.E.R' Introduction to the 1998 Reprint pp LXXI-LXXX.
[81] A.S.C 'D' 1050/1049.

Ralph's earldom may have been instigated by Earl Harold from Ireland,[82] but there is no evidence for this. It is far more likely that, as J. E. Lloyd says, Gruffydd was flexing his muscles in a reaction to the Norman colony which was being installed along the border, and providing a menace to the Welsh.[83] He must have viewed with apprehension the arrival of Richard Fitz Scrob, Osbern Pentecost and their followers. Gone were the days when the previous earl, Swegn, and he could co-operate against his southern rival, Gruffydd ap Rhydderch.

Alarmed that Godwine was preparing an attempt to return by force, Edward had forty long ships stationed at Sandwich on surveillance duty. The fleet was put under the command of Earls Ralph and Odda.[84] An army was also on standby duty in the vicinity. No doubt if Gruffydd knew that Ralph was with the fleet at Sandwich with his military adherents, he would not have been slow to take advantage of such an opportunity to stage an attack. At some time during the spring or summer of 1052 Godwine sent a message to King Edward asking for the opportunity to come in peace, in order to have the chance to clear himself of the charges brought against him. This was followed by envoys from Count Baldwin and his brother-in-law, King Henry I of France,[85] but with no more success. Baldwin would have been motivated by his long friendship with the earl. The last thing the French king wanted was an over-mighty subject, and the best way, he judged, to prevent close ties between William and the childless English king was the reinstatement of Godwine and his family. At last the earl decided that the time was ripe for action. With a fleet recruited with the assistance of the Flemish count and the treasure he had been able to take out of England, Godwine left Bruges; setting sail from the river Yser he landed at Dungeness on 23 June 1052 after an absence of nine months.

---

[82] I. Walker, 'Harold' p.43.
[83] 'A History of Wales' ch xi p 357 f.
[84] A.S.C 'E' s.a 1052.
[85] 'Vita' pp 40- 41.

Family Tree of Godgifu

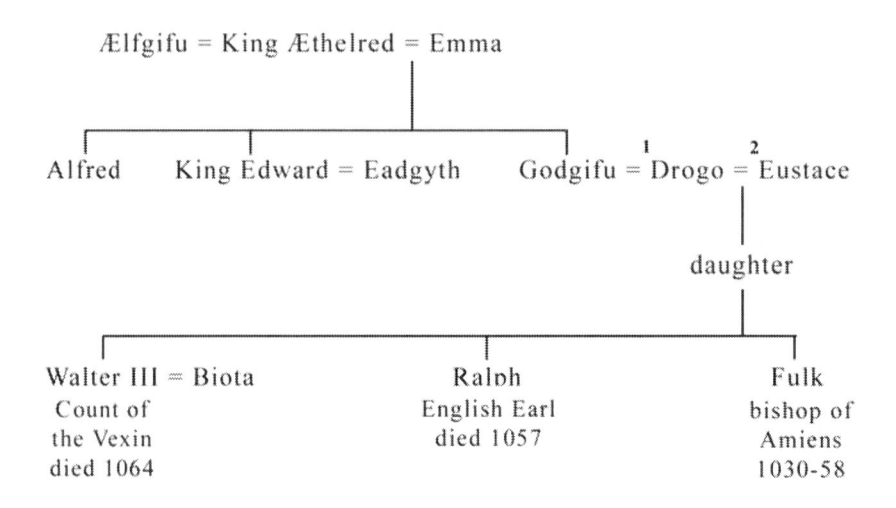

```
        Ælfgifu = King Æthelred = Emma
                      |
    ┌─────────┬───────────────────┬──────────────┐
  Alfred   King Edward = Eadgyth      Godgifu =¹ Drogo =² Eustace
                                              |
                                           daughter
                                              |
    ┌─────────────────┬──────────────────────┐
 Walter III = Biota         Ralph                 Fulk
  Count of               English Earl          bishop of
  the Vexin               died 1057             Amiens
  died 1064                                     1030-58
```

After F. Barlow, *Edward* 1979

Table 9 Sequence of Events 1051 - 1052

1051 Mid-Lent	Robert appointed as Archbishop of Canterbury
1051 Spring	Robert goes to Rome to receive his pallium
1051 June 29	Robert installed at Canterbury
1051 Summer	Marriage of Tostig and Judith of Flanders
1051 End of August	Eustace lands at Dover
1051 September 8	Edward summons Council to Gloucester
1051 September 24	Meeting of Witan in London
1051 September 25	Godwine and sons declared outlaws
1051 September 25-30	Eadgyth sent to Wherwell
1051 Oct/Nov	Possible visit of William?
1052 March 6	Death of Emma
1052 Spring	Gruffydd ap Llewelyn invades Herefordshire
1052 June 23	Godwine sets sail from Flanders

10. Godwine's Homecoming

Godwine's Planned Return

As the spring of 1052 merged into summer, Godwine at last judged the time ripe for a sortie into England in order to assess the state of the country's defences, but he also needed to assure himself of the support he was likely to receive. With a few ships he set sail from the river Yser on 22 June.[1] With a favourable east wind,[2] Godwine made his landfall at Dungeness on the spur of land to the south of Romney.[3] He had successfully eluded the royal fleet stationed at Sandwich and had already been heartened by declarations of ardent support from the men of Kent, before the earls, Ralph and Odda, became aware of his presence in the country. Ordering the shire levy to advance by land, they sailed with the royal fleet in order to cut off Godwine's escape by sea, but, warned of this danger, the earl re-embarked and sailed west along the coast to Pevensey.[4] There he had the advantage of being in his own patrimony, and he also had protection from the militia by the marshes which lay to the east, and the forest of the Weald to the north.[5] Here Godwine was able to recruit supporters in Sussex, Surrey and, according to the Worcester tradition, as far afield as Essex.[6] The seamen of the ports, particularly of Hastings, enthusiastically acclaimed their loyalty to his cause, declaring that they were ready to 'live and die' with him.[7] A fierce gale prevented the royal fleet from interfering with Godwine's recruitment, and enabled him eventually to make good his escape.[8] According to a late story, King Edward had been with the fleet at Sandwich and the same writer also records that a heavy mist fell which made it possible for Godwine to put out from Pevensey without his departure being detected.[9]

Godwine returned to Bruges inspired by the rapturous response he had received, and by the realisation that any future action would be likely to meet with success. When the news reached him that the royal fleet had been disbanded, this was the opportunity to make his comeback. He sent a message along the ship lanes of the English Channel to his son, Harold, in Ireland, advising him to commence preparations to join him at a given time and place.

---

[1] J.W. pp.568-569.

[2] 'Vita' pp.40,41.

[3] A.S.C 'E' s.a 1052, A.S.C 'F' s.a 1051; with their more intimate local knowledge; not mentioned in A.S.C 'C', 'D' J.W. or by the 'Vita'.

[4] Again mentioned by A.S.C 'E'; further evidence of their local knowledge.

[5] I. Walker, 'Harold' p.44; M. Swanton, 'A.S.C' Map, 'Areas of Swamp and Forest'.

[6] A.S.C 'D' s.a 1052; J.W. pp.568-569; A.S.C 'C', 'and all the east part, and Sussex & Surrey'.

[7] A.S.C 'C' and 'D' s.a 1052; J.W. pp.568-569.

[8] The storm is recorded only in A.S.C 'E' 1052.

[9] William of Malmesbury, 'G.R.' Bk 2 ch 199.8 pp.360-361.

Disappointed, Ralph and Odda, with their crews, returned to Sandwich. When the king realised that the earl had made good his escape, he was furious and ordered Ralph and Odda back to London in order to replace them with more efficient commanders and to obtain more loyal crews.[10] However, this was more easily said than done. Eventually, in a fit of frustration reminiscent of his father, King Æthelred, Edward abandoned the idea of a naval deterrent. Dispirited and perhaps with ships damaged during the gale, the crews were allowed to disband and return to their homes. The south coast was now unprotected and this time Godwine gathered as many ships' crews as he could enlist, with Count Balwin's assistance, and set sail for the Isle of Wight.[11] Here he sought to provision his fleet. According to the Domesday Survey, Godwine was the holder of the manor of Bonchurch,[12] of a small estate called Woolverton,[13] and of Wroxall which Gytha held.[14] Meeting with stern opposition, he was forced to raid the island until the inhabitants eventually provided him with sufficient victuals to supply his followers until more could be collected.[15] According to one version of the *Chronicle* he also commandeered any ships in the island's ports which could be of use to him and took hostages.[16] The flotilla then sailed west, presumably in order to facilitate joining the force which Harold would be bringing from Ireland. Whilst waiting for these reinforcements, Godwine put in at the island of Portland off the coast of Dorset, which was a royal estate in the hands of King Edward. This may have been the reason that he chose the island to reprovision his fleet.[17] There his followers 'did whatsoever harm they could'.[18]

After this the fleet cruised up and down the Channel waiting for the arrival of Harold and Leofwine.[19] There is no mention of Godwine's other sons, Tostig and Gyrth, being with their father either at this time or in his earlier sortie into England. They may have remained in Flanders recruiting more reinforcements; it is, however, certain that the whole family was in London at the reconciliation.[20]

By this time, Harold and his brother were sailing from an Irish port for the coast of England, with nine ships crewed by Hiberno-Danish mercenaries from Dublin.[21] Steering the fleet into the Bristol Channel, they landed at Porlock, in the hundred of Carhampton, on the Somerset coast. Porlock is situated in a haven sheltered by a range of hills, but open to the elements and the sea from the

---

[10] A.S.C 'E' s.a 1052.
[11] A.S.C 'C' 'D' 'E'; J.W. pp.568-569.
[12] Phillimore D.B. Hampshire, Isle of Wight 7.1.
[13] ibid I, W12.
[14] ibid I, W14.
[15] A.S.C 'E' S 1052.
[16] A.S.C 'F' s.a 1051.
[17] F. Harmer, 'A.S.Writs' pp.385-387, no 112 and p.526.
[18] D.B. Dorset, Phillimore 1.1; M. Swanton, 'A.S. Chronicles' p.178 note 1.
[19] A.S.C 'C' 1052, 'D' 1052; J.W. pp.568-569.
[20] F. Barlow, 'Edward' p.122 note 2.
[21] A.S.C 'E' s.a 1052; 'F' s.a 1051; 'C' s.a 1052; J.W. pp.568-569.

north. The manor and the surrounding lands were then held by Algar, perhaps the man who also possessed extensive estates in Somerset amounting to nearly 12,000 acres.[22] The village lay amidst some relatively flat pasture land of approximately five hundred acres, broken by woodland. A pebble ridge stretched some three miles along the coast and, between it and the village, about a mile inland, there was an area of marshland, lying below sea level. A field's distance from the beach and marshland there is some land now known as 'Hell byes', where, some years ago, shards of swords and other weapons were discovered; this might mark the site of the battle which ensued.[23]

Harold's intention was perhaps to reach the neighbouring manor of Selworthy over two miles distant from Porlock, which had been held before her fall from favour by his sister, Queen Eadgyth.[24] No access for his ships was available at Selworthy, owing to the steep and ragged cliffs. Harold's crew would have had to take the coastal road to reach their destination. He had no reason to expect hostility; his sole intention was to take on board enough provisions to last until he was able to join his father somewhere in the Channel. Harold was, after all, landing in territory which had been governed by his father for many years, and more recently by his brother Swegn.[25] Various reasons have been advanced to account for the antagonism which he encountered: a pronounced Celtic influence; the misdeeds of Swegn; Harold's own desire for retaliation against Odda, who had benefited by his family's disgrace and was now earl of the area; or a similar desire for revenge against 'Algar'.[26] Whatever the reasons, it is clear that, to the local thegns, the landing by Harold and his Irish recruits was regarded as a real and serious threat. Long before the fleet sailed into the Bristol Channel, the *fyrd* was alerted by a huge pyre which had been lit on the summit of Dunkery Beacon, blazing on the skyline four or five miles away. The local militia were thus well prepared for a possible landing, somewhere along the coast. Some evidence of this may be indicated by the traces of an encampment which had been excavated a mile and a half south west of the present church of Porlock, although this may have been dug against an earlier Danish attack.[27] Had Harold been expecting to obtain provisions from neighbouring Selworthy, he was unsuccessful; the *fyrd* fell upon his men before they had left Porlock. The force mustered against Harold must have been substantial, for in the conflict more than thirty thegns and their followers were killed. With the militia beaten off, Harold was then able to take whatever he required. According to John of Worcester, he plundered the surrounding townships and countryside. The author of the *Vita Ædwardi* records

---

[22] I am indebted to Dennis Corner for his advice and information. There is no need to attribute all the estates credited to 'Algar' to a single person, and the Algar is not to be identified with Earl Ælfgar, Leofric's son.

[23] J.W. pp.556-557.

[24] F.N.C. ii p.316; Walker, 'Harold' pp i ; Rev. Walter Hook for 'Ælfgar', 'History of the Ancient church of Porlock'; Dennis Corner, 'Porlock in those Days'.

[25] DB Phillimore, Somerset 32.3

[26] 'History of the Ancient Church of Porlock' p.22.

[27] ibid; D. Corner, 'Porlock in Those Days'

that Harold and Leofwine 'wasted with sword, fire and the seizure of booty all the kingdom from the farthest limits of the Western Britons or English to the place where the earl [Godwine] was stationed'.[28] This is at variance with the different *Chronicle* versions which clearly state that after the raid, loot was taken for provisions and men as captives.[29] These may have been intended to serve as galley slaves or oarsmen, and it is unlikely that, as Freeman thought probable, they were intended for the Irish slave trade. The earl's main objective at that point was to join his father and he would not have wanted to be hindered by other considerations.[30] No doubt the scribe who wrote the *Vita Ædwardi* was allowing his imagination free rein in what he mistakenly thought was a laudable victory. All versions of the *Chronicle* imply that as soon as the conflict was over and provisions gathered, the brothers sailed around Land's End and started to search for their father's fleet.

It must have been mid- or late-August when Godwine and his sons at last joined forces, either at Portland or further up the Channel towards the Isle of Wight. From then on, all raiding ended. Returning to the island, Godwine returned the hostages who had been taken earlier in exchange for the provisions that had been left behind on his previous visit. The combined fleets then sailed up the Channel putting in at Pevensey, Hastings, Romney, Hythe, Folkestone and Dover and in all these ports the earl received an enthusiastic welcome.[31] He was willingly provided with provisions and ships, hostages were given and support for his cause was confirmed. Sailing on to Sandwich the fleet made its way up the Wantsum Channel, passed the Isle of Thanet and on into the Thames estuary.[32] A small contingent dropped behind the rest and landed on the Isle of Sheppey, apparently without Godwine's knowledge, where they did a great deal of wanton damage and then proceeded to burn down the king's manor of Milton Regis. That this was done without the earl's approval seems to be indicated in the St Augustine's version of the *Chronicle* which, in recording the event, says that the perpetrators then 'took their way towards London after the earls'.[33]

---

[28] J.W pp 566-567: Vita pp 42-43.
[29] A.S.C 'E' s.a 1052, 'Captives' not in C.D. or J.W.; compare with 'C' 'D'; J.W. pp.566-567 says, 'he plundered many town ships and fields'.
[30] F.N.C.ii p.316 note 4.
[31] A.S.C 'E' 1052.
[32] M. Swanton, 'A.S. Chronicles', p.179 note 10 and p.272.
[33] A.S.C 'E' s.a 1052.

Godwine in London

The fleet weighed anchor at Southwark on Monday 14 September.[34] By this time Godwine was in command of a considerable force: one near-contemporary says 'The sea was covered with ships. The sky glittered with the press of weapons.'[35] Allowing for some exaggeration it must still have been an impressive array that arrived at Southwark that Monday morning. It has been suggested that it was Harold's mercenaries from Dublin which constituted the significant difference between the first landing at Dungeness and the earl's recent awesome strength. This is, of course, true, but surely the acquisition of the English seamen from the ports of Sussex and Kent was an even greater factor in swaying the feelings of their fellow countrymen in the events which followed in London.[36] Apparently King Edward was staying in the palace of Westminster[37] completely unaware of Godwine's successful progress until he reached Southwark.[38] Galvanized into belated action, he sent urgent messages for help and Ralph and Odda were no doubt close at hand as they were last heard of in London.[39] He summoned all the royal thegns who 'had not defected from him',[40] and couriers were sent in haste to the northern earls, Leofric and Siward.

By the time Godwine's fleet had reached Southwark the tide was at low ebb. He utilised the time to contact the leading citizens of London and apparently he had an encouraging response;[41] the earl was given assurances that his fleet would be able to pass London Bridge without hindrance. With the incoming tide, this was accomplished and the walls of the city were passed. It was then that the king's forces came in sight.[42] Edward had been able to gather fifty ships, and soldiers sufficient to line the north bank of the Thames. Also in his company were Osbeorn Pentecost, Hugh the Castellan, Richard Fitz Scrob and their Norman knights. Keeping his advancing flotilla close to the southern bank, Godwine sent a message to Edward asking that he and his family should be reinstated to their former positions and possessions.[43] The king was furious; his reply was an outright rejection and Godwine's supporters, angered at his uncompromising attitude, grew vociferously hostile. Tempers became frayed and it required all the earl's eloquence and tact to restore calm and discipline amongst his troops.[44] It becomes obvious that Godwine was in no sense desirous of deposing Edward, he merely wanted to return to the way things had been before 1050 and to work again in

---

[34] A.S.C 'C' 1052; J.W. pp.568-569.
[35] 'Vita' pp.42-43.
[36] P. Stafford, 'Unification' p.91.
[37] 'Vita' pp.42-43.
[38] A.S.C 'C', 'D' s.a 1052; J.W. pp.568-569; 'Vita' pp.42-43.
[39] A.S.C 'C', 'D', 'E' s.a 1052; J.W. pp.568-569.
[40] J.W. pp.568-569.
[41] A.S.C 'C', 'D'; J.W. pp.568-569 who adds 'that his was in return for promises given'.
[42] A.S.C 'C', 'D': J.W. pp.570-571.
[43] A.S.C 'E' s.a 1052; 'F' s.a 1051.
[44] A.S.C 'E' s.a 1052; 'Vita' pp.42-43.

harmony with his royal son-in-law and the other senior earls.[45] He gave orders for his ships to swing across the river in order to encircle the royal fleet.

At this point the northern earls arrived. Not to have obeyed the king's summons would have been tantamount to rebellion. However, during the months since the dramatic events of the previous autumn, both Leofric and Siward must have had qualms at the suddenness and completeness of their fellow earl's downfall. They both probably viewed with alarm the overwhelming influence that the Archbishop exercised, and the direction in which it was leading Edward. There is no reason to think that they were sympathetic to the idea of a Norman duke being nominated heir to the English throne. Leofric in particular must have resented the Norman colony and Norman castles that were springing up in what had been his family's sphere of influence. It says much for him that, in supporting Godwine's restoration, he was also paving the way for his son's loss of the East Anglian earldom on Harold's return, yet Ælfgar did relinquish it according to William of Malmesbury willingly and without rancour.[46]

Both Leofric and Siward must have made it perfectly clear that they were not prepared to fight in order to protect Edward's foreign friends or their ambitions.[47] Instead they advised moderation and Bishop Stigand was, as in the previous autumn, elected to act as an intermediary.[48] Accompanied by some 'wise men' he crossed the river and boarded Godwine's vessel. As a way out of the impasse, it was suggested that hostages be exchanged as a preliminary to Godwine and Harold going ashore with a considerable following.[49] It was then agreed that a meeting of the Witan be arranged for the following morning, Tuesday 15 September, in the open air outside the city walls.[50] Normally the Archbishop of Canterbury would have occupied the premier position next to the king himself, but on this occasion Robert realised that there was no future left for him in England. He dared not stay to face the earl whose career he had set out to ruin and, with the two Norman bishops, Ulf and William, he set off on horseback to escape. The southern roads to the coast were too dangerous so with their followers they made a dash for the East Gate of the city, where they forced their way through a crowd of young men who attempted to stop them, killing and wounding several. Making their way to the Naze on the Essex coast, away from the throngs of Godwine supporters who were attempting to bar their escape, they boarded the first boat that could be found and crossed to Normandy.[51]

---

[45] F. Barlow p.125.
[46] G.R. Bk 2 ch 199 pp.360-361.
[47] A.S.C 'C', 'D' s.a 1052; J.W. pp.570-571.
[48] A.S.C 'E', 'F'.
[49] ibid.
[50] A.S.C 'E'.
[51] A.S.C 'C' Robert, William and Ulf; 'D' Robert, William and Ulf; A.S.C 'E' Robert and Ulf; A.S.C 'F' only Robert; J.W. Robert, William and Ulf pp.570-571.

At the meeting of the *Gemot*, presided over by the king were the five earls: Leofric, Siward, Ælfgar, Ralph and Odda. Amongst the prelates, Stigand was doubtless one of the most notable; also present were 'the best men who were in this land.'[52] Godwine was given the opportunity to clear himself of all the charges which had been brought against him and his family.[53] First and foremost of these was the charge which Robert had resurrected the year before of his complicity in the ætheling Alfred's murder. There was also the claim that Godwine and his sons, Swegn and Harold, had gone to Beverstone intending treachery towards the king.[54] The earl was able to satisfy, on oath, his innocence and that of his sons. The Witan proceeded to proclaim him guiltless of all charges, and then outlawed Archbishop Robert and all those Frenchmen who had been responsible for spreading lies and fomenting trouble between the king and his earl. Included were Bishop Ulf, Osbeorn Pentecost, Hugo the Castellan and their followers: the latter were given permission by Earl Leofric to travel through Mercia to offer their services to King Macbeth in Scotland. For Bishop William, on the other hand, there were voices raised in his defence. It was remembered that, although he had fled with Robert and Ulf, his attitude had been less of a troublemaker and, Norman though he was, more Christian and zealous in his care for the well-being of his flock. It was agreed that messages should be sent inviting him to return.[55]

Godwine's Restoration

The Witan agreed to Godwine's restoration to his 'whole earldom'.[56] Odda, who had been given jurisdiction over the western provinces, was now compensated with an earldom which included Worcestershire and possibly Gloucestershire.[57] Ralph was appointed to Herefordshire.[58] It was approved that Godwine and Harold be re-instated, and the family restored to favour. There was then further work to be considered. The office of Archbishop had to be filled and it was perhaps natural that Ælfric, Christ Church's choice in 1050, should be overlooked in favour of Stigand, who had played such an important part in the recent negotiations. A successor had to be elected for Ulf, the bishop of Dorchester and Wulfwig, a royal priest, was nominated.[59] The following year he travelled in the company of Leofwine, the abbot of Coventry, to be consecrated overseas.[60] He held the see until his death in 1067. Harold's restoration to East Anglia meant that Earl Leofric's son lost the earldom, so to make amends to Leofric, his nephew and namesake was appointed to the abbacy of Peterborough.[61]

---

[52] A.S.C 'E' s.a 1052.
[53] A.S.C 'E' 1052, 'F' 1051; 'Vita' pp.42-45.
[54] A.S.C 'E' s.a 1048/1051; 'Vita' pp.32-33, 34-35 for Alfred's murder.
[55] J.W. pp.570-571.
[56] A.S.C 'C', 'D', 'E' s.a 1052.
[57] A.J. Robertson, 'A.S. Charters' No CXI p.456; A. Williams, 'Odda of Deerhurst' p.2.
[58] A. J. Robertson, 'Charters' No CXV pp.214-215, 466-467; A. Williams 'The King's Nephew' p.338.
[59] S. Keynes, 'Atlas' Table LXXII; for evidence that he had not been an abbot, Table LXXIII.
[60] A.S.C 'C' s.a 1053.
[61] N. J. Higham, 'Death of Anglo-Saxon England' p.138.

The findings of the Witan caused King Edward intense anger.[62] The outlawry of his Norman friends, having to swallow his pride and then being compelled to take back into favour his father-in-law was too much for him, but in the face of the council's deliberations he had no choice. Gradually he was able to gain control over his emotions and eventually he was able to make some outward show of giving the family his 'full friendship'.[63] This was made easier for him by Godwine's attitude of appearing as a supplicant rather than a victor. In order to appease Edward, the Witan agreed to allow him to keep with him some of those Normans who had given no offence in the troubled months which had just passed. Among these were Richard Fitz Scrob and his father-in-law, Robert the deacon.[64] Soon after this, Eadgyth was accompanied from Wilton with due ceremony and restored to her former dignity. The events of the former year were as if they had never been.

After the family had become reconciled with the king, Godwine was taken ill.[65] At this time he must have been over sixty and the trauma of the past year could well have been a contributory factor. The hostility and venom shown by Archbishop Robert, the suddenness and completeness of the family's downfall, his exertions during the comeback campaign, had all taken their toll and it may be that he had suffered a minor stroke. At any rate he seems to have recovered sufficiently to enable him to carry out his official duties. We find King Edward addressing a writ to 'Stigand and Godwine and all the citizens of Winchester' which must belong to this period. The writ concerns confirmation of a messuage in Winchester which the dowager, Queen Emma, had bequeathed in her will to the Old Minster. This document has to be dated sometime between the death of Emma (on 6th or 14th March 1052)[66] and the death of Godwine on 15th April 1053. This can be narrowed down still further to sometime after Godwine's reinstatement in September 1052.[67]

The Christmas *Gemot* met at Gloucester that year and presumably Godwine was at court as usual. During the Christmas festivities a severe gale started to rage on 21st December and continued all through the Christmas period. According to John of Worcester it tore trees from the ground and destroyed churches and dwelling houses.[68] Presumably it affected the midlands a great deal more than the south as it is mentioned in the Abingdon and Worcester versions of the *Chronicle* but not in the annals which were compiled at St Augustine's ccriptorium. The Witan agreed that the constant raids that were being inflicted on the area by Rhys ap Rhydderch had to be stopped by capturing him, dead or alive. On 6th January his severed head was brought to King Edward as proof of the success of the mission.[69]

---

[62] 'Vita' pp.44-45.
[63] ibid.
[64] J.W. pp.570-571.
[65] A.S.C 'C' s.a 1052.
[66] A.S.C 'C' s.a 1051 March 14th ; A.S.C 'D' March 6th ; 'E' and 'F' no actual date mentioned.
[67] F. Harmer, 'Writs' No III pp.382-385, 399-400, 526.
[68] J.W. pp.572-573.
[69] ibid.

It must have been about this time that the news reached England that Earl Swegn had died during his pilgrimage to Jerusalem. It will be remembered that he had arranged to have a ship fitted out and provisioned in readiness to sail to Ireland to recruit mercenaries. While at his father's manor at Southwark, Swegn abruptly changed his mind. Instead his place was taken by his brother, Harold, who took Leofwine with him; Swegn rode with his father to Bosham. The young earl had sinned against God's laws, he had transgressed the ordinances of the church and the sacred ties of kinship and it has been implied that a penance was laid upon him, perhaps by Bishop Ealdred, or by Godwine himself. His actions tend to prove, however, that his pilgrimage was self-imposed by sincere and genuine feelings of remorse. He would certainly have been aware of the dangers attendant on a journey to the Holy Land: both Robert, duke of Normandy, and Drogo, count of the Vexin, had died whilst on pilgrimage to Jerusalem only seventeen years earlier. They had been attended by forty Norman knights and the company had caused comments on their magnificent bearing.[70]

Swegn undertook the journey barefoot and alone against the oncoming winter.[71] His journey took him through the territory of the Magyars of Hungary, a people who had recently been involved in a period of unrest, civil war and a return to paganism. Journeying further south he would have passed through the land of the Bulgars, a nation Slavonic in outlook and language if not of descent.[72] He would have found both the Magyars and Bulgars alien to his Anglo-Danish ways and speech. Leaving the busy streets and crowded marts of Constantinople behind, the exiled earl found himself amongst a people who were becoming increasingly hostile: the armies of the Seljuk Turks were already at the gates of Baghdad. Their presence was engendering an atmosphere of fanatical fervour directed against the presence of Christian pilgrims. At last, reaching his destination, he prayed for forgiveness at the Holy Sepulchre then, renewed in spirit, Swegn set off on the long and tiring return to his native land. But the combined effects of hunger, fatigue and exposure to extreme cold had undermined his constitution: he became ill and died alone among strangers in Lykia on 29th September 1052.[73] (The *Chronicle* records his death in Constantinople, but John of Worcester, as Freeman suggests, must have had 'a sound reason for mentioning Lykia instead of the better known Constantinople.')[74] William of Malmesbury claimed that Swegn was murdered when returning from Jerusalem 'by the Saracens'.[75] John of Worcester, drawing on earlier Chronicles, has to be the more reliable authority.

---

[70] Adam Bk 2 p.92, Schol 40[41]; F. McLynn '1066' p.25.
[71] J. W. pp.570-571; A.S.C 'C' 1052 merely records, 'Swegn had earlier gone from Bruges to Jerusalem, and died on his way home at Constantinople on Michealmas Day'.
[72] H. R. Loyn, 'The Middle Ages' p.62; Lynn Thorndyke, p.134.
[73] A.S.C 'C' 1052; J.W. pp.570-571.
[74] F.N.C.ii note T pp 603, 604, particularly p.604
[75] G.R. Bk 2 ch 200-202 pp.362-365.

Godwine's Death and Legacy

The Easter feast in 1053 was celebrated at Winchester. On Easter Monday, Earl Godwine was seated as usual at the king's table when he was suddenly taken ill. He collapsed speechless and was carried into the king's chamber. He lingered for three days, unable to move or speak, and passed away on Thursday 15th April, apparently the victim of a fatal stroke. The fullest account of Godwine's death appears in the *Abingdon Chronicle*; the other versions do little more than record his death. John of Worcester supplies the information that it was his sons - Harold, Tostig and Gyrth - who carried him into the king's chamber.[76] The Abingdon annalist does mention that Harold and Tostig were with their father at the feast.

Godwine was buried in the Old Minster, Winchester, next to King Cnut, Queen Emma and his nephew, Beorn. We are told that at his funeral 'amidst scenes of great grief' he was mourned by all people as a father and a protector of the kingdom.[77] Godwine had been the foremost earl in England for thirty years, and had been loved and respected by those who knew him best.[78] The ordinary people remembered him as a champion of their rights. He was revered by all as a bulwark against the influence of foreigners who had been increasingly gaining the ascendancy in Edward's court.

As the years passed the simple and straightforward entry in the *Abingdon Chronicle*[79] became distorted in a manner which was calculated to portray the earl's death in a completely different light. One Anglo-Norman chronicler after another enlarged and falsified the story until in the early thirteenth century Roger of Wendover, the prior of Belvoir, adding details of his own to earlier embroideries wrote the following under the year 1054: "Edward, king of England, kept the festival of Easter at Winchester, and as he sat at meat, his butler, while carrying the king's goblet of wine to the table, struck one foot against the floor, but recovering himself with the other, saved himself from falling. On seeing which, Earl Godwin, who, as was his custom, sat with the king at table, remarked 'One brother has helped the other'. To whom the king gave this cutting reply, 'And my brother would now be able to aid me, had it not been for Godwin's treachery'. Godwin, who had betrayed the king's brother, not enduring this reply, said 'I know, O king, that you have me in suspicion touching the death of your brother; but, as God is true and righteous, may this morsel of bread choke me if ever your brother received his death or bodily harm through me or by my counsel.' The king then blessed the morsel, which Godwin put into this mouth, and, being conscious of his guilt, he was choked and died. Seeing him pale and lifeless the king exclaimed 'Take this dog and traitor, and bury him in a cross-way for he is unworthy of Christian burial'."[80] Roger of Wendover attempts to get over the difficulty of the earl's burial in the Old Minster alongside King Cnut by claiming that Godwine's sons buried him there without the king's knowledge!

---

[76] J.W. pp.572-573.
[77] 'Vita' pp.46-47.
[78] ibid; S. Keynes, 'Cnut's Earls' pp.84-87.
[79] A.S.C 'C' s.a 1053.
[80] Roger of Wendover s.a 1054 pp.311-312.

The story first appearance is in William of Malmesbury's *History of the Kings*, followed by a version in the work of Henry of Huntingdon. C. E. Wright published a fragment attached to the *Liber de Hyde* in his *Cultivation of Saga in Anglo-Saxon England* narrative as did Ingulf of Croyland writing towards the end of the thirteenth century. There are both similarities and variations in the five accounts mentioned, but the one factor in which all are in agreement is that Godwine died by 'ordeal by bread'.

Wright suggest that 'the legend of Earl Godwine's death is of very early origin; there is no reason why it should not indeed be the true account of Earl Godwine's death, which some vernacular saga has preserved with slight variations into the early years of the twelfth century'.[81] However, among the sources which William of Malmesbury used were the *Chronicle*, the *Vita Ædwardi Regis* and John of Worcester. In none of these sources was there any mention of this slanderous story. Henry of Huntingdon also used the *Chronicle* and also Gaimar's '*Histoire des Engleis*' and the same is true of Roger of Wendover, who drew on material from John of Worcester amongst others. The fact is that William, Henry and Roger, although they were using sources untainted by this scandal, did not hesitate to incorporate it in their writings. They were all authors who loved to enliven their histories with idle gossip, as indeed did Ingulf. By contrast, some Anglo-Norman authors did not consider the story worth repeating. John of Worcester, Simeon of Durham, Roger of Hoveden, Roger of Hexham and the author of the chronicle of Melrose were sober, conscientious historians more dedicated to the truth. Both Gaimar and the Winchester Chronicler shrank from using what was, after all, Norman propaganda invented with the express purpose of blackening the name of the man who so nearly founded a new royal dynasty.[82]

The origin of the fabrication is to be found in the pages of William of Malmesbury. After writing that the English regarded Godwine and his sons as men of liberal mind and steadfast defenders of Edward's government, he then goes on to say that the 'Normans, not being able to tolerate this, set out to destroy their characters.' William then proceeds to relate the spurious details of Godwine's death, clearly indicating that the story was simply a product of Norman lies.[83] Many were the charges laid against the earl's character. Eadmer, the monk of Christ Church, Canterbury, accused him of being a bitter enemy of the church, 'for he stole from that church her manor of Folkestone.'[84] The Abingdon chronicler complained, when writing of Godwine's illness in 1052, 'he made all too little

---

[81] 'Cultivation of Saga' p.236.
[82] For William of Malmesbury see A. Gransden, 'Historical Writing' pp.166-185; Henry of Huntingdon pp.193-200; for Roger of Wendover pp.359-368 and C. Tyerman, 'Who's Who' p.357; for Ingulf, J. Stevenson's Introduction to his translation of the 'Historia Croylandensis' but see also 'The Historia Croylandensis; A Plea for Reassessment' by D. Roffe, E.H.R col 10 pp.93-108.
[83] G.R. Bk 2 ch 197 pp.354-355.
[84] 'Historia Novorum' p.6; 'Vita' pp.32-33.

reparation for God's property which he had taken from many holy places.'[85] It is only fair to admit that the author of the *Vita Ædwardi* says that, in connection with some Christ Church lands which ran parallel with the earl's, he thought that 'right was on the bishop's side.'[86]

Godwine has also been accused of lacking any religious sentiments in an age when his fellow earls were renowned for their piety. He has been described as a traitor, 'guilefully scheming to attack him [Edward] just as once he had attacked his brother; and as cunning, unscrupulous and grasping.' C. E. Wright gives numerous examples of his supposed greed and convenient change of loyalties. Godwine's part in Alfred's betrayal 'can only be interpreted as an attempt to win the favour of Harold.' Later, when Harthacnut was accepted as king, 'Godwine's subsequent acts show that he became a willing tool to the new king.'[87] His actions on his return in 1052 are described as 'indefensible.'[88] Another historian commented of the earl: 'it is hopeless to make a national hero out of him.'[89] How far can these accusations be verified? Or can we, with Freeman, say 'to know what Godwine was, we have but to cast away the fables of later days, to listen to the records of his own time, to see how he looked in the eyes of men who had seen him?'[90]

The anonymous author of the *Vita Ædwardi Regis* paints a completely different picture of him from that portrayed by some Norman and Anglo-Norman writers. King Cnut, he writes, appreciated his wisdom, courage in war, and his eloquence; in temperament he was gentle and humble. As a revered father he saw to it that his children had a good education to prepare them for their futures; he was also patient and long suffering.[91] It may be argued that the *Vita* was commissioned by Queen Eadgyth, and was biased in her father's favour and this may be partly true. However, the author was honest enough to point out that in his opinion, regarding the Christ Church lands, Godwine was in the wrong. Again, when the earl's fleet reached Sandwich in 1052 he writes of 'this hostile and unlicensed entry into the kingdom.'[92]

The charge that Godwine was guilty of sacrilege raises several arguments, and Freeman deals with the subject at some length,[93] pointing out that a legal claim against a monastery or ecclesiastical foundation runs a fair chance of being regarded as fraudulent. Professor Barlow also states that 'it is axiomatic in the *Chronicles* and other memorials produced by the clergy that no church held an

---

[85] A.S.C 'C' s.a 1052.
[86] 'Vita' pp.32-33.
[87] 'Cultivation of Saga' p.216.
[88] F. Stenton, 'A.S.E' p.569.
[89] C. Oman, 'England Before the Norman Conquest', 9th edition p.622.
[90] F.N.C.ii p.353
[91] 'Vita' pp.10-11.
[92] ibid pp.42-43.
[93] F.N.C.ii note E pp.542-552.

estate illegally or was deprived of it with justice.'[94] The main case against the earl seems to have been Robert's charge of his being in possession of lands that rightly belonged to Christ Church, Canterbury. The problem originated in 1044 when Eadsige, then Archbishop, was forced to give up most of his official duties owing to ill health. In return for Godwine's assistance in procuring the services of Siward of Abingdon as his deputy, and in protecting the rights of Christ Church in the courts, he was rewarded with gifts of land. At some stage he received the 'third penny' of Kent, traditionally the earl's fee, which had been received by both Archbishops Æthelnoth and Eadsige.[95] Godwine's assistance in upholding the rights of the church must have been invaluable to the frail Archbishop.[96] But when Robert was appointed as his successor, he set out to reclaim all the lands which had been given to Godwine. These properties included Richborough, Sundridge, Longport, Saltwood and Folkestone.[97] Robert was undoubtedly imbued with zeal to reclaim these lands for the church and he was certainly motivated with a grim determination to challenge the earls' authority. Initially King Edward had co-operated with Godwine and Eadsige,[98] but by 1050 he had come under the influence of Eadsige's successor.

In reviewing the claims against Godwine it must be remembered that the evidence of the Domesday Survey is likely to be both biased and flawed. When the commissioners were collecting information about land held in King Edward's reign, they had to rely on what could be remembered from twenty years earlier.[99] In any case, the Domesday record is hardly likely to be impartial when it was sufficiently hostile to deny Harold his rightful title of 'King'. There is also the undeniable fact that the charter evidence is often unreliable. In their enthusiasm to procure properties for their church, the monks were inclined to invent documents which purported to prove that estates had been granted by kings of an earlier age. An examination of such claims, as judged by the leading authorities,[100] shows that Christ Church had no fewer than eight spurious royal charters and five doubtful ones. Nor was Christ Church alone in this respect: St Augustine's, Canterbury had six spurious charters and as many doubtful ones, and a bishop's charter classed as a late forgery. Old Minster, Winchester had no less than twenty spurious charters and thirteen which have been classified as dubious. Westminster Abbey's record is not much better with fourteen spurious royal charters, twelve doubtful and two bishop's charters also not genuine. The same may be said in greater or lesser degree of Worcester, Crowland, Malmesbury and Abingdon.

---

[94] F. Barlow, 'The English Church' p.175.
[95] F. Barlow, 'Edward' p.115 note 2.
[96] A. Williams, 'Kingship and Government' p.212 note 108.
[97] Robin Fleming, 'Kings and Lords' p.81; Domesday Morochorum.
[98] A.S.C 'C' s.a 1044; 'E' s.a 1043/1044.
[99] I. Walker, 'Harold' p.56.
[100] ei Napier and Stevenson, F. Harmer, A.J. Robertson, C. Hart, H.P.R.Finberg and the invaluable works of P. Sawyer and S. Keynes.

Regarding Eadmer's claim about Folkestone, it is note-worthy that in AD987 King Æthelstan is supposed to have given Folkestone to Christ Church.[101] This charter is itself doubtful.[102] A later charter recording King Cnut's grant of the town to Christ Church following the death of Eadsige has been considered a forgery.[103] It is of some interest that it says that Cnut's counsellors 'told him that it had formerly belonged to Christ Church in the time of King Æthelstan and was afterwards alienated from it with great injustice'; thus perpetuating the story of the church's ill founded claim. Another charter, this time one of King Edward's, records that he gave the church estates at Chartham and Folkestone in Kent as well as other grants of land in Kent, Surrey, Sussex, Suffolk and Oxfordshire.[104] In this case we have the authority of Dr Cyril Hart that this is only genuine in so far as Chartham is concerned, the remainder having been added after the conquest.[105] Yet another, dated AD1038, concerning King Cnut, Christ Church and Folkestone is probably a forgery.[106] It transpires that its claim was, at the best, doubtful. In 1086 Folkestone was in the possession of the Bishop of Bayeux, not Christ Church and it appears, therefore, that there is no real evidence of any genuine royal charter that provides evidence that the estate was ever granted to Christ Church.[107]

Godwine has also been charged with being involved in the dissolution of the nunnery at Berkeley. Walter Map tells a story which has a great deal in common with the fate of Leominster, and how Godwine is supposed to have gained by its suppression is not clear.[108] The lands belonging to the nunnery passed into the hands of the king, not Godwine, and the evidence against him seems to rest on the Domesday Book statement that Gytha refused to eat any food produced from its lands and the earl was obliged to buy an estate from Azur in order to provide for their needs.[109] This does not necessarily imply that Godwine was to blame for its dissolution; there may have been other reasons. According to the Domesday survey, in 1066 it was King Edward who held Berkeley, not Godwine's family (see D B Gloucestershire i, 15.).

Godwine was not the only one blamed for stealing church property. Worcester suffered losses at the hands of Earl Leofric and his family. Hemming, a monk of Worcester, presents a different picture of the Mercian earl from the one given by the Worcester version of the *Chronicle*.[110] According to him Leofric was in possession of six estates which belonged to the monastery in Worcester.

---

[101] S 398.

[102] P. Sawyer, 'A.S. Charters' p.168.

[103] Robertson, 'A.S. Charters' No XXXV. 'Grant of Land by King Cnut to Christ Church, Canterbury' pp.168-171 and pp.416-419; F. Harmer, 'Writs' p.239.

[104] S 1047.

[105] 'The Early Charters of Eastern England' no 117.

[106] M.K. Lawson, 'Cnut' p.235; S 1643.

[107] See also S 1439.

[108] 'De Nugis Curialum', v c3 pp.416-419 and p.416 note 1; F.N.C.ii pp.544-545.

[109] Phillimore D. B. Gloucestershire 1.63; Ellis vol i pp.309-310 and note 3.

[110] A.S.C 'D' s.a 1057.

Eventually he restored two, the others were left to Godgifu, his wife, and were eventually seized by their grandsons.[111] The estate of Salwarpe was held by Leofric's brother, Godwine. A forged charter of 1043 claimed that King Edward had confirmed a grant of privilege of numerous estates, including Salwarpe, to Coventry Abbey. On his death Godwine bequeathed Salwarpe to the church, but Leofric himself aided his nephew, Æthelwine, to overturn his brother's bequest.[112] Furthermore, according to Hemming, Leofric used his influence to pressurize Prior Æthelwine to grant land to one of his retainers, Simund.[113] Earl Siward too was accused of seizing land from Peterborough.[114] In all of these charges, we hear only one side of the story: the church was in a position to back up its claims by producing charters of doubtful authenticity.[115] Added to this, there may well have been cases where stewards employed by the earls were arranging private deals of their own without the knowledge or assent of their masters. Steorra's deal with Ælfstan, the abbot of St Augustine's, regarding 'the third penny of the toll of Sandwich' without the knowledge of King Harold Harefoot is a case in point.[116]

In stark contrast to Earl Leofric and his fellow earls, Godwine was given the reputation of being completely devoid in any religious belief. Is this view justified, or is there another side to Godwine's character that has become obscured by the Anglo-Norman chronicles which failed to give him his just dues? According to the *Evesham Chronicle* Leofric and his wife Godgifu had as their spiritual adviser and confessor the hermit, Wulfsige.[117] As an anchorite he would not have been allowed to travel and Leofric and Godgifu would have visited him from time to time for guidance.[118] It is also quite possible that Earl Godwine and also Gytha sought spiritual guidance from one of their ecclesiastical friends, as their son, Harold, did with Bishop Wulfstan. It is probable that the earl founded the splendid new church in Dover, built within the *burh* on the hill top. He was certainly its patron and was involved, with Leofwine the priest, for the well-being of the community of St Mary in Castro.[119] He was also well remembered at St Augustines. A charter of 1044 or 1045 records an agreement between Ælfstan, abbot of St Augstine's, and the priest, Leofwine, regarding St Mildred's property which was witnessed by Archbishop Eadsige, Bishop Siward his coadjutor and Earl Godwine. It was worded 'the

---

[111] A. Williams, 'Spoliation of Worcester' pp.386-388; Hemming pp.261-2.
[112] Hemmingi for Leofric and his family's encroachment of the lands of Worcester church pp.259-260.
[113] Hemmingi pp.259-260.
[114] D. Roffe, 'Lady Godiva, the Book and Washingborough' p.9.
[115] F. Barlow, 'The English Church' p.175; A. Williams, 'The Spoliation of Worcester' p.391.
[116] A.J. Robertson, 'A.S. Charters' No XCI pp.174-179 and 422-424.
[117] 'Chronicon Abbatiae de Evesham' p.83.
[118] Emma Mason, 'St Wulfstan of Worcester' p.67.
[119] Tim Tatton-Brown in 'Churches of the Canterbury Diocese' in 'Ministers and Parish Churches; p.110; I am indebted to Dr Ann Williams, 'Kingship and Government' p.134 and 'Lost Worlds' p.59 for this reference.

agreement that Earl Godwine has made between Abbot Ælfstan and the community of St Augustine's and the priest Leofwine…'[120] Godwine also had good relations with the religious houses of Worcester, Christ Church and Winchester.[121] In spite of the unfavourable tone of the Abingdon annalist, the earl's relations with the church there were cordial.[122] The author of the *Vita Ædwardi* claimed that Godwine was 'loyal and devoted to God'.[123]

Leofric's wife, Godgifu, was well known for her good works and gifts to the Abbeys of Coventry and Stow St Mary. Gytha too was not wanting in liberality to the church. According to the *'Annals of Winchester'* she bestowed a great sum in alms upon many churches including the manors of Bleadon and Crowcombe in Somerset, and in addition several ornaments to Winchester's Old Minster.[124] She also gave St Olave's church in Exeter land at Sherford in Devon. This must have been made after AD1057 because it was witnessed by Tostig and by Gyrth, who is designated as 'earl'.[125] Gytha also founded a collegiate church at Hartland in Devon, apparently in the early 1050s, in thanksgiving for Godwine's rescue from shipwreck. The present parish church is built on the spot where Gytha's foundation stood.[126] The earl's rescue may have occurred when he was escaping from the storm in 1052 off the Pevensey coast. Later, after the defeat at Hastings, she gave her estate at Werrington to Tavistock Abbey[127] and the *Liber Eliensis* records that the countess made a gift of 'a wonderfully wrought chasuble' to the monastery of Ely.[128] According to the *Vita*, Godwine himself gave to the Old Minster at Winchester 'many ornaments and rents of land'.[129] There is also some reason to believe that he gave Sandford-on-Thames to Abingdon Abbey on the evidence of two charters. This may have constituted Godwine's posthumous bequest.[130]

---

[120] S 1472. A.J. Robertson, 'A.S. Charters' No CII pp.191, 438-439.
[121] Evidenced by his friendship with Lyfing and Ealdred; Christ church's appeal for Godwine's intervention and their wish to nominate his relative in 1050; and A. J. Roberton's 'Charters' No CII and A. Williams, 'Kingship and Government' p.134.
[122] E. John, 'the Anglo-Saxons' ed. J. Campbell p.221.
[123] 'Vita' pp.42-43.
[124] 'Annals of Winchester' in 'Church Historians' vol IV, part one, 'Gytha, the wife of Godwin, a woman of considerably wealth, bestowed a great sum in alms upon many churches for the benefit of his soul; and gave to the church of Winchester two manors, Bleodone and Eramkumbe with ornaments of varying sorts', p.355 s.a 1053.
[125] S 1236.
[126] 'Devon and its People', by W.G. Hoskins p.47.
[127] 'Tavistock Abbey', by H.P.R Finberg pp.6-7; Exon D. B. Phillimore Bk 2 1.35; 1.50.
[128] 'Liber Eliensis' ch 50 p.293, 'ET: infula rubea bene parata, quam Gioa domina, uxor Godwine comitis, mater regina Ædgioe, uxorus gloriose Regis Ædwardi dedit'.
[129] 'Vita' pp.46-47.
[130] S 1022, 1025; Robin Fleming, 'Kings and Lords' p.83.

Nor is it correct to say that Godwine was hostile towards clerics. Bishops Lyfing and Ealdred were among his friends. Eadsige had worked amicably with him, as did Siward of Abingdon. His estrangement with Christ Church only commenced when Robert took office at Canterbury. Stigand, we are told, broke down and wept bitterly when delivering Edward's ridiculous message at Southwark in 1051,[131] and was instrumental in mediating to attain Godwine's pardon the following year.

The earl's character, according to Norman propaganda, is of a man who was both cunning and unscrupulous. It is difficult to reconcile this with the way he was thought of by the men of his earldom. While in exile in Flanders messengers were sent to him entreating him to return, assuring him that if need be they were ready to die for him.[132] When he arrived in London, 'the whole city went out to help and protect the earl'. Some[133] allowance may be made for the author's bias but for the corroboration of the *Chronicle* which records that on Godwine's return the men of Kent, Sussex and Surrey 'all declared that they would live and die with him.'[134] This was not the welcome one would have expected for an exile who had alienated his people by unscrupulous and cunning actions. His detractors called him treacherous and disloyal, but what we know of his behaviour does not support this. His friendship with Baldwin V of Flanders was maintained throughout his life. When Cnut chose the men who were to govern England under him, he selected Godwine and Leofwine who had 'served Edmund faithfully without deceit.'[135] When King Cnut died, Godwine upheld what he believed to be Cnut's wishes in supporting Harthacnut. When it became obvious that the latter was not coming to claim the English throne, he transferred his allegiance to Cnut's other son, Harold and in this he was being loyal to Cnut's wishes. A country without a king was an invitation to every aspiring adventurer, as events were to prove. It was only when both the Danish princes were dead that he gave his support to Edward. During the crisis of 1051 and again in 1052 Godwine showed clearly his aversion to bloodshed, or going to extremes, either in humiliating Edward or forcing an unacceptable situation upon him.[136] When restored to his earldom, he displayed great restraint and moderation, showing no signs of vindictiveness against those who had been in arms against him.

The one blot on Godwine's memory during his lifetime - and which has persisted to this day - is his complicity in the death of Alfred and his companions. If this was justified, surely Emma would have been first and foremost in denouncing him. The distracted mother was vehement in her condemnation of Harold Harefoot. She was even accused of entertaining ideas of urging Magnus of Norway to lay claims on the throne of England. Presumably in her frenzied state of mind this was to spite Edward for his lack of support in 1038. Godwine had supported Harold, whom she hated intensely, and yet in the work she herself commissioned it merely relates that

---

[131] 'Vita' pp.36-37.
[132] ibid pp.40-41.
[133] ibid.
[134] A.S.C 'C', 'D' s.a 1052; J.W. pp.568-569.
[135] E.E.R Bk 2 ch 15 p.31.
[136] A.S.C 'E' 1048/1051; 1052.

he met Alfred, lodged him and his companions in Guildford and then left for his night's lodgings. On his return in the morning he found that Harold's men had arrived and taken control of the situation and there is no mention at all of Godwine being to blame for what followed.[137] The *Encomium* was written sometime between 1041-1042[138] and is therefore strictly contemporary and before slanderous accusations started to circulate to sully the earl's memory.

Godwine's Line

The closing years of Edward's reign saw further advances in the fortunes of Godwine's kin. The year following Godwine's death Earl Siward led a Northumbrian army into Scotland in an effort to assist his kinsman, Malcolm. The young Scot was the son of Duncan and a kinswoman of Earl Siward. When Duncan was killed at the battle of Pitgaveny the boy had eventually found sanctuary with Siward in York. King Macbeth was driven northwards but not deposed. Within a year, Siward died either of wounds received in the campaign or of dysentery. Before the close of the year 1057 Odda, Leofric and Ralph were all dead. The decease of all the senior earls resulted in the appointment of Harold to the earldom of Wessex; two years later Tostig succeeded Siward in Northumbria, and in due course on his father's death, Ælfgar was transferred from East Anglia to the family's hereditary earldom on Mercia. This left East Anglia vacant, an office which was filled by Gyrth, and an earldom was created for his brother, Leofwine, in the East Midlands. Thoughts of divorce proceedings were forgotten and Eadgyth's position at court was secure. The family were, with the exception of Wulfnoth, restored to positions of authority. Gunnhildr was at Wilton preparing for her religious vocation, and the delicate Ælfgifu was still only a girl not yet in her teens.

All this was changed by the traumatic events of 1065/66, which flared up when Tostig became embroiled with the Northumbrian nobility, and which ended with his death on the flats at Stamford Bridge, and when Harold, Gyrth and Leofwine gave their lives in England's defence on Senlac ridge. Shortly afterwards Gytha, Gunhild, Eadgyth Swannehals, and four of Gytha's grandchildren, were gathered within the walls of Exeter. Before the city finally surrendered the family escaped and found shelter on the island of Flatholme in the Bristol Channel. We are told that with Gytha went 'the wives of very many good men.'[139] This would seem to imply that their husbands went with Harold's sons to the court of King Diarmait as their father had done sixteen years earlier.[140]

---

[137] E.E.R Bk 3 ch 4 pp.42-43.
[138] E.E.R, Introduction pXXI; F. Barlow, 'Edward' p.340.
[139] A.S.C 'D' 1067.
[140] A. Williams, 'The English and the Norman Conquest', pp.20,21.

These sons of Harold are named by John of Worcester as Godwine, Edmund and Magnus.[141] In 1068, after attempting to take Bristol, they raided in Somerset, and then returned to Ireland. The following year two of the sons returned with a large fleet,[142] but were again unsuccessful in gaining a foothold. It seems reasonable to suppose that one of them, probably Magnus, was either wounded or perhaps killed the previous year.

Stones built into the walls of the church of St John sub Castro in Lewes bear this inscription: 'Here is immured a soldier of the Royal Family of Denmark whose name was Magnus, indicates his distinguished lineage. Relinquishing his greatness, he assumes the deportment of a lamb, and exchanges for a life of ambition that of a humble anchorite.'[143] Legend linked this Magnus with the son of Harold. Through his grandmother he could in a sense be said to be connected with the Danish royal house but, 'a soldier of the royal family' does not necessarily imply that the anchorite was himself of royal stock. That Godwine and Edmund were the brothers who returned in 1069 seems correct in view of the fact that Gaimar knew their names but not that of Magnus[144] whose subsequent fate must remain a mystery.

Orderic says that Gytha 'secretly collected vast wealth,'[145] which she probably put at the disposal of her grandsons in order to recruit mercenary forces from Ireland. After the failure of their second expedition the Godwinesons left Ireland and Flatholme for Flanders. According to Saxo[146] the two sons and their sister went from Flanders to Denmark. It seems certain that the trio were Godwine, Edmund and the young Gytha. Orderic says that their grandmother and aunt accompanied them.[147] The elder Gytha may have hoped to persuade her nephew, King Swein, to launch another attack on England on behalf of her grandsons. After the failure of the previous Danish attempts of 1069 and 1070 she met with no success. It must have been then that she and Gunhild returned to Flanders and entered the nunnery at St Omer. At some time after this, possibly on her mother's death, Gunhild left St Omer and spent her last years at Bruges.

Meanwhile, Harold's second wife, Ealdgyth, the daughter of Earl Ælfgar, had been sent for safety to Chester by her brothers Edwin and Morcar.[148] Probably when William's army reached the outskirts of Chester in 1070 she fled for safety into Wales. After the death of her first husband, Gruffydd ap Llewelyn, his half-brothers, Bleddyn and Rhiwallon, were appointed by King Edward to succeed him.[149]

---

[141] JW iii pp.6-7.
[142] JW iii pp.8-9.
[143] 'Sussex' by Esther Mayrell, information supplied by the kind courtesy of Alison Swan for the church wardens of Southover, Lewes, East Sussex.
[144] Gaimar lines 5400-5403.
[145] O.V. ii pp.224, 225; A. Williams, 'The English and the Norman conquest' p.21 note 99.
[146] 'Saxo' p.58.
[147] O.V ii pp 224-225
[148] JW ii pp.604-605.
[149] A.S.C 'D' s.a 1063.

Rhiwallon died in 1069, but his brother continued to support Ealdgyth's brothers until their fall in 1072.[150] Bleddyn had the reputation of being a kindly man and Ealdgyth would have felt at home in Wales. She had lived there for several years as Gruffydd's queen; she had a daughter by him, Nest, who may have been brought up at Bleddyn's court when her mother left to marry Harold in early 1066. Some writers have thought that Ealdgyth was also the mother of Gruffydd's three other children, Maredudd, Ithael and Owain but as they were all dead by 1069, the first two being of fighting age, this is impossible. Nest was to marry the Norman, Osbern son of Richard Fitz Scrob. Their daughter, another Nest, would in time become the wife of Bernard of Neufmarché. It would seem from this that Ealdgyth might have settled in Wales.

Godwine's other daughters-in-law, Eadgyth Swannehals and Tostig's wife, Judith, were both on the continent. Eadgyth had accompanied her mother-in-law and her own children to Flanders. Judith had been left in the care of her step-brother, Baldwin V.[151] Tostig left his treasure with her when he set out on his fatal meeting with Háraldr Harðráða. In 1071 Judith was married secondly to Welf IV [Welf II of Bavaria] and with her went the treasure which Tostig had accumulated. From the Welf (or Guelph) dynasty are descended the house of Windsor.

Eadgyth's movements are uncertain. When the rest of the family set off for Denmark, it seems likely that she went as a pilgrim to visit the religious foundations in Europe. Her extensive estates in England would have ensured that she was reasonably wealthy. The links between England and Aquitaine by the mid-eleventh century make it quite possible that she was the 'Lady Edith' who came to La Chaise-Dieu in the Auverge. Different hypotheses have been advanced as to the identity of 'Lady Edith'. As she is said to have been buried there, this rules out Edward's queen. There is no evidence to indicate that it was Ealdgyth either, although both suggestions have been put forward.[152] The presence of 'Lady Edith' in the town is dated to the latter half of the eleventh century; a tomb is pointed out as hers and a fresco on the abbey walls is unique in that one of the characters is a woman.[153] La Chaise-Dieu is situated on a granite plateau, high up between the Auverge and Veley amidst forests of conifer trees. During the medieval period the monks each year commemorated an English queen who was supposed to have paid to have their dormitory built. It was apparently the widespread reputation of the founder of the abbey, Sir Robert of Turland, who had recently died, that attracted pilgrims to visit La Chaise-Dieu.[154] The town lies about ninety miles from Conques, where an Englishman named Ælfwine, claiming to be the son of Harold, King of England, arrived as a pilgrim in 1060-1062. His

---

[150] K. L. Maund, 'Ireland, Wales and England' pp.139, 208.

[151] O.V. ii Bk 3 pp.138-141.

[152] George Beech, 'England and Aquitaine', pp.94-95 for a discussion of these, and note 57 on p.95.

[153] I am indebted for this information to the Office de Tourisme, Canton, De la Chaise-Dieú.

[154] G. Beech, 'England and Aquitaine' p.95.

father has been identified tentatively as Harold Harefoot.[155] Eadmer, the Canterbury monk, was staying at La Chaise-Dieu when he received the news of the death of William Rufus.[156] All this shows that English pilgrims were making the journey into Aquitaine at this period. The name, circumstances and dating make it possible that it was Eadgyth Swannehals who found sanctuary and a last resting place in the small town situated high up in the Auverge.[157]

Godwine's son, Wulfnoth, could have been little more than fourteen when he was taken hostage in 1051. From then on he spent his life confined in a Norman prison. Knowing little of his father's death or his country's overthrow, William ordered him to be released on his death-bed in 1087 after thirty six years incarceration but his freedom was short-lived. William Rufus took him back to England and immediately imprisoned him again. According to Orderic he died as a monk at Salisbury.[158] William of Malmesbury thought that he was kept in chains in Salisbury during the Conqueror's reign.[159] It seems from the evidence available that during the reign of Rufus he was transferred at some stage to Winchester and that as he became more frail through years of hardship and deprivation he was given into the keeping of the prior of Winchester Cathedral. From there he was brought to court on occasion to witness charters. The prisoner seems to have won the respect of the prior, Godfrey of Cambrai, who composed an epitaph which reflected his respect and sympathy for the last of Godwine's sons. Wulfnoth apparently died in 1094.[160]

Two of Harold II's sisters survived the Conquest. The first is Eadgyth, whom the Conqueror liked to portray as the Dowager Queen, if only to buttress his claim to be Edward's legitimate successor. After 1066 she dwelt in comfort at Winchester, in possession of all her lands,[161] while her mother and the rest of her family were in exile or prison. Towards the end of her life she retired to the nunnery at Wilton.[162] On her death bed she is supposed to have taken an oath affirming that she was innocent of adultery.[163] It could be that her weak and troubled mind was harking back to the malicious and unfounded charges which Archbishop Robert had made in his efforts to secure her divorce in 1051. She was buried with all honour and respect by her husband's side in Westminster Abbey in 1075.[164] The second of Harold's sisters, Gunhild, accompanied her mother to Flanders. Gytha must have died sometime after 1072, and Gunhild left St Omer to live in the nunnery attached to the church of St Donatius in Bruges. A lead plate was found in

---

[155] 'An Alleged son of Harold Harefoot' p.114.
[156] 'Historia Novorum', pp.116-117.
[157] but see A. Williams, 'The English and the Norman Conquest' p.53 note 33.
[158] O.V. ii Bk 3 pp.178-179.
[159] G.R. Bk 2 ch 197 pp.362-363; F. Barlow, 'The Godwins' p.118.
[160] F. Barlow, 'William Rufus', pp.65, 66 and note 58; the Godwines p.118
[161] P. Stafford, 'Queen Emma and Queen Edith' pp.125-128.
[162] ibid p.278; A. Williams, 'the English and the Norman Conquest' p.132.
[163] William of Malmesbury ch 197 pp.352-353.
[164] A.S.C 'D' 1076/1075; 'E' AD 1075.

the Old Cathedral in Bruges in 1786 on which the Latin inscription records her noble parentage, her chaste life, the stay at St Omer and her 'gay, modest disposition, her kindness and generosity to the poor, renouncing all the pleasures of life for one of self denial and austerity.'[165] Gunhild died on 24th August 1087.

A possible third sister, Ælfgifu, is recorded in the Domesday record as 'Ælfeva, Earl Harold's sister' holding land in Buckinghamshire.[166] (She was certainly one of the earl's younger children because of her Anglo-Saxon name; probably the youngest.) According to Eadmer[167] in the oath that Harold allegedly made in 1064 William asked him, amongst other demands 'that you will at a time agreed between us send your sister to me that I may give her in marriage to one of my nobles...' In 1066 after Harold's accession to the throne, in an exchange of messages, William reproached him for not keeping the promise made in Normandy. The king replied 'my sister, for whom according to our pact you ask is dead. If the duke wishes to have her body, such as it is now, I will send it, that I may not be held in violation of my oath.'

Among Godwine's grandchildren were the sons of Swegn. Hákon, as we have seen, was given as a hostage in 1051 and according to Eadmer[168] was released and returned from Normandy with Harold in 1064. Freeman suggests that he fought at Senlac and that he may have died there in the last rally around the standards.[169] J. M. Lappenberg identified him with the Jarl Hákon who came to England in 1075 as commander of the Danish fleet which entered the Humber, looted St Peter's Minster and then returned to Flanders. Amongst the slain was Hákon's son.[170] Freeman doubted this on the grounds that if Hákon was born in 1047, he would not have had a son of an age to be fighting in 1075.[171] This assumes that Hákon was the child of the abbess Eadgifu. On the other hand, if he were the offspring of an earlier relationship, he could have been born as early as 1040-1042. According to Gaimar, Swegn had another son, named Tostig,[172] who came to England with Godwine and Edmund in 1068. There is no other mention of this, but his existence has been accepted by Michael Swanton and Ben Hudson.[173]

---

[165] The Latin original was published by Sir Henry Ellis in his 'Introduction to D.B.' vol 2 p.136 note 2 and p.137; for her gifts to the church of St Donation in Bruges see I. Walker, 'Harold' p.193 p.233 note 2.
[166] D.B. Bucks 4.21.
[167] 'Historia Novorum' p.7.
[168] ibid p.8.
[169] F.N.C.iii p.476, volume IV p.142.
[170] A.S.C 'D' 1076.1075, 'E' 1075; F.N.C.iv p.142.
[171] F.N.C. iv pp.585 - 586 and note 5 on p 585; J.M. Lappenberg, 'Norman Kings' p.168.
[172] 'L' Estoire, lines 5400-5403.
[173] M. Swanton, 'A.S. Chronicles', Genealogical Tables, 'Descendants of Godwine, Earl of Wessex'; Ben Hudson, 'The Family of Harold Godwineson and the Irish Sea Province' p.94; but see I. Walker, 'Harold' p.233 note 2.

When the battered remnants of the Norwegian army sailed back to Norway in 1066, with them went Tostig's sons, Skule and Ketel Krok. According to Snorri Sturluson[174] they were both in great favour with King Ólafr. Ketel Krok was given lands to the north in Halogoland, the king arranged a good marriage for him, and he became the father of a large and prosperous family. Skule became the king's foster son and played an important role in the affairs of the country; he was given some of the richest lands in Norway which his descendants still held in Snorri's time. With the king's blessing Skule married Gudron, whose mother was Ingegerd, a full sister of Háraldr Harðráða, and half-sister of Saint Ólafr. Gudron was thus a first cousin to both King Ólafr and to his brother, King Magnus. From this marriage were descended many prominent Norse magnates and ultimately King Inge who reigned from 1204 until 1217.

Relationship of Skule, Tostig's son and the Kings of Norway

according to Snorri Sturluson; *Saga of Harald Hardrada* ch xcviii

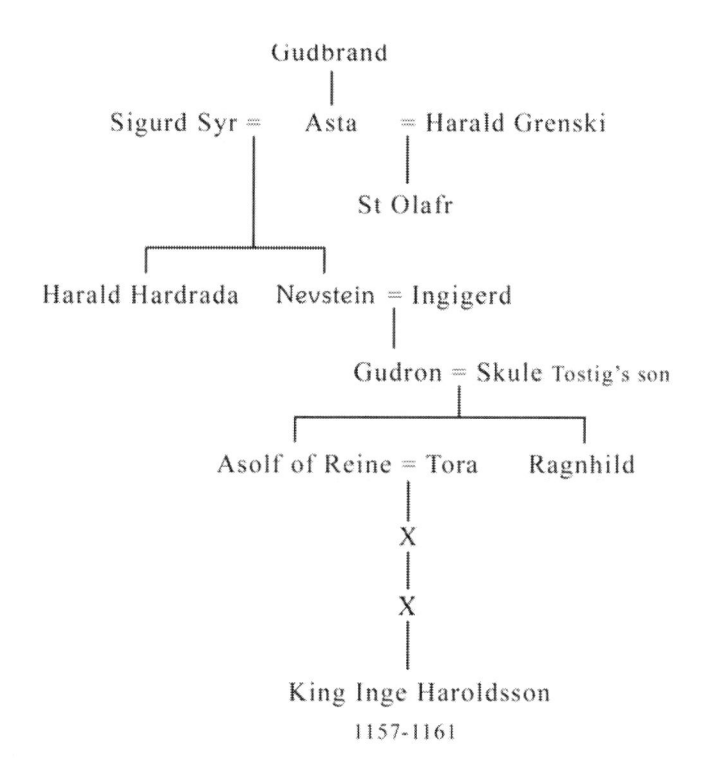

```
                    Gudbrand
                       |
    Sigurd Syr  =   Asta   =   Harald Grenski
         |                          |
         |                       St Olafr
    ┌────┴────┐
Harald Hardrada  Nevstein = Ingigerd
                           |
                    Gudron = Skule Tostig's son
                           |
              ┌────────────┴────────┐
       Asolf of Reine = Tora     Ragnhild
                    |
                    X
                    |
                    X
                    |
            King Inge Haroldsson
                 1157-1161
```

---

[174] 'Saga of Harald the Stern' ch XCVIII pp.237-238; Ch XCVII p.236.

As far as is known, Gyrth and Leofwine had no children, nor did Queen Eadgyth or either of her sisters. Harold, however, in addition to Godwine, Edmund and Magnus had two other sons. John of Worcester relates that when the Conqueror was dying, amongst the political prisoners whose release he ordered, was 'Ulf, the son of Harold'. There has been some doubt whether Ulf's mother was Eadgyth or Ealdgyth - if the latter, he must have been one of twins as Freeman surmised. There seems no evidence to support this and it is probable that he was the son of Harold's earlier marriage. (I have hesitatingly suggested in an earlier chapter that he may have been Harold's eldest son and was given as a hostage in 1051, although this too is largely uncorroborated.) Alternatively, maybe he was captured between 14th October and the time when the remainder of the family were gathered in Exeter.

Ealdgyth's son, named after his father, returned to England in the company of King Magnus Barefoot. The king was touring his island possessions of Shetland, Orkney, the Hebrides and the Isle of Man. Harold Haroldson had received a cordial welcome by the King of Norway who was grateful for the clemency shown by King Harold to Ólafr Haraldsson, his father.[175] When the Norse fleet reached Anglesey they found it overrun by Normans under the command of Hugh of Montgomery and Hugh of Chester, who had been inflicting the most barbarous cruelty on their hapless victims. Magnus attempted to land and in the skirmish that followed, Hugh of Montgomery was slain by an arrow reputedly shot by Magnus himself.[176] The young Harold must have been born in Chester in December 1066 or January 1067. At some point he presumably left Wales and went to the northlands as the Norman hold on Wales tightened. Nothing more is heard of him after 1098; presumably he lived on in Norway thereafter.

Godwine had two granddaughters, the children of Harold and Eadgyth. Both may have been born after his death. In 1066 Gunhild was still at Wilton completing her education. She remained there to avoid the unwanted attentions of Norman adventurers eager to marry an English princess in order to legitimise the seizure of the lands which would come with her. Edith, the daughter of King Malcolm of Scotland, was also at Wilton. Both claimed that although they had worn the veil they had never become professed nuns. The King of Scots had plans for his daughter to marry Count Alan of Richmond who had apparently accompanied him to Wilton. William Rufus refused to permit the marriage for political reasons. Alan was enamoured by Gunhild who had become disenchanted with her life in the nunnery. The position of abbess had been suggested but had failed to materialise. The prospect of a different sort of life appealed to her and she eloped with Alan, who was already in possession of a great proportion of her mother's lands. The story is preserved in two letters which Anselm, the Archbishop of Canterbury, wrote to her urging her to return to the cloister. Not long after their elopement in 1093, Alan died. His brother, Alan Niger, inherited the property and Gunhild continued to live there. Although she was no longer a virgin, Anselm pressed her

---

[175] William of Malmesbury, GR Bk 3 ch 329 pp.570-571.
[176] F. Barlow, 'William Rufus' pp.389-390; A.S.C 'E' s.a 1098.

to return to Wilton.[177] Eventually she did return and spent her last years there. William of Malmesbury relates that St Wulfstan cured Gunhild of a malignant tumour in her eye when visiting Wilton some years earlier.[178]

The sister mentioned by Saxo, who went with her brothers to Denmark, was Gytha. He further states that her uncle, King Swein, gave her in marriage to 'Waldemarus, King of the Russians.'[179] Waldemarus has been identified with Vladimir II Monomakh, the son of Vesovolod, Prince of Kiev, and the daughter of the Emperor Constantine Monomakhos of Byzantium. His paternal grandfather was Yaroslav the Wise and his grandmother Ingegerd, the daughter of King Ólafr of Sweden. From 1076 Vlademir had been the ruler of Smolensk. Five years later he was promoted to Chernigov, the second most important city in Russia, which he ruled until 1094. After his father's death he succeeded to the position of Grand Prince of Kiev, which he ruled wisely and well until his own death at the age of nearly eighty years.[180]

Vladimir and Gytha were wed sometime between 1073 and 1075.[181] Their first son was born in 1076, and was named Msistislav. The Scandinavian world knew him as Msistislav-Harald, after Gytha's father.[182] Gytha was the mother of eight sons and three daughters. She died on 7th May 1107. Msistislav-Harald succeeded his father as Grand Prince of Kiev and earnt the by name of 'the Brave' when he succeeded in halting an advancing attack of the Polovtsy on the cities of the Dniepr.[183] He married

---

[177] F. Barlow, 'William Rufus' pp.313-314; OV iv Bk VII p.48; 272-273 St Wulfstan of Worcester; Emma Mason p.226f.

[178] 'Vita Wulfstani' ch 11 p.36; ch 20 p.84 in the abridgement of the Life of Wulfstan in the Library of the Dean and Chapter of Durham.

[179] Saxo Bk Eleven ch VI p.58 and note 20 pp.228-229.

[180] According to the Russian Primary Chronicle p.142 he governed in succession Pereyslavl, Chernigov, Pereyslavl again and Kiev from 1113-1125. His mother, according to the R.P.C, was a relative of Constantine IX Monomachus [p285 and note 192 p.263]. Dimitri Oblensky [Six Byzantine Portraits p.185 note 4] identified her as the child of Constantine IX's second wife. Boris Rybakov [Kievan Rus pp.221-222] goes further and calls her Princess Maria. Norah Chadwick [the Beginnings of Russian History p.133] sums up Vladamir's character saying, 'The prompt and resolute character of Vladamir II, his undoubted military gifts, his single minded devotion to his people, his personal integrity and his sound judgement mark him as a sound leader'.

[181] For the later date see E. Christiansen, Saxo Note 20 p.229. At any rate Msistislav's birth in 1076 is recorded in the R.P.C pp.164-165.

[182] The career of Msistislav is covered in the 'Chronicle of Novgorod' p.7 to his death on 14th April 1132. The Norse sources knew him as Harold after his grandfather. According to Dimitri Oblensky ['Six Byzantine Portraits' p.108] he was regarded as a saint. Snorri ['Saga of the sons of Magnus' ch XX p.292] writes of Malmfrid, 'a daughter of King Harold Valdemarson'. The Morkinskinna records that Haraldr Valdimarsson's second daughter was Ingiborg who was married to King Knutr Lávaror' [p329 ch 66].

[183] F. Maclean, 'Holy Russia'; The death of Gytha is recorded on 7th May 1107 [P.RC. p.203]. According to a Genealogy contained in the latter Vladamir may have been married three times, firstly to Gytha, secondly to an unnamed lady and thirdly to a daughter of AEPA, Khan of the Cumans.

Christina, the daughter of King Inge Steinkelsson of Sweden. By her he had two daughters, Malmfrid and Ingeborg. The latter married Cnut Lavard, the ruler of South Jutland, and amongst their children was Waldemar I, who became the King of Denmark in 1157, the ancestor of Queen Alexandra, and thus of our own royal family. Msistislav-Harald died in 1132.

Genealogy of Vladimir Monomakh and Gytha

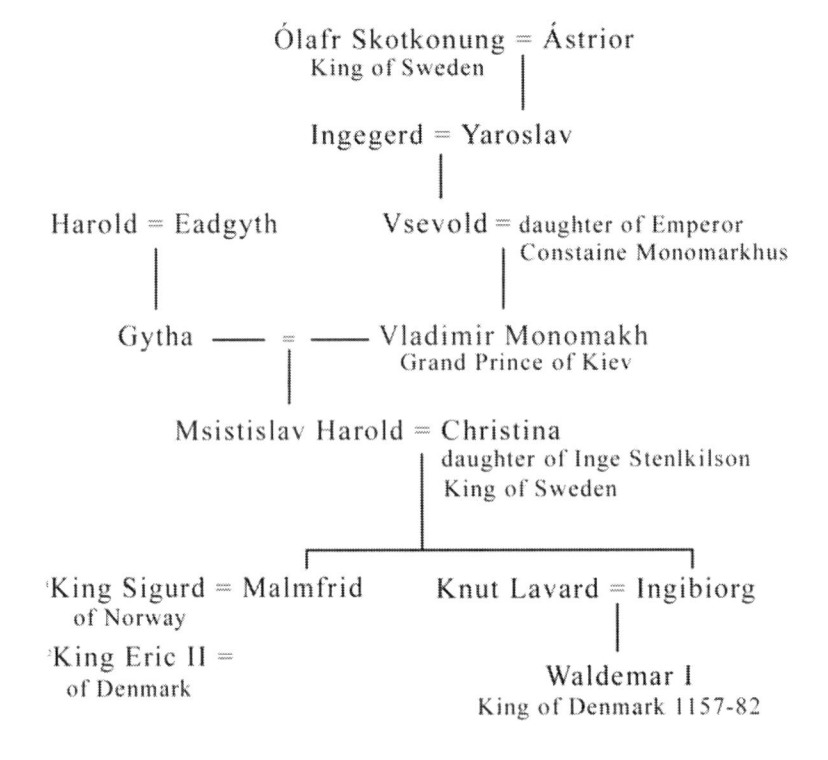

Ólafr Skotkonung = Ástrior
King of Sweden

Ingegerd = Yaroslav

Harold = Eadgyth   Vsevold = daughter of Emperor
                                Constaine Monomarkhus

Gytha ——— = ——— Vladimir Monomakh
                Grand Prince of Kiev

Msistislav Harold = Christina
                    daughter of Inge Stenlkilson
                    King of Sweden

King Sigurd = Malmfrid   Knut Lavard = Ingibiorg
of Norway
King Eric II =   Waldemar I
of Denmark   King of Denmark 1157-82

England after Harold

The England that Godwine knew was gone forever. The English were now regarded as an inferior race to be taxed and exploited to the point of starvation. Their homes and churches were razed to the ground in order to extend forests for the new nobility. Forest laws were harsh; blinding and castration were the penalty for killing royal game. Castles and dungeons were built, stark and menacing, from which the *Frenchmen* sallied forth to terrorise the neighbourhood.[184] During the Conqueror's reign there were well over thirty of these dotted over England. In 1085 William instituted the Domesday Survey in order to discover how much wealth it was possible to squeeze out of his unfortunate subjects. The *Chronicle* reflects the deep resentment caused by the oppression endured by the forest laws, the castles and the burden of heavy taxation. At the time of the survey only four principal English landowners remained, and only two bishops still held office.[185]

Under the Conqueror's successors the burden of colossal taxation intensified. It is little wonder that the annalist wrote: 'the wretched people are oppressed with every injustice, robbed of their goods, and afterwards killed. The man who had any property was robbed of it by severe taxes and by severe courts; he who had none died of starvation.'[186] But worse was to come. For nineteen years in the reign of the Conqueror's grandson, Stephen (1135-54), it was as though 'Christ and His saints slept',[187] such were the horrors of civil war. A century before, civil war had been averted, but now there were no Leofrics, Siwards or Godwines to put the interests of their country first. Nor was there any improvement when Henry of Anjou succeeded to the throne. His lands in western France stretched from Normandy down to the Pyrenees in the south and involved England in constant warfare with the French kings in a battle for supremacy. From 1078 when the Conqueror employed Englishmen as well as Normans to conquer Maine, England was drawn into continental warfare which did not cease until 1558 when Queen Mary Tudor, in alliance with the Spanish, was fighting the French.

Thorkell Skallason aptly summed up the plight of the English of his time when he wrote: 'Cold heart and bloody hand now rule the English land.'[188] A study of the contemporary chronicles must surely lead to the conclusion that 'the triumph of the Norman Conquest is a triumph of things evil, a state which will never be adequately cleared up until in the end of this world when the tares are separated from the wheat'[189] to quote the words of L.G Pine, sometime editor of *Burke's Peerage*.

---

[184] O.V. iv Bk vii pp.202-203, 268-269, 298-299; H. Loyn, 'the Making of England' p.97.

[185] A. Williams, 'The English and the Norman Conquest' pp.98, 126.

[186] A.S.C 'E' 1124.

[187] A.S.C 'E' s.a 1137.

[188] Snorri, 'Saga of Harald the Stern' ch XCVII(a) p.235.

[189] L. G. Pine, 'Heirs of the Conqueror' p.67. L.G. Pine sometime c early 1950s, editor of Burke's Peerage.

Table 10. Sequence of Events 1052 - 1107

1052 June 22	Godwine sails from Flanders
1052 Mid or late Aug	Godwine and Harold join forces
1052 Mon. Sept 14	Godwine's fleet at Southwark
1052 Tue. Sept. 15	Meeting of Witan, Godwine and family pardoned
1052 Late September	Godwine's illness
1052 September 29	Death of Swegn in Lykia
1053 January	News of Swegn's death reaches England
1053 Mon. April 12	Godwine's stroke
1053 Thur. April 15	Death of Godwine
1054 July 27	Siward defeats King Macbeth
1055	Death of Siward
1056 August 31	Death of Odda
1057 Aug 31or Oct 30	Death of Leofric
1057 December 21	Death of Ralph
1064/5	Death of Ælfgifu, Godwine's daughter
1066 Sept 25	Battle of Stamford Bridge; Death of Tostig
1066 October 14	Battle of Hastings; King Harold, Gyrth and Leofwine slain
1067 early	Gytha, wife of Godwine, left Exeter for the Flatholme
1068 summer	Harold's sons attempt to take Bristol
1069 summer	Harold's sons raid in Devon and Somerset
1070 spring	Gytha, Gunhild and Harold's children travel to Denmark
1070 summer	Ealdgyth leaves Chester for Wales Gytha and Gunhild return to St Omer
1071	Judith marries Welf of Bavaria
c1072/1074	Death of Gytha; Gunhild at Bruges
1075 December 18	Death of Eadgyth
1073/1075	Marriage of Harold's daughter Gytha to Vladimir Monomakh
1087 August 24	Death of Gunhild Release of Wulfnoth and Ulf in early September
1093	Elopement of Harold's daughter Gunhild with Count Alan
1094	Probable death of Wulfnoth
1098	Harold Haroldson with King Magnus Barefoot of Anglesey
1107 May 7	Death of Gytha, Godwine's granddaughter

Genealogy of Godwine's Descendants

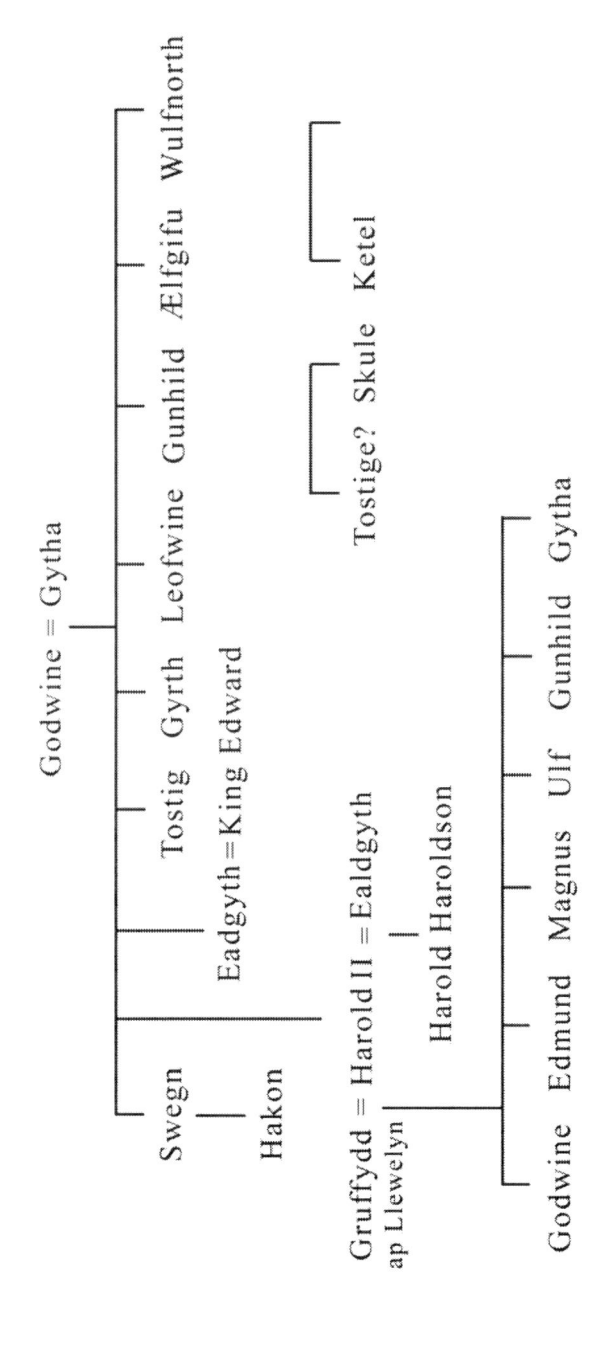

```
                    Godwine = Gytha
     ┌──────┬─────────┬──────┬──────┬────────┬────────┬────────┬──────────┐
   Swegn   Tostig   Gyrth  Leofwine Gunhild  Ælfgifu  Wulfnoth
     │       │
   Hakon   Eadgyth = King Edward
                                              ┌────────┬──────┬──────┐
                                            Tostige?  Skule  Ketel

Gruffydd = Harold II = Ealdgyth
ap Llewelyn    │
               ├──────────────┬────────┬──────┬──────┬────────┬──────┐
         Harold Haroldson  Godwine Edmund Magnus  Ulf  Gunhild Gytha
```

Adapted from:-
Ben Hudson, *The Family of Harold Godwineson and the Irish Sea Province*
JRSAI, 109, 1979, pages 92-100
and Frank Barlow, *The Godwines*, Pearson Education Ltd, Longmans, 2002, page 17

Appendix 1

The Lands of Godwine & Gytha

A summary of the lands held by Godwine and Gytha according to the testimony of *Domesdæg*.

Sussex		Lands of Godwine	
Bosham	1.1	Paid tax for 38 hides	56½ hides
Rotherfield	1.2		3 hides
Uckham	8.3		6 hides
Hooe	9.1		12 hides
Udimore	9.104	Algar held from Godwine	6 hides
Lidham	9.106	Leofred held from Godwine	1 hide
Quarter	9.107	Wulfmar held from Godwine	6 hides
Evebentone	9.108		½ hide
Higham	9.121		2½ hides
Willingdon	10.27		50½ hides
Ratton	10.31	Wulfhun held from Godwine	6 hides
Wilmington	10.39	Alnoth held from Godwine	8 hides
Wilmington	10.40	Wulfnoth held from Godwine	4 hides
Wilmington	10.41	Wulfstan held from Godwine	2 hides
Terring (Neville)	10.43	Azor held from Godwine	8 hides
(Frog) Firle	10.45		1 hide
Frog) Firle	10.46	Heming held from Godwine	2 hides
Rodmell	10.61	Paid no tax	1½ hides
Laughton	10.93		10 hides
Barkham	10.115	Godwine held from King Edward	3 virgates
Singleton	11.3		97½ hides
Lavant	11.5	Godwine held from E. Godwine	9 hides
Lavant	11.5	Godwine held from E. Godwine	1 hide
Treyford	11.8	Aethelhard held from Godwine	11 hides

Chithurst	11.9	Aelmar held from Godwine	4 hides
Stedham	11.10	Ediva held from Godwine	14 hides
Buddington	11.13	Edwin held from Godwine	1 hide
Selham	11.14	Cuthwulf held from Godwine	4 hides
Todham	11.16	Wulfnoth held from Godwine	4 hides
Westbourne	11.30	Answered for 12 hides	36 hides
Compton	11.36	Esbern held from Godwine	10 hides
Stoughton	11.37		36 hides
Mundham	11.41	Gytha held from Godwine	9 hides
Itchenor	11.45	Leofwin held from Godwine	1 hide
Angmering	11.65		5 hides
Climping	11.75 11.76		22 hides
Binstead Hundred	11.95	Herewulf held from Godwine	1 hide
Binstead Hundred	11.96	Ansgot held from Godwine	2 hides
Binstead Hundred	11.97	Ansgot held from Godwine	1 hide
Binstead Hundred	11.98	Two Englishmen held from Godwine	¾ hide
West Hampnett	11.105	Two freemen held from Godwine	9 hides
Orleswick	12.9	7 freeholders held from Godwine	6½ hides
Rottingdean	12.10	Heming held from Godwine	2 hides
Brighton	12.13	Brictric held by gift from Godwine	5½ hides
Perching	12.28	Belling held from Godwine	2 hides
Poynings	12.30	Cola held from Godwine by gift	8 hides
Seddlescombe	12.33	Godwine priest from Godwine	17 hides
Hurstpierpoint	12.36	Godwine held himself	41 hides
Plumpton	12.42	Godwine priest from Godwine	32 hides
Barcombe	12.48	Azor held from Godwine	13 hides
Truleigh	13.6	Belling held from Godwine	4 hides
Wiston	13.13	Azor held from Godwine	12 hides
Chaneton	13.17	Essocher held from Godwine	4 hides
Chancton	13.18	Werun held from Godwine	1 hide
Applesham	13.20	Leofwin held from Godwine	7½ hides

Heene	13.31	Leofred held from Godwine	2½ hides
Worthing	13.35	7 freeholders held from Godwine	11 hides
Dankton	13.42	Auti held from Godwine	5 hides
Hoe	13.46		6 hides
Ashington	13.47	2 freeholders held from Godwine	2½ hides
In lands of Washington	13.51	Edwin held from Godwine	1 hide
Eatons	13.53	Thorgot held from Godwine	3½ hides
Sussex		**Land Held by Godwine, Gytha and Grandchildren**	
Binderton	11.4	Gytha held	7 hides
Harting	11.6	Gytha held from King Edward	80 hides
Trotton	11.7	Gytha held from King Edward	9 hides
Marden	11.33	Leofsi held from Gytha	3 hides
Mundham	11.41	Gytha held from Earl Godwine	9 hides
West Meston	12.41	Gytha held	12 hides
Woodman Cote	13.22	Gytha held	3½ hides
Kent		**Godwine's Lands**	
Dover	D1	Godwine held the third penny	
Leybourne	5.40	Thorgil's held from Godwine	2 sulongs
Fairbourne	5.64	Alwin held from Godwine	1 sulong
Shelborough	5.65	Alwin held from Godwine	1 yoke
Boughton (Malherbe)	5.79	Alwin held from Godwine	1 sulong
Harbilton	5.84	Aelfric held from Godwine	1 sulong
Broomfield	5.85	Alwin held from Godwine	1 sulong
Chatham	5.89	Earl Godwine held	6 sulongs
Hoo	5.93	A manor Earl Godwine held	50 sulongs
Henhurst	5.109	Godwine held from E.Godwine	½ sulong
Folkestone	5.128	A manor Earl Godwine held	40 sulongs
Stalisfield	5.142	Thorgils held from Godwine	2 sulongs
Romney	5.178	Alfsi held from Godwine	?
Fordwich	7.10	Third part belonged to Godwine	1 yoke

(South) Ashford	9.4	Thorgils held from Godwine	1 sulong
East Bridge	9.10	Alfsi held from Godwine	1 sulong
Westerham	10.1	Godwine held from King Edward	4 sulongs
Boughton (Aluph)	10.2	Earl Godwine held	7 sulongs
Sundridge	2.5	(D. Monachorum 87)	1½ sulongs
Saltwood	2.41	(D. Monachorum 92)	7 sulongs
Langpor	2.43	(D. Monachorum 92)	1½ sulongs
Statenborough		(D. Monachorum 89)	?
Stoke	4.16		5 sulongs
		(No lands entered for Gytha)	

Hampshire		**Godwine's Lands**	
Soberton	1.13	Leofman held from Godwine	4 hides
(Nether) Wallop	1.19	Gytha held from Godwine	22 hides
Woolverton	W.12	Edeva held from Godwine	½ hide
Wroxall (I of W)	W.14	Gytha held from Godwine	5 hides
Funtley	18.2	Wulfward held from Godwine	1 hide
Headley	20.2	Earl Godwine held	3 hides
Chalton	21.6	Earl Godwine held	60 hides
Sunwood	21.7	Tunbi held from Godwine	3 hides
Hambledon	21.10	Edward held from Godwine	1 hide
Buckland	23.32	Alfward held from Godwine	3½ hides
Copnor	28.2	Tovi held from Godwine	3 hides
Sutton (Scotney)	28.7	Tovi held from Godwine	5 hides
Funtley	66.1	Thori held from Godwine	1 hide
Sutton (Scotney)	69.1	Alfward held from Godwine	5 hides
Bonchurch (I of W)	7.1	Estan held from Godwine in freehold	1 virgate
Gytha held (Nether) Wallop from Godwine	1.19		22 hides
Gytha held Wroxall from Godwine	W.14		5 hides

Wiltshire

Ugford	48.12	Godwine took from St Mary's Wilton	2½ hides
Rushall	1.9	Gytha owned	37 hides
Aldbourne	1.10	Gytha owned	40 hides
Coombe (Bissett)	1.13	Gytha owned	23½ hides

Berkshire

Chaddleworth	10.1	Gytha and Gyrth owned; 2 manors	16 hides

Surrey

Southwark	5.28	Godwine had third penny from Waterway	
Witley	24.1	Godwine held	20 hides
Oxted	15.1	Gytha held	20 hides

Dorset

Burton Bradstock	1.2	Edwin in error for Godwine	Not taxed
'Hawcombe' scrubland	1.2	Godwine had third oak	
Little Puddle	1.14	Gytha held	5 hides
Frampton	17.1	Gytha held	25½ hides

Cornwall

Poundstock	5.7.6	Manor Gytha held	Paid tax for 1 virgate
St Gynnys	5.7.9	Manor Gytha held	½ hide paid tax for 1 virgate

Somerset

Brompton (Regis)	1.11	Gytha held	10 hides
(Queen) Camel	1.22	Gytha held	8½ hides taxed 15 hides
Coker	1.23	Gytha held	8½ hides taxed 15 hides
Hardington (Mandeville)	1.24	Gunhild, Godwine's daughter	10 hides

Greech (St Michael)	1.18	Gunhild, Godwine's daughter	10½ hides
Nettlecombe	1.14	Godwine son of Harold held	2¾ hides
Longford (Budville)	1.16	Godwine son of Harold held	5 hides

Devon

Tawton	1.29	Gytha held	4 hides
Hartland	1.30	Gytha held	9 hides
(Little) Torrington	1.31	Gytha held	¼ hide
Witheridge	1.32	Gytha held	¼ hide
Woodbury	1.33	Gytha held	10 hides
Chillington	1.34	Gytha held	7 hides
Tiverton	1.35	Gytha held	3½ hides
Werrington	1.50	Gytha held	6½ hides
Otterton	11.1	Gytha held	14 hides

Herefordshire

Staunton	1.74	A manor Godwine held	1 hide
Pembridge	19.8	The Canons of St Guthlac claim this manor; they state that Godwine and his son Harold wrongfully took it from St Guthlac's	10¾ hides

Gloucestershire

Woodchester	1.63	Godwine bought from Azur	

Worcestershire

Wychbold	19.12		10 hides

Discussion

The first question is: who held those properties listed as Godwine's in the Domesday survey during the years between 1053 and 1066? The same applies to the holdings of Earl Siward who died in 1055, and of Earl Leofric and Earl Ralph who both died in 1057. There seems to be a general agreement among our best authorities that, where applicable, their estates passed to their wives and, to a lesser extent, to their children and other relatives. The wills that have survived prove this.[1] It seems that, in Godwine's case, Gytha retained most of his holdings, and no doubt administrated them with the assistance of her son, Harold. Another factor is that many of the lands listed as Harold's in the Domesday survey would have been owned by his father when he was Earl of Wessex.[2] Williams has shown, through the evidence of the manor at Frampton in Dorset, that Earl Godwine had been in possession of the third oak of Hawcombe Wood which was attached to that manor, but the estate itself was held by Gytha in 1066. 'This suggests that Gytha held at least a life interest in the land attributed to Godwine in addition to the land entered in his own name.'[3]

A second question relates to why it was so important for the survey to stress Godwine's ownership in the shires of Kent and Sussex. The answer lies in the claims made against Bishop Odo, who had been appointed as the Earl of Kent after the Conquest. The bishop was intent in claiming all the lands possible while his rival, Archbishop Lanfranc, was determined to obtain possession of all he deemed rightfully to belong to the church. The bone of contention centred largely on those lands which Archbishop Eadsige had given to Godwine in return for his valued support. The Penenden Heath Inquiry was held at Maidstone in Kent, almost a decade after the Battle of Senlac, to investigate the dispute. To provide some show of deference to Anglo-Saxon law and procedure, the aged Æðelric, the recently deposed Bishop of Selsey, was brought to the hearing. The pleas of Lanfranc and the church were upheld. In the process, Godwine's former possessions in the southeast were a matter of prime interest. In the western shires of Wessex there had not been the same need to prove what had rightly been the earl's and what had passed, on his bequest, to Gytha.[4]

How did Godwine acquire his exceptional landed wealth? In 1009 when Wulfnoð was outlawed, his lands would automatically have been forfeited. Godwine, his son, still in his teens, would have been virtually landless. It seems certain from the evidence of the aetheling Æthelstan's will, he gave his services to the aetheling and to his brother, Edmund. The first step in the recovery of his fortunes came when the

---

[1] S 1485, 'Wills' No 9; S 1487, 'Wills' No 13; S 1501, 'Wills' No 16; S 1505, 'Wills' No 12; S 1498, 'Wills' No 10; A.J Robertson, 'A.S Charters' No xxvii pp 54-55, 309-10
[2] A.S.C 'C', 'D', 'E' s.a 1053
[3] A. Williams, 'Land and Power' p.177 and note 33 on p 231
[4] D. Raraty, 'Earl Godwine of Wessex,' p.8-9; 'Reports of the Trial on Penenden Heath' p.15-26

former bequeathed his father's estate at Compton to Godwine as a reward for the loyalty and valour he had displayed. In 1017 when Cnut had apportioned England among his followers, he retained Wessex for himself and the following year he made Godwine the earl of central Wessex, which probably included the shires of Sussex, Hampshire, Surrey and Berkshire. It is extremely unlikely that the king would have advanced him to this position unless he already held more land than the 10 hides at Compton which Esbern held from Godwine as recorded in the Domesday survey of Sussex. This substantiates the view that Edmund, after his succession to the throne, restored Godwine to all his father's former possessions, and these are likely to have been substantial in view of the fact that Wulfnoð was able to command the loyalty of the crews of twenty ships. The Latin recension of the Canterbury version of the *Chronicle* calls him 'the noble man'; Swanton translates *Wulfnoð Cild* as 'Prince Wulfnoth'. Nor would Cnut have given Godwine his sister-in-law in marriage had he not been holding a considerable area of land by 1018. This inheritance formed the basis of his landed wealth.

Godwine would have been given comital estates to meet his increased responsibilities. His would have been the task of eventually ensuring the defence of the whole vulnerable coastline from the Thames estuary on the east to the western seaboard of Devonshire. In 1018 this would have given him Southwark in Surrey, Over Wallop in Hampshire and Aldermaston in Berkshire.[5] In addition, at some point he was given Hurstpierpoint, Rotherfield, Singleton, Washington, Angmering and Harting - all of these occupied strategic positions on the high ground in Sussex overlooking the Channel.

- Hurstpierpoint never paid tax;[6]
- Rotherfield and Angmering were left in King Alfred's will to Osferth;[7]
- Singleton incorporated Dean,[8] which Alfred left to his youngest son Æðelweard, who died in AD922[9] (the estate would then have reverted to the royal demesne);
- Washington had been granted to Eadric by King Eadred in 947.[10] Sixteen years later King Edgar gave land there to Bishop Æþelwold which the bishop exchanged for land in Huntingdonshire.[11] The estate amounted to 59 hides but it may not necessarily have been the same parcel of land.[12]
- That Harting was the King's to dispose of is shown by King Edgar's grant to Bishop Æthelwold.[13]

---

[5] I Walker, 'Harold' pp.58,59
[6] Phillimore DB 12-36; Sussex 13-46.
[7] S 1507, F. Harmer, S.E.H.D No 11 pp.49-53
[8] R. Fleming, 'Kings and Lords' p.89 and note 195
[9] J.W. pp.382-3
[10] S 525
[11] S 714
[12] S 1377
[13] S 776, 779

All these estates were royal demesne land and eventually were given to Godwine to facilitate his task of guarding the coast.

When Cnut and Godwine returned from Denmark, the ealdorman of the Western Provinces, Æthelweard, was banished and the territory which he had governed was added to Godwine's earldom. It was then that he would have been allotted the comital land of Puddletown which was responsible for the third penny of the whole of Dorset as well as the scrubland at Hawcombe.[14] In Somerset he would have been entitled as earl to Old Cleeve and Brompton Regis;[15] in Devon Godwine received the comital dues from Moretonhampstead and Molland.[16] All these estates Harold held when he succeeded his father in 1053.

In 1044 when Archbishop Eadsige became ill, Godwine was given authority over Kent and shared with the King and the Canons of St Martin a portion of the third penny of the revenue of Dover as well as the dues of Fordwich. In gratitude for the Earl's championship of the rights of Christ Church in the shire courts and of guarding against those who wished to usurp the Archbishop's office, Eadsige gave him *'Rateburg'*, (Richborough), Longport, Niewendene and *'Saltwde'*[17] (Saltwood). According to the Domesday Manachorum 89, 'Eadsige gave Godwine Statenborough and Sundridge, (D. Mon 87).[18] It also records that Saltwood, Sundridge, Longport and Statenborough were all held by Godwine from Archbishop Eadsige.[19] Newenden was held *T.R.E* by Leofric from Archbishop Stigand. It was attached to Longport; presumably the former held it after Godwine's death. Domesday records that Godwine held the manor of Folkestone, which Eadmer claimed he had stolen from Christ Church, but which Archbishop Eadsige also gave to him. All these estates were the subject of the plea at Penenden Heath, as a result of which they were restored to Christ Church.

Godwine's holdings in Hampshire included Chalton which had been left to King Æthelred by his son, Æthelstan, and was thus a part of the royal demesne. Similarly Hambledon was left to Ælfmaer, who Alfred Anscombe identified as Æthelmaer, Ealdorman for the western provinces. This may not be correct, but the very phraseology of the bequest suggests a different and more important Ælfmaer from the others mentioned in the will.[20] In any case the estate passed to Godwine three or four years later. Chalton was certainly demesne land. Æthelstan bequeathed 52 hides to his father,[21] this was granted to Godwine by either Edmund, Cnut or Edward. So too was probably Wroxall on the Isle of Wight. A charter of AD1043 or 1044 records the agreement that Bishop

---

[14] Phillimore DB Dorset 1.8
[15] Old Cleeve 1.13; Brompton Regis 1.11
[16] Moretonhampstead 1.45; Molland 1.41
[17] 'Reports of the Trial of Penenden Heath'; John Le Patoural pp.21-26. 7.4, 2.27, 2.41; 'The Early History of the Church of Canterbury,' Nicholas Brooks, pp.300-301.
[18] D. Douglas, 'Domesday Monachorum of Christ Church Canterbury.'
[19] 2.41, Dom Mon 93; 2.5, Dom Mon 87; 2.39, Dom Mon 89 and 2.27, Dom Mon 92
[20] But see D. Whitelock, 'Wills' No 20 pp 167-174; S 1503 pp 56-63
[21] S 1503

Æthelwine of Winchester made with Osgod when they exchanged an estate at Alderbury, Oxfordshire, for Wroxall. It seems a reasonable assumption that this Osgod was Osgod Clapa, and that when he was outlawed in 1046, Wroxall was granted to Godwine. Aldbourne, the 40-hide estate in Wiltshire held by Gytha, comes in the same category. In Ealdorman Ælfheah's will[22] he left to Ælfhere, his brother, the property. On the latter's death in 983 he was succeeded as ealdorman of Mercia by his brother-in-law, Ælfric Cild, who was outlawed two years later, and his lands passed to the crown. Chaddleworth, which Gytha held, in Berkshire had been forfeited by the thegn, Wulfric, and then restored to him by King Edgar in AD960.[23] In Devon, Hartland and Tiverton were both demesne lands mentioned in King Alfred's will.[24]

Only four charters are now extant which record royal grants to the earl. The earliest concerns *Lytlacotan*, a location which has not been identified, a grant by King Cnut. Towards the end of his reign the King gave Godwine Poolhampton in Overton, Hampshire. Ten years later Edward bestowed Millbrook in the same shire to him and in 1050, the year before the crisis, he was awarded Sandford-on-Thames.[25] According to a later legend, Godwine acquired the manor of Bosham by tricking the Archbishop, who owned Bosham, into giving it to him.[26] But the owner before Godwine had been King Cnut, not the Archbishop, and it is far more likely that it was granted to the earl by the king. There were also the gifts given by the wealthy to ensure that the bequests made were carried out by invoking the support of a powerful magnate. An example of this is the will of Wulfgyth, who left a great deal of property to her sons and daughter in Norfolk, Suffolk and Essex and 'at Fritton to Earl Godwine and Earl Harold.'[27] This may be typical of many which are no longer extant. In addition Godwine bought some property in straightforward transactions. He bought Woodchester in Gloucestershire from Azur and gave it to his wife. The purchase of Stoke in Kent, however, may have been more reminiscent of the deal between Abbot Ælfstan and King Harold Harefoot's steward in relation to Sandwich.[28]

It must be remembered that, valuable as the Domesday record undoubtedly is, the Survey was carried out twenty years after the Conquest. The commissioners who were gathering information could well have been misled owing to the fallibility of human memory. Confusion could also have arisen when the members of a family were in possession of estates joining, or even in some case different parts of the same estate.[29] Given the time lapse between 1066 and the Survey it would be surprising if some discrepancies and inaccuracies were not

---

[22] S 1485
[23] S 687
[24] S 1507
[25] S 983, 970, 1009, 1022
[26] Walter Map, 'De Nugis Curialum,' DIST V ch 3 pp.418-421.
[27] Will of Wulfgyth S 1535, D. Whitelock. 'Wills' No 32 pp.84-87, 197-199.
[28] A.J Robertson, A.S Charters No XCI pp.174 179, 422-424.
[29] A. Williams, 'Land and Power' p.177

present. For instance, Hawcombe Wood is recorded as being held by Earl Edwin but the Exon Domesday makes Godwine the owner. This is undoubtedly correct as the third oak of Hawcombe belonged *T.R.E* to Frampton, which Gytha held. Similarly, due presumably to a scribal error, Wychbold in Worcestershire is attributed to ownership by Godwine, where Earl Edwin is intended.[30] There were probably also cases in which both Godwine and Harold were not given their titles as earl, and where confusion arose between Gytha, Godwine's wife and Earl Ralph's. A more serious charge against the Domesday Book is its express purpose of vindicating the wanton destruction which resulted from the Norman conquest by denigrating the names of Godwine and Harold at every opportunity. Unlawful seizures of property are claimed against them many times. We would expect the family of Earl Leofric to come in for the same measure of condemnation.[31] On this, however, the commissioners are silent and it is left to Hemming of Worcester to relate a different picture.

It seems possible that Godwine did make a will. Some evidence of this is afforded by the charters, S 1022 and 1025. After his death the land at Sandford-on-Thames was given to Abingdon Abbey. According to the *Chronicon Monasterii de Abingdon* King Edward made this grant at Harold's instigation.[32] In Somerset, Gunhild, Godwine's daughter, was in possession of 10 hides at Hardington (Mandeville) and almost certainly of 10½ hides at Creech (St Michael). The earl's grandson and namesake held two estates at Nettlecombe and Langford (Budville) amounting to nearly 8 hides. These could well have been bequests in Godwine's will. Probably most convincing as evidence of a will is Poolhampton, in Overton, Hampshire, the estate granted to Godwine by King Cnut in 1033. The Domesday record shows that this was held in 1066 by Tostig.[33]

Note

In preparation of the Appendix I am indebted to the Phillimore edition of the Domesday Book; to Robin Fleming, 'Kings and Lords in Conquest England,' Ann Williams for the invaluable, 'Land and Power in the Eleventh Century; the Estates of Harold Godwineson,' and Ian Walker, 'Harold, the Last Anglo Saxon King.

---

[30] ibid p.182
[31] ibid
[32] 'Chricon Monasterii De Abingdon' pp 466-9; M. Gelling, 'Early Charters of the Thames Valley,' pp.141-2 and particularly A. Williams 'Land and Power' p.183 and note 81 p.233.
[33] S 970; DB Hampshire 31.1

Appendix 2

Sources for the Life of Godwine

The Anglo-Saxon Chronicle (ASC)

Manuscript 'C'

The *A.S.C* manuscript 'C' was compiled at Abingdon in Berkshire. There is a gap in the annals from 1056 until 1065 and then, after commencing with the battle of Stamford Bridge, they break off abruptly part way through. This version is generally considered to be hostile to Godwine and his family, which is surprising; Godwine had good relations with Abingdon. However, Pauline Stafford and Ian Walker have both pointed out that some of the entries show both the earl and his son, Harold, in a favourable light. For instance, when Godwine returned in 1052, the men of the south-east 'all declared that they would live and die with him.'[1] In 1053, his death is recorded in a very sympathetic tone, and in 1049 Harold is recorded as giving his cousin, Beorn, an honourable funeral.

The anti-Godwine tone - where it does exist - may possibly be due to the influence of Rotulf, King Edward's Norman kinsman. He had been the bishop of Nidaros in Norway, and possibly also acting as such in Iceland. On his return to England, he was appointed briefly as the Abbot of Abingdon in succession to Spearhafoc. The following year he was followed by Ordric, who remained in office until 22 January 1066.[2] The annal for 1052 which states that Godwine 'made all too little reparation for God's property which he had from many holy places,' could well have been influenced by the Norman abbot. It has been suggested that manuscript 'C' was written in retrospect up to 1016, possibly even up to 1042, and from then on entered annually.

Manuscript 'D'

The chronicle known as 'D; has a great deal in common with 'E': either they both used a common source, or 'D' was copied from 'E' during the period that covered the early days of Godwine's public life. After this, 'D' and 'C' are identical for some entries. 'D' ends in 1079, except for a late annal dated for the following year which rightfully belongs to 1130.

---

[1] A.S.C 'C' s.a. 1052. A.S.C D either copying form 'E' or both copying from the same source.
[2] F. Harmer, 'Anglo-Saxon Writs', 2nd edition p.569

'D' alone mentions that Swegn Godwineson 'ruined himself with the Danes.' His is the only mention of Duke William's visit in 1052/1051, except for John of Worcester, and that Bishop Ealdred and his retinue 'either could not or would not' endeavour to overtake Harold and Leofwine in their flight to Bristol in the annal for 1052/1051. Ealdred and Worcester figure prominently, and the manuscript also shows an interest in Scottish and Scandinavian affairs. In 1045-6 the writer alludes to war in Denmark between Magnus of Norway and Swein of Denmark, and in 1048-9 mentions King Swein's return to Denmark after the death of King Magnus. He does not mention Godwine in connection with Ætheling Alfred's death in 1036; the manuscript's 'he' could refer to Harold Harefoot, and in fact probably does.

Manuscript 'E'

A.S.C. 'E', known as *The Peterborough Chronicle*, was written from the year 1031 until 1121, maybe at St Augustine's, Canterbury. Prior to this, it shows a close affinity to 'D', but after its arrival in Kent it becomes an independent and contemporary record. It has been considered to be pro-Godwine in outlook, but an examination of this chronicle shows this to be only partly true. Its main preoccupation is now shown to be the south-eastern areas, particularly Kent, evidenced by its detailed knowledge of the region. The graphic account of the affray at Dover in 1048-9 is a good example of this. These entries seem to have been entered within a short time of their taking place.

Alone of the chronicles, manuscript 'E' makes no mention of the death of the Ætheling Alfred, nor of Godwine's involvement in it. This version distinctly mentions that Earl Swegn, on his return from Denmark 'made peace with the King, and he was promised that he would be entitled to all those things of which he had formerly been possessed.' (Neither 'C' nor 'D' mentions this.) 'E' is the only annalist to mention the battle of Val-ès-Dunes, and other entries concerning Normandy such as the death of Duke Richard II, his elder son, Richard, and the younger son, Robert, and the death of the latter 'while on a pilgrimage.'

Manuscript 'F'

A.S.C 'F' is a product of the late 11th century. It is an abridged edition of 'E' compiled at Christchurch, Canterbury. For the purpose of this book, its most significant entry is the one for 1009, concerning Wulfnoth who is called by 'E' 'Wulfnoth Cild, the South Saxon.' In the English version of 'F' is added, 'the father of Earl Godwine.' Admittedly, this was penned approximately ninety years after the event and nearly fifty years after Godwine's death, but the Earl was extremely popular and well-liked in Kent and it is unbelievable that the chronicler would have wished to identify him falsely with Wulfnoth, whom some people believed was a traitor.

Anglo-Norman Sources

John of Worcester

Among the Anglo-Norman historians John of Worcester stands out as pre-eminent. In a sense his work is another rendering of the *Anglo-Saxon Chronicle*, resembling 'D' in some respects, but including a great deal of information from other material. John has the reputation of copying from his sources with painstaking accuracy. He shows an awareness of Norman propaganda and, in places, distinctly refutes it, for eample in his account of King Harold's coronation in 1066.

According to Orderic Vitalis, when he visited Worcester he saw a Latin chronicle in preparation which had been started at the suggestion of Bishop Wulfstan. Originally, it was thought that its author was the monk, Florence, whose death is recorded in John's chronicle in the year 1118. It is now accepted that it was written by John, and that Florence supplied a great deal of local and topical detail.

John is the only annalist to record Queen Eadgyth's part in the murder of Gospatric at Edward's court at Christmas 1065. With 'D' he is our informant that King Swein of Denmark asked for naval assistance from England in 1047 and 1048. John, unlike the *Anglo-Saxon Chronicle* or for that matter other histories, points out under the year 1008, that Wulfnoth; ealdorman of the South Saxons 'was accused unjustly of treason.' It is surprising that Earl Leofric is portrayed in such a favourable light in view of the depredations made by the Earl and other members of his family of lands claimed by the Abbey of Worcester.

William of Malmesbury

By comparison with John, William of Malmesbury and Henry of Huntingdon are of less value. It is true that William endeavours to provide an account which reflects his own mixed parentage. However, this did not prevent him from using his imagination to explain the confusion caused by references to Gytha as being King Cnut's sister instead of his sister-in-law. To do so he invented a first wife for Godwine who he claims was Cnut's sister. According to William's story she met a well-deserved death by being struck with lightning. This was in divine retribution for the slave trade with which she was involved of selling beautiful girls in Denmark. There was also a son – according to William – who was drowned in the river Thames. Curiously William was unable to discover the name of Godwine's real wife and the mother of all their children, although it was well known from other sources which he had himself consulted.

Henry of Huntingdon

Henry of Huntingdon's claim that some of his information had been gained from eye witnesses, old men who relayed their boyhood memories probably gives his *'Historia'* some value, but like William, Henry could not refrain from embellishing accounts with flights of fancy from his own resourceful mind.

Encomium Emmae Reginae

The works commissioned by Queen Emma and her daughter-in-law Queen Eadgyth, although biased, are valuable for revealing the innermost thoughts of their patrons and the intrigues of the court circles. The author of the Encomium of Queen Emma was most probably a monk of St Omer or St Bertin. Although he must have known Emma, his knowledge of English affairs was slight. In spite of this it is only true to say that his impressions of some of the leading English magnates such as Edmund Ironside and Eadric Streona agree well with what we know of them from other sources. The book was commissioned by Emma in order to answer the accusations which were circulating and to vindicate her for having encouraged her sons by King Æthelred to make their attempts to seize the English throne. In order to exonerate herself, it was necessary to claim that it was Harold Harefoot who had caused a forged letter to be sent to them. The Encomiast was also instructed to fashion the events after Cnut's death to her advantage and to falsify the truth wherever required. Her first marriage is completely suppressed. Perhaps it is even more important that its aim was to justify Harthacnut's claim to be the rightful heir to Cnut's throne and to discredit Edward's. The Encomium was being finalised at a time when Emma and Harthacnut were faced with a rapidly deteriorating situation. Her son had become extremely hateful to his subjects.[3] It was necessary to enlist Edward in an attempt to salvage their position, and for Emma to distance herself from her actions of six years earlier. She comes over as an unscrupulous and extremely ambitious woman who was quite prepared to invent scurrilous rumours regarding Harold Harefoot's parentage. However, the Encomium does have its value: it corroborates the Chronicle in many places; it has a good knowledge of Scandinavian affairs; and the interpretation of Godwine's actions in 1036 is illuminating. There was no reason for Emma to exonerate him; Harthacnut had no qualms about trying to ruin the earl.

Vita Ædwardi Regis

The other biography, that connected with Queen Eadgyth, was also written by a Flemish monk or cleric but, unlike the scribe who wrote at Emma's command, the author of the *Vita Ædwardi Regis* was living in England and familiar with Edward's court. A great deal of controversy surrounds the date when it was

---

[3] A.S.C 'C' 1040, 1041; A.S.C 'D'; A.S.C 'E' 1039; J. W. pp 528-533.

written. The early years of the twelfth century has been suggested,[4] but it now seems certain that the work was started in 1065 and the second part completed after the battle of Hastings, probably in 1067, certainly before 1070. Its value as an historical record lies in the events which are lacking in the Chronicle. Without it, we would know nothing of the wishes of the community of Christ Church to elect Ælfric to the archbishopric of Canterbury; that Queen Eadgyth, having been sent to Wherwell according to the testimony of the chronicle, was brought back to Wilton when Godwine's fleet sailed into the Thames; or the part that Robert, the Archbishop of Canterbury, played in endeavouring to persuade the king to divorce Eadgyth. It cannot be claimed that the monk who wrote the *Vita* was prejudiced in favour of the queen's family. Although Godwine is portrayed as a patient, gentle man, fond of his family and loved by the men of his earldom, in the controversy over Canterbury lands, as a churchman, he says bluntly that right was on the Archbishop's side. He also makes a reference to Godwine's part in the death of the Ætheling Alfred. He is writing from Eadgyth's viewpoint. Tostig is obviously her favourite brother. The rebellion of the Northumbrians is represented as the crisis point, when the unity of the family disintegrated and brought about the ruin of the kingdom. The one point which reveals the personal feelings of the writer is his obvious dislike of Stigand which seems at variance with Eadgyth's sympathies.

The religious works composed at establishments contain some interesting details. Abingdon, Durham, Ely, Evesham, Peterborough, Ramsey and Waltham all contribute items which either corroborate or add to the Chronicle. There are also the Welsh and Irish chronicles, as well as the Norse and Russian literature dealing with the period in which Godwine and his family lived. A further source of valuable information is to be found in the Anglo-Saxon charters, the wills and the writs of the relevant period.

Scandinavian

Knytlingasaga

The 'saga of the descendants of Cnut' was written in Iceland in the mid-13th century and tells the story of the family from which Cnut sprang and of his descendants down to the late 12th century. It is one of a number of 'kings' sagas' composed at this time, probably by Olafr Þorðarson a relative of Snorri Sturluson.

Gesta Danorum

Saxo Grammaticus's sixteen-volume tale of the 'Deeds of the Danes' – a national origin myth and historical source, probably written in the 12th century. Although it focuses on the Danes, the story concerns the whole of Scandinavia. The first nine

---

[4] M. Bloch, 'La Vie de S. Edourd Le Confesseur,' par Osbert De Clare' in 'Analecta Bollandiana' vol 41 pp 5-131 vol 41, 1923; P. Stafford. 'Queen Emma and Queen Edith' p.40 notes 31, 33.

books deal with mythical and legendary matters, but from the story of King Gormr the narrative emerges into history. Saxo's sources seem to have included folktales, memories of euhemerised myth and, for the 11th century, some ecclesiastical records dealing with Archbishop Absalon who was appointed in 1178.

Heimskringla

Snorri Sturluson's narrative concerning early Scandinavia, dealing with both mythic and historic matter – the gods of Ásgarðr and Vanaheim, the legendary Yngling kings of Sweden and the rise of Háraldr Hárfagr (Harald Fair-hair) in the 9th century.

Abbreviations & Citations

ADAM	Adam of Bremen – *History of the Archbishops of Hamburg-Bremen*
ANS	*Proceedings of the Battle Conference* in *Anglo-Norman Studies*
A.S.C	The Anglo-Saxon Chronicle
	(a) ed. D. Whitelock, D.C. Douglas and S.I. Tucker
	(b) ed. G.N. Garmonsway
	(c) *Anglo Saxon Chronicles* Michael Swanton
Atlas	*An Atlas of Attestations in Anglo-Saxon Charters* S. Keynes
BT	The Bayeux Tapestry
BRUT	*Brut Y Tywysogion*, Peniarth M S 20 version
CRAWFORD COLLECTION	*The Crawford Collection of Early Charters and Documents* ed. A.S. Napier and W.H. Stevenson
'Dark Age Britain'	*A Biographical Dictionary of Dark Age Britain: England, Scotland and Wales* Ann Williams, Alfred P. Smyth and D.P. Kirby
DB	*Domesday Book* ed. J Morris 34 volumes
DOM MON	*Domesday Monachorum of Christchurch Canterbury* ed. D.C. Douglas
Eadmer	Historia Novorum in Anglia
Edward	*Edward the Confessor* F. Barlow
E.E.R	*Encomium Emmae Regina* ed. A. Campbell
E.H.Di	*English Historical Documents 500 – 1042* ed. D. Whitelock
E.H.Dii	*English Historical Documents 1042 – 1189* ed. D.C. Douglas and G.W. Greenway
E.H.R	English Historical Review
English Church	The English Church 1000 – 1066 *F. Barlow*
Finberg 1953	The Early Charters of Devon and Cornwall
Finberg 1961	The Early Charters of the West Midlands
Finberg 1964	The Early Charters of Wessex
F.N.C	The History of the Norman Conquest of England *E.A. Freeman*
G.N.D	Gesta Normanorum Ducum of William of Jumieges
G.R	De Gestis Regum Anglorum of William of Malmesbury

Harold	*Harold the Last Anglo-Saxon King* I. Walker
Hart 1957	The Early Charters of Essex: The Saxon Period
Hart 1966	The Early Charters of Eastern England
Hart 1975	The Early Charters of Northern England and the North Midlands
Hemming	*Hemingi Chartularium Ecclesiae Wigornensis* vol. i
Historia Anglorum	*The Chronicle of Henry of Huntingdon*
J.W.	*The Chronicle of John of Worcester* (vol. 2 unless stated as JWiii)
Battle of Hastings	*The Battle of Hastings, England and Europe 1035 – 1066* by Sten Körner
Land and Power	*Land and Power in the Eleventh Century; The Estates of Harold Godwineson* A. Williams
O.M.T	Oxford Medieval Texts
OV	The Ecclesiastical History of Orderic Vitalis
Charters	Anglo-Saxon Charters *A.J. Robertson*
R.P.C	The Russian Primary Chronicle
Sawyer 'Charters'	Anglo-Saxon Charters: An Annotated List and Bibliography *P.H. Sawyer*
Saxo, Saxo Grammaticus	*Danorum Regum Heroumque Historia*
SEHD	*Select English Historical Documents of the Ninth and Tenth Centuries* F.E. Harmer
Unification	*Unification and Conquest* P. Stafford
Vita	*Vita Ædwardi Regis: The Life of King Edward who rests at Westminster* ed. and trans. F. Barlow
Wills	*Anglo-Saxon Wills* D. Whitelock
W.P.	*Histoire de Guilaume le Conquérant* W. Poitiers
WRITS	Anglo-Saxon Writs *F.E. Harmer*

Bibliography

Primary Sources

Adam of Bremen, 'History of the Archbishops of Hamburg, Bremen', trans. J. Tshan, New York, 1959

Ágrip, Af Noregs Konunga Sogum', ed. and trans. by M.J. Driscoll, University College of London, 1995

'Anglo-Saxon Charters', ed. A.J. Robertson, Cambridge, 1939, 1956

'Anglo-Saxon Charters: An Annotated List and Bibliography' ed. P.H. Sawyer, University College, London, 1968

'The Anglo-Saxon Chronicle' ed. and trans. G.N. Garmonsway, 1953

'The Anglo-Saxon Chronicles' ed. and trans. M. Swanton, London 2000

'Anglo-Saxon Wills', D. Whitelock, Cambridge 1930

'Anglo Saxon Writs' ed F.E Harmer, Manchester, 1952

'Annals of Inisfallen' ed Sean MacAirt, Dublin, 1951' 1977

'Annals of Tigernach' to Whitley Stokes, Llanerch 1993

Annals of Ulster' ed Sean MacAirt and G. MacNiocaill' Dublin 1983.

'Annals of the Church of Winchester', trans. J. Stevenson, Church Historians of England

'Annals Cambriae', ed. John Williams (AB ITEL), London, 1860

'Atlas of Attestations in Anglo-Saxon Charters c. 670 – 1066', S. Keynes, Cambridge, 1995

'Bayeux Tapestry', ed. D.M. Wilson, London, 1985

Birch W. de Gray, 'Cartularium Saxonicum', 3 vols. 1885 – 1899

'Brut y Tywysogyon, Peniarth' MS 20 version, ed. J. Jones, Cardiff, 1952

'Brut y Tywysogyon, Red Book of Hergest' version ed. J. Jones, Cardiff, 1955

'Chronica Johannis de Oxenedes', ed. H. Ellis, London, 1859

'The Chronicle of Æthelweard', ed. A. Campbell, London, 1962

'The Chronicle of Hugh Candidus', ed. W.T. Mellows, London, 1949

'The Chronicle of John of Fordun of the Scottish Nation', 2 volumes ed. by W.F. Skene, Lampeter, 1993

'The Chronicle of John of Worcester', ed. R.R. Darlington and P.J. McGurk, trans. J. Bray, Oxford, vol ii 1995, vol iii 1998

'The Chronicle of Melrose', trans. J. Stevenson in 'Church Historians of England' vol. iv Part 1

'The Chronicle of Novgorod' 1016 – 1471 trans. from the Russian by Robert Mitchell and Nevill Forbes, London, 1914

'Danish Kings and the Jomsvikings in the Greatest Saga of Ólafr Tryggvason', by Ólafur Halldórsson, the Viking Society for Northern Research, University College, London, trans. A. Faulkes, 2000

'Domesday Book', ed. J. Morris, 34 volumes, Chicester, 1975 – 1986

'Domesday Monachorum of Christchurch, Canterbury', ed. D.C. Douglas, R. Historical Society, London, 1944

Eadmer, 'Historia Novorum in Anglia', trans. G. Bosanquet, London, 1964

'Early Sources of Scottish History AD 500 – 1286' ed. A.O. Anderson, 2 volumes, Edinburgh, 1922

'The Ecclesiastical History of Orderic Vitalis', ed. M. Chibnall, 6 volumes, Oxford, 1969 – 1980

Ellis H. 'A General Introduction to Domesday Book', Record Commissioners, 2 vols. London, 1833

'Encomium Emmae Reginae', ed. A. Campbell, London, 1949

'English Historical Documents c. 500 – 1042' vol. i, ed. D. Whitelock, 1979

'English Historical Documents 1042 – 1189' vol. ii, ed. D.C. Douglas and G.W. Greenway, Oxford, 1981

'Fagrskinna Konunga Tal', ed. Bjarni Einarsson, Reyjavik, 1984

Finberg H.P.R., 'The Early Charters of Devon and Cornwall', Leicester, 1953

Finberg H.P.R., 'The Early Charters of the West Midlands', Leicester, 1961

Finberg H.P.R., 'The Early Charters of Wessex', Leicester, 1964

'Flatey Jarbók', ed. Siguróur Nordal 4 volumes Akranes, 1944 – 5

Gaimar, 'L'estoire des Engleis', ed. Alexander Bell, Oxford, 1960

'Gesta Normannorum Ducum' of William of Jumieges, Orderic Vitalis and Robert of Torigni, ed. E.M.C. van Houts, OMT 1992 – 5, 2

'Gesta Guillelmi of William of Poitiers', ed. and trans. R.H.C. Davis and M. Chibnall, O.M.T 1998

'Gesta Pontificum of William of Malmesbury' trans. David Preest as 'The Deeds of the Bishops of England', Woodbridge, 2002

'De Gestis Regum of William of Malmesbury', ed. N.E.S.A. Hamilton and trans. Mynors, R.A.B., Thomson, R.M. and Winterbottom, M., OMT, 1998

Geraldus Cambrensis: The Historical Works of, Revised and edited by T.Wright, London 1887.

'Hemingi Chartularium Ecclesiae Wigorniensis' vol. i ed. T. Hearne, Oxford, 1723

'Henry of Huntingdon, The Chronicle of', trans. T. Forester, Lampeter, 1991

Ingulf, 'The History of Ingulf', Church Historians of England', vol. ii Part ii ed. J. Stevenson, London, 1854

'De Inventione Sanctae Crucis', in 'The Foundation of Waltham Abbey', ed. and trans. W. Stubbs, Oxford, 1861

'Jomsviking Saga: Icelandic texts', trans. N.F. Blake, Liverpool, 1968

'Knytlinga Saga', trans. Hermann Pálsson and Paul Edwards, Odens, 1986

'Laws of the Kings of England from Edmund to Henry I', Part One, 'Edmund to Cnut', ed. A.J. Robertson, Cambridge, 1925

'Liber Eliensis', ed. E.O.Blake, Camden Society 3rd series 92, 1962

'Liber Monasteri de Hyda', ed. E. Edwards, R.S., 1866

'Morkinskinna,' trans. and edited by Theodore M. Anderson and Kari Ellen Gade, Cornell University, New York, 2000

'Orderic Vitalis', 'The Ecclesiastical History of Orderic Vitalis', edited and trans. M. Chibnall, Oxford, 1969 – 1980, O.M.T.

'The Peterborough Chronicle of Hugh Candidus', trans. by C. Mellows and W.T. Mellows, 1966, 2nd edition, Peterborough

Plummer, C. and Earle, J., 'Two of the Saxon Chronicles Parallel' vol. ii, Oxford, 1899

Ralph de Diceto, 'The History of the Archbishops of Canterbury', trans. J. Stevenson, 'Church Historians of England' vol. iv Part 1

'Roger of Hoveden', trans. H.T. Riley, vol. i Part 1, Lampeter, 1994

Roger of Wendover, 'Flowers of History', trans. J.A. Giles, Lampeter, 1993

'The Russian Primary Chronicle', trans. Samuel H. Cross and O.P. Sherbowitz, Cambridge, Massachusets, 1973

Saxo Grammaticus, 'Danorum Regum Heroumque Historia', Books x – xvi, vol. i, trans. and edit. by E. Christiensen, Oxford, 1980

'Select English Historical Documents of the Ninth and Tenth Centuries', ed. F.E. Harmer, Cambridge, 1914

Simeon of Durham, 'A History of the Kings of England', trans. J. Stevenson, Lampeter, 1987

Simeon of Durham, 'A History of the Church of Durham', trans. J. Stevenson, Lampeter, 1988

Snorri Sturluson, 'Heimskringla, The Norse Kings Sagas', trans. Samuel Laing, London, 1930

Snorri Sturluson, 'Heimskringla, The Olaf Sagas', trans. Samuel Laing, London, 1930

Sven Aggesen, 'The Works of Sven Aggesen', trans. by Eric Christiansen, University College, London, 1992

'Theodoricus Monachus: Historia de Antiquitate Regum Norwegiensium,' trans. and annotated by David and Ian McDougall, University College, London, 1998

'Three Lives of the Last Englishmen', trans. M. Swanton, London, 1984

'Vita Ædwardi Regis: The Life of King Edward who Rests at Winchester', ed. and trans. F. Barlow, Oxford, 1992, O.M.T.

'Vita Haroldi', trans. and edited by W. de Gray Birch, London, 1885

'Vita Wulfstani: the Vita Wulfstani of William of Malmesbury', Camden Society 3rd series 40, ed. R.R. Darlington, 1928

Secondary Sources

ALFORD, D.P., 'The Abbots of Tavistock', Plymouth 1891

BARLOW, F., 'Feudal Kingdom of England', London 1961

BARLOW, F., 'The English Church 1006 – 1066', London 1963

BARLOW, F., 'Edward the Confessor', London 1970

BARLOW, F., 'William Rufus', London 1983

BARLOW, F., 'The Godwins', London 2000

BRONSTED, J., 'The Vikings', trans. Kalle Stov, London 1865

BROOKS, F.W., 'The Battle of Stamford Bridge', York 1956

BUTLER, D., '1066, The Story of a Year', London 1966

CAMPBELL, J., ed. 'The Anglo-Saxons', London 1991

CHADWICK, N.K., 'The Beginnings of Russian History', Cambridge 1949

CLARKE, P.A., 'The English Nobility under Edward the Confessor', Oxford 1994

CLEMOES, P., ed. 'The Anglo-Saxons', London 1959

CORNER, D., 'Porlock in Those Days', Tiverton 1992

DAVIES, Wendy, 'Wales in the Early Middle Ages', Leicester 1982

DAVIS, R.H.C., 'The Normans and their Myth', London 1980

DAVIS, R.H.C., 'A History of Medieval Europe', London 1988

DEVRIES, Kelly, 'Norwegian Invasion of England 1066,' Boydel Press 2003

DOUGLAS, D.C., 'William the Conqueror', London 1964

DUNCAN, A.A.M., 'Scotland: The Making of the Kingdom', Edinburgh 1975

FINBERG, H.P.R., 'Tavistock Abbey', Cambridge 1951

FLEMING, Robin, 'Kings and Lords in Conquest England', Cambridge 1991

FLETCHER, R., 'Who's Who in Roman Britain and Anglo-Saxon England', London 1989

FREEMAN, E.A., 'History of the Norman Conquest of England', 6 volumes Oxford 1869 – 1879

FREEMAN, E.A., 'The Reign of William Rufus and the Accession of Henry I', Oxford 1888

FRYDE, E.B., GREENWAY, D.E., PORTER, S., and REY, I., 'Handbook of British Chronology', 3rd edition, London 1986

GELLING, M., 'The Early Charters of the Thames Valley', Leicester 1979

GRANSDEN, A., 'Historical Writing in England c. 550 – c. 1307', London 1974

GREEN, J.R., 'The Conquest of England', 2 vols., London 1899

HART, C.R., 'The Danelaw', London 1992

HIGHAM, N.J., 'The Death of Anglo-Saxon England', London 1997

HOLLISTER, C.W., 'Anglo-Saxon Military Institutions on the Eve of the Norman Conquest', Oxford 1998

JONES, Gwyn, 'A History of the Vikings', London 1968

KAPELLE, W.E., 'The Norman Conquest of the North', London 1979

KENDRICK, T.D., 'A History of the Vikings', London 1968

KEYNES, S., 'The Diplomas of King Æthelred the Unready 978 – 1016', Cambridge 1980

KEYNES, S. and LAPIDGE, M., 'Alfred the Great', Harmonsworth 1983

KNOWLES, D., BROOKE, C.N.L. and LONDON, V.C.M., 'Heads of Religious Houses in England and Wales 940 – 1016', Cambridge 1972

KÖRNER, S., 'The Battle of Hastings, England and Europe 1035 – 1066', Lund 1964

LANCASTER, J.C., 'Godiva of Coventry', Coventry 1967

LAPPENBERG, J.M., 'A History of England under the Anglo-Saxon Kings', trans. B. Thorpe, 2 vols.,London 1845

LARSON, L.M., 'Canute the Great', New York 1912

LAWSON, M.K., 'Cnut, the Danes in England in the Early Eleventh Century', London 1993

LLOYD, J.E., 'A History of Wales from the Earliest Times to the Edwardian Conquest', volume 2, London1939

LOYN, H.R., 'Anglo-Saxon England and the Norman Conquest', London 1962

LOYN, H.R., 'Harold, Son of Godwine', Bexhill 1966

LOYN, H.R., 'The Middle Ages: A Concise Encyclopaedia', ed. London 1991

MASON, Emma, 'St Wulfstan of Worcester', Oxford 1990

MASON, Emma, 'The House of Godwine', London 2004

MAUND, K.L., 'Ireland, Wales and England in the Eleventh Century', Woodbridge 1991

McLYNN, F., '1066, The Year of Three Battles', London 1998

Ó CORRAIN, Donncha, 'Ireland before the Normans', Dublin 1972

OLESON, T.J., 'The Wilenagemot in the Reign of Edward the Confessor', London 1959

OMAN, C., 'England before the Norman Conquest', London 1949

PINE, L.G., 'Heirs of the Conqueror', London 1965

ROESDAHL, Else, 'The Vikings', London 1991

RONAY, G., 'The Lost King of England', Woodbridge 1989

ROUND, J.H., 'Feudal England', London 1895

ROWLEY, T., 'The Normans', Stroud 1999

RUMBLE, A., ed. 'The Reign of Cnut, King of England, Denmark and Norway', London 1994

SAWYER, Birgit and Peter, 'Medieval Scandinavia', Minnesota 1993

SAWYER, P.H., 'Anglo-Saxon Charters: an Annotated List and Bibliography', London 1968

SAWYER, P.H., 'Charters of Burton Abbey', London 1979

SEARLE, W.G., 'Anglo-Saxon Bishops, Kings and Nobles', Cambridge 1889

SOUTHERN, R.W., 'St Anselm and his Biographer', Cambridge 1963

STAFFORD, Pauline, 'Queens, Concubines and Dowagers', Athens 1983

STAFFORD, Pauline, 'Unification and Conquest', London 1989

STAFFORD, Pauline, 'Queen Emma and Queen Edith', Oxford 1997

STENTON, F.M., 'Anglo-Saxon England', 3rd edition, Oxford 1968

STUBBS, W., ed. 'The Foundation of Waltham Abbey', Oxford 1861

STURDY, D., 'Alfred the Great', London 1995

THORNDIKE, Lynn, 'Medieval Europe', London 1920

TOUT, T.F., 'The Empire and the Papacy 918 – 1273', London 1932

TURVILLE-PETRIE, G., 'The Heroic Age of Scandinavia', London 1951

TYERMAN, C., 'Who's Who in Early Medieval England', London 1996

VERNADSKY, G., 'The Origins of Russia', London 1959

VERNADSKY, G., 'Kievan Russia', London 1973

WALKER, I., 'Harold the Last Anglo-Saxon King', Stroud 1997

WATKIS, L., and CHIBNALL, Marjorie, 'The Waltham Chronicle', ed. and trans., Oxford O.M.T. 1994

WEIR, Alison, 'Britain's Royal Families: The Complete Genealogy', London 1989

WHITELOCK, D., 'The Norman Conquest: Its Setting and Impact', ed.; foreword by C.T. CHEVALIER, London 1966

WILLIAMS, Ann, SMYTH, A.P., and KIRBY, D.P., 'A Biographical Dictionary of Dark Age Britain, England, Scotland and Wales c. 500 – c. 1050', London 1991

WILLIAMS, Ann, 'The English and the Norman Conquest', Woodbridge 1997

WILLIAMS, Ann, 'Kingship and Government in Pre-Conquest England c. 500 – 1066', London 1999

WILLIAMS, Ann, 'Æthelred the Unready: the Ill Counselled King', London 2003

WRIGHT, C.E., 'The Cultivation of Saga in Anglo-Saxon England', Edinburgh 1939

YORKE, Barbara, ed. 'Bishop Æthelwold, his Career and Influence', Woodbridge 1988

Articles

ANSCOMBE, A., 'The Pedigree of Earl Godwine', Translations of the Royal Historical Society, 3rd series, vii pp. 129 – 150

ARVIDSON, R., 'Source Criticism and Literary History: Lauritz Weibull, Henrik Shück and Joseph Bédier. A Discussion', in Medieval Scandinavia, 5, 1972 pp. 96 – 138

ASHDOWN, M., 'An Icelandic Account of the Survival of Harold Godwineson', in 'The Anglo-Saxons' ed. P.Clemoes, London 1959

BARLOW, L.W., 'The Antecedents of Earl Godwine of Wessex', 'New England Historical and Genealogical Register' LXI, 1957

BATES, D., 'Lord Sudeley's Ancestors: The Family of the Counts of Amiens, Valois and the Vexin in France and England during the Eleventh Century'; 'The Sudeleys, Lords of Toddington', The Manorial Society, London 1987

BEECH, G., 'England and Aquitaine in the Century before the Norman Conquest' in 'Anglo-Saxon England' 19, Cambridge 1991

CAMPBELL, M.W., 'Queen Emma and Ælfgifu of Northampton; Cnut the Great's women', in 'Medieval Scandinavia', 4, 1971

CAMPBELL, M.W., 'Earl Godwine of Wessex and Edward the Confessor's Promise of the Throne to Duke William' in Traditio 28, 1972

CAMPBELL, M.W., 'The Rise of an Anglo-Saxon King Maker', 'Godwine of Wessex', Canadian Journal of History, 13, 1978

CUTLER, K.E., 'The Godwinist Hostages: The Case for 1051' in 'Annale Mediavale', 1971

CUTLER, K.E., 'Edith, Queen of England 1045 – 1066', Medieval Studies 35, 1973

DOUGLAS, D.C., 'Edward the Confessor, Duke William of Normandy and the English Succession', EHR LXVIII, pp. 529 – 45

FLEMING, R., 'Oral Testimony and the Domesday Inquest', ANS XVII ed. C. Harper-Bill, Woodbridge 1995

GILLINGHAM, J., 'William the Bastard at War', in C. Harper-Bill et al editors, studies in 'Medieval History for R. Allen-Brown', 1989

GRIERSON, P., 'A Visit of Earl Harold to Flanders in 1056', EHR LI, 1936

GRIERSON, P., 'Relations between England and Flanders before the Norman Conquest', T.R.H.S. 4th series 23, 1941

HART, C., 'Athelstan Half-King and his Family', A.S. England 2, Cambridge 1973

HASKINS, C.H., 'King Harold's Books', E.H.R. XXXVII, 1922

HASLAM, J., 'Saxon Exeter', in 'Anglo-Saxon Towns in Southern England', ed. J. Haslam, Chichester 1984

HUDSON, B., 'The Family of Harold Godwineson and the Irish Sea Province',

J.R.S.A.I, 109, 1979

JESCH, Judith, 'In Praise of Ástrior Ólafs Dottir', Saga Book of the Viking Society, University College, London, Volume XXIV, Part 1, 1994

JOHN, E., 'Edward the Confessor and the Norman Succession', E.H.R. XCIV, 1997

KEYNES, S., 'The Crowland Psalter and the Sons of Edmund Ironside', Bodleian Library Record 11, 1985

KEYNES, S., 'The Æthelings in Normandy', ANS XIII, 1991

KEYNES, S., 'Cnut's Earls in the Reign of Cnut', ed. A. Rumble, London 1994

KING, Vanessa, 'Ealdred, Archbishop of York: the Worcester Years', ANS XVIII, 1995

LUND, Niels, 'Cnut's Danish Kingdom' in 'The Reign of Cnut', ed. A. Rumble, London 1994

MAUND, K.L., 'The Welsh Alliances of Earl Ælfgar of Mercia and his Family in the Mid-Eleventh Century' ANS XI, 1988

McNULTY, J.B., 'The Lady Ælfgyva in the Bayeux Tapestry', Speculum 55, 1980

Ó CORRAIN, Donncha, 'The Career of Diarmait Mac Máel na Mbó', 'Journal of the Old Wexford Society' 3, 1970 – 1971

OLESON, J.T., 'Edward the Confessor's Promise of the Throne to Duke William of Normandy', EHR LXXII, 1957

RARATY, D.G.J., 'Earl Godwine of Wessex: The Origin of his Power and his Political Loyalties', History LXXIV, 1989

ROFFE, D., 'Lady Godiva, the Book and Washingborough' in 'Lincolnshire Past and Present', 12 Summer, 1993

ROFFE, D., 'The Historia Croylandensis: A Plea for Reassessment', EHR CX, 1995

SEARLE, E., 'Emma the Conqueror', in C. Harper-Bill et al 'Studies in Medieval History for R. Allen-Brown', 1989

STEVENSON, W.H., 'An Alleged Son of Harold Harefoot', EHR vol. 28, 1913

TANNER, H.J.,' The Expansion of the Power and Influence of the Counts of Boulogne under Eustace II', ANS XIV, 1992

TATTON-BROWN T., 'The Churches of Canterbury Diocese in the Eleventh Century' in 'Ministers and Parish Churches: The Local Church'

WHITELOCK, D., 'The Dealings of the Kings of England with Northumbria in the Tenth and Eleventh Centuries' in P. Clemoes ed. 'The Anglo-Saxons', 1959

WILLIAMS, Ann, 'Some Notes and Considerations on Problems Connected with the English Royal Succession 860 – 1066', ANS 1977/1978

WILLIAMS, Ann, 'A West Country Magnate of the Eleventh Century: The Family, Estates and Patronage of Beorhtric son of Ælfgar', in K.S.B. Keats-Rohan ed. 'Family Trees and the Roots of Politics', Woodbridge, 1997

WILLIAMS, Ann, 'Cockles Amongst the Wheat: Danes and English in the West Midlands in the First Half of the Eleventh Century', 'Midland History' 11, 1986

WILLIAMS, Ann, 'Land and Power in the Eleventh Century; the Estates of Harold Godwineson', ANS 3, 1981

WILLIAMS, Ann, 'Land, Power and Politics: The Family and Career of Odda of Deerhurst', Deerhurst Lecture, Deerhurst, 1997

WILLIAMS, Ann, 'Princeps Merciorum Gentis: the Family, Career and Connections of Ælfhere, Ealdorman of Mercia', ASE 10, 1982

WILLIAMS, Ann, 'Lost Worlds: Kentish Society in the Eleventh Century', 'Medieval Prosopography', 20, 1999

WILLIAMS, Ann, 'The Spoliation of Worcester', ANS 19, 1996

WILLIAMS, Ann, 'The King's Nephew: The Family and Career of Earl Ralph of Hereford' on 'Studies in Medieval History for R. Allen Brown,' 1989

YORKE, Barbara, 'Æthelwold and the Politics of the Tenth Century', in B. Yorke edit. 'Bishop Æthelwold:

Index

Abingdon, 18, 19, 38, 97, 101, 103, 105, 109, 113, 114, 115, 116, 120, 125, 131, 143, 147, 156, 158, 161, 162, 170, 171, 174, 183, 185, 187, 198, 200, 201, 203, 206, 207, 230, 231, 235
Adam of Bremen, 49, 55, 58, 89, 111, 115, 137, 138, 152, 156, 157, 237, 239
Ælfgar, 20, 36, 79, 86, 106, 132, 134, 148, 177, 186, 193, 196, 197, 208, 209, 247, 248
Ælfgeat, 76, 105
Ælfgifu, 17, 18, 20, 27, 31, 34, 37, 43, 73, 83, 88, 89, 92, 93, 94, 106, 107, 108, 109, 123, 128, 133, 135, 141, 163, 180, 186, 187, 208, 212, 218, 246
Ælfgifu of Northampton, 93, 94, 128
Ælfheah, 18, 19, 20, 46, 48, 50, 68, 80, 109, 229
Ælfhelm, 21, 25, 26, 27, 34, 36, 43, 93, 107, 118, 187
Ælfmær, 28
Ælfmaer, 16, 19, 22, 26, 29, 34, 36, 40, 228
Ælfric the Homilist, 17
Ælfsige, 22, 34, 36, 40
Ælfstan, 18, 106, 143, 162, 205, 229
Ælfthryth, 11, 25, 34, 107
Ælfweard, 18, 20, 22, 76, 161, 186
Æthelflaed, 11, 31, 32, 163
Æthelfrith, Ealdorman, 17, 18, 19, 128
Æthelgifu, 18, 19
Ætheling, 10, 12, 15, 19, 22, 26, 28, 31, 33, 34, 36, 43, 48, 49, 63, 75, 79, 89, 97, 100, 112, 115, 120, 128, 147, 166, 232, 235
Æthelmaer, Bishop, 19

Æthelmaer, Ealdorman, 15, 16, 17, 19, 20, 21, 24, 26, 43, 48, 74, 75, 76, 79, 228
Æthelnoth, 22, 32, 39, 49, 79, 84, 89, 90, 92, 108, 109, 112, 122, 136, 143, 163, 186, 203
Æthelred, 10, 11, 14, 15, 16, 17, 18, 19, 21, 22, 24, 25, 26, 27, 28, 29, 31, 33, 34, 36, 37, 38, 43, 46, 71, 75, 76, 77, 81, 89, 94, 96, 97, 99, 100, 102, 108, 117, 123, 128, 135, 141, 150, 163, 165, 172, 180, 185, 188, 192, 228, 234, 244, 246
Æthelstan, 15, 16, 18, 19, 21, 26, 27, 28, 33, 34, 36, 37, 39, 70, 75, 76, 89, 102, 162, 204, 226, 228
Æthelstan, Ætheling, 15, 26, 28, 31, 33, 34, 43, 75, 89, 128
Æthelweard the Chronicler, 16, 17, 18
Æthelwine, 11, 15, 19, 28, 75, 76, 77, 79, 86, 138, 205, 228
Æthelwold, 34
Æthelwold, Abbot, 17, 18, 19, 20, 150, 164, 227, 246, 248
Æthelwold, Bishop, 18, 75
Alfred, 8, 12, 16, 17, 19, 29, 63, 73, 78, 80, 92, 97, 98, 99, 100, 101, 103, 104, 107, 108, 112, 118, 123, 127, 140, 145, 147, 163, 166, 172, 175, 178, 197, 202, 207, 227, 228, 232, 235, 237, 244, 245
Alfred the Great, 8, 244, 245
Andredesweald, 135, 157
Anglo-Saxon Chronicle, 10, 14, 50, 53, 91, 231, 233, 237, 239
Annales Cambriae, 51
Annals of St Mildred, 104, 139
Annals of Tigernach, 184, 185, 239
Annals of Winchester, 164

Ánundr, 52, 53, 55, 57, 61, 66, 68, 71, 152
Ashingdon, 38, 39, 46, 64, 84, 142
Athelney, 75, 86
Azor, 136, 220, 221
Bamburgh, 10, 21, 25, 36, 84, 117, 118, 121, 122, 127, 135
Beorhtric, 48, 248
Beorn, 58, 60, 61, 83, 106, 120, 136, 137, 138, 144, 146, 151, 156, 157, 158, 159, 170, 176, 183, 185, 200, 231
Berkhamstead, 18
Bernicia, 10, 84, 117
Boleslav, 59, 70
Bosham, 12, 135, 156, 157, 179, 199, 220, 229
Brihthelm, Bishop, 18
Brihtric, 15, 16, 21, 23, 26, 27, 28, 39, 40, 41, 186
Bristol, 179, 183, 184, 192, 193, 208, 209, 218, 232
Bruges, 90, 104, 106, 108, 109, 111, 123, 131, 141, 148, 156, 158, 159, 183, 189, 191, 199, 209, 211, 212, 218
Brut y Tywysogyon, 51, 55, 122, 184, 239
Bury St Edmunds, 56, 73
Byrhtferth of Ramsey, 18
Byrhtnoth, 31
Byrhtnoth, Ealdorman, 11, 18, 21, 23
Byzantium, 55, 139, 153, 215
Canterbury, 14, 20, 24, 32, 39, 40, 49, 56, 71, 79, 80, 89, 92, 101, 103, 106, 109, 113, 114, 122, 143, 157, 160, 162, 165, 168, 170, 171, 174, 175, 176, 179, 180, 185, 187, 190, 196, 201, 203, 204, 205, 207, 211, 214, 227, 228, 232, 235, 237, 240, 241, 248
Carmen de Bello Hastingae Proelio, 60
Chichester, 135, 136, 179, 247
Chronicon Roskildense, 58

Cnut, 8, 9, 15, 19, 27, 31, 33, 37, 38, 39, 40, 41, 43, 45, 46, 47, 48, 49, 50, 51, 52, 53, 54, 55, 56, 57, 59, 60, 61, 62, 63, 64, 65, 66, 68, 69, 70, 71, 73, 75, 77, 78, 79, 80, 81, 83, 84, 85, 86, 87, 88, 89, 90, 92, 93, 94, 96, 98, 100, 101, 102, 103, 105, 106, 107, 108, 109, 110, 112, 113, 116, 118, 119, 120, 122, 123, 124, 125, 126, 128, 129, 131, 133, 135, 137, 138, 141, 142, 143, 144, 145, 147, 151, 152, 155, 157, 162, 163, 165, 178, 184, 185, 187, 188, 200, 202, 204, 207, 216, 227, 228, 229, 230, 233, 234, 235, 241, 244, 245, 246, 247
Compton, 29, 221, 226
Conrad II, 54, 68, 69, 87, 93
Constantine VIII, 68
Cookham, 25
Count Baldwin IV, 28
Count Baldwin of Flanders, 104
Count Enguerrand II of Ponthiu, 166
Coventry, 77, 78, 122, 197, 205, 206, 244
Danegeld, 11, 21, 23, 114
Danelaw, 9, 18, 22, 34, 84, 120, 122, 124, 125, 144, 148, 244
De Gestis Herewardi Saxonis, 184
De Inventione S. Crucis apud Waltham Historia, 125
De Obsessione Dunelmi, 36
Deira, 10, 84
Destructio Monasterri de Hydâ, 32
Diarmait Mac Máel Na Mbo, 184
Domesday Survey, 15, 19, 22, 133, 150, 184, 192, 203, 217
Domnall Mac Donnchada, 184
Donnchad Mac Gilla Patriac, 184
Dorchester, 160, 161, 197
Dover, 97, 98, 100, 168, 170, 171, 174, 190, 194, 205, 222, 228, 232
Dreux of the Vexin, 80
Dreux, Count of the Vexin, 166
Drogo, Count of the Vexin, 99
Dublin, 184, 185, 192, 195, 239, 244

Duncan, 73, 105, 108, 117, 119, 121, 145, 208
Dungeness, 189, 191, 195
Eadgyth, 16, 19, 22, 45, 49, 79, 107, 128, 132, 135, 141, 144, 145, 146, 147, 150, 162, 163, 164, 171, 177, 178, 179, 180, 181, 186, 187, 190, 193, 198, 202, 208, 210, 211, 214, 218, 233, 234
Eadmer of Canterbury, 14, 129, 133, 134, 143, 162, 163, 181, 201, 204, 211, 212, 228, 237, 240
Eadred, 21, 22, 83, 85, 117, 118, 126, 141, 227
Eadric, 14, 15, 16, 17, 18, 21, 22, 23, 25, 28, 37, 38, 39, 43, 48, 51, 62, 75, 76, 85, 87, 100, 111, 144, 187, 227, 234
Eadric Streona, 14, 15, 16, 21, 23, 25, 26, 28, 34, 36, 37, 38, 39, 45, 48, 62, 74, 75, 85, 100, 187, 234
Eadsige, 32, 80, 106, 136, 142, 143, 146, 149, 160, 162, 203, 204, 205, 207, 226, 228
Eadulf, 85, 105, 117, 118, 119, 120, 121, 124, 127, 186
Eadwig, King, 17, 18, 19, 26, 48, 49, 62, 76, 79, 83, 90, 102, 128, 186
Eadwin, 25
Edgar, King, 11, 20, 34, 117, 118, 128, 150, 163, 227, 229
Edith Swan-Neck, 181
Edmund, 9, 22, 26, 27, 28, 34, 36, 37, 38, 39, 41, 43, 46, 65, 68, 75, 76, 89, 90, 118, 120, 128, 129, 138, 139, 141, 207, 209, 212, 214, 226, 228, 234, 241, 247
Edward, 8, 9, 10, 11, 14, 15, 16, 20, 21, 22, 27, 29, 31, 33, 43, 48, 78, 79, 80, 81, 83, 90, 97, 98, 99, 102, 104, 108, 112, 115, 116, 121, 122, 123, 126, 127, 128, 129, 132, 133, 136, 137, 138, 139, 140, 141, 142, 144, 145, 146, 147, 148, 149, 150, 152, 153, 154, 155, 156, 159, 160, 161, 162, 163, 164, 165, 166, 167, 168, 169, 170, 171, 172, 173, 174, 175, 176, 177, 178, 179, 180, 181, 182, 184, 185, 186, 187, 188, 189, 190, 191, 192, 195, 196, 198, 200, 201, 202, 203, 204, 205, 207, 208, 209, 210, 211, 220, 222, 223, 228, 229, 230, 231, 233, 234, 237, 238, 242, 243, 245, 246, 247
Edward the Confessor, 9, 20, 21, 31, 108, 121, 122, 139, 166, 181, 237, 243, 245, 246, 247
Edwy, 48
Eilifr, 32, 41, 45, 47, 50, 51, 52, 53, 54, 55, 56, 58, 61, 62, 75, 85, 86, 109, 122
Einar Tambar-Skelve, 110
Eirikr Bloodaxe, 70, 118
Elmham, 19, 91, 142
Emma, 15, 21, 26, 27, 43, 56, 57, 58, 80, 83, 84, 87, 88, 89, 90, 92, 93, 94, 96, 97, 98, 99, 100, 101, 103, 104, 106, 107, 108, 109, 110, 111, 112, 116, 123, 127, 128, 129, 131, 139, 140, 141, 142, 145, 146, 150, 151, 155, 162, 164, 165, 172, 180, 188, 190, 198, 200, 205, 207, 211, 215, 234, 235, 244, 245, 246, 248
Encomium Emmae Reginae, 38, 39, 91, 97, 101, 115, 123, 234, 240
Esbearn, 29
Estrith, 56, 57, 81, 110, 144, 151, 152
Ethelred, King, 9
Eustace II, Count of Boulogne, 171
Eustace of Boulogne, 166, 168, 170
Evesham, 76
Evesham Chronicle, 78, 205
Exeter, 7, 41, 107, 130, 136, 159, 206, 208, 214, 218, 247
Exon Domesday, 131, 229
Eynsham, 20, 24, 28
Fagrskinna, 20, 53, 54, 58, 240
Fécamp', 81

Flanders, 28, 33, 38, 97, 99, 104, 108, 111, 123, 127, 129, 132, 135, 148, 151, 154, 155, 156, 158, 159, 166, 169, 170, 172, 173, 181, 183, 190, 192, 207, 209, 210, 211, 212, 218, 247

Flateyjarbok, 20

Folkestone, 23, 40, 162, 194, 201, 203, 204, 222, 228

Fyris Plain, 59, 60, 62

Gainsborough, 33, 94

Geoffrey Gaimar, 65

Geoffrey of Monmouth, 61

Gisela, 69, 139

Gloucester, 15, 38, 78, 79, 85, 140, 141, 171, 174, 175, 176, 177, 179, 180, 186, 187, 190, 198

Godgifu, 78, 80, 92, 99, 121, 166, 171, 172, 186, 205, 206

Godwine Brytael, 41

Gospatric, 118, 119, 121, 122, 135, 233

Gottfried, Count of Upper Lorraine, 154

Grimketel, 107, 108

Gruffydd, 25, 76, 79, 105, 134, 149, 169, 170, 186, 188, 190

Gruffydd ap Llewelyn, 148, 209

Gruffydd ap Rhydderch, 148, 158, 160, 189

Guelph, 210

Gunnhildr, 21, 68, 69, 70, 72, 93, 110, 124, 137, 151, 152, 155, 208

Gunnor, 141

Gyrth, 128, 132, 133, 134, 135, 179, 192, 200, 206, 208, 214, 218, 224

Gytha, 9, 47, 49, 50, 52, 54, 58, 61, 64, 78, 87, 124, 125, 128, 135, 136, 144, 151, 184, 192, 204, 205, 206, 208, 209, 211, 215, 218, 220, 221, 222, 223, 224, 225, 226, 229, 230, 233

Hákon, 56, 68, 70, 71, 72, 73, 75, 85, 86, 87, 95, 110, 119, 129, 151, 152, 158, 181, 212

Hamlandene, 28

Hárald Harðráða, 79

Háraldr Fairhair, 70

Haraldr Gormson, 23

Haraldr Gormsson, 59, 60, 61, 62

Háraldr Harðráða, 148, 210, 213

Harefoot, 55, 78, 89, 91, 93, 97, 100, 106, 111, 117, 133, 147, 187, 205, 207, 211, 229, 232, 234, 248

Harold, 9, 25, 29, 32, 33, 50, 55, 58, 64, 69, 78, 79, 88, 89, 90, 91, 92, 93, 96, 97, 98, 99, 100, 101, 103, 104, 106, 107, 108, 109, 111, 112, 113, 116, 117, 119, 123, 126, 127, 128, 129, 130, 131, 132, 133, 134, 135, 136, 144, 146, 147, 148, 149, 152, 156, 157, 160, 165, 168, 172, 175, 176, 178, 179, 180, 181, 183, 184, 185, 186, 189, 191, 192, 193, 195, 196, 197, 199, 200, 202, 203, 205, 207, 208, 209, 210, 211, 212, 214, 215, 217, 218, 225, 226, 227, 228, 229, 230, 231, 232, 233, 234, 238, 244, 245, 246, 247, 248

Harthacnut, 46, 52, 53, 55, 56, 57, 58, 62, 69, 73, 78, 83, 88, 89, 90, 92, 93, 96, 97, 100, 101, 104, 105, 106, 108, 109, 110, 111, 112, 113, 114, 115, 116, 117, 119, 123, 126, 127, 136, 137, 139, 140, 141, 146, 147, 151, 152, 163, 175, 185, 188, 202, 207, 234

Hastings, 9, 32, 116, 153, 158, 165, 166, 180, 185, 188, 191, 194, 206, 218, 235, 238, 244

Hemming, 38, 76, 77, 78, 129, 149, 150, 152, 204, 205, 230, 238

Hemmingr, 32, 45, 50, 62

Henry I, King of France, 154

Henry of Huntingdon, 14, 38, 46, 63, 100, 102, 103, 119, 126, 201, 233, 234, 238, 241

Hereford, 14, 38, 76, 79, 105, 117, 125, 171, 176, 248

heregeld, 113, 159, 165

Herluin, Vicomte de Conteville, 81

Hlathir, 70, 72, 85, 151

Holy River, 46, 47, 51, 53, 54, 55, 57, 61, 62, 68, 70
Hrani, 39, 41, 45, 51, 71, 76, 85, 117, 144
Hugh of Chester, 214
Hugh of Montgomery, 214
Hugh the Castellan, 176, 195
Hugo the Castellan, 197
Hwicce, 34, 45, 75, 85
Ingulf, 86, 91, 92, 111, 187, 201, 241
Ivo Taille Bois, 187
John of Worcester, 15, 16, 20, 26, 33, 37, 38, 45, 50, 58, 63, 68, 74, 76, 78, 79, 80, 83, 90, 91, 94, 98, 99, 100, 111, 113, 114, 115, 117, 119, 120, 124, 125, 126, 129, 132, 137, 138, 140, 141, 144, 148, 149, 156, 165, 171, 174, 176, 177, 180, 183, 193, 198, 199, 200, 201, 209, 214, 232, 233, 238, 240
Ketel, 132, 213
Kingston, 11, 40, 131
Knuts Drapa, 53
Knytlinga Saga, 15, 20, 55, 57, 58, 59, 61, 83, 88, 134, 145, 241
Leofric, 55, 73, 74, 76, 77, 78, 79, 83, 85, 86, 87, 88, 89, 92, 105, 107, 117, 122, 128, 133, 134, 140, 142, 144, 145, 147, 148, 153, 159, 160, 162, 165, 166, 175, 176, 177, 180, 186, 193, 195, 196, 197, 204, 205, 206, 208, 218, 226, 228, 230, 233
Leofwine, 22, 26, 31, 34, 37, 39, 40, 45, 51, 74, 75, 76, 79, 85, 86, 89, 109, 128, 131, 132, 133, 135, 143, 144, 179, 183, 185, 192, 194, 197, 199, 205, 207, 208, 214, 218, 232
Leominster, 77, 129, 149, 150, 162, 183, 188, 204
Lewes, 7, 209
Liber de Hyda, 15
Liber Eliensis, 122, 206, 241
Liber Vitae, 56, 58, 152
Limfjord, 68
Lindisfarne, 68
Llewelyn ap Seisyll, 105
London, 11, 21, 23, 32, 33, 37, 38, 50, 51, 56, 80, 88, 99, 100, 109, 111, 121, 124, 136, 159, 160, 161, 164, 168, 170, 171, 176, 177, 180, 185, 187, 190, 192, 194, 195, 207, 239, 240, 241, 242, 243, 244, 245, 246, 247
Lotharingia, 154
Lyfing, 40, 48, 69, 78, 80, 92, 107, 108, 109, 112, 115, 127, 137, 141, 147, 149, 169, 206, 207
Macbeth, 105, 121, 197, 208, 218
Magnus, 7, 58, 73, 79, 83, 89, 92, 104, 108, 110, 112, 113, 115, 127, 129, 137, 138, 139, 140, 141, 152, 153, 154, 169, 170, 207, 209, 213, 214, 215, 218, 232
Maidstone, 226
Malcolm, King of Scotland, 69, 214
Maldon, 11, 18, 21, 23, 31, 76
Malmesbury, 37, 38, 47, 48, 50, 56, 58, 63, 65, 69, 77, 80, 91, 92, 100, 101, 103, 111, 112, 113, 114, 115, 117, 133, 137, 142, 145, 161, 164, 177, 186, 191, 196, 199, 201, 203, 211, 214, 215, 233, 237, 241, 242
Marchad Mac Brian, 184
Mongewell, 18
Mont Saint-Michel, 81
Morcar, 25, 26, 34, 37, 43, 79, 89, 162, 187, 209
Morkinskinna, 58, 61, 152, 153, 154, 158, 215, 241
Msistislav-Harald, 215
Nest, 210
Nidaros, 71, 73, 110, 152, 231
Normandy, 21, 27, 33, 34, 37, 43, 57, 71, 80, 81, 91, 93, 94, 112, 115, 116, 123, 127, 133, 134, 137, 141, 145, 161, 164, 165, 166, 167, 170, 171, 172, 173, 181, 182, 188, 196, 199, 212, 217, 232, 247
Northman, 48, 74, 75, 76, 77, 86
Ólafr Haraldsson, 66, 94, 132, 214
Ólafr Skotkonung, 53, 62
Ólafr Skötkonung, 138

Ólafr Skóttkonung, 66, 70, 71
Ólafr Thordarson, 15
Ólafr Tryggvason, 23, 59, 60, 62, 70, 73, 240
Ólafr Trygvason, 11
Ólafr's Saga Helga', 20
Orderic Vitalis, 102, 173, 233, 238, 240, 241
Ordwulf, 24, 26, 34
Osbeorn Pentecost, 195, 197
Osbern Pentecost, 168, 176, 177, 189
Osbert of Clare, 128, 129, 132, 145
Osgod Clapa, 56, 84, 85, 124, 138, 144, 148, 151, 154, 155, 169, 229
Ottar the Black, 53
Otto I, 68, 69
Otto II, 59, 62, 68
Oxford, 33, 37, 78, 88, 90, 92, 96, 97, 103, 108, 238, 240, 241, 242, 243, 244, 245
Penselwood, 38
Pevensey, 156, 157, 191, 194, 206
Porlock, 7, 192, 193, 243
Portland, 192, 194
Prior Wulfstan, 77
Ralph, 15, 20, 81, 99, 125, 165, 168, 172, 176, 185, 189, 191, 192, 195, 197, 208, 218, 226, 230, 241, 248
Ralph the Black, 15
Ramsbury, 18, 159
Rhyd Y Groes, 76, 108, 148
Richard Fitz Scrob, 168, 189, 195, 198, 210
Richard of Devizes, 140, 164
Risborough, 17, 18
Robert Champart, 145, 147, 161, 165, 168, 177
Robert Wace, 15
Rochester, 28, 109, 117, 168
Roger of Wendover, 14, 117, 200, 201, 241
Rögnvaldr, 52, 54
Roman de Rou, 15
Romanus III, 69
Rome, 54, 55, 64, 66, 68, 69, 70, 73, 84, 87, 132, 134, 135, 137, 143, 147, 154, 159, 164, 166, 170, 185, 190
Roskilde, 57
Saga of Harald the Stern, 20, 128, 134, 154, 158, 213, 217
Saga of Haraldr Harðráða Sigurðson', 20
Saga of Knutr, 53
Saga of Magnus the Good, 110
Saga of St Olafr, 52
Saga of St Ólafr, 52
Salisbury, 133, 211
Sandwich, 26, 28, 32, 40, 49, 88, 106, 111, 127, 139, 156, 157, 158, 162, 189, 191, 192, 194, 202, 205, 229
Saxo Grammaticus, 49, 52, 53, 54, 57, 58, 59, 61, 94, 116, 120, 145, 152, 153, 154, 209, 215, 235, 236, 238, 241
Shaftesbury, 83
Sherborne, 28, 83, 88, 120
Sherborne Abbey, 83
Sherston, 15, 38, 46, 55
Sige, 85, 117, 119, 135
Sigeferth, 26, 34, 37, 43, 89, 187
Sigeric, Archbishop, 24
Simeon of Durham, 63, 89, 102, 113, 114, 118, 119, 126, 133, 134, 171, 201, 242
Sired, 39, 40, 45, 49, 80, 84, 122
Siward, 78, 83, 85, 86, 117, 119, 120, 121, 122, 127, 140, 143, 144, 145, 146, 160, 162, 165, 166, 175, 176, 177, 180, 185, 186, 195, 196, 197, 203, 205, 207, 208, 218, 226
Skane, 59, 68, 153
Skule, 132, 213
Southwark, 109, 178, 179, 195, 199, 207, 218, 224, 227
Spearhafoc, 103, 161, 164, 170, 185, 231
St Michael's Mount, 81
St Omer, 123, 131, 209, 211, 218, 234

Stamford Bridge, 132, 153, 208, 218, 231, 243
Stigand, 19, 91, 108, 131, 142, 146, 161, 165, 178, 196, 197, 198, 207, 228, 235
Stiklestad, 72
Styrbjörn, 59, 60, 61, 62
Svenn Aggeson, 58
Svöld, 45, 60, 62, 71
Swegn, 47, 58, 61, 64, 112, 128, 129, 131, 132, 134, 135, 136, 144, 146, 147, 148, 149, 150, 151, 153, 154, 155, 156, 157, 158, 159, 160, 167, 168, 169, 170, 172, 175, 176, 177, 178, 179, 181, 183, 184, 185, 189, 193, 197, 199, 212, 218, 232
Swein Estrithsson, 58
Swein Forkbeard, 9, 23, 33, 43, 45, 50, 62, 70, 71, 72, 77, 100, 151
Swein, King, 9, 11, 16, 21, 23, 24, 32, 33, 37, 43, 45, 49, 50, 56, 57, 58, 61, 62, 69, 70, 71, 72, 73, 75, 77, 78, 81, 83, 87, 89, 92, 93, 94, 95, 109, 111, 112, 123, 126, 131, 137, 138, 139, 140, 148, 151, 152, 153, 154, 155, 158, 159, 167, 169, 170, 209, 215, 232, 233
Tavistock, 7, 24, 48, 69, 80, 147, 169, 206, 243
Theodred, 124
Thetford, 117
Thord, 50
Thorgils Sprakalegg, 45, 53, 54, 59, 60, 68
Thorkell Hávi, 22, 45, 63, 94, 109, 151
Throndheim, 71
Thurkil, 51, 105, 109
Thyra, 59, 60, 61, 62
Tostig, 79, 121, 128, 129, 131, 132, 134, 135, 156, 165, 167, 170, 173, 179, 181, 183, 190, 192, 200, 206, 208, 210, 212, 213, 218, 230, 235
Tovi, 56, 124, 125, 138, 223
Trondheim, 23, 71

Uhtred, 21, 22, 25, 36, 37, 43, 84, 117, 118, 119, 121, 135
Ulfkell, 24, 34, 37, 38, 50, 71, 84
Úlfr, 15, 45, 49, 50, 52, 53, 54, 55, 56, 57, 58, 60, 61, 62, 66, 68, 81, 84, 87, 109, 110, 129, 144, 151
Vita Ædwardi Regis, 12, 15, 26, 47, 63, 64, 65, 66, 84, 91, 119, 128, 130, 137, 171, 174, 177, 178, 186, 201, 202, 234, 238, 242
Vita Beati Edwardi, 78
Vita Haroldi, 14, 242
Vita Oswaldi, 18
Walter Map, 14, 15, 38, 136, 204, 229
Waltham Chronicle, 125, 245
Waltheof, 84, 118, 119, 120, 121, 134, 162
Welshpool, 76, 105, 148
Wherwell, 150, 164, 179, 180, 187, 190, 235
William of Jumièges, 14, 20, 81, 88, 98, 100, 187
William of Poitiers, 14, 98, 99, 115, 164, 165, 180, 182, 187, 240
William Rufus, 133, 211, 214, 215, 243
William, Count of Poitiou, 69
William, Duke, 9, 133, 181, 183, 187, 232, 246, 247
Winchester, 17, 18, 19, 32, 33, 34, 36, 83, 88, 89, 96, 98, 99, 100, 108, 124, 136, 140, 142, 144, 147, 152, 157, 164, 165, 178, 187, 188, 198, 200, 201, 203, 206, 211, 228, 239, 242
Wolverhampton, 24
Worcester, 18, 19, 38, 58, 75, 76, 77, 78, 91, 99, 100, 101, 103, 106, 107, 108, 109, 112, 113, 114, 115, 117, 127, 129, 134, 137, 141, 144, 147, 149, 150, 159, 161, 162, 169, 171, 174, 175, 176, 179, 180, 185, 188, 191, 198, 199, 201, 203, 204, 205, 206, 215, 230, 232, 233, 244, 247, 248

Wulfgeat, 24, 25
Wulfnoth, 14, 15, 16, 17, 19, 20, 21, 22, 23, 26, 27, 28, 29, 31, 32, 33, 36, 40, 43, 63, 128, 133, 134, 135, 155, 181, 208, 211, 218, 220, 221, 227, 232, 233
Wulfric Spot, 25, 187
Wulfrun, 24
Wulfthryth, 18, 128, 150, 163
Yaroslav, 54, 72, 110, 138, 139, 215
York, 10, 34, 36, 37, 50, 70, 74, 79, 83, 84, 109, 111, 112, 118, 119, 129, 134, 136, 160, 161, 165, 168, 170, 208, 239, 241, 243, 244, 247

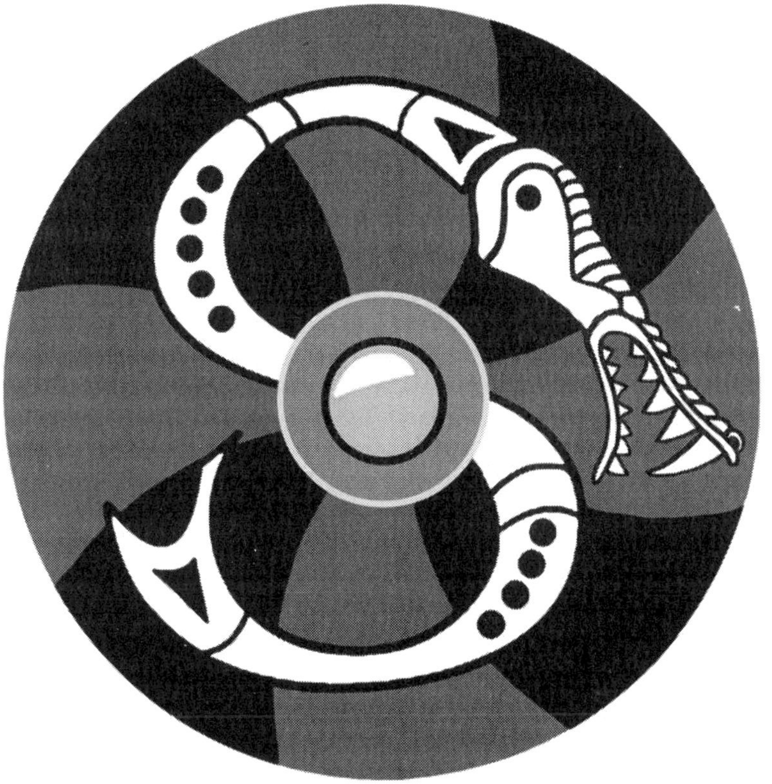

Some of our other title

Please see www.asbooks.co.uk for current availability and prices

The English Warrior from earliest times till 1066
Stephen Pollington

This is not intended to be a bald listing of the battles and campaigns from the Anglo-Saxon Chronicle and other sources, but rather it is an attempt to get below the surface of Anglo-Saxon warriorhood and to investigate the rites, social attitudes, mentality and mythology of the warfare of those times.

> "An under-the-skin study of the role, rights, duties, psyche and rituals of the Anglo-Saxon warrior. The author combines original translations from Norse and Old English primary sources with archaeological and linguistic evidence for an in-depth look at the warrior, his weapons, tactics and logistics.
>
> A very refreshing, innovative and well-written piece of scholarship that illuminates a neglected period of English history"
>
> *Time Team Booklists* - Channel 4 Television

Revised Edition
An already highly acclaimed book has been made even better by the inclusion of additional information and illustrations.

£16.95   ISBN 1–898281–42–4   245 x 170mm   over 50 illustrations   Hardback   304 pages

The Mead Hall The feasting tradition in Anglo-Saxon England
Stephen Pollington

This new study takes a broad look at the subject of halls and feasting in Anglo-Saxon England. The idea of the communal meal was very important among nobles and yeomen, warriors, farmers churchmen and laity. One of the aims of the book is to show that there was not just one 'feast' but two main types: the informal social occasion *gebeorscipe* and the formal, ritual gathering *symbel*.

Using the evidence of Old English texts - mainly the epic *Beowulf* and the *Anglo-Saxon Chronicles*, Stephen Pollington shows that the idea of feasting remained central to early English social traditions long after the physical reality had declined in importance.

The words of the poets and saga-writers are supported by a wealth of archaeological data dealing with halls, settlement layouts and magnificent feasting gear found in many early Anglo-Saxon graves.

Three appendices cover:
- Hall-themes in Old English verse;
- Old English and translated texts;
- The structure and origins of the warband.

£18.95   ISBN 1-898281-30-0   9 ¾ x 6 ¾ inches   245 x 170mm   Hardback   288 pages

First Steps in Old English
An easy to follow language course for the beginner
Stephen Pollington

A complete and easy to use Old English language course that contains all the exercises and texts needed to learn Old English. This course has been designed to be of help to a wide range of students, from those who are teaching themselves at home, to undergraduates who are learning Old English as part of their English degree course. The author has adopted a step-by-step approach that enables students of differing abilities to advance at their own pace. The course includes practice and translation exercises, a glossary of the words used in the course, and many Old English texts, including the *Battle of Brunanburh* and *Battle of Maldon*.

£16-95   ISBN 9781898281382   248 x 173mm / 10 x 6½ inches   paperback   272 pages

Old English Poems, Prose & Lessons   2 CDs
read by Stephen Pollington

These CDs contain lessons and texts from *First Steps in Old English*.

Tracks include: 1. Deor. 2. Beowulf – The Funeral of Scyld Scefing. 3. Engla Tocyme (The Arrival of the English). 4. Ines Domas. Two Extracts from the Laws of King Ine. 5. Deniga Hergung (The Danes' Harrying) Anglo-Saxon Chronicle Entry AD997. 6. Durham 7. The Ordeal (Be ðon ðe ordales weddigaþ) 8. Wið Dweorh (Against a Dwarf) 9. Wið Wennum (Against Wens) 10. Wið Wæterælfadle (Against Waterelf Sickness) 11. The Nine Herbs Charm 12. Læcedomas (Leechdoms) 13. Beowulf's Greeting 14. The Battle of Brunanburh 15. A Guide to Pronunciation.
And more than 30 other lessons and extracts of Old English verse and prose.

£11.75   ISBN 1-898281-46-7   2 CDs - Free Old English transcript from www.asbooks.co.uk.

Wordcraft: Concise English/Old English Dictionary and Thesaurus
Stephen Pollington

This book provides Old English equivalents to the commoner modern words in both dictionary and thesaurus formats. The Thesaurus presents vocabulary relevant to a wide range of individual topics in alphabetical lists, thus making it easily accessible to those with specific areas of interest. Each thematic listing is encoded for cross-reference from the Dictionary. The two sections will be of invaluable assistance to students of the language, as well as to those with either a general or a specific interest in the Anglo-Saxon period.

£9.95   A5   ISBN 9781898281535   256 pages

An Introduction to the Old English Language and its Literature
Stephen Pollington

The purpose of this general introduction to Old English is not to deal with the teaching of Old English but to dispel some misconceptions about the language and to give an outline of its structure and its literature. Some basic knowledge of these is essential to an understanding of the early period of English history and the present form of the language.

£4.95   A5   ISBN 1-898281-06-8   48 pages

The Rebirth of England and English: The Vision of William Barnes
Fr. Andrew Phillips

English history is patterned with spirits so bright that they broke through convention and saw another England. Such was the case of the Dorset poet, William Barnes (1801–86), priest, poet, teacher, self-taught polymath, linguist extraordinary and that rare thing – a man of vision. In this work the author looks at that vision, a vision at once of Religion, Nature, Art, Marriage, Society, Economics, Politics and Language. He writes: 'In search of authentic English roots and values, our post-industrial society may well have much to learn from Barnes'.

£4.95   A5   ISBN 1–898281–17–3   160 pages

Monasteriales Indicia
The Anglo-Saxon Monastic Sign Language
Edited with notes and translation by Debby Banham

The *Monasteriales Indicia* is one of very few texts which let us see how evryday life was lived in monasteries in the early Middle Ages. Written in Old English and preserved in a manuscript of the mid-eleventh century, it consists of 127 signs used by Anglo-Saxon monks during the times when the Benedictine Rule forbade them to speak. These indicate the foods the monks ate, the clothes they wore, and the books they used in church and chapter, as well as the tools they used in their daily life, and persons they might meet both in the monastery and outside. The text is printed here with a parallel translation. The introduction gives a summary of the background, both historical and textual, as well as a brief look at the later evidence for monastic sign language in England.

£6.95   A5   ISBN 0–9516209–4–0   96 pages

The Battle of Maldon: Text and Translation
Translated and edited by Bill Griffiths

The Battle of Maldon was fought between the men of Essex and the Vikings in AD 991. The action was captured in an Anglo-Saxon poem whose vividness and heroic spirit has fascinated readers and scholars for generations. *The Battle of Maldon* includes the source text; edited text; parallel literal translation; verse translation; a review of 103 books and articles.

This edition has a helpful guide to Old English verse.

£4.95   A5   ISBN 0–9516209–0–8   96 pages

Beowulf: Text and Translation
Translated by John Porter

The verse in which the story unfolds is, by common consent, the finest writing surviving in Old English, a text that all students of the language and many general readers will want to tackle in the original form. To aid understanding of the Old English, a literal word-by-word translation is printed opposite the edited text and provides a practical key to this Anglo-Saxon masterpiece.

£6.95   A5   ISBN 978 1898281481   192 pages

An Introduction to Early English Law
Bill Griffiths

Much of Anglo-Saxon life followed a traditional pattern, of custom, and of dependence on kin-groups for land, support and security. The Viking incursions of the ninth century and the reconquest of the north that followed both disturbed this pattern and led to a new emphasis on centralized power and law, with royal and ecclesiastical officials prominent as arbitrators and settlers of disputes. The diversity and development of early English law is sampled here by selecting several law-codes to be read in translation - that of Æthelbert of Kent, being the first to be issued in England, Alfred the Great's, the most clearly thought-out of all, and short codes from the reigns of Edmund and Æthelred the Unready.

£6.95   A5   ISBN 1898281149   96 pages

The Hallowing of England
A Guide to the Saints of Old England and their Places of Pilgrimage
Fr. Andrew Philips

In the Old English period we can count over 300 saints, yet today their names and exploits are largely unknown. They are part of a forgotten England which, though it lies deep in the past, is an important part of our national and spiritual history. This guide includes a list of saints, an alphabetical list of places with which they are associated, and a calendar of saint's feast days.

£6.95   A5   ISBN 1898281084   96 pages

Tolkien's *Mythology for England*
A Guide to Middle-Earth
Edmund Wainwright

Tolkien set out to create a mythology for England and the English but the popularity of his books and the recent films has spread across the English-speaking world and beyond.

You will find here an outline of Tolkien's life and work. The main part of the book consists of an alphabetical subject entry which will help you gain a greater understanding of Tolkien's Middle-Earth, the creatures that inhabit it, and the languages they spoke. It will also give an insight into a culture and way-of-life that extolled values which are as valid today as they were over 1,000 years ago.

This book focuses on *The Lord of the Rings* and shows how Tolkien's knowledge of Anglo-Saxon and Norse literature and history helped shape its plot and characters.

£9-95   ISBN 1-898281-36-X   approx. 10 x 6½ inches (245 x 170 mm)   Hardback   128 pages

Anglo-Saxon Food & Drink
Production, Processing, Distribution, and Consumption
Ann Hagen

Food production for home consumption was the basis of economic activity throughout the Anglo-Saxon period. Used as payment and a medium of trade, food was the basis of the Anglo-Saxons' system of finance and administration.

Information from various sources has been brought together in order to build up a picture of how food was grown, conserved, distributed, prepared and eaten during the period from the beginning of the 5th century to the 11th century. Many people will find it fascinating for the views it gives of an important aspect of Anglo-Saxon life and culture. In addition to Anglo-Saxon England the Celtic west of Britain is also covered.

This edition combines earlier titles – *A Handbook of Anglo-Saxon Food* and *A Second Handbook of Anglo-Saxon Food & Drink*.

Extensive index.

£25   10" x 7" (245 x 170mm)   ISBN 1–898281–41–6   Hardback   512 pages

English Heroic Legends
Kathleen Herbert

The author has taken the skeletons of ancient Germanic legends about great kings, queens and heroes, and put flesh on them. Kathleen Herbert's extensive knowledge of the period is reflected in the wealth of detail she brings to these tales of adventure, passion, bloodshed and magic.

The book is in two parts. First are the stories that originate deep in the past, yet because they have not been hackneyed, they are still strange and enchanting. After that there is a selection of the source material, with information about where it can be found and some discussion about how it can be used.

£9-95   A5   ISBN 0–9516209–9–1   292 pages

Peace-Weavers and Shield-Maidens: Women in Early English Society
Kathleen Herbert

The recorded history of the English people did not start in 1066 as popularly believed but one-thousand years earlier. The Roman historian Cornelius Tacitus noted in *Germania*, published in the year 98, that the English (Latin *Anglii*), who lived in the southern part of the Jutland peninsula, were members of an alliance of Goddess-worshippers. The author has taken that as an appropriate opening to an account of the earliest Englishwomen, the part they played in the making of England, what they did in peace and war, the impressions they left in Britain and on the continent, how they were recorded in the chronicles, how they come alive in heroic verse and riddles.

£4.95   A5   ISBN 1898281114   64 pages

Anglo-Saxon Runes
John. M. Kemble

Kemble's essay *On Anglo-Saxon Runes* first appeared in the journal *Archaeologia* for 1840; it draws on the work of Wilhelm Grimm, but breaks new ground for Anglo-Saxon studies in his survey of the Ruthwell Cross and the Cynewulf poems. It is an expression both of his own indomitable spirit and of the fascination and mystery of the Runes themselves, making one of the most attractive introductions to the topic. For this edition new notes have been supplied, which include translations of Latin and Old English material quoted in the text, to make this key work in the study of runes more accessible to the general reader.

£4.95   A5   ISBN 0–9516209–1–6   80 pages

Looking for the Lost Gods of England
Kathleen Herbert

Kathleen Herbert sifts through the royal genealogies, charms, verse and other sources to find clues to the names and attributes of the Gods and Goddesses of the early English. The earliest account of English heathen practices reveals that they worshipped the Earth Mother and called her Nerthus. The tales, beliefs and traditions of that time are still with us in, for example, Sand able to stir our minds and imaginations.

£4.95   A5   ISBN 1–898281–04–1   64 pages

Rudiments of Runelore
Stephen Pollington

This book provides both a comprehensive introduction for those coming to the subject for the first time, and a handy and inexpensive reference work for those with some knowledge of the subject. The *Abecedarium Nordmannicum* and the English, Norwegian and Icelandic rune poems are included in their original and translated form. Also included is work on the three Brandon runic inscriptions and the Norfolk 'Tiw' runes.

£5.95   A5   ISBN 978 1 898281498   Illustrations   88 pages

Anglo-Saxon FAQs
Stephen Pollington

125 questions and answers on a wide range of topics.

Are there any Anglo-Saxon jokes? Who was the Venerable Bede? Did the women wear make-up? What musical instruments did they have? How was food preserved? Did they have shops? Did their ships have sails? Why was Ethelred called 'Unready'? Did they have clocks? Did they celebrate Christmas? What are runes? What weapons and tactics did they use? Were there female warriors? What was the Synod of Whitby?

£9.95   ISBN 978 1898281504 30   128pages

Dark Age Naval Power
A Reassessment of Frankish and Anglo-Saxon Seafaring Activity
John Haywood

In the first edition of this work, published in 1991, John Haywood argued that the capabilities of the pre-Viking Germanic seafarers had been greatly underestimated. Since that time, his reassessment of Frankish and Anglo-Saxon shipbuilding and seafaring has been widely praised and accepted.

In this second edition, some sections of the book have been revised and updated to include information gained from excavations and sea trials with sailing replicas of early ships. The new evidence supports the author's argument that early Germanic shipbuilding and seafaring skills were far more advanced than previously thought. It also supports the view that Viking ships and seaborne activities were not as revolutionary as is commonly believed.

> 'The book remains a historical study of the first order. It is required reading for our seminar on medieval seafaring at Texas A & M University and is essential reading for anyone interested in the subject.'
>
> F. H. Van Doorninck, *The American Neptune*

£16.95 ISBN 1-898281-43-2 approx. 10 x 6½ inches (245 x 170 mm) Hardback 224 pages

English Martial Arts
Terry Brown

Little is known about the very early history of English martial arts but it is likely that methods, techniques and principles were passed on from one generation to the next for centuries. By the sixteenth century English martial artists had their own governing body which controlled its members in much the same way as do modern-day martial arts organisations. It is apparent from contemporary evidence that the Company of Maisters taught and practised a fighting system that ranks as high in terms of effectiveness and pedigree as any in the world.

In the first part of the book the author investigates the weapons, history and development of the English fighting system and looks at some of the attitudes, beliefs and social pressures that helped mould it.

Part two deals with English fighting techniques drawn from books and manuscripts that recorded the system at various stages in its history. All of the methods and techniques shown in this book are authentic and have not been created by the author. The theories that underlie the system are explained in a chapter on *The Principles of True Fighting*. All of the techniques covered are illustrated with photographs and accompanied by instructions. Techniques included are for bare-fist fighting, broadsword, quarterstaff, bill, sword and buckler, sword and dagger.

Experienced martial artists, irrespective of the style they practice, will recognise that the techniques and methods of this system are based on principles that are as valid as those underlying the system that they practice.

£16.95 ISBN 1-898281-44-0 10 x 6½ inches - 245 x 170 mm 220 photos Hardback 240 pages

A Guide to Late Anglo-Saxon England
From Alfred to Eadgar II 871–1074
Donald Henson

This guide has been prepared with the aim of providing the general readers with both an overview of the period and a wealth of background information. Facts and figures are presented in a way that makes this a useful reference handbook.

Contents include: The Origins of England; Physical Geography; Human Geography; English Society; Government and Politics; The Church; Language and Literature; Personal Names; Effects of the Norman Conquest. All of the kings from Alfred to Eadgar II are dealt with separately and there is a chronicle of events for each of their reigns. There are also maps, family trees and extensive appendices.

£9.95 ISBN 1–898281–21–1 9½" x 6¾"/245 x 170mm, 6 maps & 3 family trees 208 pages

The English Elite in 1066 - Gone but not forgotten
Donald Henson

The people listed in this book formed the topmost section of the ruling elite in 1066. It includes all those who held office between the death of Eadward III (January 1066) and the abdication of Eadgar II (December 1066). There are 455 individuals in the main entries and these have been divided according to their office or position.

The following information is listed where available:

What is known of their life;

Their landed wealth;

The early sources in which information about the individual can be found

Modern references that give details about his or her life.

In addition to the biographical details, there is a wealth of background information about English society and government. A series of appendices provide detailed information about particular topics or groups of people.

£16.95 ISBN 1–898281–26–2 245 x 170mm / 10 x 7 inches   paperback   272 pages

Tastes of Anglo-Saxon England
Mary Savelli

These easy to follow recipes will enable you to enjoy a mix of ingredients and flavours that were widely known in Anglo-Saxon England but are rarely experienced today. In addition to the 46 recipes, there is background information about households and cooking techniques.

£4.95   ISBN 1-898281-28-9   A5   80 pages

Anglo-Saxon Attitudes – A short introduction to Anglo-Saxonism
J.A. Hilton
This is not a book about the Anglo-Saxons, but a book about books about Anglo-Saxons. It describes the academic discipline of Anglo-Saxonism; the methods of study used; the underlying assumptions; and the uses to which it has been put.

Methods and motives have changed over time but right from the start there have been constant themes: English patriotism and English freedom.

   £9.95 A5 ISBN 1–898281–39-4 9 ¾ x 6 ¾ inches 245 x 170mm Hardback 64 pages

The Origins of the Anglo-Saxons
Donald Henson
This book has come about through a growing frustration with scholarly analysis and debate about the beginnings of Anglo-Saxon England. Much of what has been written is excellent, yet unsatisfactory. One reason for this is that scholars often have only a vague acquaintance with fields outside their own specialism. The result is a partial examination of the evidence and an incomplete understanding or explanation of the period.

The growth and increasing dominance of archaeological evidence for the period has been accompanied by an unhealthy enthusiasm for models of social change imported from prehistory. Put simply, many archaeologists have developed a complete unwillingness to consider movements of population as a factor in social, economic or political change. All change becomes a result of indigenous development, and all historically recorded migrations become merely the movement of a few hundred aristocrats or soldiers. The author does not find this credible.

This book has three great strengths.

> First, it pulls together and summarises the whole range of evidence bearing on the subject, offering an up-to-date assessment: the book is, in other words, a highly efficient introduction to the subject. Second – perhaps reflecting Henson's position as a leading practitioner of public archaeology (he is currently Education and Outreach Co-ordinator for the Council for British Archaeology) – the book is refreshingly jargon free and accessible. Third, Henson is not afraid to offer strong, controversial interpretations. The Origins of the Anglo-Saxons can therefore be strongly recommended to those who want a detailed road-map of the evidence and debates for the migration period.
>
> *Current Archaeology* 2006

   £16.95 ISBN 1–898281–40-8 9 ¾ x 6 ¾ inches 245 x 170mm Hardback 304 pages

A Departed Music – Readings in Old English Poetry
Walter Nash
The *readings* of this book take the form of passages of translation from some Old English poems. The author paraphrases their content and discuses their place and significance in the history of poetic art in Old English society and culture.

The author's knowledge, enthusiasm and love of his subject help make this an excellent introduction to the subject for students and the general reader.

   £16.95 ISBN 1–898281–37-8 9 ¾ x 6 ¾ inches 245 x 170mm Hardback 240 pages

English Sea Power 871-1100 AD
John Pullen-Appleby

This work examines the largely untold story of English sea power during the period 871 to 1100. It was an age when English kings deployed warships first against Scandinavian invaders and later in support of Continental allies.

The author has gathered together information about the appearance of warships and how they were financed, crewed, and deployed.

£14.95   ISBN 1-898281319   9 ¾ x 6 ¾ inches   245 x 170mm   Hardback   114 pages

Anglo-Saxon Burial Mounds
Princely Burials in the 6th & 7th centuries
Stephen Pollington

This is the first book-length treatment of Anglo-Saxon Barrows in English. It brings together some of the evidence from Sutton Hoo and elsewhere in England for these magnificent burials and sets them in their historical, religious and social context.

The first section comprises the physical construction and symbolic meaning of these monuments. The second offers a comprehensive listing of known Anglo-Saxon barrows with notes on their contents and the circumstances of their
discovery. The five appendices deal with literary and place-name evidence.

£14..95   ISBN 978 1898281511   272 pages

Leechcraft: Early English Charms, Plantlore and Healing
Stephen Pollington

An unequalled examination of every aspect of early English healing, including the use of plants, amulets, charms, and prayer. Other topics covered include Anglo-Saxon witchcraft; tree-lore; gods, elves and dwarves.

The author has brought together a wide range of evidence for the English healing tradition, and presented it in a clear and readable manner. The extensive 2,000-entry index makes it possible for the reader to quickly find specific information.

The three key Old English texts are reproduced in full, accompanied by new translations.

Bald's Third Leechbook; *Lacnunga*; *Old English Herbarium*.

£25   ISBN 978-1898281474   240 x 170mm   paperback   28 illustrations   544 pages

The Life and Times of Godwine, Earl of Wessex
Hubert Grills

Godwine was an independent-minded, dominant and courageous man who held a great deal of political and military power. Mediaeval kings relied on men like Godwine for support and for execution of their policies. When the interests of the king and his leading men coincided, the country could enjoy an effective administration; when these interests conflicted, ruinous and unnecessary strife resulted and it was by no means certain that the authority of the king would prevail.

The story of Godwine's life is scattered in many source documents in which fact is mingled with legend and polemic. Hubert Grills has reviewed the available sources - Anglo-Saxon, Scandinavian and Norman - and subjected them to a new analysis.

The author's familiarity with the texts - and with the inherent bias in each of them - allows him to bring a fresh approach to the little known story of a great man.

£19.95 240 x 170mm ISBN 978 1898281528 272 pages

Anglo-Saxon Art, Myth & Material Culture from the 4th to 7th Century
Stephen Pollington

In all the metalwork and archaeological oddments we have from the Anglo-Saxon period, is there anything one could call 'art'? The contributors to this book believe that not only was there considerable artistry in the output of early Anglo-Saxon workshops, but that it was vigorous, complex and technically challenging.

The designs found on Anglo-Saxon artifacts is never mere ornament: in a society which used visual and verbal signals to demonstrate power, authority, status and ethnicity, no visual statement was ever empty of meaning. The aim of this work is to prompt a better understanding of Anglo-Saxon art and the society which produced it.

Stephen Pollington, Lindsay Kerr and Brett Hammond have assembled in these pages much information and many previously unpublished illustrations which show a wide variety of artifacts, designs and motifs. It is hoped that this will help bring about a wider knowledge and appreciation of Anglo-Saxon art.

62 colour plates, 226 black & white illusrations ISBN 978 1898281566

Anglo-Saxon Riddles
Translated by John Porter

Here you will find ingenious characters who speak their names in riddles, and meet a one-eyed garlic seller, a bookworm, an iceberg, an oyster, the sun and moon and a host of others from the everyday life and imagination of the Anglo-Saxons. Their sense of the awesome power of creation goes hand in hand with a frank delight in obscenity, a fascination with disguise and with the mysterious processes by which the natural world is turned to human use.   This edition contains **all 95 riddles of the Exeter Book in both Old English and Modern English.**

£4.95 A5 ISBN 1–898281–13–0 144 pages

Anglo-Saxon Books
www.asbooks.co.uk
tel: 0845 430 4200

Ordering

Order online at www.asbooks.co.uk

See website for uptodate postal address, prices and availability.

If ordering by post please enclose a cheque or postal order payable to Anglo-Saxon Books

UK deliveries add 10% up to a maximum of £2-50

Europe – including **Republic of Ireland** - add 10% plus £1 – all orders sent airmail

North America add 10% surface delivery, 30% airmail

Elsewhere add 10% surface delivery, 40% airmail

Overseas surface delivery 5–8 weeks; airmail 5–10 days

See website for details of North American distributor.

Organisations

Þa Engliscan Gesiðas

Þa Engliscan Gesiðas (The English Companions) is a historical and cultural society exclusively devoted to Anglo-Saxon history. Its aims are to bridge the gap between scholars and non-experts, and to bring together all those with an interest in the Anglo-Saxon period, its language, culture and traditions, so as to promote a wider interest in, and knowledge of all things Anglo-Saxon. The Fellowship publishes a journal, *Wiðowinde,* which helps members to keep in touch with current thinking on topics from art and archaeology to heathenism and Early English Christianity. The Fellowship enables like-minded people to keep in contact by publicising conferences, courses and meetings which might be of interest to its members.

For further details see www.tha-engliscan-gesithas.org.uk or write to: The Membership Secretary, Þa Engliscan Gesiðas, BM Box 4336, London, WC1N 3XX England.

Regia Anglorum

Regia Anglorum was founded to accurately re-create the life of the British people as it was around the time of the Norman Conquest. Our work has a strong educational slant. We consider authenticity to be of prime importance and prefer, where possible, to work from archaeological materials. Approximately twenty-five per cent of our members, of over 500 people, are archaeologists or historians.

The Society has a large working Living History Exhibit, teaching and exhibiting more than twenty crafts in an authentic environment. We own a forty-foot wooden ship replica of a type that would have been a common sight in Northern European waters around the turn of the first millennium AD. Battle re-enactment is another aspect of our activities, often involving 200 or more warriors.

For further information see www.regia.org or contact: K. J. Siddorn, 9 Durleigh Close, Headley Park, Bristol BS13 7NQ, England, e-mail: kim_siddorn@compuserve.com

The Sutton Hoo Society

Our aims and objectives focus on promoting research and education relating to the Anglo Saxon Royal cemetery at Sutton Hoo, Suffolk in the UK. The Society publishes a newsletter SAXON twice a year, which keeps members up to date with society activities, carries resumes of lectures and visits, and reports progress on research and publication associated with the site. If you would like to join the Society please see website: www.suttonhoo.org

Wuffing Education

Wuffing Education provides those interested in the history, archaeology, literature and culture of the Anglo-Saxons with the chance to meet experts and fellow enthusiasts for a whole day of in-depth seminars and discussions. Day Schools take place at the historic Tranmer House overlooking the burial mounds of Sutton Hoo in Suffolk.

For details of programme of events contact:-
Wuffing Education, 4 Hilly Fields, Woodbridge, Suffolk IP12 4DX
email education@wuffings.co.uk   website www.wuffings.co.uk
Tel. 01394 383908 or 01728 688749

Places to visit

Bede's World at Jarrow

Bede's world tells the remarkable story of the life and times of the Venerable Bede, 673–735 AD. Visitors can explore the origins of early medieval Northumbria and Bede's life and achievements through his own writings and the excavations of the monasteries at Jarrow and other sites.

Location – 10 miles from Newcastle upon Tyne, off the A19 near the southern entrance to the River Tyne tunnel. Bus services 526 & 527

Bede's World, Church Bank, Jarrow, Tyne and Wear, NE32 3DY

Tel. 0191 489 2106; Fax: 0191 428 2361; website: www.bedesworld.co.uk

Sutton Hoo near Woodbridge, Suffolk

Sutton Hoo is a group of low burial mounds overlooking the River Deben in south-east Suffolk. Excavations in 1939 brought to light the richest burial ever discovered in Britain – an Anglo-Saxon ship containing a magnificent treasure which has become one of the principal attractions of the British Museum. The mound from which the treasure was dug is thought to be the grave of Rædwald, an early English king who died in 624/5 AD.

This National Trust site has an excellent visitor centre, which includes a reconstruction of the burial chamber and its grave goods. Some original objects as well as replicas of the treasure are on display.

2 miles east of Woodbridge on B1083   Tel. 01394 389700

West Stow Anglo-Saxon Village

An early Anglo-Saxon Settlement reconstructed on the site where it was excavated consisting of timber and thatch hall, houses and workshop. There is also a museum containing objects found during the excavation of the site. Open all year 10am (except Christmas) Last entrance summer 4pm; winter 3-30pm. Special provision for school parties. A teachers' resource pack is available. Costumed events are held on some weekends, especially Easter Sunday and August Bank Holiday Monday. Craft courses are organised.

For further details see www.weststow.org or contact:

The Visitor Centre, West Stow Country Park, Icklingham Road, West Stow, Bury St Edmunds, Suffolk IP28 6HG   Tel. 01284 728718